NEW TRENDS AND DEVELOPMENTS IN AFRICAN RELIGIONS

Recent Titles in
Contributions in Afro-American and African Studies

NEW TRENDS AND DEVELOPMENTS IN AFRICAN RELIGIONS

Edited by Peter B. Clarke

Contributions in Afro-American and African Studies, Number 186

Greenwood Press
Westport, Connecticut • London

Library of Congress Cataloging-in-Publication Data

New trends and developments in African religions / edited by Peter B.
  Clarke.
      p.   cm.—(Contributions in Afro-American and African
  studies, ISSN 0069–9624 ; no. 186.)
    Includes bibliographical references and index.
    ISBN 0–313–30128–X (alk. paper)
    1. Blacks—Religion.   I. Clarke, Peter B. (Peter Bernard)
  II. Series.
  BL2400.N485   1998
  299′.6—dc21   97–32006

British Library Cataloguing in Publication Data is available.

Library of Congress Catalog Card Number: 97–32006
ISBN: 0–313–30128–X
ISSN: 0069–9624

First published in 1998

Greenwood Press, 88 Post Road West, Westport, CT 06881
An imprint of Greenwood Publishing Group, Inc.

Printed in the United States of America

The paper used in this book complies with the
Permanent Paper Standard issued by the National
Information Standards Organization (Z39.48–1984).

10 9 8 7 6 5 4 3 2

Contents

Introduction

Peter B. Clarke

While African religions, and religions that have derived much of their cosmology, beliefs, ideology, rituals, and ethos from African religions, are becoming more international in scope and appeal—more than ethnic religions confined to people of African descent—they continue to be seen by many as either endlessly and indiscriminately adaptable, or as static traditions grounded in magic that has very particularistic and specific aims. From either perspective they are deemed to be of little spiritual and psychological value outside their original milieu when compared with the large-scale impact of the so-called world religions. They are not serious religions, it is implied, nor are their beliefs and rituals of much spiritual value for the world as a whole. Whether referring to their adaptability and openness or to their apparently changeless nature, it is usually suggested that these stem from their lack of a developed theology and/or philosophy comparable to that found in Christianity or Islam or Buddhism, and to their lack of fit with modernity.

Those who see African religions as powerless and highly vulnerable when confronted with allegedly more sophisticated belief systems point to evidence from sub-Saharan Africa of the rapid growth of Islam and Christianity there, particularly in this century. This is to ignore the continuing vitality of African religions in Africa itself and of religions derived from Africa in the Caribbean and the Americas and parts of Europe, among other places. While the question of whether African religions in Africa have been largely displaced or replaced by incoming world religions or whether the latter have been domesticated by the former is not easy to answer. It is arguable, none-the-less, that the essentially two-tiered African cosmology, and the beliefs and ritual forms most closely associated with African traditional religion have not only survived but have played and continue to play an essential role in shaping the form and content of religions of all kinds in Africa.

Those religions that descend from African beliefs and rituals found in the Americas, the Caribbean and Europe that have juxtaposed Catholic beliefs and practices alongside their own, while showing remarkable vitality and inventiveness, have also displayed considerable discrimination, when it has been necessary, to protect and preserve the African religious heritage in these regions. These religions have been the vehicle for the preservation and development not only of the spirituality and norms but also of the art, history and legends, identity, medical and psychological knowledge, and the theater and entertainment of a people, and have greatly influenced other religious traditions and cultures.

This book focuses on African and African-derived religions and how these display themselves in the contemporary world, particularly the Americas, the Caribbean and Europe and in particular on their continued dynamism and their relationship with other religious traditions, often labeled syncretism. It opens with a thought-provoking contribution from Sidney M. Greenfield on the social agendas that inform anthopological discourse and asks why, in the 1920s and 1930s, Melville Herskovits, one of the great pioneers of research on African religions in the Americas, was so convinced that Africans in the Americas would inevitably adapt to the dominant culture—a process that would give rise to, among other things, syncretic religions—while today anthropologists are persuaded of the opposite. In retrospect it appears that for Herskovits the inevitable blending of ethnic cultures with the main stream was part of a strategy to undermine the biological, cultural and social bases of prejudice. It can also be seen as a form of wish fulfilment in keeping with the social and political agenda of the most influential schools of anthropology of the day which espoused the idea of the United States as a melting pot. Today the emphasis is on the need to preserve and protect different cultures in the United States. Greenfield maintains that this position is influenced by the social and political agendas that followed on from the civil rights legislation and affirmative action legislative programs of the 1960s and 1970s in which difference has come to be seen as politically and socially advantageous.

The theme of syncretism is addressed to a greater or lesser degree in almost every contribution and is the main focus of Clarke's analysis of the nature of the relationship between Candomblé and Catholicism, and of Mundicarmo Ferretti's discussion of the complex nature of the Caboclo dimension, not often considered, to African-Brazilian religion. While there are times when syncretism in the sense of the mixing of the two traditions does occur, the more accurate term to describe this relationship between Candomblé and Catholicism is, Clarke believes, juxtapositioning, a term preferred by the late Pierre Verger, to whom all students of Candomblé owe an enormous debt. Ferretti warns against the automatic tendency to treat the Cabloclo spirits of African-Brazilian religion

as of Amerinidian origin—some are Turks—and thus uncritically labeling those
Candomblé houses such as the Tanbor de Minas in St. Luis de Maranhao in
northeast Brazil where Caboclo and African spiritual entities mingle, as centers
of African-Amerindian syncretism. Roberto Motta's discussion of the
churchification of Candomblé in Brazil, an account which complements and
takes much further a number of points made by Peter B. Clarke on this same
development, and by William Van De Berg on the process of institutionalization
of the North Carolina Rastafari movement, a bewildering development given
that there has been no better example in modern times of a movement that was
so extreme in its opposition to institutional form and structure than the Rastafari.

Community and identity construction are themes running through many of
the contributions to this book, and Valerie De Marinis presents a most
interesting account from a psychological angle of the importance of community
within the Macumba religious and ritual system in Salvador, Bahia, and of how
Macumba belief and ritual both marks and shapes the psychosocial personality
of the devotee.

Tina Gudrun Jensen is also interested in the devotee, but this time in
Umbanda. She is also, unusually and originally, interested not in the core or
initiated members, the focus of the vast majority of studies, but in the general,
more elusive category of floating member. Jensen's research reveals that the
main conduit to Umbanda, as in the case of many other new religions, is
personal contact, and that for clients this this-world-affirming religion not only
enables them to cope with the problems of everyday life and provides them with
the means to improve their material conditions, but also offers a spiritual theory
of illness and misfortune that resonates with their own understanding of these
matters.

Turning from Brazil to the Caribbean, Charles Gullick's analysis of the
multivocal aspects of Shakerism on the Caribbean island of St. Vincent
emphasises the need to consider religious symbolism in the context of the total
cultural milieu rather than purely from within the movement itself. Gullick at
the same time stresses the necessity of focusing on individual belief systems and
constructs as a means of discerning how and why the symbolic nature of actions
can fly in the face of actions studied. This approach also informs Van De Berg's
study of the Rastafari church in North Carolina.

Stephen D. Glazier's concern is with the questions of origin, genuineness,
and authenticity that have become topics of often-heated debate among scholars
of Afro-Caribbean religion, and indeed of African and African-derived religions
everywhere. He, like Gullick and others, points out that not everything about
these religions can be understood in terms of their African past. Nor can these
religions be adequately understood if interpreted as religions of protest, or, we
can add, religions of the oppressed, if oppression is understood mainly in
economic terms. Glazier argues that in the Caribbean something unique and

creative has emerged from the encounter of African traditional religion with
Christianity in its various forms.

Roland Littlewood's detailed study of the Earth People of Trinidad allows us
to see whether this is so in every case in the Caribbean. In addressing the
question of the African character of this millenarian movement which
incorporates African, Christian, and Indian elements, and of Shouter Baptism in
general, he illustrates the complexity of the issue: while worshiping Mother
Earth, the Earth People regard the Bible as central to their faith. We have here
an example of a neo-pagan, highly puritan, biblical-based movement, influenced
by Indian beliefs and practices.

While the Earth People is something of a feminist movement as well, the
Rastafarian movement decidely is not, in the opinion of Obiagele Lake. This
contributor examines the dynamics of the subordination of Rasta women in the
context of Jamaican and Caribbean and African diaspora societies. In these
societies women generally, Lake believes, are in a weak and vulnerable position
vis-à-vis men. But Rasta women, Lake argues, are particularly subject to male
domination on account of the strict adherence of Rastas to the Bible. She
concludes that a struggle by Rasta women has the potential to symbolize better
than any other group the struggle of African women as a whole for equality with
men.

William Van De Berg, while pointing out that much more research is needed
on gender in the Rastafari movement in North Carolina, makes a number of
observations on symbols of power and women's roles that lend suppport to
Lake's thesis on the position of women. His main focus, however, is on identity
and symbolism at both the group and the individual levels, providing interesting
comparisons with, among other contributions, that of Gullick. Van De Berg also
deals with the churchification process of the Rastafari movement in North
Carolina, enabling further comparisons to be made with Motta's already
mentioned discussion of this process in Candomblé and Mike Taylor's very
detailed account of the Nation of Islam.

Taylor's thorough account of the history, teachings, and principal leaders of
the Nation of Islam offers two basic ways of perceiving this movement, both of
which are, he believes, tenable: as a cult which plays upon the aspirations of the
African-American community, providing it with a powerful, albeit fanciful,
mythology, or as a pacesetting movement whose finger is on the pulse of Black
issues and one with which many Americans of African descent are proud to
identify. Still in the United States, though this time in Los Angeles, Brian
McGuire and Duncan Scrymgeour assess the contribution of Santería houses or
temples to the formation of communities among systematically marginalized
Latinos, comparing it, in this regard, to the role played by Pentecostalism in the
same city and elsewhere, including South America.

Although not her main point, Ineke van Wetering shows that the Winti cult is equally important in community building among the Creole population, mainly of Surinamese origin, in the Netherlands. While there is considerable creolization—a term van Wetering prefers to syncretism—Winti traditionists in the Netherlands share much in common with Candomble in Bahia, northeast Brazil, especially the desire, championed by women members in particular, to protect their culture from extinction by overly adapting to the western context. In both traditions there is both a process of juxtapositioning and the paradoxical trend of the simultaneous merging of traditions with a stress on self-sufficiency and separateness. This no doubt points not only to a political dimension to religious encounter but also to the fact that there probably cannot be one permanent and enduring kind of relationship between religious traditions of diverse ethnic and cultural origins, at least not for a very long period after they encounter and familiarize themselves thoroughly with each other.

Gerrie ter Haar makes effective use of Van Gennep's notion of rites of passage and Turner's idea of ritual as process, in particular the latter's idea of communitas and liminality in order to explore the present situation of African Christian communities in the relatively deprived Bijlmer area of Amsterdam. While both these elements are present in all the African churches in the area, ter Haar pays special attention to the True Teachings of Christ Temple, the largest and the oldest of the African-led churches in the district. As with Santeria, this church also provides a safe haven and a community for the marginalized, who are mainly of Ghanaian descent, and who are believed to be in greatest danger of falling into 'sin' and crime. In order to avoid being further marginalised members of this and other churches often will not use the label African when referring to their churches in order to avoid further marginalization. More generally ter Haar's contribution addresses an increasingly important and widespread development in African immigrant churches across Europe: how their ritual is defined by marginality and the struggle for security in a context of new political demarcation lines and methods of exclusion.

Italy has witnessed a rise in its African, particularly Somali, population in recent times, and in the number of new religions present there, and Vittorio Lanternari's chapter analyzes the appeal and impact of one of these, the Malingo phenomenon which derives from the healing activities of the former Zambian Archbishop of Lusaka of that name. Accused by his church of syncretism for introducing a form of faith healing similar to that found in African traditional healing practices, and ideas of ancestor veneration into the Catholic liturgy, Malingo was withdrawn to Rome where since 1983 he has continued his healing cult. Lanternari relates how the charismatic archbishop revived "archaisms" in the form of beliefs in sorcery, witchcraft and possession, normally left untouched in Catholic teaching and liturgy, and examines the reasons for the appeal of his potent mixture of Catholicism and African traditional religion to many of every age, background, and profession, including some of the clergy.

Victor Wan-Tatah, focusing on conversion to the Nazarene Church of Isaiah Shembe in southern Africa, provides a far less positive account of the role of this and other independent churches in the region. He believes that drastic changes, including greater involvement in social issues, will be needed if these churches are to have a significant impact on the developement process in southern Africa.

While the primary concern of this multidisciplinary and wideranging book has been to explore in an interesting and scholarly way many of the main developements in the world of African and African-derived religions, it also hopes to make a contribution to the wider and ongoing debate on syncretism that continues to preoccupy those in the anthropology, history, and sociology of religion.

I sincerely thank all who have contributed for their time and for the valuable insights they have provided on a fascinating if somewhat neglected area of study and research.

NEW TRENDS AND DEVELOPMENTS IN AFRICAN RELIGIONS

1

Recasting Syncretism . . . Again: Theories and Concepts in Anthropology and Afro-American Studies in the Light of Changing Social Agendas

Sidney M. Greenfield

I have taken my best pains not to laugh at the actions of mankind, not to groan over them, not to be angry at them, but to understand them.

—Spinoza

INTRODUCTION: THE DEBATE OVER SYNCRETISM

Syncretism is a term that has been used in a variety of different, and at times contradictory, ways by scholars from several academic disciplines. This has led some "to propose the abolition of the term" (Droogers 1989:7). Instead of discarding it, however, André Droogers and others (Droogers 1989, 1995; Shaw and Stewart 1994; Aijmer 1995) have attempted to, in the words of Rosalind Shaw and Charles Stewart (1994:2), "recast syncretism."

This chapter examines these recent efforts at the redefinition of syncretism in terms of changes taking place in anthropological theory and Afro-American studies. I argue that the new view of syncretism reflects the separatist social agenda of a generation of scholars who presuppose, and project into the future, a social reality that came about because of the enforcement of the civil rights laws of the 1960s and programs of affirmative action in the United States and similar legislative programs elsewhere. This social agenda will be shown to be very different from that of Franz Boas, his students (such as Melville J. Herskovits), and earlier generations of scholars influenced by them, who introduced the original concept of syncretism into anthropology. Their conceptual framework will be shown to reflect a view of a wished-for social world significantly different from the one found in the writings of those who are recasting syncretism.

In their introduction to a collection on syncretism, editors Shaw and Stewart (1994:3) contend that their "aims in [the] volume are to recast syncretism." They begin with the etymology of the word, tracing it back to its ancient Greek roots in the writings of Plutarch. Later, they note, it was used by Renaissance writers in a different way to judge and evaluate historical and contemporary events. Sixteenth- and seventeenth-century religious thinkers used it in yet another way, while late nineteenth- and early twentieth-century students of comparative religion employed it still differently.

It is surprising, however, that in that essay, in the others in their volume, and in a series of books and papers in which attempts are made to revise the concept of syncretism, the authors, many of whom are anthropologists, have not included in their reviews of previous uses of the term the way it was employed by Franz Boas and his students, and those they influenced both inside and outside anthropology (see Droogers 1989, 1995; Shaw and Stewart 1994; Aijmer 1995). Stewart (1995), for example, in another paper, mentions the work of Melville Herskovits, which he criticizes for what he calls its positive use of the term. Then, as if to discredit Herskovits, he claims, following Walter Jackson (1986), that he, and the Boas group of which he was a part, had a social agenda. Boas, Herskovits, and the other founders of American anthropology did have a social agenda. Unfortunately, neither Stewart nor others presently writing on syncretism, nor Jackson (1986) and Andrew Apter (1991), who have written critically about Herskovits and his studies of syncretism, have addressed that agenda and how syncretism, as a concept, defined as it was, related to it. Moreover, they have not made explicit their own social agenda and how their recasting of the concept of syncretism is part of a discourse promoting it.

SYNCRETISM IN THE BOASIAN SOCIAL AGENDA

The intellectual undertaking in the 1920s and 1930s that was to emerge as the anthropology of Boas and his students might be thought of in part as a byproduct of the formulation of a discourse intended to influence the social construction of the symbolic categories, including the content and meaning of those categories, used in American society to think about and, consequently for individuals to use to organize their behavior toward the members of its varied and diverse social groups. The Boasians were mostly integrationists (as opposed to separatists), although the term assimilation was used at the time. Their goal was to bring into being an integrated national society in the United States in which every citizen, no matter his or her racial, ethnic, and/or other markings, would be included as a full participant. Critical portions of what was to develop into the science of anthropology may be interpreted as part of the effort to formulate an argument, or discourse, whose intent was to attain this social policy objective.

With respect to the Boas agenda, Jackson (1986:95) begins his examination of "Melville Herskovits and the Search for Afro-American Culture" by reminding us that "In the years immediately following World War I, Franz Boas and his students faced a delicate task as they analyzed race and ethnicity in the United States." "In the aftermath of World War I," Jackson elaborates (1986:99),

race riots had broken out in more than twenty American cities. A revived Ku Klux Klan became a politically powerful force in many areas of the North and West as well as in the South. Popular magazines carried articles using IQ test scores and other "scientific" measurements to argue the inferiority of non-Nordic peoples. In 1924 Congress passed an immigration law that imposed quotas based on national origin which dramatically reduced immigration from southern and eastern Europe. (Higham 1963)

Boas, he continues,

used two conflicting strategies to oppose popular beliefs that immigrants and blacks were genetically inferior and "unassimilable" to American culture: one, universalist/ assimilationist, the other particularist/pluralist. His universal strategy denied the importance of "race" as a category for understanding the mental and emotional characteristics of individuals, and insisted that modern technology was creating a uniform culture in America to which immigrants and blacks were rapidly assimilating . . . In contrast to this universalist strategy, another strain of Boasian thought emphasized the importance of understanding each culture in its own terms and appreciating the unique contribution of each culture to human civilization.

The universalist/assimilationist strategy, which for the purposes of this chapter is better labeled integrationist, was to be the general scientific face of anthropology, while the particularist/pluralist one was to be the Boasian legacy of detailed ethnography. One side was overwhelmingly scientific, while the other was a combination of science and humanism. Boasian anthropology then, as has long been recognized, was both a scientific discipline and one of the humanities.

Boas, Jackson continues, "never confronted the contradiction between universalism and his commitment to respect minority cultures; but it would become a central issue for Melville Herskovits." Building on the impressive analysis of the Boasian legacy by G. W. Stocking, Jr. (1974), Jackson explores the Herskovits contribution to anthropology. Jackson focuses on the contradictions between the universalism (integrationism) of the Boasian social agenda and the theoretical framework, or discourse developed to rationalize it on the one hand, and the particularism of its empirical, ethnological, and historical research program on the other.

According to Jackson (1986:100), when Herskovits applied cultural analysis he realized "that the concept of 'cultural pattern' had both radical and conservative implications. On the one hand, if cultural patterns were 'unconscious in their development and capricious in the extreme,' it meant that repressive attempts to achieve 'social control' over immigrants were unlikely to succeed . . . Although Herskovits remained politically liberal throughout his life," Jackson continues, "he retained a quiet pessimism about the ease with which state intervention could alter fundamental social attitudes." "He was very optimistic in the 1920s, however, about the power of American cultural patterns to overcome ethnic particularism. Seeking to refute the racists' claim that immigrants and blacks were incapable of assimilating American culture, he at first argued [based mostly on his own experience] that assimilation was, in fact, occurring and that it was an inevitable social process" (Jackson 1986:100-101).

This optimism for the future, Jackson concludes, "was the cosmopolitan and assimilationist vision that Herskovits brought to the struggle against scientific racism in the 1920s." It began to pose problems for him, however, that were to take him in the direction of particularism and pluralism when he encountered the "Harlem Renaissance and the desire of black intellectuals to develop a distinctive cultural tradition with roots in the African past and in Afro-American folklore" (Jackson 1986:101).

When he was convinced that a knowledge of their past would help in bringing about a pride needed while the struggle against racism was being conducted, Herskovits turned his attention to the study of the histories and cultures of Africans and their descendants in the Americas. This, according to Jackson, moved him from the universalist (integrationist) position he shared with most Boasians to being a student of the particularistic details of the history and ethnography of one minority. As his career progressed, he devoted his energies more to reconstructing African and Afro-American cultures and less to trying to influence American social policy. His view of syncretism, and the use he made of it as a concept, must be understood in terms of the two contradictory dimensions of the Boasian framework.

Herskovits first proposed syncretism as a theoretical concept as part of the inquiry into what happens when carriers of different cultures come into prolonged contact with each other. This was only part of what in the anthropology of the 1930s was referred to as the study of acculturation (Herskovits 1958 [1938 original]). It is unfortunate that he selected a term that already was being used by scholars in other fields who had imbued it with meanings different from the one he proposed. Had Herskovits, or others in anthropology who built on his thinking, acknowledged that the word carried considerable baggage, perhaps they would have replaced syncretism with another term, thereby avoiding much present day confusion and the need for redefinition.

Syncretism for Herskovits (1964:190 [original 1947]) was a form of reinterpretation. He hypothesized that when acculturation takes place—that is, when peoples with different cultures are in prolonged contact with each other—each takes from what is presented to it by the other(s) certain forms and meanings that it reformulates in terms of its own beliefs and understandings.[1] Reinterpretation may lead to the borrowing and mixing—the syncretism of cultural traits and/or patterns—that enables the members of one group to better adjust to their circumstances. This was especially true for slaves in the Americas and their descendants, who were subordinated to and dominated by Europeans who scarcely acknowledged them as culture-bearing human beings, let alone recognized that they had their own systems of meaning and standards of worth and value. That studies of acculturation, reinterpretation, and syncretism focused on the dominated—the slaves and their descendants (people of color)—is understandable in that greater pressures were placed on them to accommodate and adjust since they invariably lived in societies whose major institutional structures were designed by Europeans and whose legal systems and mechanisms for their enforcement clearly privileged the latter and their cultural practices. Furthermore, in the academic division of labor of the period, anthropologists studied the poor and the marginal, who were usually referred to as "primitives." The European dominators and their descendants were the subjects of other disciplines such as sociology, history, economics, and political science.

As minorities blended with each other and with the majority, it was believed not only that they would interbreed, producing new physical types, but that their respective culture traits also would mix to become part of the new, single, unified culture that would characterize the larger national society. Syncretism in this view was neither good nor bad, but rather something believed to happen as it did every time peoples from different cultural groups came in contact with each other throughout history. This was the meaning attributed to syncretism in the textbooks and programmatic statements of an anthropology that had as its social goal the creation of a single, unified society into which all minorities were to be integrated.

A second meaning of syncretism emerged in the writings of Herskovits, however, as he moved from the realm of abstract theory—and the assimilationist/integrationist social agenda—to the particularism of ethnography and ethnohistory. It is to this second use of the term that Apter (1991) refers when he speaks of the "syncretic paradigm" of Herskovits. While some scholars cite Herskovits's general writings and textbooks for his definition of syncretism, Apter and others (including non-anthropologists), especially after the 1960s, use his ethnographies and popular publications about "the New World Negro." "Herskovits developed a number of related concepts which," as Apter summarizes the second usage, "can be glossed as the syncretic paradigm. In addition to the ethnohistorical method [by which he meant simply that ethnology and history should be combined 'to recover the predominant regional and tribal origins of the New World Negro' and 'to establish the cultural baselines from which the process of change began' (Herskovits 1966:49)], these concepts are: 1) scale of intensity, 2) cultural focus, 3) syncretism proper, 4) reinterpretation, and 5) cultural imponderables" (Apter 1991:237).

Apter's criticism of Herskovits and the conclusions he reaches about "degrees of Africanisms" in the cultures of specific New World populations is based on a combination of new historical and ethnographic data, much of which he collected himself, and its interpretation in terms of an alternative theoretical perspective.[2]

From roughly the 1920s until the beginnings of the postmodern critique, anthropologists exposed to and influenced by the Boasian perspective accepted its implicit dualism. This made them on the whole universalists, integrationists and assimilationists who supported the goal of striving in their own society for a unified national system that would accept and incorporate minorities without prejudice, at one level, and particularists and pluralists with respect to the peoples and cultures they study, at another. When after World War II the discipline moved from the almost exclusive study of "primitive isolates" to also investigating "minorities" in contemporary, complex cultures, most American scholars, as Wagley and Harris (1958:xiv) observed, focused their studies on adaptation and assimilation. In contrast to their European counterparts, who generally began with the assumption that minority groups wished to preserve their differences, American scholars presupposed integration as a goal. Four decades later, however, a new generation of researchers has adopted the European position that minority groups are and wish to remain different and separate. Why has this happened? How is it that the social groups and so many of those who study them today have become separatists, discarding the dream of integration and assimilation?

Had Boas, Herskovits, or other liberal intellectuals been asked prior to or immediately following World War II how the assimilation and integration of minorities into a unified national society without prejudice and discrimination were to be brought about, I doubt that they would have been able to provide an answer other than to express the conviction that if the symbolic foundations on which prejudice and discrimination rested were called into question and debunked, people would cease to recognize blacks and other minorities as different and therefore accept and treat them the way they do non-minority members of the society. The energies of anthropologists and other liberal intellectuals were devoted to combating prejudice. Little effort went into programs for the transformation of society that was at the heart of their social agenda.

Boasian anthropology was notoriously weak in its conceptualization and analysis of social processes. This was especially the case in its treatment of acculturation where new, reinterpreted and/or syncretic cultural forms had emerged. It was one thing to describe and reconstruct changes in the constituent parts of a culture—conceptualized in terms of traits and patterns—of a group and indicate, with the benefit of hindsight, where the mixing of elements that resulted in something new had occurred, or where elements taken from one culture had become a part of another group's beliefs and practices. Explaining how and why people changed their beliefs and behaviors and forged new social arrangements for their expression was quite another. If anthropological theory could not explain how social change came about, how could its students possibly provide a plan or blueprint for how the assimilation and integration of minorities into the mainstream of the national society might be achieved?

THE CIVIL RIGHTS MOVEMENT AND THE CHANGE FROM A DESIRE FOR INTEGRATION TO A REALITY OF SEPARATENESS

Many people believed that the immense social changes that occurred in the United States in the decades of the 1950s and 1960s would bring into being the goals of integrationists and other political liberals. Three decades later, however, this appears not to have been the case: prejudice and discrimination are perhaps more intense than ever and separatism, at times approaching confrontation and militancy, is the order of the day. I suggest that the present situation may be the result of the unanticipated consequences of the way the change was brought about: by means of the passage and enforcement of legislation to ensure the civil rights of minorities.

The driving force behind the social transformation was the civil rights movement. After at first experimenting with other options, the strategy of using the law at the federal level, and its enforcement machinery, was selected as the means to attain its objectives. The ideal of full and just participation by all, and their treatment without prejudice and discrimination, were claimed to be the "rights" of every individual as a citizen of the nation. These rights, that in practice regularly were being denied to blacks and other minorities, it was argued, should be enforced by means of the law. The elimination of discrimination and the integration of minorities, it was believed and advocated, would be brought about if the law made it clear that discrimination was illegal and that those guilty of violating it—that is those who did not treat blacks and other minorities without prejudice and discrimination—would be punished. In brief, the transformation of American society to attain what appeared at the time to be the integrationist goal, was to be brought about by punishing those who did not behave as if integration and assimilation were the norm.

American society, however, did not adopt civil rights reform as the result of reasoned debate over proposals made by the leaders of the civil rights movement (or others) followed by careful planning. Political action was taken instead in reaction to a broad range of protests and at times violent demonstrations, including those against the war in Vietnam. The new laws were enacted not as the result of reasoned decisions to confront an unjust history of prejudice and discrimination and to do the "right thing," but rather as an attempt by a beleaguered federal government to avoid further civil disobedience, divisiveness, and what at the time looked like the possible disintegration of the body politic.

Discrimination on the basis of race, color, or national origin was made illegal under the provisions of the Civil Rights Act of 1964. Furthermore, no federal agency, public university, defense or other federal contractor, or any other institution or activity that received federal funding could discriminate on the basis of race, color, or national origin. Any citizen who believed that he or she had been discriminated against could now bring legal action in order to obtain redress. Moreover, in an attempt to "make up for" past injustices to blacks, affirmative action programs were passed into law. What this meant in practice was that in the same agencies and organizations covered by the federal anti-discrimination laws, plus others that agreed on their own to accept the spirit of the law even though not technically obligated to do so, whenever the qualifications of two or more individuals for a position or a promotion were similar, preference was to be given to the one who was black or, as the law had to read, a member of a minority.

Two points must be emphasized here. One, the means, the social process, by which American society was transformed to create a new order in which discrimination based on race, color, or national origins would be eliminated— and, in the ideal, minorities would be integrated as full participants in national life—was the enforcement of the law, with its emphasis on punishment through the courts and the criminal justice system. Morality was legislated, and those who did not accept it were to be made to by the enforcement mechanisms of the law.[3] Two, the arena, or social domain, on which the law and its enforcement agencies were to focus were the occupational sector, with emphasis on employment practices and promotion procedures. Furthermore, to make up for past injustices, affirmative action programs were instituted to level the playing field and, it was hoped, to enable blacks to compete economically. This, it was assumed, would lead eventually to the full and equal participation of African-Americans in other social domains.

As soon as the new legislation was enacted and its implementation begun, however, others, as representatives of groups, or social categories, most of which had not previously been recognized in public debates about minorities, claimed their "rights" under the new laws. Categories such as American Indian, Alaskan Native, Asian, Pacific Islander, and Hispanic were quickly added to the census and used in the collection of data by the government. Their establishment as minority social categories gave them access to the benefits made available to the disadvantaged. In the following years other, previously unrecognized, categories were added to the equation. The intent here is not to question the legitimacy of anti-discrimination and affirmative action claims by new racial/ethnic groups, women, the disabled, the elderly, gays, lesbians, and others striving for equal treatment. Rather it is to point out that these were not the social groups and categories that had been center stage in whatever public discussion had been held and in the social protests that led up to the passage of the civil rights legislation. Until the 1960s, the term minority was used to refer primarily to racial and ethnic groups that had, or were believed at one time to have had, their own languages, cultures, and social practices. Many of the new minorities to bring anti-discrimination cases were not of that order. Given the way the American legal system works, an unrecognized social group or an amorphous category becomes a political reality once it wins an anti-discrimination suit. One consequence of the new politico-legal procedures was that the constituent parts of American society, its groups and categories, changed. Accordingly, for example, the term minority itself has been brought into question and replaced with identity group and other terms more reflective of the new social and political reality. In addition, older immigrants, believed to have been assimilated previously, have reemerged and redefined themselves often to emphasize their uniqueness and differences. Added to this growing number of groups and categories seeking to establish a distinctiveness that emphasized their being discriminated against have been a wave of new immigrants. Many of these new arrivals developed identities in the United States that differed from those they held when they left their Central American, Asian, and Caribbean homelands. At present there is no way to be sure just how many different identity groups there are. What is clear, however, is that in contrast to the past—before the passage of the civil rights and affirmative action laws—when it was a distinct disadvantage to be a minority, today there are benefits to a minority identity, benefits that at times may be considerable.

Conservative critics contend, for example, that a "civil rights establishment" is now in place "to fight aggressively for representation of 'minorities' in every sphere of life" (D'Souza 1995:19). Dinesh D'Souza goes on to cite the case of a business firm that now may be asked why its labor force is only 5 percent Hispanic when Hispanics are 10 percent of the surrounding population. The assumption, he claims, is that "the company is presumed guilty of illegal discrimination." He cites other cases to show that

advocates of proportional representation contend that merit standards should be adjusted when possible and abandoned if necessary to secure racially balanced results. Moreover, proportional representation extends beyond employment to virtually all sectors of public

life. If blacks are 10 percent of the population in a state, the government and the courts
expect that in order to be represented as a group, blacks should make up roughly 10
percent of all elected officials. If they do not, then the Voting Rights Act can be invoked
to reshape electoral districts in such a way that the election of black representatives is
virtually assured.

D'Souza is cited not to support the criticisms he makes of affirmative action
programs and multiculturalism. However, he represents a new breed of
conservatives who claim that the benefits that go to those able to establish a claim
to minority identity have become excessive. Not surprisingly, they see their
discourse as representing the voice of a growing political constituency that they
hope will bring about changes in the law and a dismantling of the institutions that
maintain the present situation. For now, however, not only is being a minority
"in," it also may be advantageous materially, if one has a platform from which a
claim to minority identity and past discrimination can be voiced.

Changes in anthropological theory, including the recasting of syncretism, I
suggest, reflect the post-1960s social reality of a multiculturalism as expressed
in affirmative action programs and anti-discrimination law suits. Concepts such
as power, hegemony, domination, marginalization, for example, pervade much
of postmodernist, multiculturalist, and other new thinking. The social reality
that seems to be assumed is one of suppressed groups struggling to survive in
the wake of their being dominated—usually by European authorities. The
oppressed groups tell their stories in which they make claims through discourses
that are "read" as struggles against domination and discrimination. Authenticity
and purity of tradition are used to support the continuing identity of each
subjugated group. The implication of the assumed reality appears to be that
today all groups and categories are entitled to the recognition of their "rights"
followed by "fair treatment" (to be read as benefits) under the anti-
discrimination and affirmative action laws. [4]

If Boasian anthropology is to be read as a discourse with a social agenda, as
present day critics have proposed, postmodernist and multicultural theory, I
suggest, also should be read as a discourse with its own social agenda; but that
agenda, in contrast to the integrationist ideal of Boas, is separatist. Recent
attempts to recast syncretism, and the theoretical positions on which they rest,
reflect an acceptance of the new, separatist social agenda.

THE RECASTING OF SYNCRETISM

In the introduction to *Syncretism and the Commerce of Symbols*, editor Göran
Aijmer (1995:3) speaks "against the honored Durkheimian position that
societies can be studied as integrated wholes. . . . We have no *a priori* right," he

states, "to define either society, or culture, as well integrated 'wholes.' " Arguing theoretically, in terms of the assumptions of a postmodernist, semiotic view of culture, Aijmer proposes instead an image of a social universe composed of groups that are "agglomerations of people around particular activities." These groups produce symbols that employ "systemic correspondences for bringing a society together into a union under the acceptance of a source of dominance." With this Hobbesian view of the socio-political order in place, he turns to the symbols that he assumes encode strategies and social discourses that he and others claim to be the proper subject matter of anthropological investigation and analysis. That is, after assuming a social universe characterized by dominance, hegemony, oppression, the marginality and suppression of disadvantaged groups, he turns to syncretism asking: 1. "What happens when two cultural traditions are juxtaposed in such a way and under such circumstances that they are judged as competing by those continuous social groups who are the agents of the traditions?" and 2. "Under what conditions do people in one such continuous group pay attention to symbolism upheld by another group?"

These questions seem to be not very different from those that Herskovits and other Boasian students of syncretism asked. What has changed, however, is the social universe in which the cultural subject matter is assumed to be located.

In another effort to recast syncretism Droogers asks us to look at power. "To argue that power is a dimension of syncretism," he writes, "is one thing; interpreting relations of power is another" (1989:17). Droogers distinguishes two categories of models of power, one functionalist—which sees diversity as being overcome by new synthesis—and the other Marxist, in which conflict is seen as prevailing. In the first set of models, syncretism reconciles the contradictions in the process of achieving cohesion, while in the second it "is interpreted as an instrument of oppression, creating a false unity and hiding social conflicts" (Droogers 1989:18). Droogers then makes another set of oppositions between what he calls an objective versus a subjective view of syncretism. This enables him to set off actors who may contest what scholars and others interpret objectively as syncretism.

Shaw and Stewart (1994:7) carry this further when they propose the notion of "anti-syncretism." Accepting what seems to be the postmodernist view of social reality, they see human beings as actors constantly defining themselves symbolically and redefining themselves with respect to others in the social universe. If this is the case, they ask: What use is the concept of syncretism "since all religions have composite origins and are continually reconstructed through ongoing processes of synthesis and erasure"? Implicitly accepting the position Droogers referred to as the Marxist model of society composed of social groups in conflict, which underpins most postmodernist thinking, they "recast the study of syncretism as the politics of religious synthesis...." They mean by this the study of the conflicts they assume inevitably to occur between different groups when they revise their symbolic meanings as they compete for hegemony. They define anti-syncretism as "the antagonism to religious synthesis shown by the agents concerned with the defence of religious boundaries." It is "frequently bound up with the construction of 'authenticity,' which is in turn often linked to notions of 'purity.' "

We have moved to another level. By introducing anti-syncretism while acknowledging that people always borrow, mix, and redefine social meanings, syncretism becomes the study of the symbols people in groups use to defend their boundaries vis-à-vis other groups. In a world of Marxist conflict, combined with the assumption that one social class always dominates the institutional machinery of an ever-oppressive state, the result of voicing one's differences would inevitably be their further subjugation. In the world of civil rights, multiculturalism, and affirmative action, in which the new anthropology and its broader theoretical orientation flourishes, raising one's voice in defense of difference, even where it may contradict claims made by previous generations, may be expected to bring benefits.[5] In brief, in the present day socio-political and economic realities of the United States, France, and some other European states, and in the projections of intellectuals that these ought to be the realities in all nations, advantages are offered to those who succeed in defining themselves as different and as having suffered from prejudice and discrimination. This current trend, with its emphasis on symbols and the discourses of the oppressed, I contend, does this. It is a theory that provides a voice for any group who wish to interpret or reinterpret the world in a way that enables them to claim access, under the law, to their rights.

CONCLUSION AND IMPLICATIONS

Boasian anthropology had a social agenda which in its universalistic aspect was aimed at refuting the biological and social bases for prejudice and discrimination. This was part of an effort to influence public policy in the direction of creating a single, unified society in which all citizens were to be assimilated, integrated, and treated without regard to their race, color, or national origin. This was a radical objective in that it called for the transformation of a national society. The concept of syncretism, as a form of reinterpretation or redefinition of culture in which traits and patterns are borrowed and mixed to create at times new cultural forms, has its meaning in this social vision.

Neither Boasians nor other integrationists were sophisticated when it came to analyzing and understanding social processes. Hence they were unable to provide models to implement their social agenda. What they advocated seemed at the time to coincide with the goals of the civil rights movement. When the new legislation was implemented, it resulted in a socio-political reality very different from that hoped for by liberals, including many members of the civil rights movement itself. Instead of integration, the redress of past injustices was achieved by the proliferation of identity groups each making claims to benefits under the anti-discrimination and affirmative action provisions of the law. In place of an integrated society in which prejudice and discrimination based on race, color, religion, or national origin would disappear, we have a society composed of diverse and competing identity groups and categories each demanding more as it defines and defends itself vis-à-vis: 1. the majority (believed to control the state and blamed for all past and present injustices), and 2. each other.

Multiculturalism and postmodernism are theories based on the assumed continuation of the present socio-political and legal reality whose maintenance may be considered their social agenda. Unlike Boasian theory that in its universalist aspect strove to bring about a future different from a divisive, separatist, and unjust past and present, contemporary theories seem to accept the Marxist view of inevitable and continuing conflict between social groups. Unlike traditional Marxism, however, it offers no equivalent of the integrated socialist society assumed to follow the revolution—in this case to be produced not by the workers but by the escalation of the confrontation between identity groups. It presents no vision of a better world of the future that will follow from conflict. Instead, it assumes the continuation, into an unending future, of a contentious and strife-ridden present in which its role seems to be to help provide the means for new groups to enter into the fray as contenders and claimants to anti-discrimination, affirmative action, and other benefits that are assumed to be their civil rights. Syncretism as redefined in terms of this theory reinforces the separateness of social categories and identity groups and seems to encourage their confrontation. Scholars are faced with two clearly different and opposing social agendas. They must choose between reinforcing a world of ever-present confrontation and conflict, or to helping to create one that will see an end to separatism, discrimination, prejudice, and violence. In either case, it is hoped that this analysis of the competing scholarly discourses and their social agendas will be accepted in the spirit of Spinoza's comment presented in the epigraph to this paper: not to laugh, to groan, or to be angry, but as an attempt to understand.

NOTES

1. This was especially so when one was in a position of power and domination over another, as was clearly the case in those parts of the world—like the Americas—where plantations, slavery, and colonial practices provided the backdrop for peoples from

different cultures being together.

2. Herskovits himself may not have taken this as a criticism, but rather as a revision of his work based on data not available to him interpreted in terms of a perspective with which he was not familiar.

3. A recent letter to the editor of the *Washington Post* commenting on an anti-discrimination suit in the amount of $85 million brought against the Eddie Bauer corporation expresses the philosophy of enforcing morality by means of the punitive aspect of law enforcement. "If it is shown that Eddie Bauer's corporate policy ratified or encouraged race-based misconduct of its employees, then *how better to deter future bad behavior* or to send a message to other businesses *than to assess damages* in an amount that will be meaningful to a large corporation?" (Italics added.)

4. A suggestive alternative way to think about the process would be to view many of those seeking legal redress for new identity groups as entrepreneurs mobilizing followers. A successful claim to mistreatment may obtain for both leader and others financial damages followed by jobs, contracts, and/or other benefits.

5. It is instructive to observe that these programs were instituted and are enforced by the class/ethnic group taken to be the oppressor.

BIBLIOGRAPHY

Aijmer, Göran, ed. *Syncretism and the Commerce of Symbols.* Göteborg, Sweden: The Institute for Advanced Studies in Social Anthropology, 1995.

Apter, Andrew. *Black Critics and Kings: The Hermeneutics of Power in Yoruba Society.* Chicago: University of Chicago Press, 1992.

Apter, Andrew. "Herskovits's Heritage: Rethinking Syncretism in the African Diaspora." *Diaspora* 1 (3): 235-60, 1991.

Droogers, André. "Syncretism: The Problem of Definition, the Definition of the Problem." In J. Gort, H. Vroom, R. Fernhout, and A. Wessels, eds. *Dialogue and Syncretism: An Interdisciplinary Approach.* Grand Rapids, MI: William B. Eerdmans, 1989.

Droogers, André. "Rethinking Syncretism and Revitalization." Paper presented at the Symposium "Religious Revitalization and Syncretism in Africa and the Americas" at the Annual Meeting of the American Anthropological Association, Washington, D.C., November 15-19, 1995.

D'Souza, Dinesh. *The End of Racism.* New York: The Free Press, 1995

Herskovits, Melville J. *The Myth of the Negro Past.* Boston, MA: Beacon Press, 1990 [original 1941].

Herskovits, Melville J. *Acculturation: The Study of Culture Contact.* Gloucester, MA: Peter Smith, 1958 [original 1938].

Herskovits, Melville J. *Cultural Dynamics.* (Abridged from *Cultural Anthropology.*) New York: Alfred A. Knopf, 1964 [original 1947].

Herskovits, Melville J. *The New World Negro.* Bloomington: Indiana University Press, 1966.

Jackson, Walter. "Melville Herskovits and the Search for Afro-American Culture." In George W. Stocking, ed., *Malinowski, Rivers, Benedict and Others: Essays on Culture and Personality. History of Anthropology.* Volume 4. Madison: University of Wisconsin Press, 1986, pp. 95-126.

Shaw, Rosalind, and Charles Stewart. "Introduction: Problematizing Syncretism." In Charles Stewart and Rosalind Shaw, eds., *Syncretism/Anti-Syncretism: The Politics of Religious Synthesis.* London and NY: Routledge, 1994, pp. 1-26.

Stewart, Charles. "Relocating Syncretism in Social Science Discourse." In Gören Aijmer, ed., *Syncretism and the Commerce of Symbols.* Göteborg, Sweden: The Institute for Advanced Studies in Social Anthropology, 1995, pp. 13-37.

Stocking, G. W., Jr., ed. *The Shaping of American Anthropology, 1883-1911: A Franz Boas Reader.* New York: Basic Books, 1974.

Wagley, Charles, and Marvin Harris. *Minorities in the New World.* New York: Columbia University Press, 1958.

2

Accounting for Recent Anti-Syncretist Trends in Candomblé-Catholic Relations

Peter B. Clarke

INTRODUCTION

This chapter focuses on what it means to be a Candomblé-Catholic—not a static, fixed idea—to those who are, and on whether this relationship is best described as syncretistic. By syncretism is meant here the arbitrary mixing of beliefs and rituals that theoretically do not belong together in the same religious tradition. It also addresses the "sectarian" response of official Catholicism to this cult-like dual allegiance, and more generally its understanding of syncretism. It is something of a paradox that official Catholicism adopts an exclusivist response to Candomblé participation in its worship in order to preserve its inclusivist, universalist image and pretensions while Candomblé, traditionally referred to as a sect (seita), has often adopted a more open-ended stance to the relationship.

However, there is evidence of the spread of a more defiant, oppositional attitude from a number of Candomblé leaders to members' involvement in Catholic ceremonies and rituals, and all forms of syncretism, and this is also a central concern of this presentation. This response and that of official Catholicism assume that such relationships are syncretic, which is not necessarily how they are perceived and interpreted by the actual participants themselves. The contention here is that there is selective syncretism but not on fundamentals, and that more recently cultural, economic, political, and religious changes have contributed to a rising demand from leaders on both sides for the elimination of even the most superficial levels of syncretism.

Where dual Candomble-Catholic belonging exists there is a striking degree of interest in the past and particularly in the time-honored myths of African-Brazilian religion, which is but one reason why this writer questions whether syncretism is the most appropriate term to describe this interaction. This interest also suggests that the position held by some scholars regarding the stance of popular religion toward history does not apply at least in the case of Candomblé. For example, on the orientation of popular religion toward history, Rostas and Droogers wrote: "the users of popular religion are much less concerned with where their beliefs and practices have come from and much more with the efficacy of their vision of religion" (1993:10).

It is history, a deep sense of obligation to preserve the past, and the spiritual, psychological, and sometimes material benefits that Candomblé can offer that gives it its own distinctive appeal and makes the use of the label syncretism to describe the interchange between Candomblé and Catholicism only partly applicable. The relationship is not easily defined, characterized as it is both by a degree of syncretism that never runs very deep and which is restricted to certain rites, and also by a form of separation that can be symbolically extremely rigid and unambiguous. The celebration of Candomblé-Catholic festivals and the post-initiation rituals contain elements of the former and animal sacrifice and possession are two areas characterised by separation. Why specific areas of the relationship should be open to syncretism and others not is an interesting question which for reasons of space cannot be discussed in any detail here, but some examples of obscure forms of syncretism and of unambiguous separation will be given below.

The thinking of most Candomblé devotees is both evolutionist and essentialist, and the widespread perception exists that authenticity and uniqueness ultimately derive from the origins or sources of a particular tradition which in the case of Candomblé and Catholicism are different: Africa and Rome/Europe, respectively. Furthermore, there are different forms of Catholicism, it is believed, and African-Brazilian Catholicism is one form forged in Brazil and, though different from "official" Catholicism which from an African-Brazilian perspective is seen as largely western, is, nevertheless, a genuine form.

For purposes of comparison not only are the dynamics of the relationship between African-Brazilian religion and Catholicism examined but also the processes of distancing and unification between the various African-Brazilian traditions and between these traditions and the political movement that most directly seeks partnership with Candomblé, the Movimento Negro (Black Movement), for these also throw light on the anti-syncretist trends in Candomble.

But first a brief outline of the history of the tradition.

HISTORICAL AND RELIGIOUS BACKGROUND

Essentialist and evolutionist views of the history of Candomblé that root it firmly in African soil are more existentially and experientially grounded than founded on hard fact. Candomblé is the outcome of a long encounter that began in the fifteenth century with the transatlantic slave trade between, on the one hand, indigenous African religions and Catholicism and on the other between the former and indigenous Amerindian beliefs and practices.

A number of traditions are subsumed under the general heading of Candomblé, and culturally specific practices and observances distinguish one from another. Moreover, in Brazil the different Candomblé traditions refer to themselves as nations (nacoes). The term *Nago* as applied to the Yoruba nacao or nation is a Fon expression in use in Bahia since the end of the eighteenth century to refer to the Yoruba-speaking peoples of the southeast of the Republic of Benin (formerly Dahomey) and the southwest of Nigeria, while the term *Jeje*—sometimes hyphenated with Nago to read *Nago-Jeje*—refers to descendants of the Fon and Gun peoples of the central region of the Republic of Benin (formerly Dahomey) in western Africa. The *Ijesha* nacao is a subdivision of the Nago nacao. The labels Angolan and Congo cover all Bantu traditions in Bahia.

The differences between the traditions are explained in various ways and often with reference to the way the ceremonial drums are played. Yoruba and Yoruba-derived traditions will use drumsticks to beat the sacred drums and call in the gods and/or orixa from Africa, while the Angolan traditions make use simply of the hands for the same purpose. Moreover, while the former rely almost exclusively on the Yoruba language in the chants and the liturgy generally, the latter makes much more use of Portuguese. When heavily influenced by Caboclo or Amerinidian Candomblé uses a variety of languages including German and Latin in addition to Portuguese.

The Yoruba traditions have been more reluctant than others to allow mixing with Spiritism and Amerindian religion. The Congo-Angolan tradition, on the other hand, has been more willing to accept the presence in its worship of Amerindian spirits and rituals. As Roger Bastide observed, of all the African traditions in the New World the Yoruba tradition has remained closest to its origins (1971). The Yoruba came to constitute a majority of the African population in Bahia from the last quarter of the eighteenth century when increasing numbers were shipped from western Africa to Bahia in return for cheap third grade Bahian-produced tobacco (Verger, 1976).

Despite disclaimers to the contrary, the sense and purpose of which will be discussed below, Yoruba and/or Nago Candomblé is not itself a pure tradition, having been greatly influenced by other traditions, among them those of the Jeje and Ijesha. Moreover, prior to their advent in Brazil, western African religions had already begun to interact and shape and mold each other. Robin Horton suggests that they have always shared much in common, although even in the case of shared core beliefs differences in emphasis emerged over time, the notion of destiny being a case in point (Horton, 1983).

While they share much in common there are, as previously noted, variations in the performance of rituals and in the interpretation of myths and beliefs from one Candomblé nation to another, and even each terreiro or Candomblé center, no matter what tradition it professes to uphold, has, as Bastide pointed out, "its own life, its own history and its own spirit" (1983: 262). For this reason, if for no other, specialized research will yield different conclusions on the attitudes, orientation, form, and content of Candomblé.

There are an estimated 2,800 Candomblé terreiros in Salvador, Bahia, the majority of which belong to the *Nago* tradition and are led and maintained in the main by women known as *Ialorixa* or *maes-de-santo* (mothers of the saint or holy one). While other nations will also use these terms for the chief priestess, they also have their own names, the *Jeje* employing the Fon word *humbon* and Congo and Angolan Candomblé the term *mameto do inkisi*. Where the leader of a *Nago* terreiro is a man he has the title *babalorixa,* translated into Brazilian as *pai-de-santo* (father of the saint or holy one), and this is more commonly the case outside Bahia in, for example, Recife in Pernambuco where, as in Trinidad, Candomblé is commonly known as *Xango* from the Yoruba Shango, god of thunder. The *Jeje* use mostly the same terms as the *Nago* and in Congo and Angolan terreiros one hears both this title and the term *tata do inkisi.* In Amerindian or Caboclo Candomblé the names *madrinha* and *padrinha* or *zeladora* and *zelador* are used for female and male leaders respectively (Carneiro, 1961: 128). A female devotee is known as *filha de santo* (daughter of the saint) and a male devotee as *filho de santo* (son of the saint) the *Nago, Jeje,* and Congo-Angolan equivalents for the former being *iao, vodunce,* and *muzenza* respectively. In Bahia women leaders are in the majority in *Nago* and *Jeje* terreiros and the reasons for this are complex, involving questions of history, economics, aesthetics, gender, charisma, and mythology (Clarke, 1993a).

The size of membership varies considerably from one center to another, ranging from as few as twenty to several hundred, although the question of what it means to be a member and of types and levels of membership is likewise complex. Initiation involving a period of months—the length of time can vary from one tradition and even from one terreiro to another—as a novice was once the principal path to full membership. However, the need to earn a living in a harsh and extremely difficult economic climate has reduced the length of time that can be given to training of this kind. Candomblé has had to adapt to this situation by allowing novices to work outside the terreiro during the day and by shortening the period of training. But the problem of the cost involved in becoming a novice still remains. Even to become a member of an economically middle range to poor terreiro could cost as much as $150 U.S, the equivalent of approximately one month's minimum salary, at the time of writing.

The present harsh economic climate is affecting every aspect of Candomblé from its "theology" to the quality of the material of its ritual costumes. Even the orixa or gods are losing out in that the difficult economic circumstances make it impossible for devotees to procure for them the kinds of sacrificial gifts in the form of food and other items which they demand.

Not all terreiros are affected to the same extent by these difficulties, and some of the leaders of the more historic and better known Candomblé casas or houses are benefiting from the upturn in tourism as increasing numbers of Black Americans, among others, visit and participate in the ceremonies and feasts. Certain leaders who have acquired fame throughout Brazil, Africa, the United States, and Europe are able to command remuneration for their counseling and advice, which greatly helps in the maintenance of their terreiros.

At the center of the Candomblé experience is possession. Each devotee has for guardian and protector an orixa or god whom s/he resembles closely in character and who enables the devotee to fulfil her/his destiny. The divinities are, as already mentioned, African deities called upon through the beating of drums and chanting to incorporate in their devotees the *filhas-de-santo* and *filhos-de-santo*.

While possession usually takes place during an actual ceremony and under close supervision, it can also occur outside this context and quite randomly. Initiation, thus, is not a *sine qua non* of possession; at times the one possessed is a young child or a person with no formal links with a terreiro, and in either case this can be interpreted as a sign that a god is calling such a person to be a devotee. It may also happen while a person is carrying out daily household tasks such as cooking a meal, washing clothes, or cleaning the house.

Possession can also be, among other things, a device for maintaining order and discipline in that the one possessed, whether it be during a ceremony or in other circumstances, is often the bearer of a message about a potential source of conflict within the community or a misdemeanor which is then divulged to the leader of the terreiro.

Different theories of possession in general (Lewis, 1971) and of Candomblé in particular range from the medico-psychological hypothesis of Nina Rodrigues (1935, 1977) to the strongly sociological theory of Bastide (1978). Such attempts at explanation have not always met with the approval of other experts in the field. Verger, for example, insists that there should be less concern with explanation, with the "why" of Candomblé and much more emphasis on the "how." Verger maintains that Candomblé is a distinctive religious tradition with its own philosophy of life and understanding of human nature. This view provides a suitable opening to begin the discussion of Candomblé relations with Catholicism and with other religious, political and folkloric traditions with which it has been in frequent interaction.

CANDOMBLÉ-CATHOLIC DIFFERENCES

The links between Candomblé and Catholicism are many, as previously noted. Some are of a very tenuous nature and in some measure the product of historical and political necessity, while others would appear to be much more substantial. An example of an extremely fragile link is the pairing of the Yoruba god of thunder, Xango, with the Catholic saint Jerome. The reason would seem to be that Jerome's partner in protection against lightning is St. Barbara, who resembles the Yoruba goddess Oxum. But since Oxum partners Xango in this task the latter is deemed to resemble St. Jerome.

This kind of pairing, whether flimsy or well founded, symbolizes on the one hand a society in tension, if not in conflict, a society based on a working misunderstanding between colonizer and colonized where the latter, to preserve its heritage, allowed the former to believe that he enjoyed a monopoly of all the resources, including the spiritual. On the other hand, it is a sign of belonging to two traditions both of which are an integral part of one's personal and ethnic history. This should not lead one to to perceive the relationship as essentially syncretist. Verger makes a clear and fundamental existential distinction between Candomblé and Christianity by which he means principally Catholicism, the majority Christian church in Bahia and in Brazil as a whole, maintaining that whereas the former holds an essentially optimistic view of of human nature the latter is inherently pessimistic. He is persuaded that since it does not entertain the notion of original sin, Candomblé is, as a consequence, unequivocal in celebrating the human worth and dignity of the individual. In essence Christianity burdens the individual with guilt and Candomblé uplifts him, making for a radical difference between the traditions (Clarke: *Verger Interviews,* 1986-1995).

Bastide also spoke of a "fundamental" difference between Candomblé, which he saw as a mystical tradition, and the mysticism of Christianity and Islam. He wrote, "While the mysticism of the Christian and the Muslim consists of a long ascension of the soul in the direction of God until it loses itself therein, the other mysticism (that of the blacks of Bahia) consists of making God or the Spirit come by means of appropriate rites to repose for a moment in the soul of devotee. The climax is in the trance" (1983:249).

Candomblé has also been compared and contrasted with Umbanda and found to be different. In the central ritual of trance there are, according to Renato Ortiz (1988:70), radical differences—Candomblé having a very precise model of possession derived from African sources and myths and much more collective in character, while in Umbanda the form is more indeterminate and individualistic. In Umbanda possession has shed all its links with the myths recalling the exploits and adventures of the possessing spirits, the orixa or African deities. It is Ortiz's view that while Candomblé is essentially about the conservation of the African collective memory in Brazil, Umbanda is essentially about the integration of African-Brazilian practices into the modern world (1988:71).

Many would agree with Verger and Bastide insisting, like them, that members of Candomblé—particularly *Nago* Candomblé—keep their Afro-Brazilian and Catholic cosmologies and spiritualities quite separate. Evidence that this is the case is to be found in the terreiros of Ile Axe Opo Afonja (the powerful stronghold of Afonja) in the district of Sao Gonzalo de Retiro and of Ile Axe Opo Aganju (the powerful stronghold of Xango) in the nearby town of Lauro de Freitas. The mae-de-santo of the former terreiro or cult center, Mae Stella, unusually does not permit any Catholic shrines, icons, or symbols in the Candomblé temple. And in Lauro-de-Freitas the pai-de-santo, prior to entering trance, has his crucifix removed from his neck.

However, it should be noted that even in the Ile Axe Opo Afonja terreiro there is a large white cross fronting the wooded area where the obligatory ceremonies in veneration of the ancestors are performed. Other evidence of syncretism and separation comes from Sao Luiz, capital of Maranhao, where the African-derived traditions are known collectively as *Tambor de Mina.* The separation is noticeable in certain rituals including initiation rites, funeral ceremonies, animal sacrifices, and in the music and dancing associated with the orixas or divinities. Catholic and African rituals, moreover, are practiced, as Sergio Ferretti points out (1995), in different areas of the house or temple, the former in the front room where there is an altar and the latter in "secret" spaces in the center and at the back of the house. But there is interpenetration; a Catholic ritual which begins in the front room will wind its way through the house to the verandah at the back, where African music and dance rituals are performed (Ferretti, 1995).

Among the strongest proponents of complete separation is Mestri Didi Alapini, son of the eminent priestess the late Mae Senhora and himself priest of the Ancestor Cult (Egungun). He urges members of Candomblé to abandon syncretism by making a clear choice between the Yoruba god (Portuguese: orixa) Ogum and his Catholic counterpart in Bahia St. Anthony, between Yansan and St. Barbara, between popcorn offerings and a mass in homage to St. Lazarus. These pairings were made by the older generations of Candomblé devotees, Mestre Didi explains, in order to please, in order to be accepted, in order to show that their gods had dignity and their religion worth. But African gods are Nature itself, and all such accommodations distort this truth, are unnecessary, and will end in the destruction of African religion and culture in Brazil (*A Tarde*, 9/22/90).

Even within the varied and complex world of African-Brazilian religion itself there is also a concern with boundary maintenance. The various temples of

Nago Candomblé in particular seek to distance themselves from most other forms of Candomblé and from what is seen as folklore, including Carnival. Mae-de-santo Olga de Alaketo is one of the more outspoken leaders on the subject of Carnival's links with Candomblé. She insists that, while a beautiful display, Carnival's use of Candomblé dress, symbols, and music "has nothing to do with the gods" and is "immoral" (Regis, 1984: 32).

Thus, virtually everywhere in what, to the casual observer, is a mosiac of religious belief and practice composed of Brazilianized African religion, Africanized Amerindian religion, Portuguese Catholicism, and increasing Japanese Shinto-Buddhist cults (Clarke, 1995) there is an underlying preoccupation with retaining differences, particularly where rituals are concerned, while simultaneously seeking to persuade certain of those whom one defines as "other" of one's full and total belonging to that tradition as well.

When interviewed, members of Candomblé will insist that they are full, legitimate members of the "Roman Catholic and Apostolic Church," that they have been baptized, confirmed, and have made their first solemn communion in that church. Paradoxically, it is widely acknowledged among ordinary Catholics that Candomblé practitioners are the "best" Catholics—the most regular worshippers—in Bahia. Questioned in the same context about their membership of Candomblé, the reply is usually, "I am also of Candomblé." On the other hand, participants in Candomblé when assisting at mass are routinely informed by the officiating priest that they should not receive communion if they are practicing members of Candomblé, and many do not.

African-Brazilian religions have long been involved in a contest with official Catholicism over the terms of admission to full participation in Catholic worship, and one of the main concerns of this chapter is to unpack the complex set of motivations underlying this demand for "dual allegiance" of what, as we have seen, are, in the opinion of researchers and practitioners alike two radically different religions.

The foundations of this relationship are complex, based as they are not only on theological decisions designed to ensure "authenticity" and "purity" of belief and practice but also on reactions at specific times in specific contexts to historical, cultural, and political forces. However, in line with the emphasis in this chapter on the idea that participants of Candomblé themselves have of the nature of this relationship and how it should be structured, I proceed to suggest why members themselves feel compelled to embrace both traditions.

CATHOLICISM AS DEVOTION, CANDOMBLÉ AS OBLIGATION

Candomblé is to its devotees serious religion; it is no less a religion than Catholicism. But it does not provide "Catholic" answers or solutions. It is not

Catholicism, although the latter could, it is believed, derive considerable benefit from links with Candomblé, whose gods have the capacity to energize the "saints of Rome" (Regis, 1984: 31). Opposition to this conviction from the Catholic church is deemed to be due to the latter's ignorance and lack of knowledge of Candomblé.

The character of Candomblé-Catholic relations over several centuries has often been oversimplified. They were not always hostile and they witnessed a profound change in the ninetenth century with the romanization of the Catholic church in Brazil leading to increased clerical control over those religious associations—confraternities, brotherhoods and tertiary religious orders—where from the beginning of the colonial period in the sixteenth century enslaved Africans and their descendants developed their own religious life which included the practice of African and Catholic rites (Hoornaert, 1971). Catholicism took a positive interest in the performance of these rites, which were attended on occasion by clerics. However, with the greater romanization and clericalization of the Brazilian Catholic church, Catholic attitudes changed and genuine interest was replaced by negative and derogatory comment that depicted Candomblé beliefs and rites as harmful and superstitious and of no religious or spiritual value (Hoornaert, 1971: 45-46).

To return to the present, "Catholic" members of Candomblé—resembling Max Weber's distinction between early and mature religion—will sometimes contrast the two traditions this way: Candomblé is "obrigacao" (obligation) while Catholicism is "devocao" (Clarke, *Interviews*, 1986-1995). It is easier to interpret what is meant by "obrigacao" than to unravel the meaning of "devocao" in this comparative context. But what essentially is meant is that the two traditions, African-Brazilian and Catholic, are concerned with two very different dimensions of religion and spirituality, which are seen to complement each other, the former with filial piety and the latter with worship, with paying divine honor to God. Although all ritual acts in *Nago* Candomblé are directed ultimately to *Olorun* (the Yoruba term for God), Candomblé has no special, ceremonial space for this, while Catholicism in its Brazilian form does not offer the possibility or the facilities for fulfilling obligations to African deities and ancestors, forces of nature and forces of society, respectively (Horton, 1983).

The labeling of Catholicism as "devotion" in contrast to Candomblé as "obligation" is also meant to identify the practical, this-worldy thrust of the latter compared with the more other-worldly emphasis found in the former. Candomblé directly addresses existential questions relating to identity, personal relationships, and destiny, even biological links forged in Brazil between the different races. While there is much greater emphasis on ritual than on systematic theology in Candomblé there is, nonetheless, a strong belief in destiny which involves a process of divination to discover one's "guardian angel" who guides one along the path in life decided upon by Olorun (owner of the sky) before birth. Eventually, this belief came to function as the basis of a social psychology which enables people to analyse the causes of success and failure and take the 'approriate' remedies to reconstruct their life.

Above all else, however, devotees of Candomblé have incurred the duty, the obligation to preserve the customs and traditions of their African gods who provide somewhat idealized pre-enslavement images of themselves and of their ancestors who implanted these same gods in Brazilian soil during slavery. While, as already pointed out, these African divinities are traditionally equated with Catholic saints in Bahia and throughout Brazil (Valente, 1977), they are not Catholic saints and could not be satisfied with the kind of devotion offered to the former. Their devotees are African-Brazilian Catholics who are obliged out of filial piety and in memory of a glorious past to carry out rituals in their memory that official Catholicism rejects.

These rituals are believed to have the power or *ase* to enable and uplift. Through their performance history is kept alive, communal bonds forged, and a sense of self-worth and dignity preserved. Such rituals also support an African-Brazilian system of power and status devised for people deprived of access to the necessities and benefits available in the mainsteam of society. This system has gradually penetrated and influenced much that goes on in the wider world of healing, politics, economics, art, leisure, and music in Bahia.

Obrigacao, however, has been and continues to be both burdensome in the way that preserving a minority culture through rituals that demand a great deal of time, sacrifice, and strong sense of self can be, and liberating. Examples abound and include the career of the market vendor turned mae-de-santo (high priestess) Mae Senhora, of the Candomblé terreiro Opo Afonja in the district of Sao Gonzalo de Retiro in Salvador, Bahia, Brazil. Verger recalls her struggle for survival, her pertinacity, and how on being informed that an honorary title had been conferred upon her by the Alafin (King) of Oyo in western Nigeria she exclaimed: "Now I am my ancestor" (Clarke, *Verger Interviews*, 1987). This kind of liberation that gives a sense of totally transcending the indignity of enslavement Catholicism could never provide. Yet Mae Senhora was a Catholic. But, being Catholic is not to jeopardise belonging to an "authentic" Candomblé tradition. The way such authenticity is defined and constructed has changed in such a way as to facilitate such a claim.

As previously mentioned, Candomblé nations distance themselves not only from Catholicism but also from each other and from Caboclo or Indian Candomblé. Adherents of Candomblé hold to an ideal of orthodoxy tied directly to the African origins of the oldest Candomblé centers. As centers of cultural and political resistance these Candomblé houses have tended to emphasize fidelity to ancestral beliefs, to myths of origin and to the ethnic group to which they belonged originally rather than focus on the modifications and even changes in belief and ritual that have taken place.

Thus, although the mixing of the beliefs and rituals of the various African-Brazilian religious traditions is something that they recognize, the more established Candomblé houses including the Casa Branca and the terreiros of Bogum, Gantois, Opo Afonja, and Alaketo, among others, will refer to themselves in more exclusivist terms as *Nago* or *Jeje* rather than as *Nago-Jege* or *Nago-Angolan*. And this despite the fact that, as already noted, cultural interpenetration began in the African setting and continued in Brazil gathering pace from the middle years of the nineteenth century. This process of acculturation between the various Candomblé traditions in Bahia, while an accepted part of academic research, is not always accepted by participants themselves, who refer to *Nago* or *Jeje* or *Angolan* Candomblé as if they were "pure" and "authentic" expressions, distinct from each other, of African-Brazilian culture.

The borrowing aside, these terreiros continue to see themselves as the guardians and the interpreters of those fundamental and formative principles that underlie African culture in its *Nago* or *Jeje* or *Angolan* form. However much they adapt, these terreiros see it as their foremost duty to retain the distinctive marks of their origins which constitute their special, unique source of revelation. The belief in these centers as sources of a pure experience that history or mixing or anything else cannot be allowed to corrupt runs very deep.

This interpretative framework helps, I believe, to make sense of the concern many terreiros have to trace their history back as far as possible with great seriousness and in great detail to a particular region and a particular people in Africa. Hence the use of the term nacao or nation by Candomblé members when referring to the tradition to which they belong, *nacao Nago* or *Jeje* or *Angolan,* although, as previously noted, it has become increasingly difficult to drawn clearcut lines between one Candomblé tradition and another by reference to culture.

If applied to nations as cultural formations then, the interpretative framework set out above is too rigid. Many members of Candomblé terreiros are not either culturally or by descent of the same nation as their terreiro yet will claim that they belong to a pure tradition. Such a claim was made by the venerable and esteemed Mae Aninha, the late mae-de-santo of Casa Opo Afonja whom, Vivaldo da Costa Lima (1984) tells us, stressed that her *Nago* sect was pure (minha seita nago e pura).

How could Mae Aninha who was neither born Nago nor even of *Nago* descent make such a claim? Moreover, her *"Nago"* terreiro showed considerable *Jeje* influence, including the names she gave to her devotees. She was, nevertheless, able to claim *"Nago* nationality" because of a shift in the understanding of the term "nation."

Mae Aninha took the religious route, so to speak, to "naturalization" by being formed in the fundamental principles of *Nago* belief and practice in what was historically a *Nago* terreiro. She had received the *axe* from the *Nago* gods or orixa, and it became her responsibility to ensure that the specific cultural and ethnic source of this *axe*, which empowered it, was preserved and protected, suffering no diminution in its effects through popularization or catholicization.

Her claim to belong to a "pure sect" was, thus, a theological claim and indicated a move away from the more political and cultural understanding of the notion of "Candomblé nation" and of orthoxoxy and purity prevalent in the nineteenth century to one founded more on ritual, belief, and ideology and/or theology (da Costa Lima, 1984).

One major threat to the *ase* or vital energy of which Mae Aninha was a guardian, and which derives its energy and dynamism from being grounded in a specific and particular culture, is the Catholic church which for its part sees in greater Candomblé-Catholic interaction a danger to its universalistic mission.

CATHOLIC UNIVERSALITY AND CANDOMBLÉ PARTICULARISM

Reflecting recently on the prospects for a "Catholic-Afro-Brazilian rite," the cardinal archbishop of Sao Salvador da Bahia and primate of Brazil, Dom Lucas Moreira Neves posed the question: what would be the consequences for the universal character of the Catholic liturgy if it were to be transformed in favor of ritual expressions that were limited and tied to a particular race? (*A Tarde*, 4/4/1990).

The Cardinal's relations with Candomblé have been difficult since his arrival in Bahia in 1989, largely due to his decision to publicly distance Catholicism from Candomblé, a stance that has given rise to a struggle for dominance of sacred space and for the support and loyalty of the people. This struggle is fought out on the steps of Bahia's most famous church, the Basilica of Nosso Senhor do Bomfin (Our Lord of the Good End), a traditional place of pilgrimage for both Catholics and Candomblé members—often the same people—situated on the "sacred hill" (colina sacra) in the western region of the capital city, Salvador. It is also fought out in the parish of the church of Cachoeira between the two hundred year old Irmandade da Boa Morte and the archdiocese of Salvador, Bahia, among other places.

Bomfin enters Candomblé at many points and is seen as essential to its make-up. After initiation it is traditional for the new Candomblé devotee accompanied by a more senior member to visit and mount the steps of the basilica where reverence and gratitude are expressed to Our Lord the Good Jesus of the Good End and Oxala, the counterpart of Jesus in the Yoruba pantheon. There is also an annual pilgrimage to Bomfin in January which begins seven kilometers away in the commercial quarter of the lower city at the steps of the church of Nossa Senhora da Conceicao da Praia (Our Lady of the Immaculate Conception of the

Beach) with whom Yemanja, the Yoruba goddess of the sea, is paired. The procession is followed by a mass that is traditionally celebrated by the incumbent cardinal archbishop of Salvador.

The present cardinal archbishop's position is to leave no one in any doubt that Bomfirn is a Catholic church. In his address to the large crowd gathered in the basilica and outside on the steps and in the praca or square on January 15, 1990, he spoke of the basilica as the people's cathedral as distinct from the cathedral in the upper city which canonically and liturgically is the principal church of the diocese. Then, without naming African-Brazilian religion, he left no one in any doubt that "syncretism" was intolerable, reportedly warning his listeners of the threat that the mixing of Catholicism with other beliefs presented and affirming that "God would protect 'us' from these dangers and threats" (A Tarde, Jan. 15, 1990).

The cardinal also intervened through the parish priest of Cachoeira in the Boa Morte (Good Death) festival, performed annually in August on the feast of the Assumption in that city since the early nineteenth century by the Confraternity of Nossa Senhora da Boa Morte de Cachoeira (Our Lady of the Good Death of Cachoeira). This confraternity, composed of twenty-eight irmas (sisters), all of them descendants of slaves and feitas no santo (female initiates of Candomblé), is seen by researchers as an African-Brazilian-Catholic adaptation of the Yoruba society of Aje (female possessors of an occult power which enables its human vehicles to perform effective magic) also known as Iya-mi (our mothers) and Iya-agbe (old and venerable mothers). Among the Yoruba of western Africa this society is known as the Gelede society and forms the women's section of the Egungun or ancestor cult which has as one of its main functions to guarantee individual immortality and the immortality of the community. Hence the sense, as Candomblé-Catholics, of celebrating the festival on the feast of the Assumption.

The "Catholic" liturgy for the Boa Morte festival consists of the translation of th image of Our Lady from the Confraternity to the parish church (since 1989 when the right to use the parish church was withdrawn by the archdiocese, the statue is translated to the confraternity's own church) followed by mass at which the members of the confraternity assist and take holy communion. After the mass there is the procession around the town followed by the serving of foods containing axe, spiritual power or force, that would in the setting of the Egungun cult be offered to the ancestors and the gods, such as Ogun, that are associated with them and with death. The Geled society did not survive in Brazil and the Egungun cult is limited in its force and scope and this prompts researchers to ask if the the Boa Morte festival on the Assumption of Our Lady might not be at the conceptual level an adaptation of the Yoruba understanding of death and immortality to the Catholic understanding of these phenomena, without undermining the meaning and sense provided by the former (Nascimemto and Isidoro, 1988).

The Archdiocese of Salvador, Bahia, was in no doubt that Catholicism was subjected by this festival to considerable adaptation to Candomblé and, thus, refused the use of the parish church for this event. It also disputed the ownership of the statue of Our Lady around which the cult was centered and several other religious objects, thereby giving rise to what the local press began to refer to as a "holy war." The dispute spread and the question of racial discrimination became part of it as the confraternity accused the local parish priest at the center of the conflict, Father Vilasboas, of using abusive and offensive language. The confraternity saw the conflict as a struggle for their sacred patrimony while the Movimento Negro (Black Movement) broadened it to include the defense of the rights of black Brazilians.

Both the Bomfirn and the Cachoeira disputes were about much more than "syncretism;" as already indicated, they were about questions of power and influence in society. Now the Boa Morte Confraternity, with the assistance of the State Goverment of Bahia, has new headquarters that house a museum in a large restored and refurbished nineteenth-century building, and a chapel of its own. Outside it advertises itself as the "People's Confraternity." It awaits the completion of a larger church; the parish church is in considerable disrepair.

Returning to the above question posed by the cardinal archbishop of Salvador: it reveals one of the principal differences in outlook between African-Brazilian religion and official Catholicism in Brazil. While the latter is essentially a mission-driven movement that aims to create a global religious culture that stands above any particular culture and is more than the sum of the parts of all those cultures in which it finds expression; the former has a very different perception of itself. The African-Brazilian tradition is one that does not seek in principle to convert others to its beliefs and practices, being committed, as it is, to the conservation of a specific culture preserved in sacred myth and ritual. Indeed its whole purpose is to safeguard one particular religious culture and set of values. As a spiritual and cultural resource it also has other ambitions that take it beyond these limits into the wider, more diverse, and pluralistic world of Brazil. It operates as a form of social psychology for members and nonmembers alike, and intends that its political, cultural, religious, and economic influence impact well beyond its confines. But there is no ambition in any of this to convert, at least not on a large scale. Moreover, using the imagery of the commericial market, there is in Candomblé the realization of the need for "micro-marketing" in the sense that the "religious market" in Brazil will only desire its "product lines" as long as these retain an African identity and do not come to be seen as interchangeable with the "product lines" of other traditions, including Catholicism.

It is arguable that in practice official Catholicism is tied to a particular set of values and a particular culture that are western in form and content, and for this reason is opposed to the African-Brazilian version of Catholicism. Certainly in

Brazil it has been and continues to be the case that the more Catholicism approximates to a European and/or western model the more it is esteemed and valued, and the more it approximates to African culture the less the prestige, status, and value attached to it and the more likely it is to be rejected (Hoornaert, 1971: 51).

CONCLUSIONS

Considered from the perspectives of the actors, that is Candomblé-Catholics themselves, although rituals and symbols and sacred space may be shared for certain purposes, there exist, nonetheless, unbridgeable cultural and spiritual differences between the two traditions and a clear difference in origin, source of spiritual power, and, at one important level, in aim. This is inevitable, for there cannot be simply one way and one set of rituals and symbols, however apparently integrated and symbiotic, labeled Catholic, for carrying the full content of African-Catholic derived spirituality.

Authentic Candomblé will never consciously mix myth and ritual in such a way as to obcure its fundamental role of keeping alive the presence of African gods in Brazil, although it may and does allow several myths and rituals from different traditions under the same roof. But these are mostly kept separate and participants are aware of the diversity. There is a degree of mixing, as we have noted, but to mix haphazardly is to flirt with extinction. The situation is not entirely unlike Japan, where the possibilty exists to be born Shinto, marry Christian, and die Buddhist without dissolving the three traditions, either intellectually or ritually, into one.

In the more tolerant climate of the present, Candomblé faces greater threats to its survival as an independent and powerful spiritual and cultural force than in the past when it was prohibited and persecuted. It is now widely seen by many different interest groups, including certain elements of the Catholic clergy, as an extremely valuable resource. Contemporary theology and environmentalists and New Agers see it as a relational philosophy with a deep understanding of the appropriate forms of interaction between the human and natural worlds. For others it is an effective system of personal and social psychology. Artists, academics, politicians of all persuasions, and medical and tourist and folklore agencies are fast becoming in their different ways the interpreters of modern Candomblé, threatening its *ase* or vital force which is in danger of suffering a rapid process of demystification. To put it another way Candomblé charisma is in danger of turning graceless.

This realization does as much as the spiritual/ theological differences and the differences in aims and purposes outlined above to strengthen the case for distancing and the insistence by Candomblé-Catholics that the relationship between the two faiths that they subscribe to is equal and complementary: no one tradition has a monopoly of sacred space; Candomblé members belong to both traditions by virtue of a shared history and in virtue of the fact they have supported and maintained spiritually and morally as well as materially the institutions of both traditions.

Ideally, thus, from the perspective of the actors themselves, in genuine authentic expressions of Candomblé there should be no confusion of teaching, nor of purpose, and no hodge-podge mixing of ritual. For its part, Catholicism at the official level, given its aims, is seen either to be essentially universal or nothing. Overexposure to any one specific tradition and it loses its dynamism. It must tread that fine line between over- and under-adaptation which Geertz spoke about in his study of the development of Islam in Indonesia and Morocco where he wrote:

Religious faith, even when it is fed from a common source, is as much a particularizing force as a generalizing one, and indeed whatever universality a given religious tradition manages to attain arises from its ability to engage in a widening set of individual, even idiosyncratic, conceptions of life and yet somehow sustain them all. When it succeeds in this, the result may indeed as often be a distortion of these personal visions as their enrichment, but in any case whether deforming private faiths or perfecting them, the tradition usualy prospers. When it fails, however, to come to grips with them at all, it either hardens into scholasticism, evaporates into idealism, or fades into eclecticism; that is to say it ceases, except as a fossil, a shadow or a shell, really to exist. *The central paradox of religious development is that, because of the progressively wider range of spiritual experience with which it is forced to deal, the further it proceeds, the more precarious it gets. Its successes generate its frustrations* (my italics) (1968:14).

Official Catholicism fears in the contemporary Bahian context in which it no longer has the political power and moral authority it once enjoyed, and the same degree of control over the education system, that the success it would achieve by developing a "Catholic-Afro-Brazilian" ritual would adversely affect its ability to remain a generalizing force and avoid over-particularization. Paradoxically, with globalization, diaspora, migration, and the search for identity, the traditional religions of African origin, such as Candomblé, are themselves turning into international universalist religions precisely because of the specificity of their belief content and ritual. And as this process gathers momentum Catholicism becomes increasingly relativized and particularized. But this is not so obvious to those on the ground in Brazil, where Catholicism, though challenged by a growing appeal of Pentecostalism remains the dominant religious force. Candombe members are increasingly concerned about the threat from Catholicism and from all sides to Candomblé's particular vision—even from some of those 'missionaries' of traditional African religion from western Africa now visiting Brazil in ever-growing numbers.

Candomblé is about sustaining that unique vision and version of the African world long since brought to Brazil by the ancestors and partially and selectively Catholicized and Brazilianized. In the words of Mae-de-Santo Olga de Alaketu, Candomblé has for its raison d'etre: "para nao cair este pedaco de ceu da Africa que nos temos no Brazil: (Candomblé) exists so that piece of African sky that we have in Brazil does not fall down" (my translation of Regis, 1984: 28).

This priestess, while fully aware that Africa is historically and spiritually indispensable to Candomblé, acknowledges that it has undergone a process of Brazilianization and Catholicization and has moved away from its African prototype in various ways. Singling out the differences between Africa and Brazil, she points to variations in music, dance, and dress, with no mention, however, of differences in belief (1984: 31). Africa remains, despite the changes, the source and the reservoir of Candomblé *ase,* but Candomblé is not best defined as African, but as African-Brazilian.

In a similar way she explains that African-Brazilian Catholicism is not the Catholicism of Rome which is likewise permanently indispensable to that religion. And in this case her obligation is to keep alive that version of Catholicism that her ancestors forged in slavery in Brazil, an aim official Catholicism in Bahia does not at present share, and for this and other reasons discussed in the foregoing, selective anti-syncretism will continue.

Official Catholic opposition is not necessarily detrimental to Candomblé, given Catholicism's much greater resources and influence, and it may contribute, as seems to have been the case in Cachoeira, to the emergence of a more dynamic and independent African-Brazilian tradition.

But while avoiding the dangers from over-Catholicization, those of falling prey to the secularizing demands of the state and tourism increase for, although not as yet the main financial supports of Candomblé, these institutions offer easier access to resources and more substantial returns than the traditional ones, founded as they are on initiative and self reliance, can provide.

Meanwhile, Candomblé will remain open to certain aspects of Catholicism, which it has "purified" and "integrated" without stripping them of their original symbolism and significance, while closing itself off to others. It will, further, expect to share the sacred space that is common to its Candomblé-Catholic heritage, as the Bomfim and Cachoeira disputes illustrate.

Larger issues are of course being addressed in the response of Candomblé-Catholics to Candomblé-Catholic interaction including the problematic—which is by no means a purely modern phenomenon at least where religions are concerned—of the global and the particular, of "totalizing" and "anti-totalizing" religious stances.

BIBLIOGRAPHY

Bastide, R. *African Civilizations in the New World*. New York: Harper and Row, 1971.

Bastide, R. *O Candomblé da Bahia*. São Paulo: Companhia Editora Nacional, 1978

Bastide, R. *Estudos Afro-Brasileiros*. São Paulo: Editora Perspectiva, 1983.

Carneiro, E. *Candombles da Bahia*. São Paulo: Editora Technoprint LTDA, 1961.

Clarke, P. B. "Why Women Are the Priests and Teachers in Bahian Candomblé," in Elizabeth M. Puttick, and Peter B. Clarke, (eds.), *Women as Teachers and Guides in Traditional and New Religions*. Lewiston/ Queenston/Lampeter: Edwin Mellen Press, 1993a.

Clarke, P. B. "The Dilemmas of a Popular Religion: The Case of Candomblé," in S. Rostas and A. Droogers (eds.), *The Popular Use of Popular Religion in Latin America*. Amsterdam: Center for Latin American Research and Documentation (CEDLA) 1993b, pp. 95-109.

Clarke, P. B. "The Cultural Impact of New Religions in Latin and Central America and the Caribbean with Special Reference to Japanese New Religions," *Journal of Latin American Cultural Studies*. Vol. 4, no.1, 1995, pp. 117-126.

Clarke, P. B. *Verger Interviews: Fieldwork Notes*. Salvador, Bahia, 1986-1995.

da Costa Lima, V. "Naçoes-de-Candomblé," in *Encontro de Naçoes de Candomblé*. Salvador, Bahia: Ianama and Federal University of Bahia, 1984, pp. 7-26.

Ferretti, S. "Religious Syncretism in an Afro-Brazilian Cult House in Maranhao, Brazil." Paper presented at the American Anthropological Association Meeting in Washington, D.C., November 1995.

Geertz, C. *Islam Observed*. Chicago: Chicago University Press, 1968.

Hoornaert, E. "Presuppostos Antropologicos para a Comprehencao do Sincretismo" in *Revista de Cultura Vozes*, Vol. LXXI, No. 7, 1971, pp. 43-52.

Horton, R. "Introduction" to: M. Fortis, *Oedipus and Job in West African Religion*. Cambridge: Cambridge University Press (CUP), 1983.

Lewis, I. M. *Ecstatic Religion*. Middlesex, England: Penguin, 1971.

Nascimento, L., and C. Isidoro. *A Boa Morte Em Cachoeira*, Cachoeira: Centro de Estudos, Pesquisa e Açao Socio-Cultural de Cachoeira (CEPASC), 1988.

Ortiz, R. *A Morte Branca do Feiticeiro Negro*. Umbanda e Sociedade Brasileira, São Paulo: Editora Brasiliense, 1988.

Regis, Olga F. (Olga de Alaketu). "Nacao-Queto," in *Encontro de Naçoes de Candomblé*. Salvador, Bahia: Ianama and Federal University of Bahia, 1984, pp. 27-33.

Rodrigues, N. *O Animismo Fetishista dos Negros Bahianos*. Rio do Janeiro: Civilizaçao Brasileira SA, 1935.

Rostas, S., and A. Droogers (eds.), "The Popular Use of Popular Religion in Latin America," Amsterdam: CEDLA, 1993.

A Tarde. This is a quality daily newspaper published in Salvador, Bahia.

Troeltsch, E. *The Social Teachings of the Christian Churches.* New York: Macmillan, 1931.

Valente, W. *Sincretismo Religioso Afro-Brasileiro.* São Paulo: Companhia Editora Nacional, 1977.

Verger, P. *Trade Relations Between the Bight of Benin and Bahia from the Seventeenth to the Nineteenth Century.* Ibadan: Ibadan University Press, 1976.

3

Non-African Spiritual Entities in Afro-Brazilian Religion and Afro-Amerindian Syncretism

Mundicarmo Ferretti

AFRICAN-BRAZILIAN RELIGION IN MARANHÃO

We cannot talk about African-Brazilian religion in Maranhão without mentioning Tambor de Mina and the two oldest *terreiros* (worship centers) under such religious designation: *Casa das Minas-Jeje* (Minas-Jeje House), dedicated to the worship of the voodoo Zomadonu, and *Casa de Nagô* (Nago's House), dedicated to the worship of the orisha Shango, both of them located in the capital, in the middle of the 19th century, by Africans. In the past, *Casa das Minas-Jeje* was frequently visited by people belonging to a *Cambinda terreiro* (Cambinda worship center) located in a black village in Codó, in the interior of the state, and we have very little information about it.

Tambor de Mina began in São Luis and spread throughout the interior of the states of Maranhão, Pará, and Amazonas, as well as to other states of the region, and also to those capitals in the southeast, such as Rio de Janeiro and São Paulo, that received a great number of immigrants coming from the north and northeastern regions. Although hegemonic in the state of Maranhão, *Tambor de Mina-Jeje, Nago,* and *Cambinda* in the past have been strongly syncretized with a religious manifestation of indigenous origin, called *Cura/Pajelança* (healing rites), and with an African-Brazilian religious tradition, born in Codó, in the interior of the state, called *Encantaria de Barba Soera, Mata,* or *Terecô.*

From the nineteen sixties on, *Mina* and *Mata* were also influenced by *Umbanda* in the capital and in the interior of the state. In our days, even though the oldest *casas de Mina* (Minas houses) did not affiliate to Federações de Umbanda (Umbanda Societies), many of the *terreiros de Mina* and *Mata* (Mina and Mata worship centers) adopted Umbanda, and though they continue to carry on traditional *Mina, Mata,* and *Cura* rituals, they present themselves as umbandistas, and take part in the activities promoted by the Umbanda Society, as for instance: the Yemanja Feast, the New Year's Day Procession, and the Orishas Procession, celebrating the anniversary of the foundation of the city of São Luis. After the nineteen seventies, *candomblé* became more visible in the state of Maranhão, with *Casa Fanti-Ashanti* (Fanti-Ashanti center) in the capital.

Tambor de Mina worships voodoos and orishas (Africans), noble folks (European gentlemen or African entities with Brazilian names related to the orishas), and *caboclos* (entities born in Brazilian terreiros, generally not related to the orishas). These entities are organized in "nations" and families, and they display well marked differences concerning age. Although more prestige is given to the eldest, the youngest (sometimes mere children) can also be "donas da cabeça" (owners of the head), and they can be possessed while in a state of trance in all *toques* or religious ceremonies of the beating of the drums.

In the state of Maranhão, *terreiros de Mina* settled by Africans are spiritually headed by voodoo or orisha (Zomadonu and Shango); nevertheless, to have a *caboclo* (indigenous spirit) as head of the terreiro is a very old practice in the terreiros of São Luis, probably born in the *Terreiro da Turquia* in 1889, according to its present leader.

In *Mina,* celebrations are very frequent, following the Catholic saints calendar, and they generally cover three nights of *toques* (beating of the drums). Some of the feasts are celebrated in almost all the terreiros, and others are celebrated in only a few of them; but in Maranhão, during Lent drums are seldom beaten.

Mediums in the state of Maranhão, except for *Casa das Minas-Jeje*, embody more than one spiritual entity through a state of trance; in *Mina,* generally people dance, possessed by the same entity all night through—the *"dona da cabeça"* (owner of the head) or their *guia-chefe* (leader guide), caboclo (indigenous spirit). In those terreiros (worship centers) several entities incorporate in mediums, and these entities belong to different categories. Generally there is an annual *toque* for each category of entity. Such *toques* may follow the ritual structure, as for instance *Festa das Moças* (Young Ladies Celebration), or a completely different structure, as happens with: 1) *Tambor de Borá* (Drum of Borá), for Indians, generally preceded by a camping "in the forest," 2) *Tambor de Fulupa* (Drum of Fulupa) for the *Surrupiras,* where a "thorns bed" is fixed for the *encantados* (spirits); 3) *Baião,* for female entities related to *Cura/Pajelança* (healing rites), where the accordion, the guitar, the tambourine, and the castanets are played; 4) *Tambor* (Drum) for Mina's *pretos-velhos* (old African slaves), carried on the day emancipation of slaves in Brazil is celebrated, when *Tambor de Crioula* (Drum of Crioula), a folkloric merrymaking, is organized for them.

A few terreiros carry on especial rituals for some categories of entities:

Bancada (without drums) for the most relevant female entities, generically called Tobossas.

In *Mina,* there are no *toques* for Eshu, and neither he nor *Pombagiras* (female malefic Eshus) are embodied through a state of trance. Nevertheless, some *caboclo* entities possess features common to these entities. Among *caboclos,* some, like the Turks, the members of *Legua Boji* family and the *Surrupiras* are simultaneously frolicsome and strong, dangerous and vindictive. Some of them enjoy liquor, and in a few worship centers they employ dirty words and gestures, although this is strongly repressed in most of the terreiros.

As Sérgio Ferretti (1985) exposed, in the oldest Mina terreiros, Légba is respectfully and discreetly praised in order "not to disturb the works," and other entities perform some of the roles they traditionally are supposed to carry out under other African religious traditions. In *Mina-Jeje Averequete,* he speaks on behalf of voodoos from the *Queviosô* family, like *Sobô, Badé,* and others that, being Nago, cannot speak in a *Jeje* terreiro. In *Tambor da Mata* (Terecô) and in *Mina-Nago,* he is the one in charge of "opening the doors" to the *caboclo*; in *Terecô,* he is honored at the opening of rituals, and in *Mina-Nago* he is honored when *"o tambor vira prá mata"* (the drum turns to the forest), the moment when there is a break in the beating of the drums and, instead of singing to the voodoo, the congregation sings to the *caboclos,* and the voodoos "give passage" to them (mediums leave the state of trance with the voodoo and fall in a state of trance with *caboclo*).

THE PRESENCE OF NON-AFRICAN SPIRITUAL ENTITIES IN AFRICAN-BRAZILIAN RELIGION: A CASE OF AFRICAN-AMERINDIAN SYNCRETISM?[1]

Researchers and coreligionists have commonly interpreted the presence of non-African spiritual entities in African-Brazilian religion as the result of the contact of African slaves and/or their descendants with the indigenous culture (pertaining to the "natives," first "owners of Brazilian land"). This notion is reinforced by the observation of trance rituals involving the embodiment of non-African entities, many of whom have Amerindian names, and due to the fact that in several African-Brazilian religious manifestations, mediums embodying *caboclos* through a state of trance typically wear clothes of Amerindian origin or inspiration. It certainly cannot be stated that the *caboclo* worshiped in African-Brazilian religion came from Africa, like the orishas and voodoos; nor should one deny the impact of the absorption of indigenous culture by the Africans and the recognition of the Indian as a Brazilian hero and national symbol post-Independence on Afro-Brazilian religion. Nevertheless, researches on *Tambor de Mina*—African-Brazilian religious manifestation prevailing in the North of

Brazil—suggest the ineffectiveness of the idea of African-Amerindian syncretism for the understanding of *caboclo* entities. The abovementioned studies also show the need for developing a concept of *caboclo* less dependent on ethnic factors, and less biased by an ideal of African purity that has led many researchers to consider the non-African elements of such religion as a "contamination" by indigenous culture.

THE CABOCLO IN AFRICAN-BRAZILIAN RELIGION

The non-African spiritual entities worshiped in terreiros of Candomblé, Shango, Mina, Batuque, and Umbanda are classified in the following categories, in accordance with the myth of the "three formative races of Brazilian society": 1) caboclos, representing the native/indigenous population or low classes of Brazilian society living in rural areas; 2) pretos-velhos (old blacks), representing the former African slaves; and 3) senhores or "gente fina" (gentlemen or "noble folks"), representing the white European colonizer.

The *caboclos* appear to be the oldest group, and emerged in the states of Bahia and Maranhão, in terreiros Nago (Yoruban) and Bantu (Congo, Angola, and others). However, dating from the end of the last century, there are in Bahia as well as in Maranhão, worship centers devoted to the *caboclos*, as for example the *Terreiro da Turquia* located in São Luis, capital of the state of Maranhão.

The *pretos-velhos* (old black spirits) are more closely related to *Umbanda* (Brazilian religion with elements of African-Brazilian religion, indigenous religion, and Kardecist spiritism), and seem to have emerged initially in the city of Rio de Janeiro, in terreiros of *Macumba,* from which *Umbanda* apparently derives.

The *brancos/senhores* (white/gentlemen spirits), also known in *Umbanda,* are very old entities of the African-Brazilian religion of the state of Maranhão, where they were syncretized with the *orishas* (African divinities); this is the case of Sebastian, King of Portugal, syncretized with *Xapanã* (Shapanan) in the terreiros of São Luis, capital of the state of Maranhão.

In African-Brazilian religion, there is another kind of spirit constituting either a form of caboclo or perhaps an altogether different category of spiritual entity, born in Brazil: the *boiadeiros* (herdsmen), well known in *Umbanda* and terreiros of *candomblé.* Such entities, though related to rural works, do not have an indigenous origin, and several among them declare to be Angolan (coming from Bantu worship centers?) or to have Hungarian descent (gypsies?).

In *Tambor de Mina* of the state of Maranhão, *caboclo* is not a term designating exclusively indigenous spiritual entities, like *Caboclo Velho* (old indigenous spirit), or those involved in cattle raising, connected with the *Legua-Boji* family, for instance. It is also used to designate Turks, Europeans of noble lineage (like the encantados {spirits} from the family of Don Louis, King of France), and entities "coming from the forest" who have an uncertain Amerindian ancestry, not related to cattle raising, like the *Surrupiras* (classified as "fulupa/felupe"? or as "from Gangá"—Africa?).

The widely spread idea of an indigenous origin for the non-African entities, also classified as *caboclo*, either in the researchers' work or in the speech of *pais-de-santo* (high priests in African-Brazilian religion), has been reinforced by the hasty interpretation of observed ritual elements, when such spirits may be embodied through a state of trance, and show themselves up with Amerindian names and occasionally even with corresponding vestments. A more thorough examination of the attributes of the entities embodied through a state of trance during observed rituals, an analysis of the lyrics of songs sung by them or for them, and a careful reading of the mythic narratives collected in those terreiros may lead the researcher to see these entities from a quite different perspective.

In *Mina* of the state of Maranhão, the name of the mythic entity embodied through a state of trance, and the wearing of clothes of indigenous origin during rituals are not sufficient evidence of an Amerindian root, although these features affirm the recognition of the Indian in *Tambor de Mina* and suggest a kind of connection between them. Therefore, the explanation for the adoption of indigenous names by the Turks should not be sought in the ethnic origin or through a possible indigenous borrowing process. It must be rather searched in the historical and social context surrounding their birth as spiritual entities in *Tambor de Mina*.

The use of indigenous names by several non-adopted children of the King of Turkey ("true Turks") may be interpreted:

1. As a strategy employed by African descendants to divert the attention of the dominant Catholic class from their non-Christian origin (Moslem or plainly pagan), an origin that must have been responsible for their stigmatization and, occasionally, according to Brazilian folklore, for their connection with the devil;

2. As a result of the need for assertion of their difference in relation to African spiritual entities—voodoos and orishas (for whose worship the two oldest terreiros of the state of Maranhão were opened: Casa das Minas-Jeje (Minas-Jeje House), devoted to Zomadonu, and Casa de Nagô-iorubana (Yoruban-derived Nago House), devoted to Shango;

3. As a consequence of the need for assertion of their Brazilian identity—encantados (spirits) who started to embody through a state of trance in Brazil—thus facilitating the opening of another terreiro in the city of São Luis (for Turks), proceeding still forbidden, in our days, by Casa das Minas, and discouraged at Casa de Nagô.

It is highly probable that Turks adopted names and cultural traits derived from Brazilian Indians, similarly pagans at least until the arrival of the Jesuits, due to the Amerindian idealization following the independence of Brazil, an interpretation sponsored by Roger Bastide (1974) and so many other researchers in order to explain the emergence of the *caboclo* in African-Brazilian religion. Another explanation for such emergence of the *caboclo* could be the opening of the *Terreiro da Turquia* [1889?], just one year after the emancipation of Brazilian slaves; at that moment, probably the former slaves were highly motivated to identify themselves as Brazilians rather than as Africans, driven by the desire for social integration and the urgency to efface the marks of slavery.

In *Tambor de Mina* of the state of Maranhão we find other *caboclos* who may be more closely related to the indigenous culture than the Turks. One of them is undoubtedly Surrupira do Gangá, leader of another caboclos family less accepted than the Turks in the oldest and more traditional terreiros of the capital, as for instance the prestigious Casa de Nagô, Yoruban matrix. The name *Surrupira do Gangá* reminds simultaneously its connection to Africa (Gangá), and its relation with the *Curupira,* an entity pertaining to the folklore of indigenous origin, portrayed as a small black-skinned inhabitant of the forest, of non-human origin, whose feet are twisted backwards; the *Curupira* protects the forest and the hunt, and is feared by the people of the forest. (Cascudo, 1962:262).

The *Surrupira* of *Tambor de Mina*, as the *Curupira* of Brazilian folklore, shows features of the forest spiritual entity, bearing the same name, feared by the Indians, and mentioned by Jesuit Father José de Anchieta in his letters dated from the 16th century (Leite, 1954): dangerous and feared, responsible for unexplained rumors, sudden frights, death, disappearance, and for hunters losing their way in the forest. In the scope of a future work, we intend to center our attention on such a complex entity.

CONCLUSION

The case of Turks in Tambor de Mina discloses the risks we take when interpreting the presence of the caboclo in African-Brazilian religion in terms of Afro-Amerindian syncretism. They hardly can be seen as entities of the indigenous mythology or Indian ancestors (spirits of dead Indians—heros, tribal chiefs, shamans, etc) who entered the African religion through contact between Africans or Creoles and the native population, and the subsequent assimilation of the latter's culture, or through the African custom, upon arriving in foreign territory, of honoring the local ancestors, the "owners of the land."

Nor can Turks be characterized as spiritual entities belonging to terreiros settled by Indian descendants or religious specialists related to Amerindian culture, like *curador* (healer) or *pajé* (shaman). They were rather introduced into African-Brazilian religion through terreiros led by Creoles and African descendants. The primary matrix of their mythology is the historical feats (stories) of Charlemagne, widely divulged throughout the Iberian Peninsula, and not the mythology of Tupi Indians, like the legend of *Surrupiras*. The mythology of the Turks is not a mere reproduction of the "Story of Emperor Charlemagne and the Twelve Pairs of France" which continues to be narrated, in the present, in *Cordel* booklets (cheap literature), and in folkloric performances, like *Cheganças;* however, the names, the story, and the attributes of many Turks match with the characters of that literary work. In *Tambor de Mina* of the state of Maranhão, the personages of Admiral Balão, Ferrabrás from Alexandria, or Princess Floripes are not merely literary characters or folkloric representations; they are *encantados* of non-indigenous origin. In *Tambor de Mina*, indigenous cultural borrowings must be sought in the *Cura/Pajelança* rituals (healing rites) carried out in several terreiros of the city of São Luis, and in the mythology of other spiritual entities such as the *Surrupira*.

NOTE

1. This section was a paper originally presented in the Symposium "Revitalization and Syncretism in Africa and the Americas"—AAA, Washington, DC., 11/15 to 11/19 in 1995. This paper gave birth to a work to be edited in a book coordinated by the organizers of the event in the USA: Greenfield, S. & Droogers, A, under the title Syncretism and the Syncretic Process: Africa and the Americas. The text to be edited in the USA gives more information about Terreiro da Turquia (Turkey Center) and the encantados (spirits) from the family of Rei da Turquia (King of Turkey) in Tambor de Mina.

BIBLIOGRAPHY

Bastide, Roger. *"La Rencontre des Dieux Africains et des Esprits Indiens."* In: Henri Desroche and Roger Bastide, "Ultima Scripta." *Archives de Sciences Sociales des Religions* (Paris), 1974, n.38, pp. 19-28. Also edited in Roger Bastide, *Le Sacré Sauvage*. Paris: Payot, 1975.

Cascudo, Luis da Câmara. *Dicionário do Folclore Brasileiro*. Segunda edição revista e aumentada. Rio de Janeiro: INL/MEC, 1962.

Ferretti, Mundicarmo. "Rei da Turquia, o Ferrabrás de Alexandria?: A importância de um livro na mitologia do Tambor de Mina." In: *Meu Sinal Está No Teu Corpo*. São Paulo: Editora e Consultaria Ltda/Editora da Universdade de São Paulo (EDICON/EDUSP), 1989, pp. 202-218.

Ferretti, Mundicarmo. *Repensando o Turco no Tambor de Mina*. AFRO-ÁSIA, 1992, pp. 56-70, n.15.

Ferretti, Mundicarmo. *Desceu Na Guma: O Caboclo do Tambor de Mina no processo de mudança de um terreiro de São Luis—a Casa Fanti-Ashanti.* São Luis: Servico de Imprensa e Obras Graficas do Estado (SIOGE), 1993.

Ferretti, Sérgio. *Repensando o Sincretismo.* São Paulo: Editora da Universidade de São Paulo (EDUSP); São Luis: Fundaçao de Amparo a Pesquisa do Estado do Maranão (FAPEMA), 1995.

Historia do Imperador Carlos Magno e os Doze Pares de França. (Translated from the Spanish by Jeronimo Moreira de Carvalho. Followed by Flaviense, Alexandre Gomes. Bernardo del Carpio que venceu em batalha aos doze pares de França.) Rio de Janeiro: Livraria Império, n.d.

Leacock, Seth, and Ruth Leacock. *Spirits of the Deep: A Study of an African-Brazilian Cult.* New York: Anchor, 1975.

Leite, Serafim S. I. *Cartas dos primeiros jesuítas do Brasil-III: 1558-1563.* São Paulo: Comissão do IV Centenário, 1954.

4

The Churchifying of Candomblé: Priests, Anthropologists, and the Canonization of the African Religious Memory in Brazil

Roberto Motta

The Afro-Brazilian religion commonly known as Candomblé has been turning into a church in its own right, repudiating its previous syncretic dependence vis-à-vis the Catholic church. This process, which accompanies a certain number of changes in the social and demographic structure of Brazil, entails the development of an independent theology both by the faithful themselves and by anthropologist-theologians like Edison Carneiro and Roger Bastide, who are the main authors of the concept of an African, in fact Yoruba, paradigm of ritual authenticity.

INTRODUCTION

The Afro-Brazilian cults are in a process of *churchifying* themselves. That is, they are passing—and here I adopt some of the concepts of Joachim Wach in his classic book *Sociology of Religion* (Wach, 1944)—from the stage of the more or less informal "secret" or "mystery society," or of the "brotherhood" which, in spite of some peculiarities of their own, consider themselves as part of a larger church whose superiority they recognize, to that of a full-fledged church, with its own standardized corpuses of doctrine and ritual, and its own priesthood appointed or ordained according to more or less conventional rules of succession or transmission of the priestly or hierarchical charisma. The following quotation from Wach, except for its mention of Christianity and Islam, would seem to be based on a direct observation of Candomblé.

The [. . .] group, if united and organized enough to act as a body, must justify its existence and demonstrate its will and capacity to survive. This necessity creates the beginnings of apologetics and polemics. In the early Christian church, Jewish and Greek ideas contributed to the growth of a systematic theology; all three—Christian, Jewish, and Greek elements—are combined in the development of Mohammedan theology. There follows with continued reflection and discussion, systematization, and elaboration of doctrine, the careful and comprehensive formation of a rule of faith or creed, the standardization of forms of collective worship, and eventually the establishment of a constitution to sustain the new stable organization. The oral tradition is written down, the written tradition is collected and standardized, the doctrine is redefined, and hereafter all deviations and opinions at variance with the officially accepted teachings are classed as heresy. (Wach, 1944: 142-143)

TRADITION, MEMORY, AND POWER

Let us remark that the theological and ritual models that come eventually to dominate in the churchifying process are connected with some traditions that compete with other traditions. But the concept of tradition implies the concept of a memory. And there is no memory but the memory of a group or a community. This means that the competition between traditions for the control and definition of the rule of faith is actually the competition between groups of people, with their vested interests of a political or economic character or simply striving for that subtle form of power—perhaps the subtlest and most precious of all—that consists in the control and manipulation of ideas, representations, and symbols. Whenever, therefore, a memory claims a primacy over other memories, a group is also trying to impose its authority over other groups. To give but one example –certainly a powerful one—when the church of Rome (or the church of Peter), claims (Matthew 16: 13-20) the primacy of memory, that is, of purity, "authenticity" or, as it is said in theological parlance, orthodoxy, it eventually also comes to claim a primacy of government over the other churches, as well as the primacy of its priesthood, with the power of appointing, confirming, deposing, and replacing the hierarchy of the whole church.

The attitude of many members—especially of some of their anthropologist-theologians—of Candomblé *terreiros*[1] of Bahia, such as Axê Opô Afonjá, Engenho Velho, Gantois, Alaketu, and some others, who claim a primacy based on the African "purity" and "authenticity" of their traditions, is not unlike that of Rome. They also revindicate the power to define what is right and what is wrong concerning doctrine, morals, and metaphysics[2] for all the so-called "African diaspora"[3] the supposed cultural whole which would consist of the Yorubas of West Africa and their presumed racial and/or cultural descendants in the New World. Similarly, the priesthood[4] of those terreiros claim the power to confirm and to ordain the priests of all the other terreiros of the "diaspora." Indeed, there has been a tendency to accept this claim as valid throughout the whole domain of Candomblé, as shown by the number of believers, some of them priests and priestesses of the highest prestige in their own communities, who come to Salvador in order to pay their visits "ad limina,"[5] seizing the occasion to have their rites of initiation and ordination renewed by the dignitaries of Salvador.

WHO IS THE GREATEST?

The claims of the Bahianos, often honored by "filhos" and "pais-de-santo" all over Brazil, do not preclude, nevertheless, the voicing of other claims elsewhere in Brazil. Thus, in my city of Recife the terreiro known as Sítio de Pai Adão is held, by their own members and their disciples, as the rule of the good memory and the good practice for all terreiros of Brazil. Its present paramount priest, babalorixá Manuel da Costa, has sound genealogical reasons, grandson as he is of the late Pai Adão, to consider himself not only as the leader Nação Nagô[6] for the whole of Brazil, but also, by right of his grandmother, the late Lydia de Orixalá, as the Prince of Nação Xambá.[7] In São Luís—even apart from from the famous Casa das Minas and Casa Nagô, which, if Pierre Verger's historical conjectures are right, would rival (at least the former) with the Engenho Velho of Salvador for the title of the oldest terreiro of Brazil (Verger, 1952)[8]— Father Euclydes Ferreira, chief of Casa de Fânti-Ashânti,[9] has no qualms about declaring himself the supreme guide, at least of his variety of the African memory in Brazil. He has often expressed, in both oral and written form, the opinion that his House, with its present denomination, was founded, near the end of the eighteenth century, by, in spite of ethnic differences, a carnal, not simply a ritual, sister of Iá Nassô, the Yoruba priestess held as the founder of Engenho Velho.

In his terreiro Iansan Egun Nitá, located in the outskirts of Rio de Janeiro (Jacarepaguá), the revered José Ribeiro—the most literarily prolific babalorixá of Brazil, a genuine "doctor of the faith" (in the theological, not the academic meaning of this expression, since Senhor Ribeiro holds no doctor's degree from the Sorbonne)—plays with brilliance the role of the guardian of the Afro-Brazilian, indeed of the Afro-Indian-Brazilian, memory.[10] His many published books (it is likely that Ribeiro surpasses all other Brazilian authors in sheer volume of sales) exhibit not only the mark of oral traditions of Recife, in which he was raised,[11] but also the clear influence of erudite authors, such as Pierre Verger (from whom he borrows his characterization of the saints or gods, the *orixás*) and René Ribeiro (no relation), whose description of ritual divination he wholly reproduces. (see Ribeiro, [José] n.d. [1963]; Verger, 1957; Ribeiro [René], 1952).

SOCIAL ROOTS OF THE PROCESS

The *churchifying* of the Afro-Brazilian cults, entailing a complex process of
selection, organization, and standardization of the religious memory, when did it
begin? Basing myself on the presumed dates of the establishment, in Salvador,
of Engenho Velho and Alaketu[12] and, in São Luís,[13] of Casa das Minas, my
supposition, reinforced by a brilliant intuition of Gilberto Freyre (1963),[14] is that
the process goes back to the first decades of the nineteenth century, advancing,
at its earliest stages, slowly and tentatively. It seems to have been in that period,
as a consequence of the increase of social distance as a result of the weakening
of the rural patriarchalism (also, no doubt, a slow process that has not even now
reached its completion), that the first terreiros were established with a permanent
character,[15] with their own organization and ritual cycles, essentially separated,
in spite of many syncretic links, some of which have lasted up to the present
day, from the Catholicism of the *engenhos* (sugar cane plantations) and of the
urban brotherhoods. On the level of ideology, that was also the period in which
the Catholic Church, due, among other factors, to the penetration of free thought
in Brazil and to the suppression of the Inquisition, lost its religious monopolistic
hold over Brazilian society. Indeed, the first Protestant churches with a Luso-
Brazilian membership, as well as the first Kardecist (spiritualist) groups also
date from the first half of the nineteenth century.

The rise, in the 1940s, of terreiros connected with the Goméia[16] movement in
the periphery of Rio de Janeiro city increased the impetus of the *churchifying*
tendency of Candomblé. This not so much a consequence of a deliberate project
of *babalorixás* like João da Goméia, who always remained, as put by one of his
biographers, "very religious", that is, very much attached to the Roman Catholic
Church,[17] but is rather due to the social and economic characteristics of the new
congregations, whose membership consisted of migrants who had lost their
traditional "support structures",[18] including brotherhoods and feasts of local or
regional patron saints. In point of fact, the establishment of terreiros generally
preceded that of Catholic churches and parishes in the low-income suburbs of
Rio de Janeiro and of other cities in Brazil. Like the Pentecostal churches that
spring up almost spontaneously in this kind of milieu, Candomblé terreiros have
played the role of a major source of socialization and cultural orientation for the
uprooted migrants in the new townships.[19]

PRIESTS AND SOCIAL SCIENTISTS

But perhaps most interesting of all, at least for social scientists interested in
the dynamics of their own profession, one can still point out another major
influence on the "ecclesification" of Candomblé. This is found in the writings

and activities of anthropologists, sociologists, and other social scientists. For I contend that the conception of an African, especially of a Yoruba, purity ("pureza nagô") is, as it came to be adopted as the theological basis of the churchifying process (or "ecclesiogenesis")[20] of Candomblé, is to be attributed directly to researchers, chief among them Edison Carneiro and Roger Bastide. No doubt Candomblé has always been a religion in itself. Yet, it has not always been a religion for itself. That is, it lacked the kind of theological rationalization that can be furnished by scientific research, with its taxonomies and explanations. Researchers run then the risk of turning into Ersatz theologians. In fact, they do not become so always in spite of themselves. They are often very happy with their new status. For a symbiotic process is not uncommon, in which researchers, who, in addition to information also benefit from the spiritual and psychological gratifications that terreiros are able to offer, reciprocate with virtual certificates of "authenticity," that is, of faithfulness to tradition—in the nature of the case to African tradition—that represent a major advantage in the competition of terreiros with one another and with other churches for the same potential "market" of believers and religious clients.

I will now just highlight some of the important anthropological contributions that have played such a major role in turning Candomblé into a respectable religion, endowed with its own systematic theology, now virtually on an equal footing with the Christian churches and Kardecism. I begin with Arthur Ramos, a psychiatrist by training, who had a keen interest in the mythology of the cults, which he submitted to a thorough work of interpretation, in which the ideas of Lévy-Bruhl, Freud, and Jung were used with relish. A full analysis of his conclusions would be well beside the point here. Suffice it to say that, while taking into account a few Brazilian data, drawn from his own or from other researchers' field work, Ramos's interpretations rest, to a far greater extent, on purely African myths that he found mainly in the books of T. J. Bowen (1857) and Ellis (1897). He attempts to justify his methodology with the Jungian-flavored notion of a hereditary collective unconscious. Thus, while he acknowledges that "Afro-Brazilians no longer know who is Odudua," he manages to add that this deity "is buried in their collective unconscious, since it belongs to the primitive stages of mythical seriation" (Ramos, 1940: 318).[21] The whole—or almost—of the later Afro-Brazilianist research would inherit Ramos's postulate, if not in what concerns the survival (or the emtombment) of Odudua, at least regarding the notion of an underlying structure, the African mind, which would eventually develop into the theology of ase[22] with the corollaries of a purity or "authenticity" that represents a basic founding myth in the *churchifying* process of Candomblé.

AUTHENTICITY AND DEGENERATION

It is, however, rather to the Bahiano folklorist and ethnologist Edison Carneiro, often working in close association with the North-American anthropologist Ruth Landes, that is due the first consistent work of canonization and standardization of the Afro-Brazilian memory. But only of a special kind of Afro-Brazilian memory, to which Carneiro does not hesitate to attribute a normative status for the whole of Candomblé. He upheld the thesis that the authentic African religion would have been introduced in Brazil by people of Yoruba (Nagô in Brazilian parlance) ethnic origin; that it would have been properly preserved only in a few very old terreiros of Salvador (where Carneiro and his friends were particularly well received and even made honorary members of the ritual hierarchy); and that it can only "degenerate" as it undergoes diffusion through centers of Afro-Brazilians of other ethnic extractions and through Brazilian society at large (Carneiro 1937, 1938, 1948, 1959).

Carneiro, for reasons that cannot possibly be grounded in scholarly research, considered that

Non-Yoruban candomblés are religious forms that are undergoing a process of rapid decomposition. . . . Those candomblés, by adopting so many strange elements, lose their vitality and degrade themselves. They can only survive under the shadow of the Yoruban cult centers, using the latter's mystique and ritual. The very broad liberties that the Bantus have allowed themselves can only rapidly lead to the diffusion of the worst forms of quackery. (Carneiro, 1937: 33)

Let us now take a brief look at Ruth Landes's usage of such Yoruba-philic concepts. To her, Yoruba *mothers* are paragons of virtue and religious seriousness, "who underwent at least seven years of strenuous training and whose ascension to their lofty charges had to [be] approved by their peers" (Landes, 1967: 290), whereas "schismatic" Bantu cult leaders are mostly male and, at that, "youthfully handsome and indeed all mulatto . . . recruited from among male whores, juvenile delinquents, and city booms" (Landes, 1967: 292). According to her, "uncommon circumstances encouraged certain passive homosexuals to forge a new and respected identity to themselves" (284), that is, as *pais-de-santo* in the bad "Bantu" terreiros, so different, according to the Carneiro-Landes model, from the good Yoruba ones.

This model would so influence Roger Bastide as to become the kernel of one of his major books on Candomblé, entitled *The Candomblé of Bahia (Nagô Rite)*. Indeed, as he states, "since the beginning we faced Candomblé in terms of an African civilization and of an African system of metaphysics" (Bastide, 1961: 77), which "in Brazil . . . unfortunately underwent as many losses as metamorphoses" (289). And the agents of this corrupting process are often to be found (it is obvious that Bastide had very well read, or very much conversed with, Edison Carneiro) in the cult houses tainted with Bantu admixtures. For, asserting that "trance is very real" (251), Bastide immediately qualifies this statement by adding that "we do not deny that cases of simulation take place in non-traditional [i.e. Bantu] cult centers." And how—to his mind—could it ever be different, since "cases of passive homosexuality are fairly common in Bantu cult houses" (309), which would thus be rather whorehouses than worship houses?

On the other hand, in the good cult houses, all, of course, Yoruban,

The head priestess is the spiritual guide of the cultists. Due to her moral ascendency, the cult head, by friendly persuasion, directs even the private affairs of the faithful. . . . These leaders also have the duty of assisting their flock both morally and financially and thus the Candomblé houses are true associations of mutual aid and brotherly succor, quite in agreement with their original communal spirit. . . . Religious life is guided by reciprocity and exchange. Only in the overly decadent Bantu—or Indian—derived houses does the opposite occur, but this is strongly repudiated by the true Africans. (Bastide, 1961: 67-8)

SOCIETY AS MEMORY

Bastide adopted Carneiro's paradigm of African, or rather, Yoruban memorial purity all the more easily as Bastide seems to have received a strong theoretical impact from Émile Durkheim and Maurice Halbwachs. According to the former, religion is but society's consciousness or representation of itself (Durkheim, 1915). To the latter, if society manifests itself as consciousness, then society is, above all, consciousness (Halbwachs, 1952). And consciousness, as it lasts through time, is nothing else but social memory. As Bastide put it: "African social structures were shattered, but the values were preserved. . . . Thus the superstructure had to create a whole new society. It is not an upward movement . . . but rather it is the reverse that happens. It starts with values and collective ideas and flows down into institutions and groups" (Bastide, 1971: 82).

Therefore, as Bastide eventually concluded, Candomblé is but African memory in Brazil. "To the extent as Blacks feel African, they belong to a different mental world" (Bastide, 1961: 20). Thus, "when the *orixá* [god] comes down [in trance], the Black man regains his African status and once again partakes of the tribal life of his fathers" (Bastide, 1961: 20).

In point of fact, Bastide, following the lead of Carneiro, confused two rather different issues: the mythological role of social memory and the scientific study of tradition. In strictly Halbwachsian terms, there could hardly exist a degenerated social memory, because all social memories are but the a priori grounding of a form of society. Whatever its historical origins, all memories, from a social standpoint, are but mythological paradigms in competition with other mythological paradigms. Social memory is only marginally affected by the issue of the confirmation of its contents by research of a scientific kind. Indeed, due to their necessarily mythological, hence sacred, character, it is likely that social memory would rather be harmed should it pretend to be based purely on science.

MEMORY AND SCIENCE

This does not exclude, of course, the scientific critique of memory by social scientists and historians, who could very well apply, to the field of Afro-Brazilian studies, the methods of the "history of forms" (Formgeschichte) and of the "history of redaction" (Redaktionsgeschichte), used, mainly by German-writing scholars, in the analysis of the traditions canonized in the Bible. These methods can indeed give a decisive contribution to the elucidation of certain issues related to the formation of a collective memory and the canonization of its traditions. Thus Rudolf Bultman stresses the usefulness of the study of the Sitz im Leben, the concrete social circumstances from which religious traditions originate: "The basic principle underlying this task—i.e., the scientific study of tradition or social memory—consists in the idea that the literature that expresses the life of a community . . . has its source in the manifestations and needs of this community" (Bultman, 1979: 18-19). Gerhard von Rad applies similar principles to study of the Pentateuch: "Most ancient stories had an etiological character, serving to explain some tribal, local or cultural peculiarity. . . . Their existence could not at first be conceived far from the shrine to which they were related. . . . One can easily imagine the enormous transformation that took place when the collection of materials from different cultic centers was begun, which entailed a change in their contents by the introduction of coordinating and their submission to a full-fledged process of literary manipulation" (Rad, 1968: 18-19).

And this quotation leads us back to the quotation of Wach at the beginning of this chapter and to the problem of the *churchifying* or "ecclesification" of Candomblé. Let us repeat that, from a strictly scientific point of view (as opposed to a religious or a mythological one), the question of defining what is "authentic" in the Afro-Brazilian religion has little or no meaning, as, for one thing, whatever exists cannot but exist authentically "and as part of reality Science is bound to take note of it" (Lowie, 1920: 2). And science is also bound to take note of the fact that researchers—indeed some of the foremost among them—have actively participated in the process of the creation of a mythical-religious African memory in Brazil, which supplied the *churchifying* tendency of Candomblé with its main theological guiding and legitimizing principles. Yet, a very important question remains to be answered. What are the social forces, what are the collective interests that lead certain terreiros to search their legitimacy as churches in their own right (with a consequent rejection of their role as bastard or syncretistic forms of folk Catholicism) in a logos provided by the philosophy or the social sciences of the Western world? And why does it so happen that so many researchers, often of recent European extraction, try to gain a new personal, ethnic, and religious identity by converting to Candomblé? What forces, what circumstances of a social, economic, political, and cultural kind can help us understand the *churchifying* trend, the *ecclesiogenesis* of Candomblé?

NOTES

1. *Candomblé* is used here as a general name to designate not only the *Candomblé* of Bahia, nowadays transplanted to many other states of Brazil, but also the *Xangô* of Pernambuco (where the city of Recife is located) and of other states of the *Nordeste*, as well as the *Tambor de Mina* of São Luís (Maranhão). Individual congregations of *Candomblé* are called *terreiros*, although the word *candomblé* (written here always with a lowercase) may have the same sense.

2. Roger Bastide (1961), under the influence of French ethnologist Marcel Griaule, often speaks of the "metaphysics" of Candomblé. As we are about to see, Bastide's ideas have become the normative, orthodox paradigm of theological interpretation of the Afro-Brazilian religion.

3. The idea of an African, mainly Yoruban, diaspora in the Americas, in continuity with West African traditional religion, and even conserving some elements of this religion that have been lost in Africa itself, is found in Bastide, 1961, Jean Ziégler, 1972, and Juana Elbein dos Santos, 1976.

4. Priests of Candomblé are known both as *pais-de-santo* or, in a more formal style, as *babalorixás*. Priestesses are *mães-de-santo* or *ialorixás*. Plain devotees are *filhos-de-santo* and *filhas-de-santo*.

5. Visits "ad limina" in the Roman Catholic Church are the visits all bishops must pay to the Pope in specified periods.

6. Every terreiro of Candomblé claims affiliation to a given African ethnic tradition, such as its memory has persisted in Brazilian popular lore. There are thus in Recife Nagô (Yoruba), Xambá , Congo, and Moçambique terreiros, all of which, as a matter of fact, follow the religious traditions of the Nagô (Yoruba) of West Africa, whose language (in an archaic and simplified version) they have adopted as their common liturgical language. Vivaldo da Costa Lima (1977) has written extensively (and sensibly) about the concept of 'nação' in the Candomblé.

7. The exact African roots of so-called "Xambá" nation are rather unclear.

8. Pierre Verger's conjectures, which have percolated the Afro-Brazilian memory, are the basis of a North-American writer's novel, *Agotime: Her Legend* (Gleason, 1970).

9. The appelation Fanti-Ashanti does not belong to the popular lore of Brazil, but is rather a creation of British anthropologists. I could never ascertain through which erudite sources it reached the ears of Senhor Euclydes.

10. Like João da Goméia (see below), José Ribeiro is less of an orthodox African purist than some *babalorixás* from Bahia, and he has always given a place to the worship of Indian spirits in his terreiro.

11. Yet, like many apparently non-Bahiano *pais-de-santo*, Ribeiro admits to having been born in Bahia, whence his parents would have moved to Recife shortly after his birth.

12. See Lima, 1977.

13. See Verger, 1952.

14. "When our social environment began to change in the sense that the plantation manors became city mansions more after the European manner . . . settlements of shanties and slums sprang up alongside the mansions, but with almost no communication between them . . . African cults diverging more from Catholicism than had been the case on plantations and ranches. A new distribution of power came about, but still resting for the most part in the hands of white landowners. . . . There was a greater economic gap between the extremes" (Freyre, 1963: 24). Bastide is in full agreement with Freyre (as he generally is with his Brazilian sources): "After the decadence of the mines, and during the whole nineteenth century, Brazil's social structure underwent changes under the effect of urbanization. Gilberto Freyre devoted a whole book to this problem, *The Mansions and the Shanties*. This new structure would very much widen the distance between the exploiting and the exploited classes" (Bastide, 1971: 95).

15. Luiz R. Mott (1986) has shown that practices similar to those of Candomblé existed in Brazil much earlier than my estimated approximate period of the rise of the first *permanent* terreiros. But it is precisely their permanent character that is the hallmark of the terreiros founded in the early nineteenth century (or very late in the eighteenth century); this character is due either, as Freyre assumed, to a lesser social, cultural, and racial interpenetration than in earlier periods, or to the wane of the Inquisition, or to both factors at the same time. Concerning the latter, with its relative leniency toward Africanisms (which were not taken too seriously as heresies), see Mott's article. For a general view of the problem surrounding the relationship between Candomblé and Catholicism, see Donald Warren, 1970, and Peter Clarke, 1995.

16. This movement, the history of which has yet to be written in detail, had other leaders beside the late João da Goméia. It generally accepted some elements of Umbanda theology, which in turn entailed the influence of some European spiritist (Kardecist) tenets. Yet the Goméia model involved no essential change in the ritual and in the hierarchical system borrowed from the Candomblé and from its twin cult in Recife, Xangô. This is why I have considered Goméia as "Xangô Umbandizado" in my general typology of the variety of Afro-Brazilian cults in the area of Recife (see Motta, 1988). The terreiro of Goméia, located in Nova Iguaçu (near Rio de Janeiro), is the object of an eminently readable dissertation by Giséle Binon-Cossard (1970).

17. We read in a popular biography of João da Goméia (he died in 1971) that "[s]ince his childhood years he was a very religious person [i.e., Catholic]. He often went to [Catholic] churches and was friendly to [Catholic] priests and nuns. He was very devoted to Our Lady of Aparecida [the Catholic patroness of Brazil]. . . . Although he consecrated most of his life to Candomblé, he never abandoned his [erstwhile] religion" (Siqueira, 1971: 91).

18. Concerning these structures, see Bastide, 1971: 171, 179, and so forth. However, Bastide, concerning this topic, is in close dependence upon Ribeiro, 1956, 1957.

19. Another source of the *ecclesiogenesis* of Candomblé is to be found in the Umbanda Branca movement, understood as the effort to rationalize the Afro-Indian-Catholic popular cults through the use of some theological principles *(karma,* reincarnation, spiritual development, mediumship, mutual indoctrination of the living and the dead, etc.) borrowed from Kardecist spiritualism, which came to affect deeply the ritual, the hierarchical system and the very conception of the gods, now viewed as disincorporated spirits of a given rank and still capable of further advancement. (For an outline of Umbandista beliefs as contrasted to those of "pure" Candomblé, see Motta, 1988.) But here, too, several conflicting paradigms can be found, and the constitution of a self-sufficient Afro-Brazilian church under Umbandista auspices is still far from being completed; and it is doubtful whether it will ever be completed. Indeed, a strong tendency toward *disumbandization,* that is, a tendency away from white Umbanda Branca and back to Black Candomblé (albeit in syncretic synthesis with anthropological theory) has won the day in São Paulo and elsewhere in Brazil in the last fifteen years or so. Thus Renato Ortiz's announcement of the "white death of the Black sorcerer" (Ortiz, 1978) was no doubt an exaggeration. Reginaldo Prandi's studies of the spectacular growth of fundamentalist (my term) Candomblé in São Paulo, which so often appeals to a clientele of a pure, or nearly pure, European extraction, rather points to a kind of Black birth of the White *babalorixá* (see Prandi, 1991).

20. This word is used by Leonardo Boff in his *A Igreja Se Fez Povo—Eclesiogênese: A Igreja Que Nasce do Povo* (Boff, 1986), who borrows it from the field of New Testament studies and early Church history. With the utmost probability, the word "ecclesification" (meaning more or less the same) was also used by a previous author.

21. But thanks to authors, such as Ramos, Afro-Brazilians have now learned everything about Ododua.

22. Although in this chapter I do not deal with authors later than Bastide (which means that I stop at the beginning of the 1970s), I ought to add that the theory, eventually transformed into the theology, of *ase* (or *axé* in a Brazilianized spelling) comes to its fullest development with the anthropologist Juana Elbein dos Santos, who was Bastide's student in Paris. In her view, there is "a driving force called *ase;* this power, which allows existence to be and to become is constantly being actualized, maintained, and alimented at the cult house. . . . Through ritual activity ase is liberated, directed toward, and temporarily set upon, all kinds of beings and objects, making them holy. Every individual, due to his initiation and ritual behavior, is a receiver and impulsor of *ase*" (Santos, 1976: 36-37).

BIBLIOGRAPHY

Bastide, Roger. *O Candomblé da Bahia (Rito Nagô)*. (Braz. transl.) São Paulo: Companhia Editora Nacional, 1961.

Bastide, Roger. *As Religiões Africanas no Brasil*. (Braz. transl.) São Paulo: Livraria Pioneira Editora, 1971.

Binon-Cossard, Gisèle. *Contribution à l'Étude du Candomblé du Brésil: Le Candomblé Angola*. Doctoral thesis. Paris: University of Paris, 1970.

Boff, O.F.M., Leonardo. *E a Igreja Se Fez Povo-Eclesiogênese: A Igreja Que Nasce da Fédo Povo*. Petrópolis. R.J.: Vozes, 1986.

Bowen, T. J. *Central Africa*. Charleston: Southern Baptist Publication Society, 1857.

Bultman, Rudolf. *L'Histoire de la Tradition Synoptique*. (French trans.) Paris: Seuil, 1973.

Carneiro, Edison. *Negros Bantus*. Rio de Janeiro: Civilização Brasileira, 1937.

Carneiro, Edison. *Religiões Negras*. Rio de Janeiro: Civilização Brasileira, 1938.

Carneiro, Edison. *Candomblés da Bahia*. Bahia: Publicações do Museu do Estado, 1948.

Carneiro, Edison. *Os Cultos de Origem Africana no Brasil*. Rio de Janeiro: MEC, 1959.

Clarke, Peter B. 'Candomblé and Catholicism: Syncretised or Juxtaposed?' Paper presented to the symposium on "Religious Revitalization and Syncretism in Africa and the Americas," annual meeting of the American Anthopological Association, Washington, D.C., 1995.

Durkheim, E. *The Elementary Forms of the Religious Life*. (Eng. transl.) London: George Allen and Unwin, 1915.

Freyre, Gilberto. *The Mansions and the Shanties*. (Eng. transl.) New York: Knopf, 1963.

Gleason, Judith. *Agotime: Her Legend*. New York: Viking, 1970.

Halbwachs, *Les Cadres Sociaux de la Memoire*. Paris: Presses Universitaires de France, 1952.

Landes, Ruth. "Matriarcado Cultural e Homossexualidade Masculina," in R. Landes, *A Cidade das Mulheres*. Rio de Janeiro: Civilização Brasileira, 1967: 283-296.

Lima, Vivaldo da Costa. *A Família de Santo nos Candomblés Jeje-Nagô da Bahia*. Salvador: Universidade Federal da Bahia, 1977.

Lowie, Robert. *Primitive Society*. New York: Boni & Liveright, 1920.

Mott, Luiz R. "Acotundá: Raízes Setecentistas do Sincretismo Religioso Afro-Brasileiro." *Revista do Museu Paulista* XXXI, 1986: 124-147.

Motta, Roberto. "Bandeira de Alairá: A Festa de São João Xangô e Problemas do Sincretismo Afro-Brasileiro." *Ciência & Trôpico* (Recife) 3 (2), 1975: 191-203.

Motta, Roberto. "Carneiro, Ruth Landes e os Candomblés Bantus." *Revista do Arquivo Público* (Recife) 30 (32), 1976: 58-68.

Motta, Roberto. "De Nina Rodrigues a Gilberto Freyre: Estudos Afro-Brasileiros." *Revista do Arquivo Público* (Recife) 31/32, 33/34, 1978: 58-68.

Motta, Roberto. "Indo-Afro-European Syncretic Cults in Brazil: Their Economic and Social Roots." *Cahiers du Brésil Contemporain* (Paris) 5, 1988: 27-48.

Ortiz, Renato. *A Morte Branca do Feiticeiro Negro.* Petrópolis (R.J.): Vozes, 1978.

Prandi, J. Reginaldo. *Os Candomblés de São Paulo: A Velha Magia na Metrópole Nova.* São Paulo: Hucitec, 1991.

Rad, Gerhard von. *La Genèse.* (French trans.) Genève: Labor et Fides, 1968.

Ramos, Arthur. *O Negro Brasileiro.* (2nd ed.) São Paulo: Companhia Editora Nacional, 1940.

Ribeiro, José. *O Jogo dos Búzios e as Grandes Cerimônias Ocultas da Umbanda.* Rio de Janeiro: Editora Espiritualista, 1963.

Ribeiro, René. *Cultos Afro-Brasileiros do Recife.* Recife: Instituto Joaquim Nabuco, 1952.

Ribeiro, René. *Religião e Relações Raciais.* Rio de Janeiro: MEC, 1956.

Ribeiro, René. "As Estruturas de Apoio e as Reações do Negro ao Cristianismo na América Portuguesa." *Boletim do Instituto Joaquim Nabuco* (Recife), 1957: 59-80.

Santos, Juana Elbein dos. *Os Nagô e a Morte.* Petrópolis: Vozes, 1976.

Siqueira, Paulo. *Vida e Morte de João da Goméia.* Rio de Janeiro: Nautilus, 1971.

Verger, Pierre. "Le Culte des Vodoun d'Abomey aurait-il été Apporté à Saint-Louis de Maragnon par la Mère du Roi Ghézo?" in Verger, *Les Afro-Américains.* Dakar: IFAN, Mémoire 27, 1952: 59-80.

Verger, Pierre. *Notes sur le Culte des Orisa et Vodun.* Dakar: IFAN, Mémoire 51, 1957.

Wach, Joachim. *Sociology of Religion.* Chicago: University Chicago Press, 1944.

Warren, Jr., Donald. "Notes on the Historical Origins of Umbanda." *Universitas* (Salvador) 6-7, 1970: 155-163.

Ziégler, Jean. *O Poder Africano.* (Braz. trans.) São Paulo: Difusão Européia do Livro. 1973.

5

With Dance and Drum: A Psycho-Cultural Investigation of the Meaning-Making System of an African-Brazilian, Macumba Community in Salvador, Brazil

Valerie De Marinis

The western-trained researcher who is approaching the world of Macumba would do well to keep in mind the academic caution expressed by French anthropologist Roger Bastide, one of the most influential sociological researchers on Afro-Brazilian religion, "with a way of thinking . . . shaped by three centuries of Cartesianism . . . an ethnocentric mode of thought, . . . I [realized that I] would have to 'convert' myself to a new way of thinking if I ever hoped to understand it. . . . the sociologist who studies Brazil no longer knows what set of concepts to use. The ideas he has learned in Europe or North America are no longer valid, Cartesian distinctions between past and present, sacred and profane, the living and the dead, no longer hold" (Bastide, 1978, Foreword, p.viii). This caution holds true for the researcher in psychology as well.[1] And so it was with an awareness of the need to proceed with caution and a critical suspicion of the limits and often limitations of my research tools that I began, in the summer of 1984 an on-going psychosocial, field research study of a Macumba community in Salvador, Brazil.[2] As a psychologist of religion my interests have been directed primarily to an investigation of phenomenological and functional dimensions of individual and community existence and the role of religious experience in that existence.[3]

This research paper focuses on the Macumba community's way of making meaning in its Afro-Brazilian cultural context.[4] The community's meaning-making system is analyzed through five central points relating psychosocial function to religious ritual experience. First, an overview is presented of the use of religious ritual and its psychosocial function for the Macumba community within the larger context of Afro-Brazilian culture. Second, attention is given to the nature and role of ritual in developmental and lifecycle perspective, including attention to gender issues and to the involvement of children in the community's ritual process. Third, an analysis is given of ritual process as a community-wide process of empowerment and energy-containment. Fourth, the use of ritual trance and communication with the Yoruban spirits in the development of preventive and interventionist strategies for addressing the particular needs and problems of community members is explored. And fifth, attention is focused on the larger social impact of such Macumba communities through their grass-roots projects for social change; and through the use of Macumba religious rituals and symbols by Afro-Brazilian practitioners in the healing arts of medicine and psychotherapy in Salvador, Brazil. Before proceeding to these points, a brief community profile is given.

PROFILE OF MACUMBA COMMUNITY

This chapter is based upon the findings of my field research in Salvador, Brazil, with a Macumba community of men, women, and children, composed of families and single individuals numbering approximately fifty persons. Females and males are equally represented in the membership. Though the members live separately, it is a community-based model of existence and development that predominates. Afro-Brazilian communities such as this can be found throughout Salvador and Brazil.

Macumba is best understood as both a cultural and a religious system whose roots are in the African, Yoruban tradition. In this particular community the interweaving of Yoruban, Christian and Amer-Indian symbols is prevalent.[5] Ritual dancing and drumming in community religious services are essential dimensions of communication and energy-containment for the community. It is the community's task, in coordination with the work of the priestess and priest and the trance elders, to provide preventive as well as interventive psychosocial care for each of its members.

The community (terriero) is under the direction of a priest Ezechial (babalorixá)(over age seventy-five) and a priestess Jupira (yalorixá) (in her middle thirties).[6] The community has five trance mediums, three female and two male. Both priest and priestess use the term Macumba because this particular community represents a more syncretistic grouping of African, Christian, and Amer-Indian traditions. There are also certain rituals of Macumba magic used in a limited number of ritual practise. This community's religion and culture may also be argued to fall under the term Candomblé because of the focus and direction of the gods (orixás). However, for our purposes Macumba will be the term used as a more-or-less umbrella term for the variety of Afro-Brazilian religious and cultural communities in the Bahia area of Brazil, with the understanding that differences do exist between communities and that each community needs to be studied as a special unit.

There is a saying in Brazil: "Afro-Brazilians are 98% Christian and 150% Macumba." Whatever varieties of cultural and cross-cultural adaptation and acculturation, Afro-Brazilians remain, from a functional standpoint, within the Macumba worldview. As Bastide observes, "As long as acculturation has not penetrated the mentality, or as long as the compartmentalization principle confines the change of mentality to the domains of politics and economics and excludes it from the domain of religion, reinterpretation always occurs in terms of the African values, norms, and ideals" (1978, p. 388). As we proceed with our five points, the nature and necessity for both historical and contemporary adaptation yet foundational preservation of the Afro-Brazilian traditions, values, and religious rituals in community context will, it is hoped, become clear.

An Overview of the Use of Religious Ritual and Its Psychosocial Function for the Macumba Community within the Larger Context of Afro-Brazilian Culture

An overview of Macumba religious ritual, psychosocial function, and Afro-Brazilian culture can be constructed with reference to the words of Afro-Brazilian psychologist Roberto Derceao, "There are three words to keep in mind: slavery, survival and deep symbols."[7] In the 1500s African persons, from different areas on the eastern coast, were brought as slaves to the Portuguese plantations in Brazil. The objective of the plantation owners was to, as Derceao explains, "destroy the communication systems of the slaves at every level: familial, social, cultural and religious. But the white man and the black man communicate and live differently. And this helped to keep the traditions of Macumba alive despite the slaughter and dehumanizing treatment of African men, women and children. Our music and dance provided a way to communicate and to keep alive our hope and our traditions. We survived through our deep symbols of music and dance."

In psychosocial terms, slavery effected a breach between the superstructures and the infrastructures. The African social structures were shattered, the values preserved. "In brief, the superstructures had to secrete a society. The movement is not an upward one from the morphological base toward the world of symbols and collective representations but the opposite: a downward movement of those value, and collective representations toward the institutions and groupings" (Bastide, 1978, pp. 56-57).

The values and core dimensions of the African worldview existed in the collective memory and through the religious and social rituals of Macumba. Communication of values took place through dance and drum. These functioned as the deep symbols for cultural and spiritual survival during slavery. Communication through African tribal music and dance took place without the

knowledge of the Portuguese colonists. Mistaking Macumba music and dance
for a means of surface entertainment, the colonists unwittingly allowed
communication to continue and for the Macumba traditions to be passed from
generation to generation. Communication here needs to be understood at every
level. As priestess Jupira notes, "Our music and dance and symbols are not split
between soul and body. To dance this way will give a message about some
need, something to be done, and will also give us energy and a kind of food
inside. There are always many layers of meaning."[8]

The historical methods of cultural and spiritual survival captured in
Derceao's "slavery, survival, deep symbols," accurately describe as well the
contemporary struggle for survival of Afro-Brazilian communities. As Jupira
notes, "Slavery is still here, not in chains of iron but in poverty, political torture
and pressure, and a lack of education for our children and ourselves. For a time
I tried to find a way to fight all this and not use Macumba. This was not
possible for me. Not only is that like trying to ride a bicycle without wheels but
more Macumba is life and resource. We need to keep from going crazy here,
with all this suffering and dying. Macumba lets us see without becoming blind
and do without becoming dead inside."

The Nature and Role of Macumba Ritual in Developmental and Lifecycle Perspective, Including Attention to Gender Issues and to the Involvement of Children in the Community's Ritual Process

To begin to understand the nature and role of ritual in lifecycle perspective
for this Macumba community, we must first understand the nature and role of
ritual. Recent developments in the umbrella field of Ritual Studies, especially
the contribution of historian of religion Catherine Bell's ritual features provide a
means of entry into ritual experience. These features include: "strategies of
differentiation through formalization and periodicy, the centrality of the body,
the orchestration of schemes by which the body defines an environment and is
defined in turn by it, ritual mastery, and the negotiation of power to define and
appropriate the hegemonic order" (Bell, 1992, p. 220).

In the Macumba community established rituals and evolving ritualizing
activities (see Driver, 1991) both mark and shape psychosocial reality. This
double function of ritual process, marking and shaping, is evident in the four
types of ritual or ritualizing activity within the community.

TYPOLOGY OF MACUMBA RITUALS [9]

Type 1. Containment rituals for initiated and mediums—preparation of initiates at the highest level in the wisdom of the orixás, use of sacred herbs and powers. Inside the terreiro or at designated sacred places.

Type 2. African-based rituals of the gods (orixás)—community-wide participation, coordinated with Macumba calendar of holidays and feasts usually coordinated with Catholic feast days. Inside the terreiro, sometimes coordinated with special ceremonies at sacred places.

Type 3. Healing and renewing rituals—community-wide weekly participation, focusing on specific issues, problems drawing on the resources of the community's orixá Yemanjá, Yoruba goddess of the sea. Inside the terriero. Smaller gathering are sometimes coordinated between the weekly celebrations. Smaller gatherings can be at terriero or outdoors or in someone's home.

Type 4. Ritualizing containment for children—meetings organized by priestess with the community's children. Older children meet in the terriero. Younger children meet outside in nature and on occasion at sacred places.

Rituals of Types 1 and 2 can be considered as rituals which mark events, feasts, communal celebrations. These draw upon and engage the collective memory of the community. The collective memory includes both the intellectual and the motor memories. The intellectual memories contain the myths and sacred stories. The motor memories, stored in the body, contain the rituals, movements and actions. And as Bastide notes, "The more closely collective representations and myths are interwoven in the web of actions, the more resistant to change they will be" (1978, p. 258). It is important to note that in Macumba, a primarily oral tradition in itself and as demanded through its beginnings in Brazil, the motor memory, rituals and movements, has had a more predominant role than the intellectual memory, myths and stories. "Myth's principal function is now to justify or explain rites or the forms and types of sacrifices, taboos, and ceremonial sequences" (Bastide, 1978, p. 258). Memories inherited from the ancestral tradition(s) survive to the degree that "they can insinuate themselves into the existing framework of society" (Bastide, 1978, p. 258).

Rituals of Types 3 and 4 actively shape the identification and use of community resources. Here the focus is on using the rituals as resources in themselves and as resources for shaping the outcome of a certain situation or problem. Type 4 rituals, with the community children, can best be understood as an expression of the community's preventive and anticipatory approach to development which is itself an expression of Macumba's logic as culture and religion. Here the concerns of individual community members are "worked on" through the ritual use of shells, herbs, animal sacrifice, trance, and other ritual components in community context. It is not uncommon for dimensions of these healing and renewal rituals to become over time a part of the collective memory.

In this sense the different types of Macumba ritual serve in the preservation and evolution of collective memory as well.

Macumba's logic, as its rituals embody, is compactly described by the words of Macumba priest Ezechial, "What happens after we die is unknown to us now. What has taken place before we are born is also unknown. What happens between birth and death is our concern. And this is hard enough!!! We use what we have, all that we have, the dance and drum, and the help of the powers to live between birth and death."[10]

Macumba rituals provide a microcosm of Macumba meaning-making. The microcosm as found in the community (terriero) of Ezechial and Jupira is concerned to address false and destructive dualities and power asymmetries including: the mind over the body; male over female; light over darkness, intellect over instinct, and virginity over sexuality. Through a functional and phenomenological analysis of the typology of rituals in Macumba as practiced and experienced in this community, the conclusion must be reached that ritual serves as one of the bases, if not *the* foundational and developmental base upon which meaning-making throughout the lifecycle is grounded. From the perspective of a psychology of religion which will be outlined in points 3 and 4, the nature and function of ritual in Macumba can be thought of as the primary resource for Macumba psychosocial ecology.[11]

The Dynamics of Macumba Psychosocial Ecology: Approaching Ritual Process as a Community-Wide Process of Empowerment and Energy-Containment

The perspective of psychology of religion used both to coordinate the research process and to analyze the data builds upon a clinical and theoretical framework begun by the late Dutch-American Paul Pruyser. Central to this framework is the understanding that human, multidimensional reality is concerned with three worlds: autistic, realistic and illusionistic. An individual's psychological function is dependent upon how these worlds interact.

Pruyser's framework places religion and culture in the illusionistic world. Religion and culture, when functioning in the service of psychological health, will serve as creative resources for the tutored imagination. The illusionistic world can serve to balance the autistic and realistic worlds.[12]

The autistic (inner) world, dominated by primary process, is subjective, solipsistic and dominated by ineffable fantasy (Pruyser, 1991, p 174). This is the world of the infant and child, but this world does not disappear as the child develops psychosocially. Instead, the autistic world learns to live in interaction with the realistic (outer) world. The realistic world is dominated by secondary process activity, coordinated through sense perceptions, reality testing, logic, facts and external objects. (Pruyser, 1991, p. 177)

Interaction between the autistic world and the realistic world comes through the function of the third world, the illusionistic world. In this world of tutored fantasy, orderly imagination, cultural needs, symbols, playing, creativeness, transcendent object and inspired connections (Pruyser, 1991, p. 177) the negotiation process between the autistic and realistic world takes place. Ritual can be understood as one of the primary resources of the illusionistic world which serves to balance the processes of the autistic (inner) and the realistic (outer) worlds. Ritual activity takes place in the transitional space between persons, unlocking the creative imagination, restoring psychological energy and providing active engagement of person in the context of community.

The illusionistic world is the shared, transitional world which has the symbols of religion and culture contained therein. Religious experience in general and religious ritual experience in particular are among the resources of the illusionistic world. Through religious ritual experience an individual joins his or her world as part of a community of meaning-making. The ritual experience together with its symbols and actions serve a transformative purpose for the community, a means by which multi-level communication and organizing take place. (De Marinis, 1994, pp. 12-13)

Pruyser's framework is appropriate for understanding the nature and function of ritual in Macumba because its phenomenological and functional means of assessment can be responsibly adapted to the Afro-Brazilian context. As both culture and religion Macumba can be understood as functioning in the illusionistic world. In this adaptation we need to understand the illusionistic world's functioning in a model which includes both intra-personal, inter-personal, natural and cosmological dimensions. The model, illustrated in Figure 5.1, is termed Macumba Psychosocial Ecology.

At the core of the psychosocial model of both intra-personal development and of inter-personal development, lie the deep symbols, powers, and collective wisdom of Macumba, the ritual core. To understand how a person can safely gain access to this core, an appreciation of three operative concepts is necessary. These concepts are: community, energy and containment. In the model, community is featured as two of the circles surrounding the individual person. Community wisdom is needed for access to the Macumba ritual core. Community also surrounds the individual as a means of approach to the larger circles of life and to the world of nature, animals, and spirits. Though the individual person is certainly recognized, the psychosocial ecology of Macumba psychology always locates the individual within a community context for understanding both intra-personal and inter-personal development. And every individual in the community is located simultaneously in the three, different circles of the diagram locating the individual and community functions.

The concept of energy together with the related concepts of movements and process capture the heart of Macumba psychology. Whether we are discussing personal development, social development, or understandings of psychological or physiological conditions of health and illness, the operative concept of energy is

Figure 5.1
Model of Macumba Psychosocial Ecology

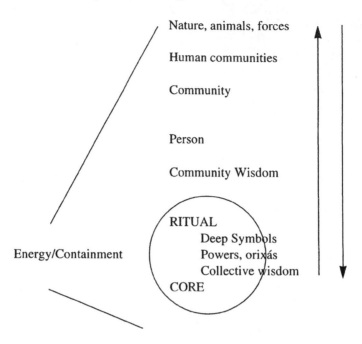

Note: Community appears twice in the model, as a single term and then as community wisdom. This is to indicate the impact of the community both as a physical presence and as a spiritual presence that provides wisdom and guidance for interpreting the contents of the ritual core.

found. In the words of psychologist Derceao, "We think in terms of energy, that is as you say a metaphor for us as African-Brazilian persons, believers, Macumba practitioners and as psychological or medical professionals. Energy is a cultural metaphor for us. This has to do with the way we live and approach reality. It is not the static way of thinking sometimes found in North America. We live and work with movement, energy, dance and drum. Finding and diagnosing how energy is working, where and how things are in balance and out of balance is critical for prognosis and for treatment whether it be in the terreiro or in my clinic."

Derceao's words signal the need for investigating energy's function as pivotal for approaching the provinces of psychological or spiritual diagnosis. And the emphasis in both provinces is on finding energy's proper balance. Why is the balancing of energy necessary? This leads us to the third operative concept, that of containment. Energy, in the Macumba psychological worldview, is the medium operative at all levels and dimensions of interaction.

Energy in itself is not good or evil. The human use of energy or the energies available determine how assessment will be made. In any case energy is in a pure and powerful form which requires, for human use, containment and safe passage. Without such containment, which is accomplished for the individual person through community wisdom and participation, access to energy may be lethal, this includes energy emerging from the Macumba ritual core. Community functions both literally and symbolically as the containing apparatus for ritual core energy as well as for other forms of energy entering from the outer levels represented in the model. The function of community containment of energy allows for the process of energy empowerment for community members. A parallel process of energy containment and empowering release takes place within each individual person as he or she, from childhood onward, learns how in the words of community member Maria, age twelve, "to pull the community inside us so that when we are in a bad situation or afraid or something we can use the community strength to stop this time and get energy in a safe way to decide what to do." As Maria's words indicate, Macumba psychology and its operative concepts of community, energy, and containment allow for the Macumba psychosocial ecology model to operate whenever and virtually wherever it is needed. An illustration of how this takes place is offered in the next point, which focuses on the psychosocial function of trance in Macumba.

The Use of Ritual Trance and Communication with the Yoruban Spirits in the Development of Preventive and Interventive Strategies for Addressing the Particular Needs and Problems of Community Members

Ritual trance, the mystical possession process (santidade),[13] provides an opportunity to illustrate the inner working of the three operative concepts of Macumba psychosocial ecology outlined above: community, energy and containment. Ritual, ecstatic trance within the context of Macumba involves a long process of training and initiation. The process continues throughout the medium's lifecycle. The community's priest and/or priestess, themselves mediums, work to nurture the gift and responsibility of becoming a medium. The individual person cannot be forced into this role, but must come to this role by choice. The community members are there to encourage those members with this gift, and to discourage members who may wish to be mediums but who are unable to function in this way. The mediums, several levels of whom are represented in any given community, are the responsibility of the community. It is a two-way process of responsibility, as the mediums help to provide access to and translate the Macumba ritual core for the community members. Likewise, the community members need to care for the mediums to ensure their safety during the trance state as well as to assist with providing for physical needs of food and shelter whenever possible and necessary.

Trance is involved as a part of the rituals in the entire Macumba typology, with a somewhat lesser frequency in the Type 4 rituals involving children, although children as well can themselves be mediums in training after the age of seven. The mediums and initiates-in-training have their own rituals during which strategies of containment are learned as well as developed. Though the entire community is not present at these rituals, the "community wisdom" (see Figure 5.1) is assumed to be present. This wisdom is necessary to strengthen the containment process as the energy of the gods and/or spirits (orixás) is very powerful and the medium needs to be ready to be "mounted" by the god. If unready or ill-prepared, containment may not be possible and both the medium and the community members may be harmed.

Let us briefly examine the three-stage trance process that takes place during a Macumba Type 2 ritual (celebrating a feast of one of the orixás). It is worth noting that during the ritual there is a specific ordering of persons in the terreiro. An outside circle at the edge of the room is comprised of community members considered very wise and experienced. The next circle in is of newer community members and younger members. Then comes the circle of the mediums together with the priest and priestess. Though there is a great deal of movement, dance, and exchange during the course of the ritual, these three circles of persons remains. The three-circle assignment of space is significant for the containing process. When the ritual has advanced to the point that the mediums are beginning the trance process, the priest and priestess as well as the community members in the outer circle make a final decision together with each medium as to her or his readiness. In the rare case of conflict, the community's assessment is final. As the trance process begins, specified community members (yaba) assist the mediums physically by holding them by the waist or shoulders. Meanwhile the community elders and priest and priestess prepare the mediums to "be safely mounted" by the god or spirit. The next stage in the trance process is the giving of messages by the spirit in a variety of open, coded, and/or physical forms. The mediums begin with messages to those in the outer circle working inward. The priest and priestess are frequently the last to enter the trance process and appear to enter it in a somewhat different manner. Likewise, they are often the last to "return" to the group. In this second stage of the trance process the community members use special rhythms, movements, and drum-beating patterns to assist with the containing process as well as to, in the words of the sacred drummer José, "help the god or spirit keep moving and not get too attached to the body of the medium."

The third stage of the trance process involves the community's help to assist the mediums to return to the group. This stage can have a great number of surprises, as the god or spirit may temporarily refuse to "leave" the medium. In such cases the community members try a number of different strategies including special music, dance, and offerings to negotiate with the god or spirit. When the mediums and priest and priestess have "returned" the work of the community has just begun. The community must together decipher and interpret the various coded message from the gods or spirits for each person in the community. This is done together with attention to both individual and community problems and concerns. After many hours of exchange which includes both verbal and nonverbal forms, the community members have decided just who will do what and how in both short-range and long-range planning. Analysis of this decoding and application process of the messages from the trance state result in two types of working assignments for community members. There are intervention assignments related to specific problems or situations needing immediate attention. And there are preventive assignments where community members direct efforts toward anticipating needs in the community or larger social context, especially directing efforts to the developmental concerns of children and young adults. Community members often work in coordinated small groups to address these interventive and preventive assignments. Macumba ritual, dance, and drum are virtually always a part of the process helping members to contain, focus energy, and be guided by community wisdom as they go about the work they need to do. Two of these assignments, representative in nature, are discussed in the following final section.

The Larger Social Impact of Such Macumba Communities Through Their Grass-Roots Projects for Social Change; and Through the Use of Macumba Religious Rituals and Symbols by Afro-Brazilian Practitioners in the Healing Arts of Medicine and Psychotherapy in Salvador, Brazil

Time and space permit us only a brief look at the larger social impact of this and other Macumba communities' grass-roots projects. Two will be presented here.

Project 1. This Macumba community has an ongoing project for a group of former street children (ages ranging from three to thirteen) providing a place to live, study, learn simple agricultural skills, and participate in the working of a small farm attached to the housing unit. Priest Ezechial together with various community members visits the children, provide clothing and food for them, and coordinate the children's learning about the African and Afro-Brazilian culture. Children are also invited to participate in a specially designed program of Type 4 rituals (see above) to give them a sense of belonging to a Macumba community and for their own self-development. Coordinated with these rituals is special training for boys in the capoeira, and for girls in female rites of protection and care for the body.

Project 2. This Macumba community, through the central efforts of Priestess Jupira and ten community members, is involved in a region-wide effort to coordinate the healing work of visiting nurses and healers from the variety of Afro-Brazilian folk-healing traditions. Several healing teams have been working successfully for the past five years in some of the most needy and desperate areas in Salvador. In keeping with Macumba philosophy, wherever possible the healing team tries to use interventive and preventive approaches in their visits.

Finally, the work of another group connected to Afro-Brazilian culture and religion needs to be mentioned. Through the coordinating efforts of psychologist Derceo, mental health professionals of Afro-Brazilian heritage are bringing in and transforming the services of the mental health clinic through the attention to and responsible inclusion of dimensions of Macumba philosophy, psychology, and ritual experience. Working in this way professionals are making a significant impact on addressing issues of intra-familial abuse, recovery after rape and abuse, psychosomatic illness, and in the treatment of neurotic patterns. As Derceo notes, 'In my training I had to place both feet in the Western way, this did not allow me to use the toll of dance in my work. Now I try with one foot in the Western and one foot in my Afro-Brazilian way, I can begin to see and use dance and drum in my work with my people. In the future maybe we can create our own way bringing in the knowledge from the outside ways of diagnosing but healing through the wisdom of our culture and Macumba and Candomblé communities.'

CONCLUDING NOTE

It is hoped that through this five-point presentation the reader has at least an initial understanding of the nature and importance of community within the Macumba religious and cultural system. In this Macumba community context ritual, through dance and drum, serves as the basic multi-dimensional vehicle for psychosocial and spiritual development. As a researcher permitted to conduct field research and continuing research projects with this particular Macumba community, I need to express my gratitude and appreciation for the community members and for their decision to trust an outsider to be present and to be privy to the inner workings of Macumba religion and culture.

GLOSSARY

babalorixá—cult (sect) leader in northeastern Brazil popular name (pae de santo).

caboclo—an Indian god. Person of mixed Indian and white blood.

candomblé—Afro-Brazilian religion in Bahia region. The great ceremonies honoring the orixás. The sanctuary in which these ceremonies are held.

capoeira—African contest and special training, considered also as a dance form in certain regions, introduced by Angola blacks.

lundu—dance of Afro-Brazilians.

macumba—African sect primarily in Rio. The practice of magic.

orixás—Generic name for the Yoruban deities.

santidade—mystic power that possesses a person in ecstatic trance. A seventeenth-century Indian religious movement.

terreiro—Afro-Brazilian cult center (temple).

yaba—cult member who attends those during trance.

yalorixá—High priestess of a candomblé, popular name (mae de santo).

Yemanja—Yoruba goddess of the sea.

NOTES

This paper is a reworking of two conference presentations: American Academy of Religion, Chicago, 1994, and the Scandinavian Conference of the Donnerska Symposium on Music, Dance, and Ritual, Åbo, Finland, 1992. Initial funding for this research was provided by a grant from the American Academy of Religion; further support has been provided by a doctoral faculty grant from the Graduate Theological Union in Berkeley, California, and by the Swedish Research Council (Forskningsrådsnämden).

1. For an excellent discussion of the cautions and levels of awareness needed by researchers in studying traditions other than their own, see Murphy, 1988, 1993.

2. My beginning interest in Macumba began several years earlier in my psychotherapeutic work with a young woman from Salvador, Brazil, who was able to use her tradition's rituals and resources to assist with the therapeutic process. An account of this clinical case is found in De Marinis, 1996a.

3. I am indebted to the orientation of Norwegian phenomonologist of religion William Brede Kristensen, 1971, which cautiously maintains the need for an interpretation of religious experience based on the believer's or participant's perspective.

4. See references to the works of Strum for resources on the Afro-Brazilian context and Sullivan to the South American context of religion in general. See Myskofski's work for a historical source analysis of women's initiation rites in Afro-Brazilian religions. See Verger's volume (also available in English) on the nature of the African gods (orixás) in the Brazilian context.

5. Space does not permit an exposition of the way in which these symbol systems are interwoven. However, the discussion which Murphy pursues around the Cuban, Afro-American religion and culture of Santería is applicable to the Macumba situation as well.

"The symbiosis of orisha and saint, of Africa and Europe, is the santeros' solution to Marx's problem of accommodation and resistance. It is at once elegant, creative, and clever. . . . But by steadfastly remembering that Catholicism was only a correspondence to the way of the orishas, a translation of a deeper, more puissant way of worship, they resisted the limiting and racist definition of themselves held by white Catholic society" (Murphy, 1988, pp. 124-125).

6. This male and female team of priestly direction for a Macumba community is not a very frequent pattern.

7. From a personal interview on July 17, 1984, with R. Derceao, Afro-Brazilian psychologist in private practice in Salvador, Brazil. All quotes are taken from this interview text.

8. Quotes used in the text are from recorded interviews with priestess Jupira during the summer of 1984 in Salvador, Brazil.

9. Typology is the author's categorization based on analysis of field data, in consultation with Afro-Brazilian, North American, and European consultants. An excellent resource on Yoruba ritual analyzed from the perspective of performance theory is the volume by Margaret Drewal, 1992. Like Drewal (see especially Chapter 2), I want to note here that the concrete and distinct categories used by scholars to distinguish ritual, festival, spectacle, and play are not present in the community consciousness, ontology, or approach to ritualizing activity.

10. From interview material during summer of 1984 in Salvador, Brazil.

11. Macumba psychosocial ecology is a theoretical approach and model for understanding the psychosocial function and consequences of ritual participation. The approach and model were designed in consulation with members of the Macumba comunity as well as with a group of psychological and medical consultants in Bahia, Brazil.

12. See De Marinis, 1994 and 1996b and De Marinis, Grzymala-Moszczynska, 1994, for a theoretical development of Pruyser's illusionistic world in relation to the study of religious ritual eperience.

13. The contribution of Herskovits's approach (1952) is assumed here, placing the study of trance in the Afro-Brazilian religious context in cultural context "By treating trance as a ritual element, the new [Herskovits] viewpoint not only frees us . . . from interpretations of ecstasy based on the data of mental pathology; even more important , it initiates the unification of the psychological and the cultural aspect." Roger Bastide, *The African Religions of Brazil: Toward a Sociology of the Interpretations of Civilizations*, (1960 French) trans. by Helen Sebba (Baltimore: The Johns Hopkins University Press, 1978), p. 23.

BIBLIOGRAPHY

Bastide. R. *The African Religions of Brazil: Toward a Sociology of the Interpretations of Civilizations* (1960 French trans. by Helen Sebba). Baltimore: The Johns Hopkins University Press, 1978.

Bell, C. *Ritual Theory, Ritual Practice*. Oxford: Oxford University Press, 1992.

De Marinis, V. *Transitional Objects and Safe Space: The Interaction Between Psychology of Religion and Ritual Studies*. Uppsala: Uppsala University Press, 1996a.

De Marinis, V. "The Nature and Use of Religious Ritual in Psychotherapy," *The Function of Religious Ritual as the Medium for Memory and Meaning: An Interdisciplinary Investigation*, eds. V. De Marinis and M. Aune. New York: State University New York, SUNY, 1996b.

De Marinis, V. "Psychological Function and Consequences of Religious Ritual Experience," *Tro och Tanke* (The Swedish Research Journal on Religion), vol. 4, no. 6, 1994: 11-20.

De Marinis, V. "Movement as Mediator of Memory and Meaning: An Investigation of the Psychosocial and Spiritual Function of Dance in Macumba Religious Ritual," in *Dance as Religious Studies*, eds. D. Adams and D. Apostolos-Cappadona. New York: Crossroad Press, 1990.

De Marinis, V., and H. Grzymala-Moszczynska, "The Nature and Role of Religion and Religious Experience in Psychosocial Cross-Cultural Adjustment: On-Going Research in Clinical Psychology of Religion," *Social Compass*, vol. 42, no. 1, 1995: 121-135.

Drewal, M. *Yoruba Ritual: Performers, Play, Agency*. Bloomington: Indiana University Press, 1992.

Driver, T. *The Magic of Ritual*. San Francisco: Harper, 1991.

Herskovits, M. J. "Some Psychological Implications of Afro-American Studies," in *Proceedings and Selected Papers of the Twenty-ninth International Congress of Americanists* (1948). Chicago: Univ. of Chicago Press, 1952.

Kristensen, W. *The Meaning of Religion*. The Hague: Martimus Nijhoff, 1971.

Murphy, J. *Santeria: African Spirits in America* . Boston: Beacon Press, 1988, 1993.

Myscofski, C. "Women's Initiation Rites in Afro-Brazilian Religions," *Journal of Ritual Studies*, vol. 2 no. 1, 1988: 101-118.

Pruyser, P. "Forms and Functions of the Imagination in Religion," in *Religion in Psychodynamic Perspective*, eds. H. Newton Malony and B. Spilka. Oxford: Oxford University Press, 1991.

Strum, F. "Afro-Brazilian Cults," in *African Religions: A Symposium*, ed. Newell Booth. New York: N.O.K. Publishers Int., 1977.

Sullivan, L. *Icanchu's Drum: An Orientation to Meaning in South American Religions*. New York: Macmillan, 1988.

Verger, P. *Orixás: Deuses Iorubás na África e No Novo Munde*. São Paulo: Editoria Corrupio Comercio Ltda, 1981.

6

Umbanda and Its Clientele

Tina Gudrun Jensen

INTRODUCTION

Umbanda originated in the 1920s in Rio de Janeiro. It appeared at a time of major social changes in Southeastern Brazil—changes having to do with industrialization, urbanization, immigration, and the formation of social classes, especially of the middle class as a new and influential social class.

Umbanda came about as a religious innovation that synthesized existing religious traditions of Brazil, that is, candomblé, Kardecist spiritism,[1] catholicism, and Indian religious traditions. In this way umbanda brought together the three ethnic groups that constitute the Brazilian population: the African, the European, and the Indian. The strongest characteristics of umbanda are its eclecticism, dynamics, and variation. The attempts of the umbandists to standardize its rituals and doctrine have not been quite successful. Thus, umbanda varies from one umbanda center to the other.

Umbanda has often been stigmatized as a religion of the lower classes because of the Afro-Brazilian element, which is generally strongly apparent in the ritual conduct. Umbanda started, however, within the middle class and is a forum for the middle class as well as for the lower classes (Brown 1979). From early on umbanda became widespread as a popular religion, especially in the urbanized areas of southeastern Brazil. In the state of São Paulo, the industrial hub of Brazil, it has thus gained vast popularity since the 1950s (Ortiz 1988). It is estimated that a quarter to a third of the Brazilian population has contact with the umbanda centers (Droogers 1993). The majority of these people have a "low level experience" with umbanda as accidental clients frequenting the umbanda centers (Fry 1974). They have little or no knowledge about the doctrines and rituals of umbanda, and they generally only frequent the umbanda-centers in times of difficulty.

While the majority of the research into umbanda is based on the coregroup
members of umbanda, the *pai-de-santo* and the *filhos-de-santo*, the clientele has
been somewhat ignored. During my fieldwork in an umbanda center in the city
of São Paulo, I became interested in exploring the question of what attracts the
many clients to the sessions in the umbanda center. In this article, then, I
examine what umbanda offers the clientele as regards the internal relationship
between them and the umbanda-center, as well as the worldview of umbanda
and its ritual practices. In addition, I will examine the clients' own explanations
for why they frequent the umbanda center, their modes of using the center and
their attitudes toward religion in general. The findings are, finally, treated in
relation to the social reality of the urban setting of São Paulo.[2]

THE UMBANDA-CENTER

The umbanda center consists of a *pai-de-santo*, the leader of the center, and
about twenty *filhos-de-santo*, who serve as ritual assistants and mediums in
various stages of initiation.

There are two types of organization within the umbanda center: the ritual and
the secular organization. The ritual organization is in the hands of the
charismatic leader, the *pai-de-santo*. Together with his spiritual parallel, the
guia chefe, who is the chief spirit of the umbanda-center, he instructs and
initiates his *filhos-de-santo*. The status of the *pai-de-santo* as the leader of the
umbanda-center is legitimatized spiritually, by the fact that he is the one who
incorporates the *guia chefe*.

The secular, or, administrative, organization of the umbanda-center is
prescribed by the federation to which the umbanda-center is affiliated. In
contrast to the ritual organization, this type of organization is referred to as
taking care of the material rather than the spiritual side of the umbanda-center. It
is a purely administrative hierarchy with a president, a vice-president,
secretaries, and treasurers. In this hierarchy the *pai-de-santo* has little
importance. Since he is in charge of the ritual leadership, and should not be
connected with the material side of the umbanda center, he does not function as
its president. The ritual organization, however, being defined by the spiritual
raison d´être of the umbanda center, seems to represent the most important type
of organization.

The umbanda center is characterized by autonomy. Even though the umbanda
center is affiliated with a federation, the federation only plays a small rôle with
respects to the workings of the individual umbanda center. The umbanda center
chooses its own doctrines and ritual conduct through the *pai-de-santo* and his
guia chefe, without the interference of the federation. From the point of view of

the umbanda center the affiliation with the federation is merely a question of legitimation and protection.

The autonomy is also reflected in the fact that it is the *pai-de-santo* himself and his *guia chefe* who instruct and initiate the mediums. The mediums have to obtain their knowledge through practice. The *pai-de-santo* prefers that his *filhos-de-santo* do not read umbanda literature, and he is opposed to their working in any other umbanda center.

RELATIONSHIP TO THE CLIENTELE

Clients are, per se, not initiated into umbanda. They are a rather loose and fluctuating category. The umbanda center has little control with its clients. The majority of them are not registred, they are simply accidental clients. Thus, clients come and leave the umbanda center without any obligations and commitments. As the *pai-de-santo* told me regarding the clients, "It's their own free will." The *pai-de-santo* does not care if the clients frequent other umbanda centers or other religious institutions; he believes that all religions lead to the same god. Nevertheless, the umbanda center is dependent on the clients; indeed, the prestige of the umbanda center is measured by the number of clients it has.

The *pai-de-santo* and his *filhos-de-santo* have little contact with the clients. They have contact with the clients almost solely when they incorporate the spirits during the sessions. The *pai-de-santo*, in particular, does not want to be personally involved with the clients and their problems. He prefers that the clients confide their problems to the consulting spirits during the sessions. He justifies this standpoint spiritually, by reasoning that clients in times of difficulty attract evil spirits that may cause harm to other human beings.

THE WORLD-VIEW OF UMBANDA

The umbanda cosmos consists of three levels: the astral level, the earth, and the underworld. The astral level is inhabited by the *Orixás*/saints and the more or less evolved spirits like the *Caboclos,* the unacculturated Indians, and the *Pretos Velhos*, the Old Negroes, who are the founding spirits of umbanda. Human incarnations, who are at lower stages of spiritual evolution, inhabit the earth. The earth is visited by the spirits from the astral plane, and at times by the *Orixás,* who descend to help the human incarnations on earth. The underworld is inhabited by evil and ignorant spirits, such as the *Exus* and their female counterparts, the *Pombas Giras*. They, too, visit the earth, generally causing trouble to the human incarnations (Brown 1986).

In umbanda the *Orixás* do not play the same active part as in candomblé.

They rarely incorporate in the mediums, and when they do, they are generally mute. The *Orixás,* just as the highly evolved spirits, are often said to be too "illuminated" to visit the earth. In umbanda it is the spirits of the dead that hold the greatest importance—whatever stage of spiritual evolution the particular spirit may belong to and whether or not it be a good or an evil one. These spirits are the focus of the sessions in the umbanda center, where they function as consulting spirits.

The spirits of the astral level are called spirits of the light, or of the right. They are generally good, highly spiritually evolved, and connected to the "white magic" of umbanda. The spirits of the underworld are called spirits of the shadows, or of the left. They are generally evil, amoral, ignorant, material and are connected with the forces of *quimbanda,* "black magic." They are often characterized as having been criminals in their former incarnations; one of the common versions of *Exu* is the crook *Zé Pilintra.*

The qualities of good and evil, as mirrored in the spirits of the right and of the left, are somewhat relative (Negrao 1993: 192-200). Some spirits are able to work for the good as well as for the evil. The spirits of the left are not purely evil. Some of them are even considered good. In umbanda there is a distinction between the pagan *Exus* and the baptized *Exus.* The good *Exus* are the ones who are baptized and doctrinized. Their ignorance and amorality make them naïve and child-like, so they are often treated like children who need education. Their evil character is regarded as being tied up with their lack of spiritual evolution. By being baptized and doctrinized, however, they acquire the possibility to evolve.

In contrast to the spirits of the right, the spirits of the left are more human-like and share in human weakness. It is therefore easier to make them work for human beings. The presence of these spirits at the sessions is considered a necessity; they are regarded as useful and indispensable because of their capability to resolve the material and concrete everyday problems of the clients. With respect to human matters, they are more efficacious than the spirits of the right. In addition, they resolve problems quicker than the spirits of the right, who are working with spiritual matters on a long term. Many of the problems that are interpreted as being caused by spirits of the left have to be undone by spirits of the left. Even though umbanda primarily works with the spirits of the right, the spirits of the left are as fundamental as those spirits.

The relativity of good and evil, as mirrored by the equally fundamental and indispensable spirits of the right and of the left is often emphasised by the *pai-de-santo* and the *filhos-de-santo.*They state that there is no good without evil and vice versa. The relationship between good and evil is often pictured as a balance—the one depends on the other. The relativity of good and evil is furthermore brought forward in statements to the effect that what is good for one person might be evil for another. In line with this, the question of morality and amorality is treated in a special way in umbanda. Umbanda does not perpetuate a moral hegemony that deprives the individual of his or her rights. On the contrary, the concept of morality in umbanda brings legitimacy to the rights of the individual (Negrao 1993: 220-222).

THE CONSULTATION

The umbanda center has sessions twice a week, in the evening. These sessions are open to the public. The main attractions are the consultations with spirits. As a ritual unfolding of caridade, charity—a central concept in umbanda, derived from Kardecist spiritism—the consultation bridges the interests of the clientele and of the ritual and spiritual personnel of the umbanda center. During these sessions the spirits, who are incorporated in the mediums, are consulted by clients with different kinds of problems. In helping the clients, the spirits perform charity, and, in so doing, further their own spiritual evolution.

Besides being a ritual unfolding of charity, the consultation constitutes a model for interpreting and resolving the problems of the clientele. There is a distinction between spiritual problems and material problems, that is, whether problems are caused by spiritual agencies or not. According to the *pai-de-santo*, the majority of the clientele´s problems are material. Whether the clients' problems be spiritual or material, the consultations represent solutions to these problems through the *trabalhos,* magical works, of the spirits. The consulting spirits listen to the clients and guide them. All the spirits, whether of the right or of the left, are considered excellent psychologists. Besides giving consultations to the clients, the spirits protect the clients through the *passe,* the imposition of hands (Brumana and Martinez 1989: 84). This is a cleansing ritual, which discharges evil fluids, protects and strengthens the client.

The consulting spirits represented in the umbanda center may be either of the right or of the left, but there are also spirits who are able to work for both the right and the left. The spirits that work for the left are not allowed to carry out works that are downright evil, however; the clients may not demand that murders and the like be committed through these spirits. What is offered through these spirits is the resolution of problems that, in various ways, are related to the material and concrete everyday life of the clients: financial difficulties, unemployment, unhappy love, and the like.

When the *pai-de-santo* and the mediums incorporate the spirits during the consultation, they are dressed in accordance with the spirits who incorporate in them. For instance, the *pai-de-santo*, as incorporating a *Cigana,* a gipsy, wore a décolleté red taffeta dress and a lot of jewelry. They dress up as the spirits solely because of the clientele, however. According to the *pai-de-santo*, the clientele would not believe that the spirits incorporate in the mediums if the mediums were not dressed up like the spirits.

UMBANDA'S ORIENTATION TO THE WORLD

Umbanda offers the clients a kind of model for how to perceive oneself as a human being and how to orient oneself in the world. While this model may only be an implicit one, it does seem to be both real and coherent. I shall now, by way of summarizing some of the points made earlier, try to outline the contours of this model.

Through its worldview, umbanda justifies the weakness and failures of human beings. These are mirrored by the amoral, material, and human-like spirits of the left. Human beings are perceived as not being fully evolved spiritually, something which justifies their failures. Nevertheless, human beings, just as spirits, have the opportunity to evolve spiritually. "The human factor" is likewise justified by the relativity of good and evil. In the relativity of these notions, as in the concept of morality, umbanda offers legitimacy for individual rights. Furthermore, the conception of good and evil as being equally fundamental in the umbanda worldview affirms the coexistence of good and evil in the social reality. Umbanda has been interpreted as a sacralization of a fundamental aspect of Brazilian culture, as a legitimation of the crook, of dirty tricks, and of the favor; additionally it has been seen as a dramatized and ritualized metaphor for the political and social reality of Brazil (Fry 1982: 13 & 42).

Through the consultations umbanda offers interpretations and immediate solutions to problems through short term magical manipulation. In the majority of cases the problems of the clients are interpreted as being material and not spiritual. The consultation offers solutions to problems related to the concrete everyday life, such as financial difficulties, unemployment, unhappy love, and so on. The consultations thus offer the possibility of improving the present situation of the client. In this way the consultations contribute to the this-worldly aspect, which is emphasized by umbanda. The consultation cultivates individualistic aspects—Each person is the center of his or her own private universe. The question of social responsability is a non-issue in the treatment of the individual's problems (Fry 1982: 28).

Umbanda generally emphasizes values like individualism and autonomy. These values are reflected at various levels: Each umbanda center is responsible for its own organization, the clientele have no commitments or obligations to the center; individual rights are legitimated by the umbanda worldview; and, finally, individual problems are treated through personal consultation.

My contention is that umbanda to some extent represents a world-affirming religion in the sense of Roy Wallis (1984). First of all, umbanda is world-affirming in the sense that it affirms the normatively approved goals and values of the social world. In addition, umbanda emphasizes individualism by focusing on the individual achievement, that is, the improvement of each individual's situation, whether this be his or her financial situation, personal relationships, or self-realization.

THE CLIENTELE

Most of the clients interviewed were born in the city of São Paulo. About one-third of these clients may be said to belong to the lower classes: the rest pertain to the middle class. Those who belong to the lower classes are black or mixed, while the rest are white. All these clients are Catholic-born and brought up with Catholicism, but generally they state that their parents are non-practicing. Most of the clients were introduced to umbanda and other forms of spiritism.[3] either through their parents or other relatives—many of them during early childhood.

As regards the actual religious self-definition of the clients, very few regard themselves as Catholics. Most regard themselves as being *espíritas,* spiritists, and secondarily, as being catholics. All of them have had various experiences with other kinds of spiritism as well as other religions, especially with the Pentecostal churches. These churches are strongly in opposition to umbanda and to spiritism in general. Besides the umbanda center, most of the clients simultaneously frequent other religious alternatives.

MOTIVATIONS FOR FREQUENTING THE UMBANDA-CENTER

Many of the clients made their first contact with the umbanda center through relatives or friends. Others have made their first contact singlehandedly. The majority of the clients live in the very neighbourhood of the umbanda center or in the vicinity thereof.

The clients have a rather superficial and noncommital relationship to umbanda and the umbanda center. Nevertheless, their interpretations of social events reflect a worldview that is coherent with that of umbanda. For instance, most of them believe that illnesses, financial difficulties, and domestic problems are, in part, caused by spiritual agencies and that they can be resolved through the magical works of the spirits. In addition, in the view of the majority the notions of good and evil are relative ones. I did not, however, record any experiences of conversion to umbanda. The clients do not think that their experiences with umbanda have transformed their lives spiritually. Rather, clients frequently state that their experiences with umbanda have changed their lives materially, that is, with respect to finances, employment, and so forth.

What attracts the clients to the umbanda center are the consultations. The clients frequent the umbanda center during the sessions because of problems, but also because they like the center and feel good there.

Financial difficulties, unemployment, and the quest for a better job seem to be the most urgent problems causing the clients, men and women alike, to frequent the umbanda center. Next to these there are the domestic problems and interpersonal conflicts. Women, in particular, make reference to problems of this sort. Only a few of the clients that I interviewed go because of illnesses.[4] In only one of these cases the disease was referred to as being spiritual. However, a few clients, all female, frequent the umbanda-center because of mediunidade, mediumism. They go in order to develop their mediumistic gifts, something that they take to be a spiritual necessity.

Besides problems, the other major reason for frequenting the umbanda center is that the clients like the center and feel good there. They like the atmosphere of the center and the commemoration of *Orixás* and spirits, and they also enjoy talking to the consulting spirits, lighting a candle, and knowing that the umbanda center has no interest in their money. Furthermore, the clients are attracted to the music, the hymns, the clothes worn by the *pai-de-santo* and the *filhos-de-santo*, the rituals and the consultations. What the clients consider most important in umbanda is the help given through the consultations with the spirits. They consider it important that umbanda, through the spirits, works with the human race and that it is down-to-earth.

USE OF THE UMBANDA-CENTER

The clients frequent the umbanda center approximately three to four times per month. A visit usually has the following phases. The client arrives for the session (often after it has already started), sits down, and waits until it is his or her turn to talk to the consulting spirit. He or she then pays for the session and finally goes away before the session ends. Usually only the ritual personnel participate in the final rituals. The clients are generally not well acquainted with the ritual conduct. The proper conduct includes standing or sitting down at certain points during the session, not crossing arms or legs while sitting or standing (this is said to attract evil spirits), and the like.

Generally, the client's' relationship to the personnel of the umbanda center is superficial. Most of the clients know neither the *pai-de-santo* and the *filhos-de-santo* nor the other clients, except for those who have introduced them. The existence of patronage relations between clients and *pai-de-santo* has been asserted by Diana Brown (1986). According to my own findings, however, there is no good evidence of such a relation. The clients do, however, feel very intimate with the spirits, or rather with one particular spirit. At the entrance to the umbanda center there is a bulletin board announcing the names of the spirits to appear in the forthcoming sessions of the month. The clients are thus always kept informed about the time of the appearance of a particular spirit. In most cases the clients make reservations for consultations with spirits beforehand in order to avoid going to the umbanda center in vain. The most popular spirits are *Cigana,* a Gipsy who is of the left, *Caboclo,* an unacculturated Indian of the right, *Baiano,* a Bahian from the state of Bahia who is able to work for the right as well as for the left, *Marinheiro,* a Mariner of the right, and *Cosme e Damiao*, a Child of the right. Each of them has a talent for resolving a particular kind of problem. Clients with financial problems and unemployment as well as clients with problems in love affairs generally have consultations with the Gipsy, the Bahian or the Mariner, who are known to be talented in dealing with these things; clients who suffer from illnesses generally have consultations with the Indian and the Child, which are known to be healers; and so on.

Patronage relations thus exist, grounded in the reciprocity between clients and spirits; the clients are helped by the spirits, and the spirits, in performing this charity, further their own spiritual evolution. Further, a kind of identification between clients and spirits takes place. Some spirits are less evolved spiritually, being amoral, material, close to human weakness, and full of vices. An example is the Bahian. People with drinking problems, then, will normally consult this spirit, who is known to be a drunkard himself. Thus a client said, "He drinks a lot . . . he likes to drink beer even more than I do. That's also why I like him."

The fact that the spirits are human-like and have vices makes them more attractive to clients. There is no limit to the kinds of problems that the clients can present them with—the spirits will always meet them with sympathy, tolerance, acceptance, support, and guidance.

In spite of its personal character, the relationship between client and spirit can also be charaterized as an impersonal one of client-therapist. The client is dealing with a spirit, not with a human being that he or she has to relate to in everyday life. As a client said, "It's like a person who doesn't have anything to do with your life. If you tell your daddy about a problem of yours, he reacts. There (at the center) they don't."

ATTITUDES TOWARD RELIGIOUS AND NONRELIGIOUS INSTITUTIONS

The majority of the clients rarely go to the Catholic church—only about once a year or less. They generally frequent the Catholic church at weddings, baptism, and such, together with their families. Likewise, the majority of the clients prefer their children to marry in the Catholic church, and not, for instance, in the umbanda center. In this way the Catholic church seems to represent tradition, that is, the normative institution. Nevertheless, most of the clients have very negative attitudes toward the Catholic church regarding many points. For instance, they blame the Catholic church for being far too involved in politics, for being corrupt, for moralizing concerning the individual's behavior, and for being old-fashioned. As for the other religious institutions, the pentecostal churches are blamed for being too fanatic and backward, for being extremely prohibitive, and for limiting the individual's freedom of action. Many of the clients have had experiences with a pentecostal church. Many of them also state that they ceased frequenting the pentecostal church because they could not cope with the fact that the pentecostal church wanted to interfere with their ways of living. In comparison, the clients regard umbanda and spiritism in general as more allowing and accepting, as giving the individual supreme right to live the way he or she wants to, without moralistic interference. A client said, "In umbanda you can do what you want, it's the only religion that doesn't condemn you." Likewise, the general opinion is that the individual's freedom of decision is more respected in umbanda.

In times of difficulty, seeking the umbanda center or other religious agencies in general prevails over seeking other nonreligious agencies. In cases of less serious illnesses, the reasons for seeking an umbanda center instead of a doctor are most frequently that it is too difficult and expensive to get medical attention and that the doctors are incompetent and the medicine inefficient. Many clients state that seeking an umbanda center is cheaper, easier, quicker and, last but not least, closer to their homes than a doctor or a hospital. Others find that the spirits are more powerful than a doctor, who is just a human being. In cases of financial problems, domestic problems, interpersonal conflicts, and emotional crises, seeking the umbanda center prevails over seeking family, friends, or a psychologist. The clients frequently argue that spirits have more insight into their problems than do human beings. Others say that it is a way to escape from the problems, and that this is easier than to actually resolve them. Finally, others refer to the private nature of the consultation.

CONCLUSION: UMBANDA, THE CLIENTELE AND THE SOCIAL REALITY

By way of conclusion, I would like to state two points that relate to the findings that I have presented above. First, I would argue that the things that umbanda and the umbanda center have to offer its clientele as well as the clientele's motivations for frequenting the umbanda center and their modes of using it relate to the social reality that they live and act in. Secondly, it seems that this behavior reflects aspects and values of modern urban life.

As to my first point, I would like to mention that the social reality of Brazil is one of economic instability, a lack of social security, and of inefficient social services. In São Paulo unemployment is endemic, and salaries are often very low. This situation is a threat both to the lower classes and to the middle class. Fear and distrust are inherent elements of the everyday life of São Paulo (Fry 1982: 41).

As I have reported, the majority of the clients are motivated to frequent the umbanda center by problems related to the social reality. These are primarily financial difficulties and unemployment or the quest for a better job. In this sense umbanda is, in many ways, in touch with the social reality. This is also emphasised by the clients, who find it important that umbanda is down-to-earth and describe it as working with the human race and providing help. The social reality that the clients live and act in is mirrored in umbanda. The worldview of umbanda affirms the coexisting realities of good and evil in society. Umbanda is this-worldly in its focus on human beings, their weakness, failures, and their material and concrete everyday-life problems. It offers interpretations for and immediate solutions to these problems, providing the possibility for changing and improving the situation of the client through the magical manipulation of the spirits and through their protection, support, and guidance. Correspondingly, the clients attach more importance to the material improvement that umbanda can provide than to whatever spiritual benefit there might be gained from it. It is furthermore considered cheaper, easier, and quicker to frequent the umbanda center than to seek out other agencies.

My second point concerns the relationship between the umbanda center and its clientele one the one hand, and, on the other hand, some of the values that go with living in a modern urban society. These are values such as individualism, autonomy, privacy, and the right for everyone to be the architect of his or her own fortune. As shown, umbanda mirrors these values in various ways: I have already described the autonomy of the umbanda center and its relationship to the clients, which is characterized by a lack of control, obligations, and commitments, the legitimacy of individual rights, something that is mirrored in the worldview, and, finally, the way that individual problems are treated individually, something that is mirrored in the consultation. Last, but not least, I have described the world-affirming character of umbanda, with its emphasis on individual achievement with respect to goals that are valued in the social world. Correspondingly, the clients' attitudes toward religion revolve around the importance of the freedom of the individual and of freedom of decision and action. The clients find these values in umbanda. They use their consultations with the spirits as an instrument for achieving their goals, goals such as individual progress and upward social mobility. These values also become apparent when one considers the clients' superficial and impersonal forms of contact with the personnel of the center and with the other clients. Umbanda is generally an individual affair rather than a collective affair. There is a conspicuous absence of patronage relations between clients and core group members, something which results in the nonexistence of social networks. Clients prefer to confide their problems to spirits in privacy and not to their social surroundings.

NOTES

1. This is the spiritism of Allan Kardec, which originated in France in the 1850s and soon spread to Brazil.

2. This contribution is based on field studies, interviews with a *pai-de-santo* and two *filhos-de-santo,* as well as standardized interviews with fifteen selected clients, carried out in an umbanda center in the city of São Paulo in 1992 and 1994, for a total of six months. I thank the University of Copenhagen for having supported this project financially.

3. The clients use the term "spiritism" as a broad term covering Kardecist spiritism, umbanda, and candomblé.

4. Illnesses are ofen considered the most common reason for seeking the umbanda center and intitiating into the umbanda center (Brown 1986, Camargo 1961, Montero 1985).

BIBLIOGRAPHY

Brown, Diana. "Umbanda and Class Relations in Brazil," in M. Margolis and W. Carter (eds.), *Brazil: Anthropological Perspectives.* New York: Columbia University Press, 1979.

Brown, Diana. *Umbanda: Religion and Politics in Urban Brazil.* Ann Arbor: UMI Research Press, 1986.

Brumana, Fernando Giobellina and Elda Gonzales Martinez. *Spirits from the Margin. Umbanda in São Paulo. A Study in Popular Religion and Social Experience.* Uppsala Studies in Cultural Anthropology 12. Uppsala: Acta Universitatis Upsaliensis, 1989.

Camargo, Cândido Procôpio Ferreira de. *Kardecismo e Umbanda.* São Paulo: Livraria Pioneira Editora, 1961.

Droogers, André. "Power and Meaning in Three Brazilian Popular Religions," in S. Rostas and A. Droogers (eds.), *The Popular Use of Popular Religion in Latin America.* Amsterdam: Centrum voor Studie en Documentatie van Latijns Amerika, 1993.

Fry, Peter. "Reflexoes sobre o Crescimento da Conversao à Umbanda," in *Cadernos do ISER.* Rio de Janeiro: ISER, 1974.

Fry, Peter. *Para Inglês Ver: Identidade Política na Cultura Brasileira.* Rio de Janeiro: Zahar Editores, 1982.

Montero, Paula. *Da Doenca à Desordem: a Magia na Umbanda.* Rio de Janeiro: Edicoes Graal, 1985.

Negrao, Lísias Nogueira. *Umbanda e Questao Moral: Formacao e Atualidade do Campo Umbandista em São Paulo,* doctoral thesis. São Paulo: Universidade de São Paulo, 1993.

Ortiz, Renato. *A Morte Branca do Feiticeiro Negro. Umbanda e Sociedade Brasileira.* São Paulo: Editora Brasiliense, 1988.

Wallis, Roy. *The Elementary Forms of the New Religious Life.* London: Routledge and Kegan Paul, 1984.

7

The Shakers of St. Vincent: A Symbolic Focus for Discourses[1]

Charles Gullick

The Shakers of St. Vincent have become the focus of various discourses concerning Vincentian culture. This chapter attempts to untangle the symbolic meanings attributed to them by Vincentians and other West Indians. In so doing it demonstrates how ethnographers have tended to ignore the multivocal aspects of Shakerism and to focus on single meanings in analyses. As a result it is argued that, while some anthropologists, like some Vincentians, have perceived the Shakers in terms of African Religions in the New World, this is only a small section of a complex symbolic system.

A MUSICAL DISCOURSE

During the 1976 Carnival in St. Vincent, King Brooklyn's offering for the Calypso King contest entitled *Largo Height Busy* commenced:

Ah converted girl she making fame.
Went down by the plain and spoil she name.
Went and look for work, she get ah man,
Surprise everybody—ah married man.
Now the belly big he leave and gone,
All about she hunting only for man.

Chorus
Largo Height is way dem busy,
Largo Height is way dem busy,
Largo Height is way dem busy,
Rich Ruby come see way Biggie day.

The song, among other things, is a comment on the morals of "Converted" Vincentians. While many rival sects and denominations convert the inhabitants of St. Vincent, the term "Converted" almost invariably refers to members of the Spiritual Baptist Church. Members of this church prefer the description "Converted" to "Shaker" (a term used by other Vincentians to describe them).

This chapter seeks to analyse this and other discourses concerning Converted people found among non-believers both in the West Indies and in academia in general. In so doing it attempts to balance the studies of Spiritual Baptists that have emphasised the participants' views (e.g., Henney 1974). The chapter commences with a discussion of Vincentian discourses and then passes via Trinidadian ones to an overview of the anthropological perspectives mentioned in the discussion of the Vincentian discourses.

DISCOURSE AND PERFORMANCE IN ST. VINCENT

The Vincentian Shakers had become powerful symbols of Vincentian culture when I was undertaking anthropological fieldwork in St. Vincent in 1970-1971, 1974, and 1976. They were discussed in many varied contexts and discourses. The discussion of their morals, as exemplified by the calypso, was a major theme.

Whenever there was an open-air Shaker meeting in one of the two villages I studied during the early 1970s, spectators would comment on the hypocrisy of various worshipers and they followed this with details of their morals and/or sex life. The negative attitude of the song was typical of such views. In St. Vincent, as in Trinidad, calypso "is a means of disclaiming responsibility for one's words. It is only because the norms of the event are shared by members of the community—political leaders included—that many a calypsonian does not end up with a law suit filed against him" (Sealy quoted by Saville-Troike 1989: 34). While the theme of male/female conflict was as common in St. Vincent as in Trinidad (Elder 1968), anthropologists studying calypso in St. Vincent have tended to emphasise their political (e.g., Manning 1986, 1990) and economic (e.g., Gearing 1988, Gullick n.d.) roles. Songs concerned with gender conflicts and politics had overlaps with general gossip, which also had shared conventions that reduced recourse to the law.

Gossip was an art form in St. Vincent. The conventions whereby Vincentians gossip about other Vincentians have been explored by R. D. Abrahams and R. Bauman (1971), Charles Gullick (1976) and G. M. Fraser (1979). The negative views of Shaker morals expressed by audiences of their services are the only discourses concerning the Converted that have not been given theoretical respectability by such ethnographers.

Other Vincentian commentaries on the Shakers focused on seven major areas:

(i) their performances during services, (ii) their roles in the local curing system, (iii) their history, (iv) their role in politics, and (v) their employment at wakes, with subtexts on (vi) class and (vii) ethnicity. In addition, items from the five major discourses could occur as subtexts to one another. In order to tease out the major discourses (i-v) in the following analysis. the minor ones (vi and vii) are underplayed. All seven factors have been adopted by anthropologists in their discussions of Spiritual Baptism.

DISCOURSES CONCERNING SHAKER SERVICES AND TRANCES

The majority of discourses concerning Shaker trance behavior by non-Converted Vincentians occurred when they were observing open air services held by the Shakers.[2] As a result I collected far more such comments when I was undertaking field research in a village without any Shaker buildings, than in one which was relatively well supplied with such facilities (Gullick 1985: 20). In the former village there were frequently more than one such service per week (and more when the moon was full), while in the latter they were rare except for occasional wakes.

Shaker services have been described in detail elsewhere (cf. Henney 1974, Gullick 1971, 1974, 1981, 1985:14-5, 163, 1988, 1993, etc.) and all that need be explained herein is that there is no fixed order of service but most commenced with prayers from the Anglican or Methodist communion services interspersed with hymns with a strong beat. As each Shaker arrived (s)he shook hands with all the other Converted present. They then took it in turn to lead the prayers and/or hymn singing. After about an hour the Holy Spirit possessed some of the worshipers, who then shook to the rhythms of the service and occasionally talked in spirit language.

Discussions of Shaker trances were the main occasions when outsiders considered Shaker beliefs, insofar as most explained that the Holy Spirit was possessing them. This was generally taken as the basis of discussions concerning the genuineness of the trances that were under observation. The most animated debate was occasioned by a dog which growled at a possessed Shaker who rapidly returned to normal! The majority view of the audience was that he had been faking the trance.

Other debates about Shaker beliefs occasionally followed their equivalent of sermons. The "sermons" that produced the most discussion were when Shakers recounted their experiences during mourning. Mourning was a period of sensory deprivation in which initiates retreat into a darkened hut with little food or drink and are expected to have a spiritual journey which they recount at the next service. Again the discussion tended to focus on the genuineness of the event, and not the content of the message. The only exception I came across was when the message concerned the evils of infanticide. This was treated as a great joke. The lack of interest in the beliefs per se may have reflected the fact that in many ways the unity of the Shakers lay in relatively uniform performances and not a unity of beliefs. Each pointer seemed to have different beliefs and while their followers frequently echoed them, there was no unity, even among local groups of Shakers.

SHAKERS IN MEDICAL DISCOURSES

In one village in 1970 there was a man who had more tales told about him than any other. He related that he had had a Jumby (spirit/ghost) set on his back. He started to become a Shaker. Once he had commenced attending services as a participant, tales about his affliction became common currency amongst the non-Shaker audience watching the proceedings from the road. Apparently he had stolen some ground provisions from the land of a woman from the neighboring village. She cursed him so that he got a "Jumby in he belly." Various doctors and Obeah men from all over the island had failed to remove it, so that he was attempting a cure by becoming a Shaker. He commenced mourning, but failed to complete it.

The man's experiences overlapped with tales about two villagers from a different community who had a dispute over some land. One put a Jumby on the other. The spell was such that every day at noon the victim's belly swelled up and started kicking like a pregnant woman's tummy. The Jumby then went up to his throat and made it swell. Half an hour later it descended to his genitals which also swelled up. The patient saw both doctors and Obeah men, but died five months later.

When preparing a flow chart (Figure 7.1) for a paper on folk-medicine in the Caribbean (Gullick 1988), I realized that the chart also gave the plot for numerous narratives about curing. Many of these tales were used to reinforce local beliefs about illness and the treatment of invalids, in rather the same ways as films, hospital soaps, and documentaries do in our culture. It should be noted that the Shakers were optional characters in the plots.

Medical data can produce great problems for ethnographers, because very different models of health, the body, and the self interact in concepts relating to disease and illness. Frequently, as K.V. Staiano (1986) demonstrates in her study of the Garifuna (or Black Caribs) in Belize, this is because religion plays a major role in defining causes of illness and in their cure. The Shakers in St. Vincent have a similar role in the local curing system. This is an area where African parallels of cures can add even more meanings. As a result, when an earlier version of this chapter was presented at a conference the majority of Africanists emphasised the parallels they saw between the Vincentian curing

Figure 7.1

Vincentian Carib Curing System in the 1970s

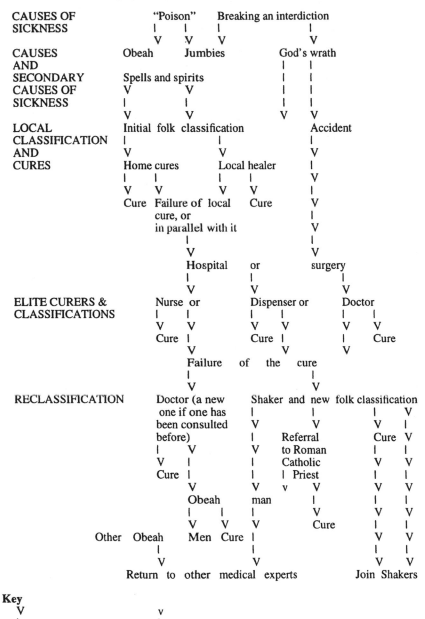

Key
```
V                        v
|                        |
V  Common selections     v    Rare selections        (after Gullick 1988)
```

system and the ones they knew best in Africa. The parallel most frequently drawn was the way in which more than one cure was attempted at a time. Such debates were rare in St. Vincent. Some young intellectuals with a tendency to search for local Africanisms did occasionally mention local cures, but not in the context of the Shakers.

Vincentian Historical Discourses

Another tale was frequently told about the Converted in the first village. Most tellings were provided just down the road from an open-air Shaker service. It was explained that a Shaker had become possessed (a noisy imitation appeared compulsory) near the Governor's carriage, causing one of the horses to bolt. As a result the Governor banned the Shakers. Their rituals and worship were consequently confined to the forest, until the law was repealed by Ebenezer Joshua, the leader of the Peoples' Political Party. Those who did not belong to the party added that this was because he was himself Converted.

The "Shakerism Prohibition Ordinance" was passed in 1912 and stated nothing about such a cause. The official reason was that Shakerism "exercise[d] a pernicious and demoralising effect upon the island inhabitants" (Ordinance no. 13 of 1912 To Render Illegal the Practice of Shakerism as indulged in the Colony of St. Vincent). The key sections of the ordinance included:

2. In this ordinance: "Shaker meeting" shall mean a meeting or gathering of two or more persons, whether indoors or in the open air at which the customs and practices of Shakerism are indulged in. 'Shakers house' shall mean any house or building, or room in any house or building which is used for the purpose of holding Shakers meetings, or any house or building, or room in any house or building which is used for the purpose of initiating any person into the ceremonies of Shakerism. . . .

3. It shall be an offence . . . for any person to hold or to take part in or attend any Shakers meeting, or for any Shaker meeting to be held . . .

4. It shall be an offence . . . to erect or to maintain any Shakers house or to shut up any person in any Shakers house for the purpose of initiating into the ceremonies of Shakerism . . .

6. It shall be an offence . . . for any person at or in the vicinity of any Shakers meeting to commit or cause to be committed or to induce or persuade to be committed any act of indecency or immorality.

From the definitions and the items forbidden it is clear that both spirit possession and mourning rituals were held in a manner similar to the modern versions discussed herein. It also suggested that discourses concerning Shaker morals were as prevalent at the beginning of this century as in the 1970s.

The ordinance also stated that

5. (1) If it shall come to the knowledge of the owner or manager of any estate or land in the Colony that a Shakers house is being erected or maintained, or that Shakers meetings are being held . . . he shall . . . notify the Chief of police . . .

7. (1) It shall be lawful for any party of police one of whom shall be a commissioned or non-commissioned officer, without a warrant to enter at any time . . . any house or place in which [an] officer may have good ground to suspect. . . that a Shaker meeting is being held or . . . person . . . being kept . . . for initiation . . . and take the names and addresses of all persons present. (2) It shall also be lawful for any . . . police or rural constable to demand the names and addresses of any persons taking part in any meeting in the open air, which he believe[s] is a Shaker meeting . . . Any person refusing to give his name shall be liable to be detained at the nearest police station until his identity can be established. . .

8. Any person guilty of an offence against this ordinance shall be liable, on . . . conviction to a fine not exceeding fifty pounds, and in default . . . imprisonment with or without hard labour for a term not exceeding six months.

The colonial authorities in their *Annual Report of 1912-3* (St. Vincent 1914: LVIII:17=413) discussed the ordinance and its impact. They referred to Shakerism as "a pseudo-religion [practiced] by persons who call themselves Shakers or Penitents" and considered that as a result of its passing Shakerism was "becoming a 'dead' letter in the colony." In practice as a result of the law the Shakers had concealed their activities. Mourning rituals and services were held in the interior of the island on Crown Land well away from the villages and they stopped calling themselves "Penitents." It is probable that the term "Converted" began to be used as it was not, at least initially, known to the authorities.

The ban was only lifted in 1965 when Ebenezer Joshua was Prime Minister (Gullick 1985: Young 1993: 162-163). In the 1970s some informants still objected to the lifting of the ban because of the claimed immorality of the Shakers or occasionally because of their African origins. The latter complaint was only expressed by aged informants and was partially a reaction to the way in which some youths were emphazising their African heritage.

RIVAL VINCENTIAN POLITICAL DISCOURSES

The occasional final commentary on the lifting of the ban on Shakerism hints at the political nature of some discourses concerning the Converted. In Caribbean political discourses "grand oratory flourishes, for West Indian politics are nothing if not oral" (Lewis 1985: 229) and most comments on the Shakers by politicians were part of their oratorical repertoire.

During my first period of fieldwork in St. Vincent, the Vincentian Labor Party was in government and the Peoples' Political Party (PPP) were the opposition. The former was mainly supported by the better-off villagers and the latter by the poor. The leader of the Labor party used the Shakers as an object of derision and commented on their pretentiousness in now calling themselves Spiritual Baptists and not being content with their old name of Shakers. This was typical of comments by the educated elite on the uneducated masses, as well as an indirect criticism of Joshua and the PPP. In contrast I never heard any of the PPP politicians use the Shakers in their political rhetoric. Their political oratory, however, was sometimes stylistically similar to Shaker "sermons."

At the other end of the political spectrum from the relatively conservative Labor Party in the early 1970s was Black Power. Its supporters were mainly young intellectuals. They tended to see the Converted as a group who had resisted colonialism and representing to a degree the African inheritance of the Vincentian population. However, since most saw Christianity as a tool of the colonialists, they were equivocal about the Shakers. According to V. H. Young (1993), the Black Power view of the 1970s merged with national consciousness in the 1980s and as a result Shakerism became part, albeit a minor part, of Vincentian cultural and national awareness (Gullick 1990).

Ethnohistorical commentaries upon the degree of Africanisms in Shakerism include J. H. Henney (1974: 80-81), who developed arguments put forward by M. J. Herskovits and F. S. Herskovits (1947) regarding Trinidad. She saw some parallels between African religious practices and the Vincentian Shakers' use of the center and corners of the area in which they worshiped, drawings on the floor, talking in tongues, the white dresses of initiates, periods of seclusion, the rhythmic accompaniment to hymns, and possession trances. G. E. Simpson (1978:121-122) held a similar view to Henney on the intermix of Africanisms with Methodism, Anglicanism, and Roman Catholicism. Stephen Glazier in addition saw links with Amerindian shamanism.[3] As my studies of Converted Vincentians were undertaken in villages whose populations mainly claimed descent from the Amerindian inhabitants of the island, my studies have tended to support Glazier's hypothesis (Gullick 1981 & 1988).

None of my informants claimed that John and Charles Wesley were the originators of Shakerism, as many of Henney's (1974: 23) stated. This may have been because the two villages studied by me had far fewer Methodists than was normal in rural St. Vincent. None of my rural informants mentioned the European input into Shakerism. However, in the discussion of the earlier drafts of this and Roland Littlewood's contributions to this volume (at the Conference on African New Religions in the West, December 1994), Littlewood pointed out that ethnohistorians have ignored the impact of the dissenters who fled to the Caribbean on the restoration of Charles II. While their specific influences on Shakerism cannot at the moment be proved (or disproved), there is certainly a large input of western practices in Shaker performances and beliefs.

The role of Europeans tended to be downplayed in most discourses concerning the Shakers. This was partially because they were seen as being in opposition to the established Christian denominations. This aspect of the Shakers was mainly highlighted in the discourses concerning wakes.

DISCOURSES CONCERNING THE PERFORMANCES OF SHAKERS AT WAKES

The Vincentians had a complex system of wakes for the dead. As these have been discussed in detail elsewhere (Gullick 1985:13-15, Young 1993: 158-159), only the wakes held on the third, ninth, and fortieth nights, six months, and a year after death, are outlined herein, as in the majority of observed rites, they were run by the Converted. These wakes were relatively similar to standard Shaker services, though they were held in the deceased's yard around a table and frequently under an awning. Another major difference was that the living and the dead were guided to the site by lighted candles, and that once the deceased spirit was present it was followed into the house by a Shaker ringing a bell. After the wake the Converted were normally fed by the deceased's family. Such services tended to provoke the most negative comments and were sometimes accompanied by local youths holding a mock Shaker meeting further down the road. The majority of the comments were those found at other services, though some would comment on the arrival of the deceased as signaled by the Spiritual Baptist with the bell. The presence of the deceased at such wakes was accepted by virtually all Vincentian villagers, whatever their religious allegiance.

While the majority of discourses concerned with the Shakers focused on them per se, those relating to wakes also included the family of the deceased. As a result when the family were not Converted the discussions highlighted the symbolic nature of the Shakers. Thus when a family, who had had no connections with the Shakers, held a wake run by the Converted, most of the audience wondered why. In one case the family were considered to be too respectable and too Anglican to do so. In these musings the commentators were referring to a common subtext of all the discourses, namely status and class. While such comments were heard throughout the service they reached a crescendo when one of the family led a prayer, albeit in a non-Shaker fashion. She knelt down at the door of the deceased's house and prayed in a quiet, still, non-rhythmic manner. It is noteworthy that there were no such criticisms when similarly ranked Vincentian villagers made use of the Shakers as curers.

In the event of a third, ninth or fortieth night wake not involving the Shakers, the absence was commented upon. The omission generally occurred when the family concerned were members of one of the stricter Christian sects that had recently been introduced by missionaries from North America. The critique normally included a list of other activities that were banned by the sect. One such household included the best local calypsonian and when they held a wake, consisting solely of prayers, it was noted that his family was not permitted to sing. Soon afterward the calypsonian joined his parents and siblings' religion and stopped composing and performing. Fellow villagers greeted this with horror, as they saw little friction between calypso and Christianity. This of course reflected the tolerance of most Vincentians (including the Shakers) who, when attacked in song, accepted their fate, laughed it off, or even composed calypsos in reply.

As the wakes after six months and a year were more expensive than the earlier ones, few criticisms were aired if they were not held. In any event the families concerned had made their views clear by whether or not they had employed Shakers at the earlier wakes.

SUBTEXTS ON CLASS AND ETHNICITY

The above discourses on the Shakers tended to have subtexts concerned with class and ethnicity. The Converted were perceived by most Vincentians as being both lower status and dark colored. Such connotations were behind the negative comments of the Shakers in many of the items highlighted above.

These aspects of Shakerism have been focused upon by various anthropologists. Their existence in the region has been explained in terms of either class or ethnic resistance to the colonial elite (Henney 1974, Betley 1976, Rubenstein 1987). While the ethnic element may well have been key until recently, the class explanation works better nowadays. The Shakers are mainly composed of lower status Vincentians. Ethnically St. Vincent's lower class consists of Afro-Americans, East Indians, and Caribs. The Indians are the descendants of indentured laborers imported from the Indian subcontinent after the abolition of slavery and the Caribs are the descents of the Amerindian population of the Windward Islands. Not only Afro-Caribbean Vincentians, but also Caribs and East Indians were Converted, so that Shaker cultural values transcended pluralistic cultural divides. However, in practice there was a tendency for Carib Shakers to prefer to take trips to other Carib areas and to ignore Afro-American ones.[4]

OTHER CARIBBEAN DISCOURSES

The Vincentian Shakers were not only a symbol to be manipulated within Vincentian discourses; they were also discussed by non-Vincentians in the

Caribbean. In contrast to the Vincentian narratives where there was frequently a mixing of discourses with subtexts from other symbolic uses of the Converted, in the intercultural use of them as a symbol there tended to be dominant discourses with little overlap.

A MISSIONARY COMMENTARY

The worry about the Shakers' use of the name Spiritual Baptists expressed by Milton Cato, the Premier, was echoed by many of the North American Baptist missionaries who visited the island. They found great problems with the sobriquet "Baptist." As the Baptist missionaries pointed out, the Spiritual Baptists were pentecostalists, while they themselves were not; but whenever they mentioned the name of their parent bodies most Vincentians equated them with the Shakers.

In general, as explained elsewhere (Gullick 1991, 1993), missionaries to St. Vincent had major communication problems, and this difficulty with adapting the name of their churches to the Vincentian situation was a relatively minor problem. It was, however, one of the few areas where expatriate missionaries realized that they had intercultural communication difficulties.[5]

A TRINIDADIAN COMMENTARY

Some of the Spiritual Baptists of Trinidad claimed Vincentian origins, and as a result studies of them have often drawn parallels with the Vincentian Shakers (e.g., Simpson 1978). Glazier's analysis (1983) of the Trindadian Spiritual Baptists accordingly comments upon parallels between his fieldwork findings in Trinidad[6] and those of Vincentian ethnographers (especially Gullick 1971 and Henney 1974). If Trinidadian tradition is correct in connecting the importation of Vincentian Shakers to the inter-island slave trade, Spiritual Baptist performances must have remained fairly stable for over two centuries.[7]

Despite the great similarities between Spiritual Baptist beliefs in both islands, there are differences, such as those concerning:

1. Possession, Trinidadian Spiritual Baptists could be possessed by the Saints or African Gods in addition to the Holy Spirit (Henney 1974:83-85);
2. Methodism. The Vincentian references to Methodist origins and the use of items from the Methodist Communion service were not found in Trinidad[8] (Henney 1974:82);
3. Their drawings. The style used by Vincentian pointers for chalk drawings produced to guide mourners was very different from that used in Trinidad (Henney 1974:190-211);
4. Pilgrimage. The Trinidadian Spiritual Baptists frequently use the term to describe travel to other parts of Trinidad to holy places run by other groups of Baptists, while

Vincentian Spiritual Baptists tend to reserve that term for spiritual journeys undertaken in trances during "mourning" rituals (Gullick 1994: 32). Mourners in both areas are, however, called "pilgrims" (Glazier 1980a; Taylor 1993);

5. Wakes. Trinidadian Spiritual Baptists were less involved with rites for the dead (Glazier 1983:31 1993); and

6. Economics. Vincentian Spiritual Baptists consider that their Trinidadian colleagues were too commercial (Glazier 1993: 128).

ANTHROPOLOGICAL DISCOURSES

Most anthropologists who have studied St. Vincent refer at least in passing to the Shakers. It is noteworthy that most, if not all, echo the views expressed by Vincentian non-Shakers. They, however, tend to privilege one of the above discourses and play down rival perspectives. Those relating to medicine, history, politics, social structures, and ethnic cultures have been highlighted herein, as have some aspects of performance.

The aspects of Spiritual Baptism highlighted by various anthropologists relate to the closeness of fit between the Vincentian and anthropological discourses. When there is an overlap the relevant factors are privileged. As a result the emphasis on the social structural elements of Shakerism and religion in general flow from Functionalism, early Structuralism, and Marxism. That these can still be successful can be seen in the works of Glazier (1980, 1983). His analysis of the Spiritual Baptists of Trinidad, however, transcends this focus, partially because as an ex-seminarian he is as interested in their varied belief systems, as he is in their role in Trinidadian culture.

There are, however, aspects of the Converted that, because there are few Vincentian discourses concerning them, have been less elaborated upon by anthropologists. These include (i) aesthetic factors, other than the performance of gossip as discussed above; (ii) the consideration of the Shakers as a symbol; and (iii) the interplay between the individual Shaker and the Shakers as a group.

AESTHETICS

The major artistic festival of St. Vincent is the Carnival in which both new calypsos are performed and varied multicolored costumes are paraded through the streets and playing fields of the Island (Abrahams 1983: 98-108, Gearing 1988, Young 1993: 179-85). Many protestant sects in St. Vincent object to this period of accepted license, but the Shakers are far more tolerant, even when performers satirize them. Other verbal arts included speech making at tea meetings (Abrahams & Bauman 1971, Abrahams 1983) and wedding receptions (Gullick

1985: 10). All included give and take between performer and audience. Political oratory was similar though there was rarely as much audience participation. In the case of Shaker services both performers and audiences reacted, but the Shakers rarely modify their performances in response to their nonbelieving observers. In many ways the members of their audiences were also performers. They were using their verbal arts to perform the discourses highlighted therein.

It should, however, be emphasized that none of these Vincentian performances are ever repeated word for word or action for action. Vincentian rituals (both religious and secular) are frameworks for creative actions and speeches which generate a great range of performances. Insofar as they are judged by aesthetic criteria, creativity is a key factor. In cases where audience participation is involved, speed of response and wit are similarly highly rated.

The role of performance in Vincentian culture has been captured in C. G. H. Thomas's novelistic account of Caribbean politics: *Ruler in Hiroona* (1972). Most Vincentians assume that Hiroona was St. Vincent and that the hero was based on Joshua. Given that the Aboriginal name for St. Vincent was given in school textbooks (eg Duncan 1941: 1) as "Hairoun (Hi-roon)" (cf. Gullick 1985: 54), and that Thomas was a Vincentian headmaster, the first pairing is obvious. There were also many parallels between the early careers of both the real and fictional party leaders. While the interplay of politics and folk religion in Hiroona is highlighted by the author, the Shakers are not mentioned by name.

The performative nature of Vincentian society partially explains why descriptions of Shaker performances have been privileged along with the performance of their audiences' discourses. The emphasis on such approaches is also a consequence of the relative lack of a uniform Shaker belief system. If the unity of Spiritual Baptism rests upon shared rituals and not beliefs, then their performances are key to any analysis.[9]

Art is an area of culture that rarely travels between cultures without losing much of its original meaning. However, the graphic arts of the Vincentian Shakers, which are drawn on the floor of mourning houses and used to guide mourners on their spiritual journey, could be used to explain the beliefs of the Shaker pointer who drew them (Henney 1974:109-111). Similarly records of Spiritual Baptist music (Glazier 1980a) introduce aspects of their beliefs and rituals to ethnomusicologists. This chapter has hopefully shown that the texts of songs, like that by King Brooklyn (above), express non-Converted Vincentians' views concerning the Shakers.

SYMBOLISM

While the anthropology of religions frequently focuses on symbolism, it tends to explore symbolism within a particular religion or even religious media (e.g., the drawings on the floor, on headbands, or their religious music) and not the religion as a symbol in its cultural milieu. I trust that this chapter has shown that this second approach has some validity. Indeed it could be argued that the symbolic nature of Shakerism reinforces the process by adding other meanings. An explanation for the many negative Vincentian comments about Shakers and their morals could accordingly be due to the way in which the Shakers form an ambiguous symbol (with the rival political, ethnic, and medical connotations), and as a result many non-Shakers attempt to distance themselves from the reality behind the symbolism by attacking the membership (but not the abstract group). In addition the explanation is also arguably that there is a contradiction between Vincentian cultural and social norms and the moralistic rhetoric of the Shakers.

Shakers: Collectives or Individuals?

As a result of focusing upon only one Vincentian discourse most analyses tend to ignore the complex role of the Spiritual Baptists. This chapter has attempted to demonstrate that as a collective the Converted are used as a powerful symbol in varied discourses. Such symbolic use of them as a category has tended to make analysts consider them uniform. Their similarity of costume for major ceremonies helps to reinforce this impression. In practice, each Spiritual Baptist leader and most followers have individual belief systems and constructs. As a consequence individual factors have to be considered in the analysis of Spiritual Baptists and a concentration upon narratives and to a lesser degree performances could save anthropologists from the illusive search for normative beliefs and dogmas.

Up to now attempts to bring in individual factors have been in the fields of psychological anthropology and transactional analysis. Studies of psychological factors have focused upon Vincentian religious trances (Henney 1974), glossolalia (Goodman 1972), and Afro-American religious mindsets (Gullick 1994).[10] The role of individuals within a sociocultural setting are also explored in transactional analyses. So far these have tended to consider the linkages between the Converted and fellow Vincentians and not to one another (Gullick 1985).

As a result of the anthropological choices of discourse both in St. Vincent and academia, little has been said on the linkages between Spiritual Baptists as individuals and as members of a group. The failure to connect the two has hidden the way in which the symbolic nature of actions can fly in the face of the social actions studied. As a result, while

Ah Converted girl, she making fame
Went down by the plain and spoil she name;
she did not spoil the name of the Converted.

NOTES

1. A shorter version of this paper was presented at the conference on *African New Religions in the West,* and I would like to thank the organizers and all those present for their helpful comments. Various drafts of this paper have been commented on by colleagues at the University of Durham and I would like to thank Peter Collins, Simon Coleman, Robert Layton, Andrew Russell, and Mary Gullick for their assistance. Mary Gullick also participated in the ethnographic research, which was undertaken in 1970-1971, 1974 and 1976. My research focused on oral history and not the Shakers per se. As a result, in contrast to J. H. Henney and H. Rubenstein, who used Shaker pointers as major informants, my information was mainly obtained from followers and not leaders. My focus on the "little historical traditions" means that the discussion of the past herein, differs considerably from that of Stephen Glazier (Chapter 8), who focuses upon the "greater historical traditions" of the Caribbean.

2. As Shaker baptisms tended to occur away from villages, there were rarely non-Converted audiences to comment on the events and Shakerism in general. As a result this major ritual of the Spiritual Baptists is not described or discussed herein. Mourning ceremonies were also undertaken from the public sphere. As a result these ceremonies, which Glazier (c.f, Chapter 8) considers key to the understanding of Spiritual Baptism, are only referred to in the context of the services that concluded mourning.

3. Glazier's views concerning the Amerindian origins of Shakers were signaled in his abstract of a paper to be presented at a conference which was, alas, never given, though the abstract was published (Glazier 1983). Glazier also sees some African influences (c.f, Chapter 8).

4. Such journeys are a method by which the Shakers break out of normal cyclical time (Gullick 1981).

5. The growing anthropological literature on the impact of missionaries and conversion marks the development of more culturally based studies of new belief systems (e.g., Bax and Koster 1993: 57-78, 91-106; Brusco and Klein 1994; Rostas and Drooger 1993; Salamone 1985; Whiteman 1984).

6. Trinidad's lower class mainly consists of Afro-Americans and East Indians. While Afro-Americans supply the majority of Spiritual Baptists, East Indians are also active within their hierarchy and congregations (Glazier 1980b: 67-80, 1983).

7. In contrast to the oral traditions suggesting a pre-emancipation migration referred to by Littlewood at the conference on African New Religions in the West, some anthropologists consider that Spiritual Baptism was introduced from St. Vincent to Trinidad during the first (Pollak-Eltz 1993:21, Simpson 1978:17) or third decade (Glazier 1993:37) of the twentieth century.

8. This omission was also partially because Henney (1974) has explored their beliefs in detail.

9. It is also possible that one of the factors maintaining the uniformity of present day performances is the response and reaction of their audiences. However, historically audience participation was less likely during the period when Shakerism was banned.

10. An analysis of mindsets could accordingly be used to explain the rival views of the Shakers found in the 1970s between youthful Black Power supporters and their elders who opposed their political philosophy.

BIBLIOGRAPHY

Abrahams, R. D. *The Man-of-Words in the West Indies.* Baltimore: Johns Hopkins University Press, 1983.

Abrahams, R. D and R. Bauman. "Sense and Nonsense in St. Vincent: Speech Behavior and Decorum in a Caribbean Community." *American Anthropologist,* vol. 73 (1971), pp. 726-771.

Bax M, and A. Koster (eds.). *Power and Prayer: Religious and Political Processes in Present and Past.* Amsterdam: VU University Press, 1993.

Betley, B. J. *Stratification and Strategies: A Study of Adaptation and Mobility in a Vincentian Town.* Ph.D. dissertation, University of California at Los Angeles, 1976.

Brusco, E. and L. F. Klein (eds.). *The Message in the Missionary: Local Interpretations of Religious Ideology and Missionary Personality;* Studies in Third World Societies No. 50. Dept. of Anthropology, College of William and Mary, Williamsburg Va., 1994.

Duncan, E. *A Brief History of St. Vincent with Studies in Citizenship.* St. Vincent; Graphic Printers, 1941 (1st ed.), 1970 (5th ed.).

Elder, J. D. "The Male/Female Conflict in Calypso." *Caribbean Quarterly,* vol. 14, no. 3. 1968, pp. 23-41.

Fraser, G. M. *The Disputing Process in St. Vincent.* Ph.D. University of Massachusetts-Amhurst, 1979.

Gearing, J. "Live from New York! Calypso! Carnival!" 87th Annual Meeting of the American Anthropological Association (Phoenix), 1988.

Glazier, S. *Spiritual Baptist Music of Trinidad,* Folkways Record and Service Corporation, New York, Folkways FE4234, 1980(a).

Glazier, S. (ed.) *Perspectives on Pentecostalism: Case Studies from the Caribbean and Latin America.* Washington, D.C.: University Press of America, 1980(b).

Glazier, S. "Aboriginal Influences on Spiritual Baptist Ritual." *Abstract of Papers, the 44th International Congress of Americanists,* 1982, p. 263.

Glazier, S. *Marchin' the Pilgrims Home: Leadership and Decision Making in an Afro-Caribbean Faith.* Westport, Conn.: Greenwood Press, 1983.

Glazier, S. "Funerals and Mourning in the Spiritual Baptist and Shango Traditions." *Caribbean Quarterly,* vol. 39, nos 3, 4, 1993, pp. 1-11.

Goodman, F. D. *Speaking in Tongues: A Cross-Cultural Study of Glossolalia.* Chicago: University of Chicago Press. 1972.

Gullick, C. R. "Shakers and Ecstacy." *New Fire: The Journal of the Society of St. John the Evangelist,* no. 9, 1971, pp. 7-11.

Gullick, C. R. *Tradition and Change Amongst the Caribs of St. Vincent.* D.Phil. Oxford University, 1974.

Gullick, C. R. "Carib Ethnicity in a Semi-Plural Society." *New Community: Journal of the Community Relations Commission,* vol. 5 no. 3, 1976, pp. 250-258.

Gullick, C. R. "Pilgrimage, Cults and Holy Places: Carib Religious Trips—Some

Anthropological Visions." *Dyn: The Journal of the Durham University Anthropological Society,* no. 6 1981, pp.1-13.

Gullick, C. R. *Myths of a Minority: The Changing Traditions of the Vincentian Caribs.* Assen, The Netherlands: Van Gorcum, 1985.

Gullick, C. R. "Chamainsmo Garifuna." *America Indigena* vol 68, no. 2, 1988, pp. 283-321.

Gullick, C. R. "A Colonial Heritage: The Politicisation of Religion in Small Commonwealth States" 12th World Congress of Sociology: Madrid, 1990.

Gullick, C. R. "Expatriate Missionaries and Local Politics in St. Vincent." *Dyn: The Journal of the Durham University Anthropological Society,* vol. 10, 1991, pp. 22-38.

Gullick, C. R. "Politics for the Powerless: conversion and politics in St. Vincent" in M. Bax and A. Koster, *Power and Prayer,* 1993, pp. 91-107.

Gullick, C. R. "Afro-American Religious Mindsets: A Review Essay." *Bulletin of Latin American Research* vol. 13, no. 3,1994, pp. 319-26.

Henney, J. H. "Spirit-Possession Belief and Trance Behavior in Two Fundamentalist Groups in St. Vincent," in F. D. Goodman, J. H. Henney, E. Pressel, *Trance, Healing and Hallucination.* New York: John Willey, 1974, pp. 1-111.

Herskovits, M. J. and F. S. Herskovits. *Trinidad Village.* New York: Knopf, 1947.

Lewis, G. K. "The Contemporary Caribbean: A General Overview," in S. W. Mintz and S. Price (eds.), *Caribbean Contours.* Baltimore: Johns Hopkins University Press, 1985, pp.219-250.

Manning, F. E. "Challenging Authority: Calypso and Politics in the Caribbean" in M. J. Aronoff, (ed.) *The Frailty of Authority,* Political Anthropology, vol v. New Brunswick N. J.: Transaction Books, 1986, pp. 167-79.

Manning, F. E. "Calypso as a Medium of Political Communication," in S. H. Surlin and W. C. Soderlund (eds.), *Mass Media in the Caribbean.* New York: Gordon Breach, 1990.

Pollak-Eltz, A. "The Shango Cult and Other African Rituals in Trinidad, Grenada and Carriacou and Their Possible Influences on the Spiritual Baptist Faith." *Caribbean Quarterly* vol. 39, nos. 3 & 4, 1993, pp.12-25.

Rostas, S. & A. Droogers (eds.). *The Popular Use of Popular Religion in Latin America.* Amsterdam: Centrum voor Studie en Documentatie van Latijns Amerika, 1993.

Rubenstein, H. *Coping with Poverty: Adaptive Strategies in a Caribbean Village.* Boulder, Colo.: Westview Press, 1987.

Salamone, F. A. *Anthropologists and Missionaries,* Studies in Third World Societies no. 26. Williamsburg, Va., 1985.

Saville-Troike, M. *The Ethnography of Communication* (2nd ed.). Oxford: Blackwell, 1989.

Simpson, G. E. *Black Religions in the New World.* New York: Columbia University Press, 1978.

Staiano, K. V. *Interpreting the Signs of Illness: A Case Study in Medical Semiotics.* Berlin: Mouton de Gruyter, 1986.

St. Vincent. "Ordinance to Render Illegal the Practice of Shakerism as Indulged in the

Colony of St. Vincent," no. 13 of 1912 in 1927 *Laws of St. Vincent 1926,* chapter 172, pp. 1091-1093. St. Vincent, 1912.

St. Vincent. *Annual Administrative Report 1912-3.* St. Vincent, 1914.

Taylor, I. A. "The Rite of Mourning in the Spiritual Baptist Church with Emphasis on the Activity of the Spirit." *Caribbean Quarterly,* vol. 39, nos. 3 & 4, 1993, pp. 26-42.

Thomas, G. H. *Ruler in Hiroona.* Trinidad: Columbus, 1972.

Whiteman, D. L. (ed.). *Missionaries, Anthropologists and Cultural Change,* Studies in Third World Societies no. 25. Williamsburg, Va.: 1984.

Young, V. H. *Becoming West Indian: Culture, Self and Nation in St. Vincent.* Washington, D.C.: Smithsonian Institution, 1993.

8

Contested Rituals of the African Diaspora

Stephen D. Glazier

INTRODUCTION

Over the past ten years problems of "origin," "genuineness," and "authenticity" have become hot topics of debate within a number of Afro-Caribbean religions. The debate has intensified with regard to alleged "African," "Asian," and "European" elements in Afro-Caribbean ritual; especially as a number of prominent Afro-Caribbean religious leaders have traveled to Africa and found there little evidence of Caribbean ritual practice. Nevertheless, many Caribbean leaders have made concerted efforts—with varying degrees of success—to purify ritual forms and to "restore" the so-called African elements within their own services, while other Afro-Caribbean religious leaders have resisted such attempts. It is therefore of interest for social scientists to examine social and political factors which serve to make "authenticity" and "genuineness" major concerns in selected Afro-Caribbean religions but not others.

Debates concerning the origins and authenticity of New World ritual are far from new to the field of African-American studies (cf. Harris, 1993). In the first half of this century notable scholars such as Melville J. Herskovits, E. Franklin Frazier, and their students staged vigorous and sometimes acrimonious debates on the possibilities for the existence of African survivals in the Americas. M. J. Herskovits (1941) argued passionately that identifiable elements of African cultures were retained and can be readily recognized in New World African religions, while Frazier argued equally passionately that the disruptive effects of slavery were so complete that few African retentions are discernible. For Frazier (1964), Africa was a "forgotten memory," and the issue of African retentions in the New World was moot.

What sets the current debate apart from previous debates is that the major participants in the current debate are themselves members of the religions in question. This sets a different tone and provides different perspectives on issues of African survivals in the New World. There is a greater perceived urgency. A major difference is that believers' assumptions vary considerably from scholarly assumptions that have hitherto informed debates on the topic. Another major difference is that the forum for debate has changed. Debate is no longer carried out in books, journals, and paper presentations—but during heated arguments taking place in the midst of worship itself.

Difficulties in establishing "genuine" African ritual practice have become more complicated since African religions in Africa have also changed dramatically as well (cf. Blackley, Van Beek, and Thomson, 1994; MacGaffey, 1986; Fernandez, 1985; Clarke, 1986). To make matters even more contentious, African religious leaders have themselves begun traveling to the Caribbean in order to attempt to "purify" their own ritual forms and/or to make African religions "more genuinely African." This raises a number of important and related questions: What makes for a genuine African ritual? What makes for a genuine Christian ritual? What makes Afro-Caribbean ritual unique?

In examining "criteria in use" for discerning genuine Afro-Caribbean religious movements, it is apparent that authenticity is very much a contested construct that takes on different meanings depending on the vantage point of the speaker. One difficulty—as Edward Sapir suggested in his 1924 essay " Culture: Genuine and Spurious"—is that participants are not in full agreement as to where exactly to put the label. While Afro-Caribbean religious leaders frequently disagree on the value of things African, they often enough agree on the particular values of the labels "African" and "European." But as Sapir (1985: 308) cleverly points out, it is "only when the question arises of just where to put the label that trouble begins."

Sapir's essay "Culture: Genuine and Spurious" is of special theoretical relevance for the study of New World African ritual because Sapir adopts an extremely broad view of "culture"—and because, as a linguist, he was meticulous in his selection of terms. "Spurious," he recognized, is a word of multiple meanings: (1) of illegitimate birth: bastard; (2) outwardly similar to something without having its genuine qualities: false; (3) superficially like but morphologically unlike; (4) of falsified or erroneously attributed origin: forged; (5) of deceitful nature or quality. In "Culture: Genuine and Spurious" he plays with the word "spurious" in its many connotations. For Sapir, genuine culture was not relative, it was an absolute. Genuine culture, according to Sapir, is "a culture in which nothing is spiritually meaningless, in which no important part of the general functioning brings with it a sense of frustration, of misdirected or unsympathetic effort. It is not a spiritual hybrid of contradictory patches, of water-tight compartments of consciousness that avoid participation in a harmonious synthesis" (Sapir, 1985: 315). He emphasizes that genuine culture has no necessary connection to efficiency and that genuine culture refuses to consider the individual as a mere cog. Individuals are the primary focus, not a means to an end.

NEW WORLD AFRICAN RELIGIONS: GENUINE AND SPURIOUS

A major thesis of this chapter is that, with respect to Caribbean religions, the religions of the white planter class were by definition spurious, while the religions created by the slaves were of necessity genuine, in Sapir's sense of the term. Sapir—always a champion of human rights—would have found the religion of slave masters less genuine than the religion of the slaves. The culture of slave masters was replete with inconsistencies (Genovese, 1974; Curtin, 1990; Raboteau, 1978; Johnson, 1994; and Earl, 1993), while the religions of slaves were characterized by traits of authenticity, genuineness, and creativity. Historian Charles Joyner (1994: 37), focusing on the early experiences of enslaved people in the low country areas of South Carolina and Georgia, underscores the genuineness and creativity of slave religion. He concludes that the originality of African-American Christianity "lies neither in its African elements nor in its Christian elements, but in its unique and creative synthesis of both." From a similar perspective, Albert J. Raboteau (1994) has argued forcefully that slaves did not simply become Christians; they fashioned Christianity to fit their own peculiar needs and experience of enslavement in the Americas.

At the same time, the case of Christianity in the New World was clearly a spurious one for many members of the white planter class (Genovese, 1969). Many whites came to the Caribbean islands to seek their fortunes. Most had fixed terms or contracts; few brought their families; fewer still intended to remain in the region after their fortunes were made and the terms of their contracts had expired. The religious situation on the islands—at least in terms of European Christianity—has been described by contemporary chroniclers as imitative, halfhearted, and bleak. As Raboteau (1994: 2) and Riggins Earl (1993: 9-23) have pointed out, planters were ambivalent about converting slaves. They often had little use for Christianity themselves, let alone proselytizing among their slaves. In addition, select Christian teachings were seen as threatening to whites. In a majority of cases, whites did not wish to accord slaves the status of fellow Christians or to acknowledge any claims to equality that such status may have implied for blacks. Planters—who were involved in a brutal and dehumanizing social and economic system—often had little use for religion and its trappings. Their social positions precluded genuine culture or genuine religious expression.

Like E. Franklin Frazier (1964), Sidney Mintz and Richard Price in their *An*

Anthropological Approach to the Afro-American Past: A Caribbean Perspective
(1992), account for much of the lack of orthodoxy in New World African
religions in terms of the brutality and disruption of the slave experience itself.
They also place considerable emphasis on the demographics of slavery; that is,
who in Africa was most likely to be taken into slavery and who in Africa was
most likely to be transported to the New World? In the early years of the slave
trade, Mintz and Price contend that high ranking religious specialists would
rarely have been enslaved. This is of considerable significance since in both the
African and New World African religious contexts religion is thought to be
processual; that is, it is revealed in multiple stages. Slaves—mostly younger
men who had yet to be initiated into higher levels of understanding—had a very
limited knowledge-base and were often left to their own devices in attempting to
reconstruct ceremonies. It is—to borrow Karen McCarthy Brown's (1991)
speculation concerning the lack of orthodoxy in Haitian *vodun* —as if American
religion and culture were to be replicated in its entirety from the knowledgebase
of eighteen-year-old boys. While Brown's statement has heuristic value,
exceptions abound. Within the Kingdom of Dahomey, for example, it was
possible for political prisoners with considerable religious knowledge to be sold
into slavery. This was a common occurrence in nineteenth-century Brazil, but it
may also have happened in earlier centuries. It is, thus, reasonable to assume
that some of these knowledgeable individuals also made it to the plantations of
Hispaniola, albeit in smaller numbers than in Brazil.

Another option for social scientists has been to articulate problems of
syncretism, creativity, and genuineness in terms of a distinction between so-
called "Great Traditions" and "Little Traditions." This approach popularized by
Redfield (1953) has been soundly criticized for its lack of applicability to the
Asian context (Dumont, 1971; Pocock, 1973; Spiro, 1994). Similar objections
could be raised concerning its applicability in the study of New World African
religions. The issue—as Robin Horton (1993: 170-171) astutely points out—is
one of translatability and boundaries. Is missionary activity on Hispaniola to be
seen as part of the Great or the Little Tradition? The religious situation in
Africa is equally complex (Clarke, 1986). Dahomean religious forms were both
imperialistic and syncretic. Which is the Great Tradition and which is the Little
Tradition?

In *Conceptualizing Religion*, Benson Saler (1993) ultimately concludes that
while the distinction between Great Traditions and Little Traditions does have
the positive value of highlighting religious diversity, it fails to adequately
characterize that diversity in a theoretically useful manner. In other words, the
distinction between Great Traditions and Little Traditions is less useful than
Sapir's "1985" (originally published in 1928) distinction between "a religion"
and "religion." In some respects, Redfield's distinction is somewhat less
precise. At least Sapir recognized that the category "religion" is an abstraction.

Advocates of the distinction between Great Traditions and Little Traditions often seem to forget that all Great Traditions are abstractions. No individual participates in a Great Tradition. Individual religious experience; alas, is always confined to a small part of the Great Tradition; that is, the Little Tradition.

HISTORICAL CONTINUITY AND RELIGIOUS KNOWLEDGE

It must be emphasized that the degree of African religious knowledge in the New World varied considerably from time to time and place to place, and that higher concentrations of slaves from one area of Africa greatly increased fidelity to traditional forms. At one end of the continuum of religious knowledge lies Salvador (Bahia). Slavery continued in Brazil long after it was abolished in the West Indies, and—unlike the Caribbean—more slaves were imported directly from Africa during the nineteenth than during the eighteenth century. Pierre Verger (1968: 31), building on a lifetime of dedicated fieldwork and meticulous archival research, provides ample evidence for extensive and continuous contact between religious specialists in Africa and their adherents in the New World. He carefully documents that this flux and reflux in the slave trade is not only in Africans (i.e., the slave trade itself) but by Africans as well. African Americans were producers and traders as well as laborers in the plantation system, and played an active role—not just a passive one—in the ongoing drama of the slave trade (Galembo, 1993: 97-98; Murphy, 1994: 48). Even after the legal abolition of slavery in 1888, Verger demonstrates that connections with Africa were maintained by trading Brazilian tobacco and other products.

Candomblé in Bahia, as Verger (1968) so skillfully documents, benefited from a continual renewal of ideas and practices brought by African emigrants and visitors, and for this reason many Brazilian rites evidence considerable fidelity to "old African" sources. Nonetheless, it is notable that Bahian leaders are not especially concerned with preserving such fidelity. While African religious leaders make frequent pilgrimages to Bahia in order to purify their own rites, Brazilian leaders evidence few such concerns. While Brazilian leaders may visit Africa, they do not consciously strive to incorporate African rituals into New World services. Nor do they believe that New World rituals would be any more genuine or have greater efficacy if they were to attempt to do so.

At the other end of the continuum of religious knowledge lies Haiti. Vodun, the Afro-Catholic folk religion of Haiti, combines an impressive continuity with selected ancestral African elements as well as a remarkable openness to change, whether from innovation or outright borrowing. An unusual aspect of vodun is that it appears to be both heterodox and orthodox; creative and conservative at the same time (Desmangles, 1992; Hurbon, 1972).

African dances were performed by slaves in the western part of Hispaniola as early as the seventeenth century, but the period 1730 to 1790—when African slaves were imported in increasing numbers—is usually interpreted as vodun's formative period. It was during this period that the religious beliefs and practices of Dahomeans, Senegalese, Congolese, Yoruba, and African tribal groups combined with selected ideas concerning the Catholic saints to form the complex religious system now known as vodun. The Yoruba influence is marked by music, chants, foodstuffs, and blood sacrifice. During ceremonies, blood—the food of the deities—flows onto sacred stones belonging to the cult leader. As in African religion, these stones are believed to be the objects through which the gods are fed and in which their power resides.

A central focus of vodun—in its many manifestations—is devotion to the *loa* or *lwa* (deities). All important members of the pantheon are said to be of "genuine" African origin as is reflected in their names: Damballah, Ezurlie, Legba, Ogun, Shango, and so on. Confusion in beliefs surrounding these deities stems in part from contradictions in the Dahomean religious system as it was taken over by the Haitians as well as the addition of members of the Yoruba pantheon to the Dahomean religious system.

The *lwa* made the transition from Africa to the New World relatively unscathed, but what did not translate from Africa to the New World was an ordained priesthood sanctified by theocratic order. Such a priesthood existed in the kingdoms of Dahomey, Kongo, and the Yoruba, but never in Haiti. Therefore, in Haiti the relationship between devotees and the *lwa* has become more or less a contractual one. It is both highly individualistic and highly flexible. If one is scrupulous in performance of offerings and ceremonies, the *lwa* will be generous in their aid. If one neglects the *loa,* one cannot expect their favors and risks their wrath. It is widely believed that neglect of one's *lwa* may result in sickness, the death of relatives, crop failures, and other misfortunes. In this respect, vodun is an intensely personal religion. Relations with the *lwa* are first and foremost an individual responsibility. This may account for the tremendous variation and creativity which has become a much noted hallmark of Haitian religious life.

There is evidence that vodun—at least in the major urban centers of Haiti—may be moving to enforce orthodoxy. UCLA folklorist Donald Consentiño (1993) reports on the efforts of Max Beauvoir, Herald Simon, and other religious leaders *(houngans)* to construct a national framework for vodun. Certainly the religion has become more international in scope. One can find variants of vodun throughout urban centers in the United States, Europe, and the Spanish-speaking Caribbean. Many American practitioners are non-Haitians (Brown, 1991). Sandra Barnes (1989) makes the case that African inspired religions are among the fastest growing new religions in the North America. I will take this assertion one step further. Among the most significant and understudied religious development in the United States over the past twenty years has been the large-scale transfer of Haitian vodun and other African-derived religions to urban centers of New York, Miami, Los Angeles, and Toronto. It is estimated, for example, that there are currently more than 100,000 devotees in New York City alone. This would make variants of Afro-Caribbean religions the largest and fastest growing religious movement in that city. Similar assessments have been made for Miami and Toronto. As Carlos Esteban Deive (1979) has documented, vodun in the Dominican Republic has become a distinct new religious movement of enormous proportions.

Despite the efforts of Max Beauvoir and others, it can still be said that Haitian vodun has no well defined body of doctrine or uniform mythology (Bourguignon, 1985), and that comparatively few participants and leaders trouble themselves with theological speculations. Nor is there a uniform mythology on which to base a formal theological system. Traditions vary dramatically from family to family and house to house, and contacts with the *lwa* are direct and intimate. Dreams and possession-trance remain the primary vehicles by which spirits reveal themselves to their devotees. Attempts to establish a hierarchy have failed, and—like Candomblé in Bahia—genuineness and authenticity do not appear to be central concerns.

CONTESTED RITUAL CLAIMS

With respect to contested claims to authenticity, the island of Trinidad is very much at the center of the debate. Much Afro-Trinidadian religious knowledge is secondary in origin, and leaders' claims to genuineness lie somewhere outside those of Brazilian and Haitian leaders since the majority of African Americans came to Trinidad indirectly via South America (Guyana, Venezuela and Brazil), other West Indian islands (Martinique, St. Kitts, Grenada, St. Vincent, and Barbados), Hispaniola, or the United States (Herskovits and Herskovits, 1947: 305). Bridget Brereton (1981: 16) argues that the bulk of Africans slaves in the eighteenth century came from the French-speaking islands of Martinique and Hispaniola.

There were some notable exceptions to the above pattern in the nineteenth century. According to historian Donald Wood (1968), between 1841 and 1861 Trinidad received 6,581 free Africans representing a number of cultural groups representing Ibo, Temme, Wolof, Yoruba, Ashanti, Fulani, and Mandingo. Among these migrants were two *vodunsi* (initiates) and a Dahomean *hubono* (high priest), Robert Antoine, who established a Rada compound in the Belmont section of Port of Spain. The late Andrew Carr (1953) observed that while Antoine was able to maintain a substantial portion of the Dahomean ceremonial calendar in Trinidad, and his compound became a center for migrant Dahomeans. In the twentieth century, adherents to the Rada movement did not seem overly concerned with orthodoxy and/or authenticity (both being tacitly assumed), But for other African-derived groups—like the *Orisha* religion and the Spiritual Baptists—these were and remain highly contested constructs.

As James Houk (1995) emphasizes, the *Orisha* religion in Trinidad may have began as a transplanted African religion, but gradually took on selected religious elements from Catholicism, Protestantism, Asian religions, and the Kabbalah (cf. Houk, 1993). He notes that over the past decade Hindu deities and paraphernalia were borrowed and incorporated into Orisha shrines and worship. While acknowledging that Orisha worshipers have a great respect for Hinduism and tolerate Indian involvement, the incorporation of Hindu elements has met with passive resistance in the form of what he sees as "a nativisitic revitalization that seeks to 're-Africanize' the Orisha religion by emphasizing its African roots" (Houk, 1993: 161). Houk reports on repeated attempts to organize over 160 Orisha shrines on the island. A group called the "Orisha Movement" was founded during the early 1970s, but organizers met with limited success. The *"Opa Orisha"* (Shango) movement which began in the mid-1980s; however, accomplished much more. By 1990, *Opa Orisha* claimed to represent over half of all shrines on the island. This is a formidable achievement in light of the highly competitive religious environment. Fragmentation would be expected since individual shrines are generally concerned with the worship of only one particular deity of the Yoruba pantheon, and few religious specialists are considered to be knowledgeable of ritual practices associated with other major Orisha.

Houk (1993) suggests that so-called "Africanization" may be a response to a perceived demographic threat because Asians have potential to outnumber Afro-Trinidadians within their own religion. Asians, too, have instigated something of a nativistic revitalization movement (Vertovec, 1992). One is struck by the irony of Hinduism—that most tolerant and supposedly unorthodox of major world religions—attempting to "purify" itself to fit preconceived notions of nineteenth-century Hinduism which probably were never practiced in Trinidad or anywhere else in the Caribbean.

Similar forces are at work among the Spiritual Baptists of Trinidad who have attempted to organize themselves along denominational lines. Like *Opa Orisha*, Baptist attempts to organize in the 1970s were aborted, but later attempts were much more successful. By 1990, over half of all Spiritual Baptist churches belonged to some denominational organization, and many Baptist churches belonged to more than one denomination (Glazier, 1991).

The Spiritual Baptists are an international religious movement with congregations in St. Vincent (where some Baptists claim the faith originated), Trinidad and Tobago, Grenada, Guyana, Venezuela, Toronto, Los Angeles, and New York City. Currently, two of the largest Spiritual Baptist churches are in Brooklyn and on the outskirts of Toronto. There are a number of religious movements on other Caribbean islands whose rituals are similar to those of the Baptists (i.e., "Tieheads" of Barbados and the "Spirit Baptists" of Jamaica), but Spiritual Baptists do not consider these others to be a part of their religion and do not participate in joint worship, pilgrimages, missions, and other activities with these other groups. They do, however, maintain active ties with brethren in St. Vincent, Guyana, Grenada, Venezuela, the United States, and Canada.

Like other religions considered in this chapter, Spiritual Baptist membership is predominantly black, and—like other Afro-Caribbean groups—the Baptists seem to have started out as a "religion of the oppressed." In recent years, however, congregations in Trinidad have attracted membership among middle-class blacks as well as sizeable numbers of wealthy East Indians, Chinese, and individuals of mixed blood. Membership has remained stable at about 10,000 over the past ten years (Glazier, 1991).

Many Trinidadians confuse Spiritual Baptists and the *Orisha* tradition (Shango) and assume that Spiritual Baptist and *Orisha* rituals are the same. Such as not the case. As Houk (1995) ably demonstrates, members of these respective traditions do not share this confusion. A percentage of Spiritual Baptists condemn Shango rituals as "heathen worship." Shangoists, for their part, claim that the Spiritual Baptists copy their ideas and try to "steal their power." On occasion, Spiritual Baptist leaders have picketed Shango centers prior to Shango ceremonies. Afro-Caribbean religious ceremonies in Trinidad are rife with conflict and dissension. It is not uncommon for participants to leave ceremonies after becoming dissatisfied with aspects of the liturgy or the way a particular leader conducts ritual. Heated arguments break out between officiants and congregants; at times, violent disagreements occur in the midst of worship. Cutlasses are brandished; leaders and participants are threatened with knives; curses are made; and objects are thrown.

Both the Spiritual Baptists and Orisha (Shango) creatively combine beliefs and rituals from many religious traditions. A major difference is that Baptist rituals are directed to their version of the Holy Trinity, while Shango rituals are ostensibly directed to African gods. Spiritual Baptists profess that they are Christians and "do not worship them others." This is not to say that Spiritual Baptists do not believe in the power of Shango deities. They do believe in the power of Shango, but do not believe that Shango deities should be venerated.

Although the Spiritual Baptists and Shango are clearly separate traditions, they are interrelated on a number of levels. Their memberships overlap. I would estimate that about 80 percent of all Shangoists in Trinidad also participate in Spiritual Baptist services and that about 40 percent of all Baptists also participate in Shango. Houk's (1993) informal survey of Shango shrines established that eighteen out of fifty-one (roughly 35%) also contained Spiritual Baptist churches. Houk's survey greatly underestimates the situation since he does not include Spiritual Baptist churches that are owned by Orisha leaders but are not located on or next to an Orisha compound. There are, of course, degrees of participation in both religions. Not all leaders in the former religion are necessarily officials in the latter, and vice versa.

SPIRITUAL BAPTIST MOURNING: GENUINE OR SPURIOUS?

A central and controversial ritual in the Baptist faith is known as the mourning ceremony. Some Baptist leaders claim that it is a "genuine" African rite; other leaders claim that it is a "genuine" Baptist and/or Christian rite. Still others suggest that it is a ritual unique to their faith and serves to differentiate the Spiritual Baptists from all other world religions.

The concept of mourning has a very different meaning among Spiritual Baptists from that which it has in many other religious traditions. Among Baptists, it does not relate directly to physical death and bereavement but is an elaborate ceremony involving fasting, lying on a dirt floor, and other deprivations. A major component of the rite is to discover one's "true" rank within the twenty-two-position church hierarchy.

Mourning rites usually last from one to three weeks, beginning when participants are blindfolded and led to the mourning chamber (usually a separate building near the main church) and concluding during Sunday worship when participants share their visions (also known as "tracts") with waiting members of the congregation. During the mourning ceremony itself, participants are expected to pray and meditate. They are given little to eat; no salt; limited water; lie on an earthen floor with a rock for a pillow; and sit, kneel, and stand in prayer as directed by their spiritual leaders.

I have witnessed rites that are much more relaxed than they have been portrayed in the literature (Henney, 1974). For example, some Spiritual Baptist leaders allow their mourners to take off their blindfolds; allow them to smoke, and allow them to talk and laugh with other participants. Participants and supervisors are often close friends outside the mourning chamber, and formalities are difficult to maintain. Such "winking at the rules" makes mourning more enjoyable and less intense for all concerned. Nevertheless, such relaxation of the rules does not make mourning rituals any more or less "African," or more or less "Christian," or more or less "genuine." "Winking at the rules" is common in many tribal religions, and it occurs with great frequency in African initiation rites. Solemnity and rigid adherence to form is not considered to be a necessary component of many African rituals.

Mourning is believed to have curative powers, and because so many individuals enter the rite in an unhealthy condition, occasionally participants die during the ceremony. This almost always results in a government inquiry. The government asserts that poor diet and damp conditions in the mourning room are contributing factors in mourners' deaths. Government officials contend that Baptist leaders should refuse to mourn participants believed to be too weak to withstand the rigors of the ceremony. Leaders defend themselves by claiming that they take every possible precaution to ensure the mourner's physical survival, but emphasize that their primary responsibility is for the "spiritual" survival of the mourner. Mourning rituals are believed to have been "spiritually" effective even when the mourner dies.

While the mourning ceremony may derive "authenticity" from its resemblance to African initiation rites (Raboteau, 1978: 29), some Baptist leaders argue that its "authority" clearly rests in the *Book of Daniel* (a decidedly un-African provenance). For these individuals, the mourning ceremony is said to be a re-enactment of Daniel 10: "I, Daniel, mourned for three full weeks." Whether the mourning rite is African or Christian, whether it is to be seen as a parallelism of ritual forms or fortuitous convergence—does this perceived lack of authenticity make the rite any more or less genuine?

The term "mourning" occurs with considerable frequency in studies of African-American religions. Herskovits (1941) suggested that Spiritual Baptist mourning was nothing less than a direct reinterpretation of an African-style initiation rite. Raboteau (1978), too, pointed to an African provenance. He postulated that many features of the Spiritual Baptist mourning ceremony closely resemble rites of cult initiation in West Africa, and asserts that death-resurrection motifs—fasting and lying quiet, reception of a new role and a new name, color symbolism, and prohibitions concerning the use of salt are unifying features in West African and African-American ritual. Raboteau cites Samuel Miller Lawton's study of African-American Sea Islanders in the Carolinas. Lawton noted that Sea Islanders customarily spoke of the period of seeking conversion as the time of "mourning." Sea Islanders also utilized blindfolds and white bands tied around the head in much the same manner as contemporary Trinidadian Spiritual Baptists. Walter F. Pitts (1993: 170-171) noted similar patterns throughout the Americas.

Charles Williams (1982: 70) personally observed similar patterns in revivals held in Lowndes County, Mississippi, where "sinners" were advised to go to the "mourner's bench" and to pray for the salvation of their souls. Periods of seclusion were important components of initiation rites in Mississippi, and Washington (1994: 67-72) has noted similar rituals and beliefs among the Gullah. In all of these cases, contested constructs are ultimately related to a highly competitive religious environment. In Trinidad— where over half the population are Asians—ethnic diversity and ethnic competition also play a major part.

While the origins of the Spiritual Baptist mourning ceremony may be ambiguous, the "genuineness" of these rites is clear. Spiritual Baptist mourning rituals are genuine in every sense of Sapir's use of the term. They focus on individuals. Like Sapir's vision of a genuine culture, individuals within the mourning rite are not seen as mere cogs but are the center of attention. "Mourners on the ground," I was told, "are like a bride at her wedding. All eyes are on the mourner."

These rites promote harmony and integration. Spiritual Baptist mourning rites capture what Sapir saw as the essence of culture and religious meaning. If religion is to be understood—following Paul Tillich (1952)—as addressing ultimate concerns, then, Spiritual Baptist mourning rites ably address such concerns. If religion is to be understood —following Emile Durkheim (1915) and Peter L. Berger (1967)—as an integrative force uniting society and the individual, then the Spiritual Baptist mourning ceremony patently serves this function. If religion is to be understood as part of the quest for the "genuine," a striving for consistency, then the Spiritual Baptist mourning ceremony admirably satisfies such a quest.

Mourning rituals provide a vehicle for the articulation, interpretation, and reinterpretation of one's life. Life, for the believer, becomes a long "sacred journey," punctuated by ritual. The mourning rite lends new meaning to every event: past, present, and future. Visions obtained on the mourning ground serve to eliminate much randomness from human existence and make everything a part of God's plan as revealed in the mourning chamber. Good fortune and misfortune, trials and tribulations, joy and suffering now "make sense" in unanticipated ways. For many Baptists, one's entire life can be understood and made meaningful in terms of experiences in the mourning chamber. Whatever its provenance, it remains a quintessential integrative religious experience.

While the mourning ceremony may contain elements "borrowed" from other religious traditions, each element is taken on its own terms. This is also true for the majority of indigenous religious movements in the Caribbean which claim to have an African or a Christian base. In all cases, Caribbean peoples have modified selected aspects, added to them, and made them their own. While much attention has been given to African influences, one cannot completely understand contemporary developments in the region solely in terms of an African past. The African past is a piece—albeit a large piece—of a more complex whole.

In closing, I would ask social scientists to keep an open mind in the study of Afro-Caribbean and African-American religions. As Vittorio Lanternari himself would acknowledge, it is not always fruitful to look at all religions in the Third World as "religions of protest" or as "religions of the oppressed" (Lanternari, 1963), not because they are not "religions of protest," or "religions of the oppressed," but because such an approach can be limiting and too one-dimensional. While there is considerable evidence to support the assertion of anthropologists Hans Baer and Merrill Singer (1992) that most African-American religions exist in a constant state of tension with the larger society, it needs to be emphasized that there has been considerable accommodation as well over the past forty years. Sometimes African-American religion has been at the forefront and not merely the respondent to change. In addition, for many religious groups in the region, there is ample evidence for both cooperation with and hostility toward dominant cultural and political forces. Many religions—formerly classified as "religions of protest" or "religions of the oppressed"—have joined the political and economic elites of their respective societies.

NOTE

Earlier versions of this chapter were presented in 1994 at annual meetings of the Society for the Scientific Study of Religion and the American Anthropological Association in 1995 at the conference "Varieties of Prayer" held at the University of Rome, "La Sapienza." Sidney M. Greenfield, Peter B. Clarke, Vittorio Lanternari, Carlos Navarro, Lewis F. Carter, Larry Greil, Miguel Leatham, Stewart Guthrie, James W. Fernandez, and James Houk provided helpful comments on earlier drafts of this paper.

BIBLIOGRAPHY

Baer, H. and M. Singer. *African-American Religion in the Twentieth Century: Varieties of Protest and Accommodation.* Knoxville: University of Tennessee Press, 1992.

Barnes, S. *Africa's Ogun: Old World and New.* Bloomington: Indiana University Press, 1989.

Berger, P. L. *The Sacred Canopy: Elements of a Sociological Theory of Religion.* Garden City, N.Y.: Doubleday, 1967.

Blackley, T. D.; W. A. van Beek; and D. Thomson. *Religion in Africa: Experience and Expression.* Portsmouth, NH: Heinemann, 1994.

Bourguignon, E. "Religion and Justice in Haitian Vodun." *Phylon* 46, 1985: 292-295.

Brereton, B. *A History of Modern Trinidad, 1983-1962.* Portsmouth, NH: Heinemann, 1981.

Brown, K. McC. *Mama Lola: A Vodou Priestess in Brooklyn.* Berkeley: University of California Press, 1991.

Carr, A. T. "A Rada Community in Trinidad." *Caribbean Quarterly* 3, 1953: 35-54.

Clarke, P. B. *West Africa and Christianity.* London: E. Arnold, 1986.

Consentino, D. J. "Vodou Vatican: A Prolegomena for Understanding Religious Authority in a Syncretic Religion." *Caribbean Quarterly* 39, 1993: 100-107

Curtin, P. *The Rise and Fall of the Plantation Complex: Essays in Atlantic History.* New York: Cambridge University Press, 1990.

Desmangles, L. G. *The Faces of the Gods: Vodou and Roman Catholicism in Haiti.* Chapel Hill: University of North Carolina Press, 1992.

Dumont, L. *Religion, Politics and History in India*. The Hague: Mouton, 1971.

Durkheim, E. *The Elementary Forms of the Religious Life*. New translation by Karen E. Fields. New York: Free Press, 1915/1995.

Earl, R. *Dark Symbols, Obscure Signs: God, Self, and Community in the Slave Mind*. Maryknoll, NY: Orbis Books, 1993.

Esteban Deive, C. *Vodu y Magia en Santo Domingo*. Santo Domingo: Museo del Hombre Dominicano, 1979.

Fernandez, J. W. *Bwiti: An Ethnography of the Religious Imagination in Africa*. Princeton: Princeton University Press, 1985.

Frazier, E. F. *The Negro Church in America*. New York: Schocken Books, 1964.

Galembo, P. *Divine Inspiration—From Benin to Bahia*. Albuquerque: University of New Mexico, 1993.

Geertz, C. "Religion as a Cultural System," in *Anthropological Approaches to the Study of Religion*. M. Banton, ed. London: Tavistock, 1966.

Genovese, E. *Roll Jordan Roll: The World the Slaves Made*. New York: Pantheon, 1974.

Genovese, E. *The World the Slaveholders Made*. New York: Pantheon, 1969.

Glazier, S. D. *Marchin' the Pilgrims Home*. Salem, Wisconsin: Sheffield, 1991.

Glazier, S. D. "When the Spiritual Baptists of Trinidad Read What I Write About Them." *When They Read What We Write*. Caroline B. Brettell, ed. New York: Bergin and Garvey, 1992.

Harris, J. E., ed. *Global Dimensions of the African Diaspora* (second edition). Washington, D.C.: Howard University Press, 1993.

Henney, J. H. "Spirit-Possession Belief and Trance Behavior in Two Fundamentalist Groups in St. Vincent." *Trance, Healing and Hallucination*. Felicitas D. Goodman, Jeannette H. Henney, and Esther Pressel, eds. New York: John Wiley, 1974: 6-111.

Herskovits, M. J. *The Myth of the Negro Past*. New York: Harper, 1941.

Herskovits, M. J., and F. S. Herskovits. *Trinidad Village*. New York: Knopf, 1947.

Horton, R. *Patterns of Thought in Africa and the West: Essays on Magic, Religion and Science*. New York: Cambridge University Press, 1993.

Houk, J. "Afro-Trinidad Identity and the Africanization of the Orisha religion," in *Trinidad Ethnicity*. K. A. Yelvington, ed. Knoxville: University of Tennessee Press, 1993.

Houk, J. *Spirits, Blood, and Drums: The Orisha Religion in Trinidad*. Philadelphia: Temple University Press, 1995.

Hurbon, L. *Dieu dans le Vaudou*. Paris: Payot, 1972.

Johnson, P. E., ed. *African-American Christianity: Essays in History*. Berkeley: University of California Press, 1994.

Joyner, C. "Believer I Know: The Emergence of African-American Christianity." in *African-American Christianity*. Paul E. Johnson, ed. Berkeley: University of California Press, 1994.

Lanternari, V. *The Religions of the Oppressed: A Study of Modern Messianic Cults*. New York: Knopf, 1963.

MacGaffey, W. *Religion and Society in Central Africa.* Chicago: University of Chicago Press, 1986.

Mintz, S., and R. Price. *An Anthropological Approach to the Afro-American Past. The Birth of African-American Culture: An Anthropological Perspective.* Boston: Beacon Press, 1992.

Murphy, J. H. *Working the Spirit: Ceremonies of the African Diaspora.* Boston: Beacon, 1994.

Pitts, W. F. *Old Ship of Zion: The Afro-Baptist Ritual in the African Diaspora.* New York: Oxford University Press, 1993.

Pocock, D. F. *Mind, Body, and Wealth: A Study of Belief and Practice in an Indian Village.* Totowa, NJ: Rowman and Littlefield, 1973.

Raboteau, A. J. *Slave Religion: The "Invisible Institution" in the Antebellum South.* New York: Oxford University Press, 1978.

Raboteau, A. J. "African-Americans, Exodus, and the American Israel." in *African-American Christianity,* Paul E. Johnson, ed. Berkeley: University of California Press, 1994.

Raboteau, Albert J. *A Fire in the Bones: Reflections on African-American Religious History.* Boston: Beacon Press, 1995.

Redfield, R. *The Primitive World and Its Transformations.* Ithaca, NY: Cornell University Press, 1953.

Saler, B. *Conceptualizing Religion: Immanent Anthropologists, Transcendent Natives, and Unbounded Categories.* Leiden: E. J. Brill, 1993.

Sapir, E. *Selected Writings in Language, Culture, and Personality.* Edited by David G. Mandelbaum. Berkeley: University of California Press, 1985.

Spiro, M. E. *Culture and Human Nature.* New Brunswick, NJ: Transaction, 1994.

Tillich, P. *The Courage to Be.* New Haven: Yale University Press, 1952.

Verger, P. *Flux et Reflux de la Traite des Negres Entre le Golfe de Benin at Bahia de Todos os Santos, du XVIIe au XIXe Siecle.* The Hague: Mouton, 1968.

Vertovec, S. *Hindu Trinidad: Religion, Ethnicity, and Socio Economic Change.* Warwick, England: Warwick University Caribbean Studies, 1992.

Washington, M. "Community Regulation and Cultural Specialization in Gullah Folk Religion" in *African-American Christianity.* Paul E. Johnson, ed. Berkeley: University of California Press, 1994.

Williams, C. "The Conversion Ritual in a Rural Black Baptist Church," in *Holding onto the Land and the Lord: Kinship, Ritual, Land Tenure, and Social Policy in the Rural South.* Robert L. Hall and Carol B. Stack, eds. Athens: University of Georgia Press, 1982: 69-79

Wood, D. *Trinidad in Transition: The Years After Slavery.* New York: Oxford University Press, 1968.

9

From Mimesis to Appropriation in Shouter Baptism and Shango: The Earth People of Trinidad

Roland Littlewood

They give us a Book to pray, Yeh!
To call on their God, me see
When they lie, they lie
And they give us a Book to pray, Yeh!
To call on their God, me see
When they lie, they lie, You!
The Earth is the Lord, the fullness
The Earth is the Life me see
That is Life, that is Life, Oui! [1]

By the early 1980s few people in the West Indian island of Trinidad had not heard of the Earth People, a small community established on its remote northeast coast. In a country long familiar with the religious charisma of the Shouter (Spiritual) Baptists, frequently gathered by the roadside in their brightly colored robes, intoning lugubrious "Sankey and Moody" hymns and enthusiastically ringing handbells, and also with the newer Rastafari movement introduced from Jamaica in the early 1970s, the Earth People remain an enigma. Fifteen years on, their appearance in the villages or in the capital Port-of-Spain still causes public outrage, for their most outstanding characteristic is that they are naked.

Public opinion favors the view that these taciturn young men, carrying staves or cutlasses and with the long matted dreadlocks of the Rastas, are probably crazy: if not the whole group then certainly their leader Mother Earth. For it is she whose visions gave birth to the movement and she who leads their annual marches to town. Alternatively, some villagers feel they are merely a rather idiosyncratic Baptist group or a particularly dangerous variant of Rastafari. Communication is hampered by the Earth People's characteristic language, their deliberate and studied use of obscenities, and Mother Earth's striking teachings.

She informs Trinidadians, a largely devout if not exactly church-going population, that while God does not exist she is the biblical Serpent, the Mother of Africa and India, Nature Herself.

Her commune, which is known by its members as Hell Valley or the Valley of Decision, lies beside a track leading from the nearest village, Pinnacle, some nine miles away, itself perhaps the most distant in Trinidad from Port-of-Spain and only to be reached at the end of a winding coastal road. The local smallholdings of coffee and cocoa, planted in the nineteenth century, have returned to forest; their owners and share-croppers either left the area for good or moved back to Pinnacle village. The mountains behind the settlement, never inhabited and seldom crossed, remain part of the island's protected forest reserves, exploited for wood only on their southern side where they meet the Caroni plateau.

The track from Pinnacle village follows the coast, occasionally passing over headlands and allowing a glimpse of the sea but usually winding through the dense bush of secondary forest, hidden from the sun, occasionally dipping down to ford small rivers and mangrove swamps. Through the tangled foliage of now-overgrown coffee and cocoa and the tall, spreading *immortelle* trees planted a hundred years ago to give them shade, the occasional traveler can make out the remains of abandoned cocoa houses and rotting wooden huts. The track starts from the village, and after passing through the valley, ends twenty miles further on at Petite Riviere, another fishing village which is usually reached directly from Port-of-Spain through a gap in the Northern Range. Few now pass along the track: some forestry workers conducting a survey or the occasional group of hiking secondary school pupils. The villagers who still occasionally gather copra from the palms along the coast prefer to visit their coconut groves by *canot*, the small high-prowed boat they use for fishing.

This coast is regarded by urban Trinidadians as the most desolate part of the island, "behind God's back" as they say, a fitting retreat for the handful of Black Power insurgents who established themselves here briefly in 1972 after blowing up the Pinnacle police station. They were tracked down in the forest and shot by The Regiment, Trinidad's small armed forces.

MOTHER EARTH IN THE VALLEY OF DECISION

A year after the rebels were killed, Jeanette Baptiste[2] a thirty-nine year old woman from Port-of-Spain, came to live on the coast, together with six of her children and her partner Cyprian. After spending two years on various estates near Petite Riviere, the family settled in the remains of one of the deserted hamlets midway along the now disused track, where on one side it overlooks a small rocky bay, and on the other a long curving beach divided by a river which, laden with mangroves, slowly enters the sea as a modest delta.

Both Jeanette and Cyprian had been Spiritual Baptists and they continued to "pick along in the Bible" and to interpret the visionary import of their dreams. From 1975, after the birth of twins in their wooden hut, until 1976, Jeanette experienced a series of revelations that have become the foundation of the Earth People. She became aware that the Christian doctrine of God the Father as creator was untrue and that the world was the work of a primordial Mother, whom she identified with Nature and with the Earth. Nature gave birth to a race of Black people, known as the *mothers*, but Her rebellious Son re-entered his Mother Nature's womb to gain Her power of generation and succeeded by producing White people. The Whites, the Race of the Son, have enslaved the Blacks and continue to exploit them. The Way of the Son is the Way of technology, war, cities, clothes, schools, hospitals, factories, and wage labor. The Way of the Mother is the Way of Nature: a return to the simplicity of the Beginning, a simplicity of lived experience, nakedness, cultivation of the land by hand and with respect, and of gentle and non-exploiting human relationships.

The Son in his continued quest for the power of generation has recently entered into a new phase. He has now succeeded in establishing himself in Africans and Indians,[3] and is also on the point of replacing humankind altogether with computers and industrial robots. Nature, who has borne his behavior out of love for all Her creation, has finally lost patience. The current order of the Son will soon end in a catastrophic drought and famine, or a nuclear war, a destruction of the Son's work through his own agency, after which the original state of Nature will once again prevail.

Jeanette herself is a partial manifestation of the Mother who will fully enter into her only at the End. Her task now is to facilitate the return to Nature by organizing the community on the coast to prepare for the return to the Beginning and to "put out" the truth to her people, the Black Nation, the Mother's Children. She has to combat the doctrines of existing religions which place the Son over the Mother, and to correct the distorted teaching of the Bible where she is represented as the Devil. As the Serpent, she stands for Nature and Life, in opposition to the Christian God who is Nature's incestuous Son, the male principle of Science and Death. She is opposed to churches and prisons, book learning and money, contemporary morals and fashionable opinions. Because God is generally seen as "right" Mother Earth teaches the Left, and the Earth People, like some other African-Americans (Gates 1988), interchange various conventional oppositions: "left" for "right"; "evil" or "bad" for "good." So-called obscenities are only Natural words and are to be used freely, for She Herself is the Cunt, the principle of Life.

The exact timing of the End is uncertain, but it will probably come in Jeanette's physical lifetime. Then Time will cease, disease will be healed, and the Black Nation will speak its one language. The Son will return to his Planet, the Planet Sun, really the Planet of Ice which is currently hidden by Fire placed there by the Mother—Fire which will eventually return to where it belongs, into the heart of the nurturant Earth.

Since her revelations in 1975 which signaled the Beginning of the End, Mother Earth's immediate family have been joined by numbers of Black Trinidadians, usually young men who bring their partners and children. The community has a high turnover and, while over fifty people have been associated with the Earth People, when I lived with them between 1981 and 1982, there were twenty-three staying in the valley, with perhaps twenty close sympathizers in town who visited occasionally. About once a year the group march into town, camp out in the Laventille area, and present their message in the central streets and parks, particularly in Woodford Square, the popular site for political demonstrations and other mass meetings next to the parliament building. After a few weeks of Putting Out The Life, explaining and arguing with bystanders, and visits to friends and relatives, they return to the Valley to Plant for the Nation.

THE BEGINNING OF THE END: THE VISIONS OF MOTHER EARTH

Jeanette's account of her childhood and early adulthood are not characterized by any extraordinary events. She had a conventional working-class life in the slum areas of Port-of-Spain, a life she recollects as hard:

Well, it was a struggle, a very hard struggle for me, because I just been living.[4] I never had to pay rent. I live with my first children's father for three years. He put me out . . . I go by my mother. I remain there. I try to live with somebody else again. It wasn't so easy. I leave, go back home, try again the third time. I leave again, go back home and I decide to stay home. So then I been living and struggling, selling, doing whatever little I could do to make a penny for my children. When I get in with somebody we last until my belly is big— I'm pregnant again. They leave me. I have to fight again to mind my children but somehow or the other the spirit always sends somebody to help me . . . My spirit always be with me so that someone would help me, come and help me. But it always usually end up I by myself, working again, selling again and feeding my children as much as I could, send them to school . . .

But the struggle was on. I go ahead with it. I wasn't finding no fault of the city. Is one thing is always in my mind since I am living in the city: is to help my people. Something always in me, when I see a sick [person] I feel I should be able to help them. When I go anywhere and somebody complain about their life, although mine's so rugged, I always think about that person and wish I could have helped them. This is always myself. I know to myself that I am a healer. As the Baptists would say, "You are a healer." I know that I had healing work to do but I don't know when.

Jeanette's maternal grandmother (with whom she lived at various times during her childhood) was a Spiritual Baptist, and Jeanette occasionally attended the services from the age of twelve. She was not particularly involved and indeed scorned conventional religious beliefs. On one occasion a burst gas pipe near Port-of-Spain caught fire and everybody fell on their knees:

... an' say Jesus come. I laugh an' walk on.

As a child I was baptise with the Baptists at the age of fourteen. And I go in the Baptists, listening to them preaching and talking about the Bible, bawling Jesus. But in my growing up, I had a lot of visions and never really see what they speaking about within my visions. So I didn't understand, I didn't query over it, I just live.

In my thirties, I went to mourn[5] and for the very first time, because I never wanted to go and mourn but they keep nagging at me why I don't come to mourn. They prepare the list for me; I took the list, buy what they said to buy, and I went to mourn.

It was terrible because I had a lot of trouble and yet myself was talking to me to help me out in my trouble. Until the day come that I there lying down and didn't see nothing too much (I hearing the rest of the mourners talking and so forth but I wasn't going nowhere) until the third day—rising day—the Mother come and tell me if I don't see myself rising I'll have to remain there! I started to cry and thing. When it turn the evening, one of the Mothers come and sit with me. A Teacher, they call her. She come and she sit with me. She say, "I come to help you see yourself" and she started to trump.[6] I started to trump with her and I started to see myself—down in a grave, swaddled from head to foot like a mummy. I tell her. She say, 'What again?' and I take off the swaddling bands, throw them in the hole and seal it but in a darkness. I saw the coffin come up. I saw myself standing on it with a very large foot. And I say "Well, look I am a giant" because my foot was very long. She say, "Go ahead— what again?" And I tell her I saw myself as a Kong.[7] I could have seen the tail of the Kong, it was brown. She turn round and said "What again?" An' I said "Well I seeing something in front of me". She said "What it is?" "It is a serpent but I afraid of it—I can't speak to it". She said "Speak to it". I said "No, I can't". I started to bawl because I was afraid of it although I know it in my sleep for many years: I was seeing it and always running from it. This life[8] it was in front of me so I couldn't run, but all I did was bawl and eventually I snatch it and I hold it. She turn around and she say "What that mean?" I said "Well, look it straighten and it turn a staff". She said "What is the meaning of that?" I said "The Christ is the Good Shepherd". She said "Thank you." She say I'm finished. So it then she left me and I was blank again. I didn't see nothing again. Yes—till then nobody didn't really tell me what it mean. I live on. I didn't really study[9] it after the mourning and thing.

Her partner Cyprian (now called Jakatan) went to mourn in 1967 after he himself joined the Baptists. "The week after I baptize I lie down and have a vision. I standing on a hill and see town destroyed by a flood. I go to a half-broken down house and see a big black box. I open it. I hear a whole set of voices. I see a white man standing by it, the people crying 'help,' and I say 'I am the True Shepherd and will lead you to true freedom.' " Cyprian took the Baptist title of Shepherd (a designation he kept in the early days of the Earth People). The following year he had another vision while mourning: "I go into a school and it have a big map of Trinidad but no pupils. A short black man point to map and say 'Go down to the valley . . . Like shooting is about to begin.' "

However, in 1970 Cyprian did join the urban Black Power rebellion (on which see Bennett 1989). After its failure he was struck by a remark which had been made by one of its leaders, who said that Trinidadians should "buy less clothes, go less to store." During the street demonstrations that year he met Jeanette, who was then thirty-seven (he was twenty-six), already with ten children. They started living together; they have since had four children.

In 1973, the 21st of May, I leave the city with my child father [Cyprian] and come in the bush with him. Well, I have to say the spirit lead me there because at the life [time] I was about to build a house. I had the land, I had galvanize, I had wood, I had everything, but I just walk out on it, pick up the smaller children (which I had eleven at the time), pick up the smaller ones and his own, and I come to the bush with him."I didn't even know I was coming in the bush! But one day he just came back and tell me "I come for you to go in the bush" and I say "Who— me? Not me! I ai' going in the bush!" Well, he said "Think it over. On Monday I'll be here with a van and be ready." Well, I didn't even take him on, but Sunday a little incident happen between one of my children and another little boy kick him . . . Within myself something was telling me "Look— this is the time for you to leave; get out of this place."

"It was so simple. I was about to build a house then. When life [time] reach to come in the bush these things come like nothing to me. I just pack up and pick up some of my children and move out . . . And something in me feel different. From that day I started to feel a kind of lightness. How you would call it a lightness in spirit, yes, because to me, myself start talking to me more freely, you know; things come in my mind, I talk to myself and it was nice, feeling a vibration in the body and I started to live.

"It was nice living, although it was hard because I knew nothing then about the bush and the life and the food, how to live, because you accustom in the city with money and buy. So it was a little rough but I continue with it. People call the bush "the jungle." I call it "life" because within the bushes you find many lives in different form, in the birds and the animals, the insects, the serpents, and they all life.

Jeanette doubtfully went along with Jakatan's attempt to return to a simple rural life; everyone who used to live along the coast between the two villages had now left. They settled by agreement on the estate where Hell Valley now lies and, after an argument with the owner who lives in Pinnacle village, squatted on the land, occupying a disused house and selling the copra they gathered to the village. A rare visitor surveying the idyllic setting said "This is the Valley of Peace." Immediately, without reflecting, Jeanette corrected him: "No, here is the Valley of Decision" (the title of a then-popular song). The name stuck.

Jeanette fasted that Lent and had a vision in which she ran away from Jesus into a river in which swam a serpent. She continued to look after her children and "do usual housewife thing" until another dream in 1975 when she was eight months pregnant:

I find well I was too heavy, you know. So I had to stay in one place. I stay one place for about two months already. What make me stay one place is I come and had a vision that the moon [come] up this place to have the baby.

The vision was I was living in a place and it look like in the city and I heard the people laughing, laughing outside, so I came outside to see what it is was going on. When I came out I see everyone looking up on the sky and laughing. When I look I saw something funny, shape in a something, it had a head but the head was funny. It had thin thin hands but yet it was the moon that was shape in that form. So when I look up it said to me "Don't bother with them, it is you I want to speak to. Get on the hill there. You will see a house. Go there and make your baby."

And when I come out [of the dream] I tell him. I say, "Well, look, I have to go to make my baby up on the hill because I is Mary." This is what the moon tells me – "Mary, you got to go and make the baby." So I say I'm Mary, say I have to go so to make the baby. The moon didn't say really mother of Jesus but I know to myself now I am the mother of Jesus since I reach to this stage . . . And then one of my sons come and had the same vision: he was leading the donkey and I on it with the baby: Mary going to make the baby.

So when I get up I was wondering where to go to make this baby? It have no house on the hill so that I could go and make this baby. Where? So I end up going upstairs in the cocoa box[10] . . . And then I come and make one night. I just feel a forcing— I didn't have no pain to make the baby. I just feel a force and when I feel a force I telling the children "Look like I going to make the baby." And rain started to fall. I made one. I telling them "Well, look, something still in my belly, I still feel something" so I make a force again and another comes out! I was so shocked, seeing two babies which I never had before. So I just them them off, one of my sons cut the navel [cord]. I show him what to do. And the next one the father cut it. I show him what to do. And they cut it, which was two boys.

And after that, when they was five months, well I started to burn everything I had. Just like that one day. It was the same as any day. It was surprising too how I started. . . . The rain started to fall that day and I went outside. I started to dance in the rain and sing an African song which they usually use in Shango tent (which I use' to go around Shango a lot so I know how to call the water). So I started to sing one of the songs:

Ehmanjah, saiy, saiy,
Ehmanjah, sanya,
Sanya roya maja,
Sanya roya . . .[11]

And I sing it, and after that I sing for the day different tunes, calling the water, calling the thunder and lightning. Well, next day the sun was shining and from then, I started burning thing. I just came inside of the house, I said "Look I want everything in the kitchen burn, the pots and pans and everything." So from then we use to roast little plantain and eat it because the pot is in the fire. I put the radio in the fire. The children take it back out. It burn a little but it was still playing. They take it back out. Well I come around all the bedding I had to wash from the twins (because I couldn't go by the river when they born so I was washing very little here, waiting until I get a little stronger to go down by the river to do the big washing). And the bundles come so high that the day I took them up and put them into the fire I feel like if something come out of me! I feel light. Two big bundles of bedding, I put them in the fire! And they burn, the sheets and everything burn! I burn everything in the house for a few days! I can't tell you exactly what day I start but I know the last thing I had to burn was the [sewing] machine. I even took down the doors and windows and burn them . . . I had no thinking, just doing. I was like a mad body. If I see a nail, I pull it out.

So Sunday morning the fire was still going for the day, things keep burning. I pick up the Bibles then for the first time for I didn't intend to burn them. I said, "Let me go, come and let me show you how your education is upside-down." So he [Cyprian] come with me to the fire. And certain things I have done by the fire, can't remember all directly but one of the main things I know: I rest my feet in the fire; I said "Just now I will be dancing in the fire." Then I took up something from the fire which is a burnt piece of something and pass it in the book, open the Book. The writing come upside down and I show it to him. I show it to them. All of us was surprised. I and all was surprised! Although it's me do it but yet I was surprised to see the writing come upside down. So I told him, I say, "Look your education is upside down."

IN SUMMARY

Jeanette's mourning visions in Port-of-Spain had been relatively conventional, similar to those of her friends and neighbors except perhaps for the recurrent serpent which she is encouraged to oppose, and for a closer identification with Christ than was usual among the Baptists (but one by no means totally outrageous). Her vague sense of mission was shared by many others, including her partner, Cyprian. She had met him at the time of the failed Black Power uprising after which, dissatisfied both with the compromises of Black Power and those of the Baptists, he proposed that they adopt a simpler and more traditional rural life away from the pressures of the town. Jeanette only reluctantly agreed to join him together with their children, for she had been gathering materials to build a house of her own in town. The family settled at the most deserted part of the coast, reading the Bible and discussing religious questions together, accepting omens in visions (visionary dreams) and continuing occasional fasts. It was a physically demanding life, but the calm and peace of the coast more than compensated for the arguments with overseers and estate owners, recalling to Jeanette the best times of her childhood when she had accompanied her godfather as he worked on his little patch of four acres. In a dream after she settled on the coast she finds herself running away from Jesus toward a snake waiting for her in the river.

Two years after they arrived, when Jeanette was forty-one years old, and eight months pregnant, she has another dream in which the moon tells her she is Mary and she should have her child on top of a hill. Not understanding why, she follows the dream and gives birth to twins under the roof of the house. Five months later, Jeanette, in a burst of energy, sings a song to the mother deity of Shango and starts burning all the disposable articles, and last of all her Bible; neither she nor her family understands what is happening, but her partner presumes some religious meaning in it and does not interfere. When questioned by him, Jeanette gives answers that flash into her head, principally that her actions are due to the natural spirit in her. The burned objects she now refers back to personal concerns, to her religion (Bible), sickness (spectacles), or to her domestic tasks (bedding, kitchen utensils, and eventually the sewing machine with which she made the children's shirts). Together with the burning of all their clothes, this results in the family going naked until she makes up some temporary garments out of sacking, later abandoning these again as uncomfortable and unnecessary. This period is now known as the Beginning of the End, the moment when Nature became incarnate in Jeanette as Mother Earth.

Friends of her older sons, half inclined to Rastafari, and who knew her in town, come out to visit the family on the coast. Amazed at what they find, they argue and discuss matters with Mother Earth. Some discard their clothes and stay in the valley, and the Earth People's beliefs are consolidated through debate. Together they interpret and reinterpret Mother Earth's visions. The commune is established, an uneasy accommodation is established with Pinnacle village, and within a year they begin their annual marches to Port-of-Spain.

APPROPRIATION FROM THE BAPTISTS . . .

It was during her Baptist mourning that Jeanette first became aware of some sense of difference from her friends and neighbors. Many other members of the Earth People have previously attended meetings of the Shouter Baptists who, like Rastafari, are regarded by her as "half way there" to the full revelation of Mother Africa. Indeed, we can place the Shouters as lying between those mainstream Baptist churches of the Caribbean still closely allied to their parent congregations in the United States, and the conscious Africanisms of the Shango cult. Shango and Shouter Baptism are closely associated and some followers of

Shango continue to refer to themselves as "Shango Baptists" (Glazier 1983).

During Baptist *mourning* as I observed it in Northern Trinidad and Chaguanas, initiates and members are secluded in a side room, lying on the earth or on pallets of leaves, and bound all over with flat cloth bands recalling the appearance of a wrapped Egyptian mummy. These *bands* are *sealed* with *signs,* and the mourner remains for a period of (generally) at least seven days, accompanied by a spiritual director, usually the Mother of the group. She feeds the *traveling children* on weak vegetable broth and guides their spirit quests, usually to India, China, or Africa where they learn a new role (Captain, Head Nurse, Labourer) often by self-perception as a Biblical figure (Joseph, Mary, Joshua) which is communicated to the Mother and, if ratified, involves them in fresh ritual costume and paraphernalia in future services.

"Mourning" is considered by the participant less as a bereavement than as a temporary bodily death in close association with the earth (Daniel 10:3), enabling the spirit to live more fully in the other world, thence to be reborn spiritually. Shouters admit that mourning can be dangerous, for the individual when traveling is vulnerable to *mauvay lespwis* (malign, usually African, powers or nature spirits) but correct sealing and guidance by the Mother can prevent mishaps. It has been argued that the style and authenticity of mourning visions determine future status in each Baptist group and that they are closely tied to internal disputes and challenges to the authority of the leader;[12] most Mothers therefore prefer to keep a close watch on the proceedings. Jeanette had rather overstepped the mark when she reported a vision of herself as Christ: not even the Baptist Mother identifies with any of the persons of the Trinity. Such identification is anyway regarded outside of the mourning as only "spiritual," and even in the vision itself it is a temporary visit or gift of higher powers, not unlike the gift of tongues from the Holy Spirit in other denominations.

How self-consciously "African" can we take Shouter Baptism? The Herskovitses (1947) regard it as transitional between West African spirituality and Protestantism. As we look at Shango and Spiritual Baptism today there appears to be some thematic and experiential elision between them, and it is likely that they continue to share key personnel as in the past, the "open" Christian service sometimes preceding a more restricted Shango meeting (Glazier 1983, Houk 1993). Small short-lived groups draw on both sources (Smith 1962) and the conventional distinction between the two is perhaps more rigid than their pragmatic and casual organization would warrant. Certainly the Baptists are regarded by other Trinidadians as being particularly close to *obeah* ("African" sorcery), and the material success of the family of the Shepherd Mother in the nearest Baptist group to the village I lived in was attributed by some of her neighbours to obeah. None of the Baptist leaders I knew admitted to practicing it but they agreed that their familiarity with the spirit world made them particularly successful at returning obeah on the senders through *guards* or *lighting a candle* (Littlewood 1988). Nor did they see Baptism as a specifically "African" form of Christianity, welcoming the occasional white participant such as myself, and maintaining that the difference between Spiritual and "Carnal" (mainstream American-based) Baptists lay in an openness to the Holy Spirit and a lack of formality which were simply more congenial to those of African descent. In the colonial period, however, some Baptists were thought to hold Black supremacist views (Simpson 1980); and Rastafari derives from the not dissimilar Revival Zion groups in Jamaica.

The absence of the sort of exorcism practiced by the new local Pentecostal groups, or of a rigid distinction between the context of good and bad spirit intrusion, together with the idea of travel in some world where the physical and spiritual meet, and the overlapping membership between Shango and Spiritual Baptism, suggest that good and evil are less dichotomized here than in mainstream Christianity. By contrast with Jamaica, where obeah and myal opposed each other in the nineteenth century, Trinidadian Shango seems deliberately more "African" in asserting a non-dualistic world, one in which the initiate can return temporarily to Africa.[13] The extent to which the Shouters incorporate themes of *high science* (Western-derived "Hermetic" magic) is uncertain: Shouter seals certainly recall those found in such Hermetic texts as *The Sixth and Seventh Books of Moses* ("Moses" n.d.); and the Herskovits' accounts of the 1930s imply that Shouters then shared the pantheistic tendencies of *science,* including invocation of ancient European nature spirits.[14] To an extent this sharing may be attributed to the strength in Trinidad of Catholicism whose syncretic and arguably thaumaturgical practices are decried by the Protestant churches: Baptists may often be simultaneously Catholics (and less often Anglicans) but only rarely Presbyterians or Pentecostalists.

Certain currents in Baptism are commented upon and developed by Mother Earth: the dynamic continuity with Africa, an affirmation of the popular working-class world as opposed to the *social*[15] churches, the physical and conceptual closeness to the earth, the organizational and nurturant role of the Mother, the association of women with the "African" center pole of the Baptist chapel rather than with its altar, the local religious community as a family, an openness to subjective imagery, personal visions as justification for daily life, and, perhaps most significantly, a notion of the ultrahuman as not that far removed from everyday experience. While Mother Earth has moved decisively away from Christian doctrine, the Bible remains for her, as it does for the Rastas, an important source for understanding the history of our world, albeit one to be interpreted with circumspection.

... AND FROM SHANGO

The origins of Spiritual Baptism lie not only in missionary Baptism but in those secret nocturnal meetings of the African-born slaves where they weighed their knowledge against what was known of the Christianity of the planters, with resulting accommodations, appropriations, and reinterpretations. Although described somewhat quaintly as "balls" by the Europeans, such assemblies are likely to have offered other opportunities rather than simply entertainment. Of what actually happened at those meetings we can know little, but out of them emerged the characteristically West Indian "sensibility" of the mainstream churches, together with such distinctive groups as the Shouters, and those popular understandings of the self, nature and the ultrahuman world which are employed in bush medicine (Littlewood 1988). To an extent, that popular body of knowledge took an institutional form in the Shango rites of spirit possession by African powers, ceremonies that shared members and ideas with Shouter Baptism. After the 1760 slave rebellion, "obeah" was in theory punishable by death until Emancipation (and it remains illegal): like the Shouters (Gullick, ch. 7, this volume), the followers of Shango continued to engage in what were illicit activities. While its formal practice continues in Trinidad, by the early 1980s it appeared to be disappearing in a society where it had never been officially recognized as embodying any characteristic national values—unlike the Baptists who were usually regarded by the Trinidadian establishment with good humored tolerance as a year-long carnival.[16]

Shango—now more genteelly described as "orisha worship"—is not opposed to obeah (sorcery) except in as much as obeah is employed for harm. Shango may indeed be said to be morally neutral in that every African *power* (or *orisha*) is potentially both malevolent and benevolent. Ritual centers which emphasized the ability of the powers to heal were once known as *balmyards,* and many popular practitioners of "obeah" (who would not now use the designation of *obeahman* but prefer *seerman, teacher* or *healer)* continue to offer advice for physical or spiritual misfortune.

Instead of the Baptists' *traveling* during mourning, devotees of the orishas were completely possessed by their *power* in full view of the audience, acting as a *horse* (or *child*) upon which the power manifests.[17] The powers themselves are named West African deities although they are often coupled with Christian saints as in Brazilian *umbanda* and Haitian *vodu*: thus the Yoruba deity Yemanja is associated with the Virgin Mary, St. Anne or St. Catherine. Shango powers are usually Yoruba, although in the Belmont area of Port-of-Spain where Mother Earth lived as a girl there was a Rada group deriving from nineteenth-century immigrants from Dahomey (Carr 1952). (And Shango itself probably has strong post-slavery African sources.) There are also powers with no distinct

African antecedents such as Mama Latay (La Terre). Compared with Shouter Baptism, there is more use of *patois* (French Creole) and many songs are in "Yoruba" although the precise meaning of the words are usually unknown to the participants. There is little similarity to a Christian service; Shango rites recall rather the traditional fetes, "African dances," communal labor entertainments (*gayaps*), and wakes of rural Trinidad (Herskovits 1947, Simpson 1980). They are sponsored activities, involving expenditure on food, various ritual objects, and animals for sacrifice, and their organization is perhaps closer to a fraternity or cult than to the conventionalized idea of a church. Shango employs domestic items regarded as more "African" than "Christian"—rum, tobacco, drums, *chacs-chacs* (gourd rattles), calabashes and cutlasses. Music characteristically employs polyrhythms, but antiphony between leader and chorus is less common than in Baptist meetings. According to my informants, greater attention is supposed to be paid to the central pole, for the altar is merely one of the resting places for a variety of ritual paraphernalia rather than the central concentration of spiritual power: earthern stools (shrines) of the individual orishas may be located around the courtyard of a Shango *palais*.

For the Earth People, Shango asserts an Africa quite independent of European Christianity. Whether the assimilation of the Shango powers to Christian saints is to be termed "syncretic" may be doubted, for the power/saint still has two distinct aspects which are not elided (Pollack-Eltz 1993), and the shrine of the *orisha* always remains distinct from the altar: a relationship Bastide (1975) prefers to term a "correspondence." In some aspects Shango is closer to everyday village life than Baptism: toward the end of a wake in Pinnacle village, the more *respectable* villagers, particularly the married women who have previously been central to the rite, return home to sleep; as rum drinking intensifies, the singing shifts from the plaintive "Sankeys" to a sharper tempo, a greater degree of improvization and the introduction of call and response, and polyrhythms, progressing to general male dancing in a moving line backed by massed *bongo* drumming in which domestic calabashes and bowls are percussed by hand.

Through its use of blood sacrifices, plants, palm oil, and "thunderaxes,"[18] and the associations between the orishas and the powers of sea and thunder, animals and trees, Shango elides the natural, human and mystical domains which Spiritual Baptism as a nominally Christian faith still prefers to distinguish. While Baptism merely accords the earth on which mourners lie a status which represents the origin and fate of man, Shango takes the ground as the continuing physical source of the gods: oblations are poured onto it, and it is from the earth that the orishas manifest up through the central pole and then onto their *child*. While earth from graves is now regarded as the material for malign obeah par excellence, it comes from what is the resting place of the ancestors, and *grave dirt* was formerly placed in the mouth of the suspected thief or practitioner of harmful sorcery to determine the truth.

As Mother Earth, Jeanette now argues that Shango is the most authentic memory we retain of the Mother of all things. She herself was never an adult participant in Shango and remembers relatively little of its rites beyond some of the songs, the sacrifices of goats (of which she disapproves), and the childrens' *tables* (feasts). She recalls how once a year the Mother of a Shango group would invite the local children, both followers of the orishas and other neighbors, African and Indian together, to a feast where they were invited to partake of large quantities of food piled on tables in a Shango *tent*. The attending children like the young Jeanette were specifically identified with the African orishas: "when you feed the children, you feed the saints" (Thomas 1987).   The Earth People now regard children as the authentic Africans, and call themselves the Children of the Nation. (The term *nation*, once used to describe particular African descent or regional groups in Trinidad, and later their organizations for mutual aid and *fetes*, as well as suggesting Africans in general, now refers in Shango to the ceremonies themselves.) "Feeding the children" appears in the Earth Peoples' cultivation of the land around the valley and their accumulation of large quantities of food surplus against any immediate needs, their emphasis on preparation for the coming famine by Planting for the Children, not to mention the centrality of the communal consumption of food, to be the only activity in the valley that could be described as in any sense a standardized ritual.

The Earth People appropriate and revise those aspects of Shango regarded as distinctively African—drums, stools, and the revering of an animate nature. Shango cultists once washed their "thunder stones" and made offerings in the sea while some devotees were said to dance with snakes.[19] There is, however, no experience of anything like spirit possession or Baptist mourning among the Earth People. Mother Earth argues that the slaves did return to Africa after their death, and that Shango possession has been a "half-way" stage of keeping in contact with these ancestral spirits, an accommodation during the Nation's exile from their Mother. This is no longer necessary, for the whole world is about to return to the original state of Nature, the "otherworldly" becoming the everyday.[20]

From fragmentary rites, visions, dreams, and recollections we shall return to the totality, for these were only a testimony, a keeping of memory until the Beginning of the End: "Your ancestor is you," says Mother Earth. We are now living in the last days, at that moment when time itself is ending, when past and present will be finally reconciled. Perhaps paradoxically it is Mother Earth herself who still seems to retain the double identity of the African power and the contemporary human on whom the power manifests.[21] In her African identity as the Earth Mother she embodies not only Yemanja but all the orishas and the ancestors, and that whole history of the separation of Nature from Her Children, the separation between Africa and the Caribbean, and indeed between woman and man.

SYNCRETISM AND THE POLITICS OF AUTHENTICITY

How appropriate is the term "syncretic" to describe the Earth People.[22] The term has recently returned to academic favour after being avoided by social scientists because, as Stewart and Shaw (1994) note, it increasingly developed pejorative implications: less a synthesis of religious traditions but rather the contamination by local cultures of a notionally standardised 'world religion' such as Islam or Christianity (and ignoring of course the extent to which such religious systems themselves had composite origins). The increasing recognition that 'tradition' has always to be recreated, together with post-modern celebrations of multivocality and improvisation, is now transforming the notion of 'cultures' as autonomous entities into more complex idioms of continually inventive process— what Clifford terms "creolising interculture." In my own writing on the Earth People I have emphasised the radical novelty of Mother Earth's own ideas as rooted in personal experiences which ironically comment on and transform her local cultural contradictions, particularly those of gender and ethnicity. Here I should, however, like to emphasize three points:

1. "Syncretism" is generally used to refer to the domain of "religion" as a belief system as if this could be taken independently of politics, a limitation particularly inept for the Caribbean;
2. Our currently fashionable use of multiplicity and heteroglossia as analytical models follows the political decline of immediate Western power and its metanarratives in the post-colonial world; but
3. Individuals may still prefer to orient their new possibilities within the language and tradition of formerly dominant ideologies.

Thus, Rastafari takes itself as Christian (indeed as the authentic Christianity, not syncretic, nor derived from Christianity), and has been accepted as such by sympathetic Catholic clergy (e.g, Owens 1976): just as other "new" religions and denominations may see themselves as revitalising or reforming the old order. Of Rastafari, Nettleford (1976) comments that "the overthrowing of the Christian faith was to be fought by weapons out of its own armoury." The extent, however, to which we take the new dispensation as overthrowing the old, or as simply revising or fulfilling it, remains arbitrary, determined not only by its later affiliations and practical contingencies but by the interests of the historian (Littlewood 1995). Syncretism, acculturation, revitalization and resistance as analytical categories may be quite at variance with the intentions of the individuals to which they are applied. The Earth People, it will have been apparent, acknowledge little affinity with Christianity (or indeed with what they term *religion*), and I myself prefer to place them with revitalist movements or neopaganism despite their evident affinities with radical Puritanism.[23] As with many other groups, their own claims to authenticity explain away as half-truths or deliberate obfuscation these sentiments and language through which they themselves have emerged.[24] And that is perhaps what any social movement we term a "new religion" must do.

NOTES

1. *Oui* as in French Creole: an Earth People's gathering song sung by Tannia. I lived with the Earth People on and off during 1981-1982. Since then there have been many changes, notably the death of Mother Earth herself in 1984. I returned again for three months in 1988 and again in 1991, but this chapter, written in the "ethnographic present," is concerned with the community in 1981. My initial stay was funded in part through an SSRC Post-Doctoral Fellowship. A detailed account of the Earth People may be found in my *Pathology and Identity: The Work of Mother Earth in Trinidad* (Cambridge University Press, 1993). In previous papers on the group (Littlewood 1984, 1992, 1995), I have emphasised social analysis. Here I offer some greater space for Mother Earth's own account of her visionary experiences in a revised version of a paper published in *Caribbean Quarterly* (1993, *39* (3, 4)): 56-73), to whose editors I am grateful for permission to reprint in part. While the Earth People have frequently been reported in the Trinidad press, the only other account of Mother Earth's visions is as a local folktale by Jerry Besson (n.d.). A remarkably similar cosmogony, however, appears as an African "fable" written by a Trinidadian student for an American university newspaper (Jean 1983), and the idiom of People of Ice (Europeans) versus the People of Fire (Africans) continually emerges as an African-American moral dichotomy (e.g., Leonard Jeffries).

2. Like most other proper names in this chapter, a pseudonym at the request of her immediate family. Members of the Earth People take *fruit names* such as Tannia, Breadfruit, Cassava; these I have retained here.

3. The local names for Trinidadians descended from Black African slaves and nineteenth-century African immigrants, and those descended from Indian indentured labourers who came in the period 1860-1914.

4. Cohabitating without marriage.

5. Baptist vision quest. See text below.

6. Or *tramping*. Rhythmic vocal expirations synchronized with slow stomping (compare Glazier 1983: 43).

7. Giant monkey as in the film *King Kong*.

8. This time: the word *time* is generally avoided by the Earth People as illusory for we have now entered the Beginning of the End when time will cease altogether

9. Worry about or preoccupy oneself with it.

10. Loft with retractable roof for drying cocoa beans.

11. A Shango song. In the Yoruba cosmogony, Ehmanjah (Yemanja) is the deity of the river Ogu who conceives Orungan by her brother Aganja, the power of the dry land. To her son Orungan himself she bears a number of *orishas* including Shango, Ogun, and Shopona. In African-American religions Yemanja is generally assimilated to St. Anne

(the mother of the Virgin Mary) or to Mary herself; her personality (as embodied in the followers through whom she manifests) is maternal, nurturant, tolerant but implacable.

12. Simpson 1980. But see Glazier 1983, who argues differently.

13. Indeed Lewis (1983: 19) talks of a "shango-obeah complex."

14. What I have referred to here and elsewhere as science or Hermeticism is termed Kabbalah by Houk (1993a, 1993b). Its association with Spiritual Baptism has not been unrecognized as he claims, but it has been termed differently (Herskovits and Herskovits 1947).

15. "Bourgeois" in its various glosses, snobbish, *high society*: in other words, the established denominations (although some Baptists have elected bishops and joined the Trinidad and Tobago Council of Churches (Thomas 1987)).

16. Compare St. Vincent (Gullick, ch.7, this volume). The 1980s saw a resurgence of Shango now known as the "Orisha Religion," backed by a renewed African-American interest in Nigerian culture in a "re-Africanisation" of a religion which had incorporated Christian and even Hindu themes (Houk 1993a): a process of purification Stewart and Shaw (1994) term "anti-syncretism." One Shango organisation, the Orisha Movement, has recently obtained government recognition.

17. From Houk (1993a), it seems that spirit possession is now less common in Shango, while mourning has been adopted from the Baptists.

18. Neolithic stone tools taken as manifestations of the orisha Shango (as in West Africa).

19. Herskovits and Herskovits 1947. The Earth People do not "dance" with snakes, but they pick them up and play with them if they are found in the compound.

20. Even more than Rastas, the Earth People are hylozoic and "this worldly": sacrifice is the process of joining the group. Ganja is smoked for pleasure, not for spiritual insight, and they ridicule the Pinnacle villagers' resort to obeah and science and their optimistic supplication of divinities. If the sentiments of the Rastas recall Calvinist revivalism, then we might regard those of the Earth People as Quaker or even neo-pagan. Whilst fairly sympathetic to Rastafari, Mother Earth still regards it as essentially the work of the Son (Littlewood 1995).

21. Mother Earth agrees that after her visionary experiences (when she was "out of myself") her awareness and actions were different, which she interprets as the entry of the Mother into her body. To use the ideal-typology which Bourguignon (1978) applies to Lienhardt's account of the Shilluk King, she originally experienced something akin to PT, possession trance (altered state of consciousness plus possession belief), which has been succeeded by P, possession (the belief alone). The Shango participant experiences PT and then returns to an everyday state; while the Baptist mourner is arguably in T, trance (an altered state of consciousness without possession belief). On the actual divinity of leaders in African-American religious groups, see my *Pathology and Identity* and also Warner-Lewis 1993.

22. As Stewart and Shaw (1994) point out, there is no consistent usage of the term, nor does its likely etymology help: "a coming together of Cretans." The now fashionable

term "creolisation" has an even less promising origin in that it referred to the dominant Europeans established in their colonial setting, but its current linguistic use is for a "contact language" which is now autonomous.

23. Radical Puritanism itself has often proceeded to similar antinomianism if not transvalorized diabolism: Ranters, New England Shakers, Oneida, Doukhobors, and other perfectionist theodicies (Littlewood 1995).

24. Like Earth People, Jehovah's Witnesses deny they are "'a religion."

BIBLIOGRAPHY

Bastide, R. *The African Religions of Brasil: Towards a Sociology of the Interpenetration of Civilisations.* Baltimore: Johns Hopkins University Press, 1975.

Bennett, H. L. "The Challenge to the Post-Colonial State: A Case Study of the February Revolution in Trinidad." In F. W. Knight and C. A. Palmer (eds.), *The Modern Caribbean.* Chapel Hill: University of North Carolina Press, 1989.

Besson, J. *Tales of the Paria Main Road.* Port-of-Spain: Creative Advertising Publications, n.d.

Bourguignon, E. "Spirit Possession and Altered States of Consciousness." In G. D.Spindler (ed.), *The Making of Psychological Anthropology.* Berkeley: University of California Press, 1978.

Carr, A. T. "A Rada Community in Trinidad." *Caribbean Quarterly,* 3, 35-54, (1952)

Gates, H. L. *The Signifying Monkey: A Theory of Afro-American Literary Criticism.* New York: Oxford University Press, 1988.

Girard, R. *To Double Business Bound: Essays on Literature, Mimesis and Anthropology.* Baltimore: Johns Hopkins University Press, 1978.

Glazier, S. D. *Marchin' the Pilgrims Home: Leadership and Decision Making in an Afro-Caribbean Faith.* Westport, CT: Greenwood Press, 1983.

Glazier, S. D. (ed.) "Spiritual Baptists, Shango and Other African-Derived Religions in the Caribbean." *Caribbean Quarterly,* special issue, *39,* 3, 4. Jamaica: University of the West Indies, 1993.

Herskovits, M. J. and F. S. Herskovits. *Trinidad Village.* New York: Knopf, 1947.

Houk, J. "Afro-Trinidadian Identity and the Africanisation of the Orisha Religion." In K. Yelvington (ed.), *Trinidad Ethnicity.* London: Macmillan, 1993a.

Houk, J. "The Role of Kabbalah in the Afro-American Religious Complex in Trinidad." In Glazier (ed.), "Spiritual Baptists . . . ," 1993b.

Jean, C. "History as Fable." Brandeis University: *The Watch,* 4, 6 (1983): 6-11, 1983.

Lewis, G. *Main Currents in Caribbean Thought: the Historical Evolution of Caribbean Society in Its Ideological Aspects, 1492-1900.* Kingston, Jamaica: Heinemann, 1983.

Littlewood, R. "The Imitation of Madness." *Social Science and Madness,* 19 (1984): 705-715.

Littlewood, R. "From Vice to Madness: The Semantics of Naturalistic and Personalistic Understandings in Trinidadian Local Medicine." *Social Science and Medicine,* 27 (1988). 129-148.

Littlewood, R. "Putting Out the Life." In J. Okely and H. Callaway (eds.). *Anthropology and Autobiography*. London: Routledge, 1992.

Littlewood, R. "History, Memory and Appropriation: Some Problems in the Analysis of Origins." In B. Chevannes (ed.), *Rastafari and Other African-Caribbean Worldviews*. The Hague: Institute of Social Studies/London: Macmillan, 1995.

"Moses," *The Sixth and Seventh Books of Moses*. Aclington, TX: Dorene Publishing, n.d.

Nettleford, R. Introduction. In Owens, *Dread . . .,* 1976.

Owens, J. *Dread: The Rastafarians of Jamaica*. Kingston, Jamaica: Sangster's 1976.

Pollack-Eltz, A. "The Shango Cult and Other African Rituals in Trinidad, Grenada and Carriacou, and Their Possible Influence on the Spiritual Baptist Faith" In Glazier, "Spiritual Baptists, . . . ", 1993b.

Simpson, G. E. *Religious Cults of the Caribbean*. Puerto Rico: Institute of Caribbean Studies, 1980.

Smith, M. G. *Dark Puritan*. Kingston, Jamaica: University of the West Indies, 1962.

Stapleton, A. *The Birth and Growth of the Baptist Church in Trinidad and Tobago, and the Caribbean*. Port-of-Spain: Stapleton, 1987.

Stewart, C., and R. Shaw. Introduction. In C. Stewart and R. Shaw (eds.). *Syncretism/Anti-Syncretism: The Politics of Religious Synthesis*. European Association of Social Anthropologists/London: Routledge, 1994.

Thomas, E. *A History of the Shouter Baptists in Trinidad and Tobago*. Port-of-Spain: Callaloux, 1987.

Warner-Lewis, M. "African Continuities in the Rastafari Belief System" In Glazier, "Spiritual Baptists, . . .", 1993b.

10

Religion, Patriarchy, and the Status of Rastafarian Women

Obiagele Lake

The genesis and evolution of the Rastafarian movement has been widely discussed in the literature (Barrett 1977, Chevannes 1990, Campbell 1990). Until recently these discussions have ignored, or given scant attention to, the statuses and roles held by Rastafarian women (see Rowe 1985; Llaloo 1981; Lake 1994). Although Rastafarians do not constitute one monolithic group, there are major tenets that are held by many Rastafarians regarding the relative status of women and men: 1) Rastafarian men are the spiritual leaders of the movement; 2) women can only become Rastafarian through Rasta men; and 3) Rasta men are the natural heads of households. These beliefs, along with the notion that women are polluted, emanate from religious and other cultural beliefs and serve to legitimate the subordination of women at every level of society. I suggest that what is at stake in these relations is male supremacy and domination, and not, as Rasta men would suggest, an enactment of what is divinely ordained.

The secondary position of Rasta women is particularly interesting in a movement that promulgates liberation as their underlying philosophy. In order to fully understand the dynamics of the subordination of Rasta women, a broader discussion of the dynamics of oppression bears a brief, but close study.

Many students of women's issues contend that women wield power in a number of ways (Leacock 1981; Sudarkasa 1987). One of the problems with this contention is that there is no basis for its support or rejection since a clear outline of the mechanics of oppression is absent from this discourse. Oppression occurs when a segment of the population is *systematically* denied equal access to material and cultural resources (Turner, Royce, and Musick 1984). While societies differ in the nature of economic (material) and cultural production, sexual oppression derives from the fact that men in any given society own and control these valuable resources. Material resources include land and technology and other assets necessary to produce commodities. Control over cultural resources entails the creation and perpetuation of an ideology that supports and validates economic relations of production (Beckford and Witter (1980). That is, women's inferior economic position is justified by a belief system that renders them innately less capable and less deserving than men.

In Jamaica, as well as in other areas of the world, women, as a group, are disproportionately at the bottom of the economic hierarchy (Harrison 1988) which, consequently, disables them from having an equal voice at the ideological level. In order to fully grasp the predicament of Rastafarian women in this regard, it is necessary to understand the broader position of Jamaican women of which they form an integral part.

That women in Jamaica are denied equal access to material resources is well known (Senior 1991; Spaulding 1993; Antrobus and Gordon 1984; Deere et al. 1990:51-85ff). They are relegated to low-paying jobs as domestics and service workers and are victims of high unemployment rates (Levitt 1991:48). Higher levels of education and jobs that are traditionally male and, therefore, higher paying, make women economically dependent on men. "Even where women have similar qualifications, perform similar tasks and have the same level of productivity, their remuneration is usually significantly lower than their male counterparts" (ibid:48). This predicament places women in a weak position and diminishes their ability to challenge traditional roles.

Women's position in the political arena is equally subordinated to that of men. While women do hold elected positions in the government, they do not serve in decision-making positions in numbers consonant with their proportion in society. This is most clearly demonstrated by the fact that, with two exceptions,[1] there have been no women heads of state in the whole of the Caribbean, where women outnumber men. This political marginalization is reified at the cultural level, where women are less valued than men. Cultural beliefs that deem women to be inferior to men are part of a superstructure that supports and sustains their marginalization at the political-economic level. This belief system is intrinsic to Jamaican culture and characteristic of other African (Obbo 1980; Brain 1978) and Diaspora African societies.

The tendency in the literature is to claim that the denigrated status of indigenous African women (Steady 1981:7-44; Okonjo 1976:45-58) and women of African descent (Terborg-Penn, Harley, and Rushing 1989) in the diaspora is a result of the imposition of European cultural norms and capitalist political-economic structures. While Europeans and European American cultures have influenced the status of women in other societies, the implicit and explicit claim that precolonial African women were not subordinated to African men (Hafkin and Bay 1976; Etienne and Leacock 1980) is unfounded (Robertson and Klein 1989; Henn 1986:3, 13-23). While it is true that women were (and are) the main agricultural producers in these societies, these roles are not tantamount to holding political-economic or personal autonomy. Indigenous African men exerted control over African women in cultural, political, and economic spheres. Domination of precolonial indigenous African women was most clearly demonstrated in polygynous marriage systems,[2] the capture and sale of women slaves for the Arabic and European slave trade, and awarding women as war prizes. When Europeans transported Africans to Jamaica, and the rest of the African diaspora, African ideology was not left behind. The capitalist economic organization in colonial Jamaica may have exacerbated women's roles and statuses, but, if so, this degraded position was a continuation of a home-grown variety. Indigenous African rituals sacralized the subordination of women (Brain 1978:176-188) in much the same way as Christian rhetoric does today.

Slavery and Christianity were imposed on Africans in the Caribbean at one and the same time. The effects of Christian religious teaching has been two-pronged. At one level it has helped to foster a degree of complacency among its adherents who believe that God will lead them to salvation. On the other, religious teachings that emphasize righteousness and brotherly love have spurred Jamaicans (Turner 1982:154ff), as well as other oppressed people, to struggle for freedom. Similarly, while a sense of Christian duty has encouraged many women to struggle for equality within the church and in society at large, the basic tenet of Christian pedagogy relegates women as inferior to men. This notion has been addressed by a number of scholars (Ruether 1974; Beers 1992; Goldenburg 1979), but has been deemphasized in academic curricula.

Although all Caribbean women are theoretically subject to degrading religious tenets, Rastafarian women are even more susceptible to living out these scriptures because of the strict interpretation that Rastas lend to the Bible. In this chapter I focus on Rastafarian women's domination in the domestic and public spheres and how this domination is reified by religious ideology. These proposals are based on my empirical research observations of male/female relations and extensive interviews (Lake 1992, 1993) in various parts of Jamaica where I gathered information from a wide range of Rastafarians representing various political, economic, and cultural perspectives.[3]

This discussion is significant in that it emphasizes the correspondence between women's struggles in the sociocultural sphere and her marginalization at the political-economic level. In this regard, the position of Rasta women resonates with the struggles of Jamaican women as a whole and with women of African descent internationally. On a broader scale, this discussion is significant in that it addresses questions of sexual equality and the role that cultural norms and institutions play in creating and maintaining stratified communities even among relatively progressive elements of society. Before discussing these inequalities more specifically, a brief summary regarding the genesis of Rastafari is instructive.

RASTAFARIAN ROOTS

In order to understand Rastafarian women's position within the movement it is necessary to take a brief look at Rastafari as a whole. Rastafarians are most often associated with dreadlocks, reggae music, and Bob Marley. While these are contemporary cultural symbols that identify this group, Rastafarians emerged from a long line of resistance to slavery and capitalism. Although the literature (Barrett 1977; Owens 1976) indicates the Rastafari began in 1930 with the coronation of Haile Selassie, this date marks a point on a continuum of discontent with foreign political-economic control. Slave revolts and maroon societies (Price 1973) were the first forms of political activity that offered resistance to a European capitalist class and a mulatto petty bourgeoisie. Significant inequalities in access to valuable resources instigated armed revolts in nineteenth-century post-slavery period. Labor disputes continued into the twentieth century, the most notable being the labor strike in 1938 (Campbell 1990:81-84). By far the most significant twentieth-century personality to wage a struggle against the interests of the elite class was Marcus Garvey (1887-1940).

When he was in his early twenties, Garvey launched a career in the labor movement that would culminate in a broader pan-African struggle. His travels to Costa Rica, Panama, and other areas where people of African descent constituted the lowest ranks of the working class provided him with a global perspective on the oppression of African people that shaped his back-to-Africa philosophy (Garvey 1967; Lewis 1988).

In 1914 Garvey formed the Universal Negro Improvement and Conservation Association and African Communities League whose purpose was to "promote the spirit of pride and love, to reclaim the fallen, . . . to assist in the development of independent Negro nations and communities; [and to] establish a central nation for the race" (Garvey 1968:38). His emphasis was on enhancing educational opportunities, commerce, and industry among diaspora Africans in order to create a climate where diaspora Africans could establish control over their own destinies (Martin 1976).

In 1916 Garvey migrated to the United States and reformulated his organization as the Universal Negro Improvement Association (UNIA). Garvey's main goals were to create pride through self-sufficiency and to promote his back-to-Africa agenda. His political message emphasized that the Black *man* (emphasis mine) had no chance for equal opportunity in the African Diaspora (Clarke and Garvey 1974:379) and that his *manhood* (emphasis mine) could only be realized in Africa (ibid:liii-liv; Martin 1976:23-24). In order to remedy this predicament Garvey and other members of the UNIA negotiated with the Liberian government to settle Diaspora Africans in that area. In spite of (or maybe because of) Garvey's ability to embolden and mobilize large groups of people in the United States and abroad, the United States government and a conservative African-American element accelerated the demise of his movement. On February 1, 1925, Garvey was convicted of mail fraud on very flimsy evidence and sentenced to five years in prison. His sentence was commuted and he was deported to Jamaica in 1927. Although Garvey was not able to resuscitate the UNIA, his impact had already been made throughout Africa and the African diaspora.

In spite of Garvey's failure to send large numbers of people back to Africa, he succeeded in reawakening diaspora African pride in their African identity (Clarke and Garvey 1974:381-383)—a pride that was to become a major emphasis in the formation of Rastafari. Garvey's cultural exhortations encompassed a religious ideology that put forth the notion of a Black god. "We Negroes believe in the God of Ethiopia, the everlasting God, God the father, God the Son and the Holy Ghost, the One God of all ages. That is the God in whom we believe, but we shall worship Him through the spectacles of Ethiopia"(Garvey 1967:34). Although Garvey was not a Rastafarian, his political philosophy laid the groundwork for Rastafarian ideology that incorporated his ideas regarding secular and religious Ethiopianism (Clarke and Garvey 1974:381-382; Chevannes 1990:140-142). Among contemporary Rastafarians, Garvey holds a central place among the pantheon of revered ancestral leaders.

Disillusioned by an increasing state of landlessness and exploitation, many Jamaicans were receptive to claims that the God of Ethiopia was realized with the coronation of Haile Selassie. That Haile Selassie (whose former name was Ras Tafari) deemed himself to be the King of Kings and Lord of Lords lent greater credibility to this notion. "The coronation was opportune since it came during a period of general unrest among Jamaican laborers and served as a catalyst for the crystallization of their discontent" (Lake 1994). Rastafarians consisted of a small percentage of the population in 1930, with Jamaican peasants and laboring classes becoming the first constituents of this group (Chevannes 1981; Owens 1976).

In the early stages of the movement, Rastafarians were spurned by the general Jamaican populace (Nettleford 1972:39-111). This antipathy was a reaction to Rastafarian political and cultural ideology which included the smoking of ganja (marijuana) and belief in its sacred properties; the wearing of dreadlocks; beliefs in the divinity of Haile Selassie; and the promulgation of repatriation to Africa. Rastas also articulated an anti-capitalist position that was antithetical to most other Jamaicans, both rich and poor. This general antipathy led to a number of violent clashes between Rastas and police. Although some contemporary Jamaicans display a greater acceptance of Rasta, this acceptance is more symbolic than ideological (Yawney 1984:95; Douglass 1992:81, 158-159).

Rastafarian ideology continues to be antithetical to mainstream Jamaican society. Although Rastafarian women have been victims of the same constraints as Jamaican women at large (Rowe 1985:16), religious beliefs and cultural practices that constitute the Rastafarian way of life work to further institutionalize their subordinate status (Austin-Broos 1987).

RELIGIOUS IDEOLOGY AND FEMALE DOMINATION

Rastafarian religious orientation is central in maintaining the roles and statuses of Rastafarian women (Rowe 1985) since the patriarchal nature of Christian dogma legitimates the secondary position of women (Ruether 1974; Dunfee 1989; Renzetti and Curran 1989: 260-283). The Christian religion is joined by a host of others (Steinfels 1992; Haddad 1985) that are replete with an ideology that is inconsistent with equality.

Throughout the history of Judaism, women have been governed by a set of laws delineated in the Talmud that encode her inferiority (Renzetti and Curran 1989:268-272). The Qur'an also hold men to be a degree above women and explicitly states that "[m]en are in charge of women because God has made one to excel over the other and because they spend their wealth" (quoted in Haddad 1985:294). Christianity is unambiguous on the relative status of men and women. Although there are passages that praise women and their virtues, the underlying tenets espouse women's inferiority. "Let the wives be subject to their husbands as to the Lord; because a husband is head of the wife, just as Christ is the head of the church, being himself savior of the body. But just as the Church is subject to Christ, so also let wives be to their husbands in all things" (Ephesians 5:22-24).

The effects of these teachings on women's everyday lives are profound. Primarily, it sends the sacralized message that women are innately inferior to men. Having laid this groundwork, it is not a great leap to exclude females from enjoying the same social and economic mobility as men do. Ways in which Rastafarian men and women have internalized religious beliefs are palpable.

The Rastafarian belief that men are the heads of households is held by women and men alike. Although a number of informants stated that they were equal to men, they also felt that men were the natural heads of households and the spiritual leaders of the movement. Rasta women, like most women everywhere, base these beliefs, in part, on the scriptures while failing to realize that the scriptures themselves were created and interpreted by men who, therefore, have the ability to write in their privileged status. Even though the majority view supported male privilege, there were several women who added their own variation to this theme as is indicated from the following interview excerpts.

Rw 1 (Rasta woman 1): It's Rasta women that's holdin' the money now. And we refuse to be treated like footstools because it's not working.

Rw 2: [In order for women to remove the impediments in front of them, they] must be clearer in their minds, having plans for their lives. Looking forward more confident. Women not requiring to have a medium between them and their God, talking to God directly. We don't need nobody to talk to God for us. Because God listens to everybody who call upon him—he, she, or it. So I mean to say that women need to take our destiny in our hands. We have to take the responsibility for that because there were many slaves who never wanted slavery to end.

Most of these views, which represent the more radical segment among Rasta women, are held by women who are relatively economically independent. One could safely say that there is an inverse relationship between the level of economic independence and the degree to which women accept the notion of male privilege (Sen and Grown 1987; Safa 1986; Gill 1984). Given the relative state of impoverishment of Jamaican women compared to men, most women are either wholly or partially dependent on male partners. Notwithstanding the exceptions, many women defer to men regardless of their economic standing (Douglass 1992).

During interviews with members of the Buba Shanti, the most orthodox of Rastafarian groups,[4] the influence of Christian dogma on reifying the privileged position of men was clear. In response to my question regarding women preachers, a male gave the following response: "A woman can't speak to the congregation. You can't have women preachers going up on a pulpit . . . her nakedness could be displayed. The man creates everything so he must be the head. That's why the world is like it is because women are doing too many things that she shouldn't be doing. It is an abomination for woman to do things pertaining to the man and vice versa." The notion that "man creates everything" is an interesting one which also has its basis in religious ideology. The closeness with which Rastas adhere to religious teachings is demonstrated by how similar the above testimony is to Corinthians 14:34-35: "Let your women keep silent in the churches, for they are not permitted to speak; but they are to be submissive. If they want to learn something, let them ask their own husbands at home, for it is shameful for women to speak in church." This passage reflects the patriarchal nature of Christianity in at least two regards. It *assumes* that a woman will have a husband and that her position is inferior to the degree that she should be voiceless. As is the case with any form of oppression if it is to be successful, the victims often internalize beliefs that legitimate their own subordination. In a general sense, this is also true of Jamaican Rastafarians. This internalization is most clear in the notion that women are unclean.

FEMALE AS NATURALLY POLLUTED

The idea of female pollution is ubiquitous among human societies (Ullrich 1992; Meigs 1991; Buckley and Gottleib 1988). Menstruation and childbirth are processes that ostensibly pollute women, making them untouchable during these periods. These beliefs are pervasiveness, in both western and nonwestern societies (Faithorn 1975:127-140; Rubin 1975; Hyman 1976:105, 110-111; Uta 1990: 192-193 [quoting *Paedagogus* II, 33,2]; Crumbley 1992:505-522), and have allowed men to point to the most common and natural female attributes in order to justify women's subordination.

The Christian religion also vilifies women by linking them closely with sex and, in turn, linking sex with sin (Bullough, Shelton, and Slavin 1988:97-101; Ranke-Heinemann 1990:192-93). The notion of the virgin birth of Jesus Christ reflects this conceptualization, the logic being that if Mary is pure, then all other women are tainted. The idea of the virgin birth, along with the power of God to bestow "rebirth" upon his disciples symbolically transfers the creative power of reproduction away from women and confers it to men. The Bible is also explicit regarding the unclean nature of women during menstruation and child birth (Leviticus 15:19f.). Christian beliefs that support the notion of women as polluted serve the purpose of denying women opportunities for equal participation in the household and in public spheres (see Steinfels 1992; Cornell 1992).

Given the embeddedness of Christian beliefs among Rastafarians, it is not surprising that women are considered unclean during menstruation and that this serves as the basis for their containment. The Buba Shanti group of Rastas are the most strict in this regard. Menstruating Buba Shanti women are not allowed to cook for other members of their group; they must be secluded from other men and non-menstruating women of the group; and they must not engage in sexual intercourse. Most Rasta women commented that they abided by these practices as much for a reprieve from household tasks as for the belief in their ideological foundation. While these rules theoretically apply to all Rastafarian women, most Buba Shanti women live in a circumscribed community and are not as free to come and go.

The significance of the rules of purdah and pollution are profound and far-reaching. The equation of woman as polluted automatically precludes opportunities for participation in activities outside of the home, given that such endeavors would always be subject to interruptions of childbirth or menstruation.

Buba Shanti women, for example, cannot be preachers based on their ability to menstruate. Neither can women enter the church when they are menstruating. The fact that women are also considered polluted seven days before and seven days after her period is a clear indication of the degree of their containment.

LANGUAGE AND POPULAR MEDIA

As stated above, the oppression of women is actualized in every sphere of society. In order for political-economic oppression to be successful, there must be a superstructure that supports and sustains the material conditions of inequality. In addition to religious rhetoric, everyday Rasta language and musical lyrics perpetuate women's subordinate status.

On the face of things, it would seem that there is a complementary language that defines male and female Rastafarians. Females can be referred to as empresses or queens, just as males are called princes or kings or king man. This complementarity breaks down given the third term for females, "daughters." Females of all ages are colloquially referred to as such and are rarely called queens or empresses in everyday parlance. The obvious question becomes why there is no complementary term, i.e., "sons," for male Rastafarians. Unfortunately, the answer is equally obvious. If men are naturally superior to women, then this must be reflected in their language—the most important element in the creation of cultural ideology.

In Jamaican society, in general, women are also depicted in stereotypical roles in music and various forms of advertisements (Antrobus and Gorgon 1984: 120; Henry and Wilson 1975:193-194; Harrison 1988:114). From calypso (Elder 1968:23-41), to ska and rock steady women are treated as sexual tools to be used for the pleasure of men or as pawns who are expected to acquiesce to men's sexual commands. Ska performer Prince Buster exemplifies this attitude in his Ten Commandments where he sings of them having to remember to honor and obey, at all times and in every situation, every desire and caprice.

In their study of female images in Jamaican music Anderson and Langley (1988) found that women were portrayed as housewomen (many women in households were not wives) whose primary role was to cater to their men's needs. "Women who do not elect or who reject the role of housewomen are portrayed as lacking in substance, as shallow, as superficial" (ibid:4). The alternative stereotype is to depict women as sex objects, without souls and without personalities. The authors explain that to be an object "means, among others, to be made a thing without a will, to be totally controllable" (ibid:13). These values, along with the notion of women's dependency, are also depicted in reggae music.

Although reggae is the medium that has popularized Rasta in many parts of the world, it is an expression that not all Rastafarians accept. The Buba Shanti, for example, do not consider it to be an expression of Rastafari. The following commentary from a Rasta woman (who is not Buba Shanti) is particularly interesting insofar as it highlights her perceptions of women's images in reggae compared to those of her mate.

Rw 3: I think the Europeans just want to see the Black race laughed at according to the things that they promote things that are not edifying to our young, singing so many derogatory things about women. When you start to underrate the woman of this world, I think you are doomed

Rm: I think it's just one aspect of reggae music.

Rw: Yes, but they are playing upon it.

Rm: I think you should tell her [the interviewer] that we still have conscious reggae music whose message hasn't changed from Bob Marley.

Rw: Yah, man, you have that, but what they are promoting now, the most popular person now in reggae, Shaba Ranks, he's not saying much. He's even leading the youths astray more than anything else. And you have great reggae artists who do not gain that popularity because of social status here.

To me I don't see many Rasta women in music and I don't know why because you have talented Rasta women. I've traveled quite a bit going to different shows. And of all the shows I've been on, maybe I might be the only Rasta woman there, sometimes I'm the only woman. I think that's why the music is getting out of hand because we don't have a lot of women even coming out and saying that we don't appreciate what they're saying about us.

Reggae music has provided social commentary which speaks to a positive African identity and social justice for oppressed people. As is true for other music that ostensibly favors social transformation, reggae also perpetuates female images of passiveness, domesticity, and sexual objectivity (Campbell 1990:199; Silvera 1980). Jamaican music is not unique in this regard and is joined by other forms, for example, African American rap music, purportedly a revolutionary genre, which is noted for its misogynist messages (Dyson 1989:45-50; Roberts 1991:141-152).

DRESS AND HAIR AS SYMBOLIC CONTROL

The physical appearance of Rastafarians is heavily influenced by Biblical teachings. One of the ways that Rastas embody these teachings is in the wearing of dreadlocks. "All the days of the vow of this separation there shall no razor come upon his head: until the days be fulfilled, in the which he separateth himself unto the Lord, he shall be holy, and shall let the locks of the hair of his head grow" (Numbers 6:5).

Most Rasta men and women wear dreadlocks in keeping with this passage and as an expression of their African identity. Interestingly, it is only women who are expected (in the case of the Buba Shanti, required) to cover their hair in public.

Rules regarding head coverings also demonstrate that Rastafari does not offer the same freedom to women as it does to men. Even though similar prescriptions existed in pre-capitalist and pre-Christian societies, Christian teachings act as a validation for women covering their hair. The longevity and ubiquitousness of this practice is evident in the promulgations of Gratian, a twelfth-century Benedictine monk, who was a strong advocate of women's subordinate position: "Man certainly must not cover his head, because he is image and reflection of God, but woman must cover her head because she is neither reflection nor image of God. They must do this as a sign of their subjection to authority and because sin came into the world through them. Because of original sin they must show themselves to be submissive" (Gratian as quoted in Raming 1976:38).

Likewise, the division of the sexes by dress codes is clearly delineated in the Christian Bible. "The woman shall not wear that which pertaineth to the man, neither shall a man put on a women's garment: for all to do so are an abomination unto the LORD thy GOD" (Deuteronomy 22:5).

All Rasta women recognize these codes to some degree and hold them up as beacons to describe what differentiates them from other Jamaican women.

Rw 4: You're supposed to wear your dress below your knee. You're supposed to wear no sleeveless clothes. Your armpit is not supposed to show. We no wear pants, we no wear shorts, you know. In the good old ancient way, that's the way we dress. In ancient livity [way of life], you cover your head, some people cover their bodies and it comes way down to their ankles. You can see the mark on I 'n I.[5] When you see a Rasta dawta, you know she's a Rasta because of the way she adorn herself.

The vast majority of Rasta women wear dresses that are ankle or calf length. Those who wear slacks wear those made of African cloth and design. Although most Rasta women felt that they should follow these dress codes, there is an emerging segment, as indicated in the interview excerpt below, that see the need for more flexibility. "At the end of the day, I'm not fighting for equal opportunity with nobody. Equal to who? I'm fighting for my freedom. And the first step in my freedom is freedom of choice. . . . So that me no want nobody tell me how to wear my hair, how to wear my clothes or how to do my body."

These aspects of Rasta women's life may seem trivial without an understanding of the ways symbolic expression serves to code relationships within society. Dress codes can be viewed as one of the many symbolic ways that females are turned into women and as an example of the sex/gender system which exaggerates the actual biological differences between males and females. That is, "[g]ender is a socially imposed division of the sexes" (Rubin 1975:179), a characterization of the sexes" which "arise[s] out of something other than a nonexistent "natural" opposition. Far from being an expression of natural differences, exclusive gender identity is the suppression of natural similarities" (ibid: 179-180).

The question of dress is an important one because dress is a symbolic gesture that expresses people's status relative to other members of society, and in the case of religious groups, in relationship to their god. While it is common for some observers to elide dress rules as only aesthetically meaningful and culturally relative, such perspectives are merely descriptive and do not add to analytical approaches to this topic. It is more useful to ask why there are rules for dress and head coverings for females and none for males.

CONCLUSION

The interpretation of cultural relativity has become a shield that prevents meaningful cross-cultural study of ways in which hierarchy and dominance are created and maintained. In an effort to strike a culturally neutral pose, many western anthropologists, and even (or especially!) some feminists, propose a laissez faire policy on the critique of other cultures. This is an unfortunate position, since its motivation derives from a kind of imperialist nostalgia (Rosaldo 1989:68-87) and fails to recognize the structural similarities in the global oppression of women.

Serious attempts at analyzing this oppression, require a clear definition of dominance and how it is actualized in everyday life. At the same time, there is a need to clearly articulate the areas where male domination occurs. What I have tried to point out in this chapter is that male domination is pervasive in all spheres of society. More specifically, we can locate it in economic relations, where women are more often unemployed, underpaid, and, therefore, dependent on men for economic support. Although a large percentage of women in Jamaica are heads of households, this confers more of a burden on them as sole caretakers of house and children, than it does power or freedom. Another locus of male power is in cultural and social arenas, as well as in physical control over women.

Violence against women is pervasive in Jamaica (Leo-Rhynie 1987:30; Jones 1987:30-37; Phillips 1987:39) as it is in other societies (Bopp and Verdalis 1987; Cross 1982; Russell 1992; Singer 1992:170-176). Christianity has a particularly powerful effect on rules regarding women's status, as well as violence against women (Fortune 1994:109-118; Matter 1994: 83-90; Fischer 1994:75-82), given the special and sacred position religious doctrine holds. Rastas have incorporated the worst elements of both African and European societies in their abuse and marginalization of women (Campbell 1990:199-

200). Pre-colonized and colonized African societies ritually denigrated women qua women in order to mystify and denigrate her creative powers and label her polluted based on her natural biological processes and functions. European society, through cultural mores that are embedded in society inside and outside of religion, has its own sexist traditions.

Unfortunately, it has been women who have been admonished to forgive "seventy times seven" (Matthew 18:22). "Forgiving and valuing suffering are not effective strategies for an oppressed group to force social change. These activities reinforce existing power disparities and encourage the disempowered to accept their real-world disadvantages as spiritual advantages" (Becker 1994:10). In order to assess ways in which this control affects the lives of Rastafarian women, and women everywhere, and how religion fits into this discussion, it is first necessary to understand that religion is ideology. Religious texts, and interpretations of these texts, are most often written and controlled by men who create mythologies to fit their own needs. This state of affairs has had debilitating effects on the position of women for centuries, but is even more curious when we look at the effects of sexual hierarchy in an environment ostensibly concerned with radical transformation and development.

If we consider Rastafari and other Diaspora African nationalist movements, such as the Nation of Islam, liberation appears to be the preserve of men, while women are relegated to second-class status. Rastafarians have a great deal to offer the diaspora African community based on its emphasis on images that reflect a people's history; proposals for links with Africa as a spiritual and psychological basis for identity; and a general ethos that promulgates natural food ways and natural living (Lake 1985). In spite of these ideals Rastafarians have not found it necessary to view women as co-determiners in their quest for liberation.

On a broader level, Jamaica's process of political-economic development is attenuated by the subordination and marginalization of women. If development is measured by the control of resources by the people and by equal distribution, then women must be co-producers and co-determiners in such a society. In a society where women are economically dependent, discriminated against in the job market, and degraded in religious and popular culture, development will continue to signify a larger GNP without concern for equality and self-determination for all of its members.

If Rastafari is to continue as a viable force within the Jamaican populace, a force that proposes fundamental change in the relations of power, then it is incumbent upon Rasta men and women to be revolutionary in thought and in deed. Whether this is possible given the patriarchal nature of Christianity and the Rastafarian movement is questionable. As one Rasta informant averred: "Rasta woman is going to have to find a path which links her with all her sisters in genuine sisterhood and relates more to the brothers as co-travellers and not the dominated and the dominator."

NOTES

1. In the history of the Caribbean, there have only been two women prime ministers, Eugenia Charles of Dominica and Maria Liberia-Peters of Netherlands Antilles.

2. The argument is often made that polygyny allows for more efficient agricultural and domestic organization.

While this may be the case, this explanation begs the question as to why women did not normally have multiple husbands for the same purpose, or why there were not other ways to engage in communal production.

3. The findings discussed in this paper pertain only to my research in Jamaica. There are also Rastafarians in other Caribbean islands, the United States, and Canada, as well as other parts of the African Diaspora, whose views and practices may not be represented here.

4. Other Rastafarian groups in Jamaica include the Twelve Tribes and the Nyabingi. Based on informants testimonies and my observations, the Twelve Tribes is the largest of the three groups. There are many Rastas who are not affiliated with any particular group.

5. Rastafarian vernacular contains a large number of "I" words, in which "I" is used as a prefix before many words, for example, I-tal for vital. I and I [usually articulated as I 'n I], refers to the unity of the speakers with the most High (Jah) and with his fellowmen. I and I simply refers to "me" and my God—one "I" is the little I and the other the Big I. The little I or me refers to the lower self of man, to his body and its ego, that part of him which is born and will die. . . . The Big I is the everliving, immortal or "true" self that was never born and can never die. It is the spirit of divinity and holiness residing in the depth of each (Forsythe 1983:85).

BIBLIOGRAPHY

Anderson, Beverly, and Winston Langley. "Women as Depicted in Music in Jamaica." Caribbean Studies Association, XIV Annual Conference, Barbados, 1988.

Antrobus, Peggy, and Lorna Gordon. "The English-Speaking Caribbean: A Journey in the Making." In *Sisterhood Is Global: The International Women's Movement Anthology*. pp. 118-126, Robin Morgan (ed.). Garden City N.Y.: Anchor Books/Doubleday, 1984.

Austin-Broos, Diane J. "Pentacostals and Rastafarians: Cultural, Political, and Gender Relations of Two Religious Movements." *Social and Economic Studies*. 36(4):1-39, 1987.

Barrett, Leonard. *The Rastafarians—Dreadlocks of Jamaica*. Kingston, Jamaica: Sangsters, 1977.

Bart, Pauline, and Eileen Mora. *Violence Against Women. The Bloody Footprints*. Sage Publications, 1993.

Becker, Mary "Religion and Equality for Women." Paper presented at the Law and

Society Meeting, Phoenix, Arizona, June 1994.

Beckford, George, and Michael Witter. *Small Garden . . . Bitter Weed. Struggle and Change in Jamaica.* London: Zed Press, 1980.

Beers, William. *Women and Sacrifice: Male Narcissism and the Psychology of Religion.* Detroit: Wayne State University Press, 1992.

Bolles, Lynn. "Kitchens Hit by Priorities: Employed Working-Class Jamaican Women Confront the IMF." In *Men, Women, and the International Division of Labor.* June Nash and Marcia Patricia Fernandez-Kelly (eds.), pp. 138-160. Albany: State University of New York Press, 1983.

Bopp, William J., and James J. Vardalis. *Crimes Against Women.* Springfield, Ill.: Charles C. Thomas, 1987.

Brain, J. "Symbolic Rebirth: The Mwali Rite among the Luguru of Eastern Tanzania." *Africa.* 48(2):176-188, 1978.

Buckley, Thomas, and Alma Gottleib. *Blood Magic: The Anthropology of Menstruation.* Berkeley: University of California Press, 1988.

Bullough, Vern, Brenda Shelton, and Sarah Slavin. *The Subordinate Sex: A History of Attitudes Toward Women.* Athens: University of Georgia Press, 1988.

Campbell, Horace. *Rasta and Resistance. From Marcus Garvey to Walter Rodney.* Trenton, N.J.: African World Press, 1990.

Chevannes, Barry. "The Rastafari and Urban Youth." In *Perspectives on Jamaica in the Seventies.* Carl Stone and Aggrey Brown (eds.), pp. 292-422, Kingston: Jamaica Publishing House, 1981.

Chevannes, Barry. 'Towards a New Approach.' *New West Indian Guide.* 64 (3 and 4), pp. 127-148, 1990.

Clarke, John H. and Amy Jaques Garvey. *Marcus Garvey and the Vision of Africa.* New York: Vintage Books, 1974.

Cornell, George. 1992. "Bishops May Table Policy on Women." *Iowa City Press Citizen.* November 18, 1992.

Cross, Phillis Old Dog. "Sexual Abuse, A New Threat to the Native American Woman: An Overview," *Listening Post: A Periodical of the Mental Health Programs of Indian Health Services* (April), 6(2):18, 1982.

Crumbley, Deidre H. "Impurity and Power: Women in Aladura Churches." *Africa: Journal of the International African Institute.* 62(4):505-522, 1992.

Deere, Carmen, Peggy Antrobus, Lynn Bolles, Edwin Melendez, Peter Phillips, Marcia Rivera, and Helen Safa. *In the Shadows of the Sun.* Boulder, Colo.: Westview Press, 1990.

Douglass, Lisa. *The Power of Sentiment. Love, Hierarchy, and the Jamaican Family Elite.* Boulder, Colo.: Westview Press, 1992.

Dunfee, Susan Nelson. *Beyond Servanthood. Christianity and the Liberation of Women.* Lanham, M.D.: University Press of America, 1989.

Dyson, Michael. "The Culture of Hip-Hop." *Zeta Magazine.* pp. 45-50, 1989.

Elder, J.D. "The Male/Female Conflict in Calypso." *Caribbean Quarterly.* September, 14(3):23-41, 1968.

Etienne, Mona, and Eleanor Leacock. *Women and Colonization.* New York: Praeger Publishers, 1980.

Faithhorn, Elizabeth. "The Concept of Pollution among the Kafe of the Papua New Guinea Highlands." In *Toward an Anthropology of Women*. Rayna Reiter (ed.), pp. 127-140. New York: Monthly Review Press, 1975.

Fischer, Irmgard "'Go and Suffer Oppression!' said God's Messenger to Hagar," In *Violence Against Women*. Elisabeth Schussler and Mary S. Copeland (eds.), pp. 75-82. London: SCM Press, 1994.

Forsythe, Dennis. *Rastafari: For the Healing of the Nation*. Kingston, Jamaica: Zaika Publications, 1983.

Fortune, Marie M. "Clergy Misconduct: Sexual Abuse in the Ministery," In *Violence Against Women*. Elisabeth Schussler and Mary S. Copeland (eds.), pp. 109-118. London: SCM Press, 1994.

Garvey, Amy Jacques. *Philosophy and Opinions of Marcus Garvey*. London: Frank Cass and Company, Ltd. New York: Atheneum, 1967, 1968.

Gill, Margaret. "Women, Work and Development: Barbados 1946-1970" In *Women and Work*. Cave Hill, Barbados: Institute of Social and Economic Research, UWI. WICP, Vol. 4, 1984.

Goldenberg, Naomi R. *Changing of the gods: Feminism and the End of Traditional Religions*. Boston: Beacon Press, 1979.

Haddad, Y. Y. "Islam, Women and Revolution in Twentieth-Century Arab Thought," pp. 275-306. In Y. Y. Haddad, and E. B. Findly (eds.). *Women, Religion and Social Change*. Albany: State University of New York Press, 1985.

Hafkin, Nancy J., and Edna G. Bay. *Women in Africa*. Stanford, Cal.: Stanford University Press, 1976.

Harrison, Faye. "Women in Jamaica's Urban Informal Economy: Insights From A Kingston Slum." *Nieuwe West-Indische Gids*, 62(3&4):103-128, 1988.

Henn, Jeanne Koopman *The Material Basis of Sexism: A Mode of Production Analysis with African Examples*. Working Papers in African Studies. No. 119. Boston University: African Studies Center, 1986.

Henry, Frances, and Pamela Wilson. "The Status of Women in Caribbean Societies: An Overview of Their Social, Economic and Sexual Roles." *Social and Economic Studies*. 24(2):165-198, 1975.

Hyman, Paula. "The Other Half: Women in the Jewish Tradition." In *The Jewish Woman: New Perspectives*. New York: Schocken, 1976.

Jones, Angella. "Battered Women." *Status of Women in the Caribbean*. Report of Regional Seminar Held at Wyndham Hotel, New Kingston, Jamaica, pp. 31-37, December 10-11, 1987.

Lake, Obiagele. *Cultural Determinants of Breast Feeding Among Jamaican Rastafarians*. Master's Thesis, Cornell University: Ithaca, New York, 1985.

Lake, Obiagele. Interviews with Rastafarian Men in Kingston, Jamaica, 1992, 1993.

Lake, Obiagele. "The Many Voices of Rastafarian Women." *New West Indian Guide*. 68(3&4) [In Press], 1994.

Leo-Ryhnie, Elsa. "The Role of Women in Caribbean Society." *Status of Women in the Caribbean*. Report of Regional Seminar Held at Wyndham Hotel, New Kingston, Jamaica. December 10-11, 1987.

Levitt, Kari Polany. *The Origins and Consequences of Jamaica's Debt Crisis. 1970-1990.* Mona, Jamaica: Consortium Graduate School of Social Sciences, 1991.

Lewis, Rupert. *Marcus Garvey: Anti-Colonial Champion.* Trenton, N.J.: Africa World Press, 1988.

Llaloo, Sister. "Rastawoman as Equal." *Yard Roots.* 1(1):7, 1981.

Martin, Tony. *Race First. Ideology and Organizational Struggles of Marcus Garvey and the Universal Negro Improvement Association.* Westport, Conn.: Greenwood Press, 1976.

Martin, Tony. *The Pan-African Connection: From Slavery to Garvey and Beyond.* Dover, Mass.: New Marcus Garvey Library, 1983.

Matter, E. Ann. "Ecclesiastical Violence: Witches and Heretics." In *Violence Against Women.* Elisabeth Schussler and Mary S. Copeland (eds.), pp. 83-90. London: SCM Press, 1994.

Meigs, Anna S. *Food, Sex and Pollution. A New Guinea Religion.* New Brunswick, N. J.: Rutgers University Press, 1991.

Nettleford, Rex. *Identity, Race, and Protest in Jamaica.* New York: William Morrow, 1972.

Obbo, Christine. *African Women. Their Struggle for Economic Independence.* London: Zed Press, 1980.

Okonjo, Kamene. "The Dual-Sex Political System in Operation: Igbo Women and Community Politics in Midwestern Nigeria." In *Women in Africa.* Nancy J. Hafkin and Edna G. Bay (eds.), pp. 45-58. Stanford, Cal.: Stanford University Press, 1976.

Owens, Joseph. *Dread. The Rastafarians of Jamaica.* Jamaica: Montrose Printery, 1976.

Parker, Rebecca. "For God So Loved the World?" In *Christianity, Patriarchy, and Abuse: A Feminist Critique.* Joanne Carlson Brown and Carole R. Bohm (eds.), 1989.

Phillips, Hilary. *Status of Women in the Caribbean.* Report of Regional Seminar Held at Wyndham Hotel, New Kingston, Jamaica, pp. 38-59, December 10-11, 1987.

Price, Richard. *Maroon Societies: Rebel Slave Communities in the Americas.* New York: Anchor Books, 1973.

Raming, Ida. *The Exclusion of Women from the Priesthood.* Metuchen, N. J.: The Scarecrow Press, 1976.

Ranke-Heinemann, Uta, *Eunuchs for Heaven: The Catholic Church and Sexuality.* England: A. Deutsch, 1990.

Renzetti, Claire, and Daniel J. Curran. *Women, Men and Society. The Sociology of Gender.* Boston, Mass.: Allyn and Bacon, 1989.

Roberts, Robin. Fall "Music Videos, Performance and Resistance: Feminist Rappers." *Journal of Popular Culture.* 25:141-152, 1991.

Robertson, Claire, and Martin Klein. *Women and Slavery in Africa.* Madison: University of Wisconsin Press, 1989.

Rodriguez, Jeanette. *Our Lady of Guadelupe. Faith and Empowerment among Mexican-American Women.* Austin: University of Texas, 1994.

Rosaldo, Renato. *Culture and Truth: The Remaking of Social Analysis.* Stanford, Cal.: Stanford University Press, 1989.

Rowe, Maureen. "The Woman in Rastafari." *Caribbean Quarterly Monograph.*

University of West Indies: United Co-operative Printers, 1985.

Rubin, Gayle. "The Traffic in Women: Notes on the 'Political Economy' of Sex." In *Toward an Anthropology of Women.* Rayna R. Reiter (ed.), pp. 157-210. New York: Monthly Review Press, 1975.

Ruether, Rosemary Radford. *Religion and Sexism: Images of Women in the Jewish and Christian Traditions.* New York: Simon and Schuster, 1974.

Russell, Diana E. H. *A Selected Bibliography on Male Violence Against Women and Girls in South Africa.* Cape Town, South Africa: Institute of Criminology, University of Cape Town, 1992.

Safa, Helen. "Economic Autonomy and Sexual Equality in Caribbean Society." Social and Economic Studies (Special Issue: *Women in the Caribbean* (June) Pt. 2; 35:2, 1986.

Sen, G., and Grown, C. *Development, Crises, and Alternative Visions: Third World Women's Perspectives.* New York: Monthly Review Press, 1987.

Senior, Olive. *Working Miracles. Women's Lives in the English-Speaking Caribbean.* Cave Hill, Barbados: Institute of Social and Economic Research, University of the West Indies, 1991.

Silvera, Makeda Patricia. *Sunday Gleaner Magazine,* February 10, 1980.

Singer, Beverly R. "American Indian Women Killing: A Tewa Native Woman's Perspective." In *Femicide, The Politics of Woman Killing.* Jill Radford and Diana Russell (eds.), pp. 170-176. New York: Twayne Publishers, 1992.

Spaulding, Gary. "MP Blasts Status of JA Women." *The Gleaner* (Kingston, Jamaica). July 15, 1993.

Standing, Guy. *Unemployment and Female Labor.* New York: St. Martin's Press, 1981.

Statistical Institute of Jamaica. *Population Census (Final Count).* Kingston, Jamaica: STATIN, 1982.

Steinfels, Peter. "Pastoral Letter on Women's Role Fails in Vote of Catholic Bishops." *New York Times.* November 19, 1992.

Steady, Filomena Chioma. "African Feminism: A Worldwide Perspective." In *Women in Africa and the African Diaspora.* Rosalyn Terborg-Penn, Sharon Harley and Andrea Benton Rushing (eds.), pp. 3-24. Washington, D.C.: Howard University Press, 1989.

Sudarkasa, Niara. "The Status of Women in Indigenous African Societies." In *Women in Africa and the African Diaspora.* Rosalyn Terborg-Penn, Sharon Harley and Andrea Benton Rushing (eds.), pp. 25-42. Washington, D.C.: Howard University Press, 1989.

Turner, Jonathan, Royce Singleton, Jr., and David Musick. *Oppression. A History of Black-White Relation in America.* Chicago: Nelson-Hall, 1984.

Turner, Mary. *Slaves and Missionaries: The Disintegration of Jamaican Slave Society, 1987-1834.* Urbana: University of Illinois, 1982

Ullrich, H. E. "Menstrual Taboos Among Hvik Brahmin Women: A Study of Ritual Change." *Sex Roles: A Journal of Research.* (January), 26(1-2):19-40, 1992.

Waters, Anita M. *Race, Class, and Political Symbols. Rastafari and Reggae in Jamaican Politics.* New Brunswick, N. J.: Transaction Books, 1985.

Yawney, Carol D. "Dread Wasteland: Rastafarian Ritual in West Kingston, Jamaica." In *Anthropological Investigations in the Caribbean,* Basil Hedrich, Jeanette Stephens, Carol Yawney, and Frank Manning (eds.), pp. 90-111. Greeley, Colo.: University of Northern Colorado Press, 1984.

11

Rastafari Perceptions of Self and Symbolism

William R. Van De Berg

The present study was an attempt to understand Rastafari perceptions of self and symbolism. Specifically the project aimed to understand the meaning that Rastafari and its associated symbolism had to the individual adherent. The issue of Rastafari identity was crucial to this study because members offered varying interpretations of the meaning of symbols associated with Rastafari, while adhering to certain central themes in the Rastafari belief system.

Respondents were chosen from the Triad House of Rastafari, a local church of Rastafari, and interviewed using McCracken's (1988) long interview format, in which in-depth interviews are conducted with a small group of respondents. Although they were considered by group members to be peripheral to an overall understanding of Rastafari, theses symbols of Rastafari adherence (such as hairstyles, diet, taboos, dress, mannerisms, etc.) were observed to have importance in the presentation and maintenance of the adherent's identity.

Members made a distinction between those who display the physical symbols of Rastafari identity and those who have internalized the deeper meaning of these symbols. Thus the project tried to understand the interaction and multi-vocality of symbols that are used to represent the adoption of a particular ideology or theology.

SETTING

My field work for the current project was carried out from May of 1995 to May of 1996 with the Triad House of Rastafari (THOR), a group of Rastafari indigenous to the Piedmont-Triad area of North Carolina. The THOR hold formal Sabbath worship services every Saturday at 6:00 p.m. at their church on North Liberty Street in Winston-Salem, North Carolina.

The city of Winston-Salem is located in the Piedmont-Triad area of North Carolina (United States), which is comprised of the cities of Winston-Salem, High Point, and Greensboro. According to the 1990 United States Census of the population, approximately 59% of the population is white and 39% is of African-American descent. There are more whites in the area than African-Americans, and there are significant differences in the socioeconomic conditions of the two groups. In 1989, the per capita income for whites in Winston-Salem was $20,203, whereas it was only $9,036 for African-Americans (1990 United States Census of Population and Housing). Additionally, African-Americans in the area have a higher rate of unemployment (7.4 %) than do whites (2.2%) (Ibid). A larger percentage of the total population living below the poverty line are African-Americans (25% as opposed to 7% for whites) (ibid). Thus, it is out of this disadvantaged socio-environmental context that the THOR arose.

The businesses in the area surrounding the THOR church consist of two meat markets, a biker bar, a bank, and an Army surplus store, all of which stand in stark contrast to the ideals of the Triad House of Rastafari. Thus, when the Overseeker (the group's leader) tells the members of the THOR that Babylon is right outside the door, he is speaking fairly literally of the surrounding businesses which support behavioral patterns that are not endorsed by the Rastafari (such as drinking alcohol, sexual promiscuity, and the eating of any type of flesh).

MEMBERSHIP

Although the majority of the members reside in the Piedmont-Triad area, a number of members live elsewhere, such as Durham, North Carolina, and Atlanta, Georgia. These out-of-town members often make the trip to the church to attend its Saturday evening services and are always in attendance at all large functions of the church.

The THOR is comprised of approximately 30 active to semi-active members (20 male; 10 female), although there are many non-attending "members" who are considered "AWOL." Most members are between the ages of 18 and 38. Members who have children (approximately 4-5 families) bring them to the services as well. The children, who are both male (n = 4) and female (n = 3), are all between the ages of 2 and 16.

Members of the THOR are primarily African-American, although there are two (one male and one female) Caucasian members who regularly attend and several guests and associate members who attend services intermittently. All of the leadership hierarchy, which is comprised of the Overseeker, the Pastor, and three deacons, are African-American males. However, this is not to say that females (nor Caucasians) do not have positions of status in the THOR. The treasurer is the Overseeker's wife, and the secretary is a Caucasian female who has been with the group since its inception.

HISTORY

The history of the THOR extends back approximately three years, when the individual who was to become the Overseeker began to feel a strong need for a united Rastafari church in the Triad area. As the Overseeker met more people who were interested in the development of an organized church of Rastafari, a small core of individuals began to develop around him . From the dedication of these individuals the THOR was created. At first the meetings were informal affairs, generally consisting of a series of cookouts and "reasoning sessions" These 'reasoning sessions' involved an intense discussion of an array of topics that were of interest to both parties in the interaction. During a reasoning session, individuals state their opinion on the topic and then relate this to their interpretation of a corresponding Biblical passage, as well as engage in open dialogue on the subject with the other participants in the session.

However, the group holds as its official date of origin July 23, 1993, which commemorates the first annual Oneness Celebration held in Washington Park, Winston-Salem, North Carolina. The Oneness Celebration is comprised of the Rastafari gathering at the park and engaging in drum and chant sessions as well as the females serving Rastafari vegetarian foods to those who attend.

During this time, the nucleus of the group was comprised of approximately seven individuals, five of whom still currently attend the church services. The new THOR then took a road trip down to Myrtle Beach, where they became involved in a rescue of a drowning child (who unfortunately died shortly after he reached the hospital). The members felt that: "From all the spiritual vibes that happened then, we thought it was very important to form a leadership organization, and the leadership organization became the Abyssinian Assembly of the Living God. Jah gave me like a whole page of names."

The Abyssinian Assembly of the Living God [AALG], which is the umbrella organization under which the THOR operates, holds both nonprofit and tax exempt status. As the AALG grows larger and new churches are opened, the new churches will become new chapters of the AALG. The Overseeker explained:

See, right now we are functioning in Atlanta and are trying to put together a house in Durham. We really need to because we have so many members of the THOR that live in Durham. Whatever the (local church's) name pops up to be, it'll be an AALG. AALG holds the non-profit vibrations that holds the tax exempt vibrations. Everything else is chartered right under it and falls right into those vibes. Any charity organizations that we start, like say we start a drug rehab, it'll fall under the AALG.

Since its inception, the church has grown in membership substantially. After the Oneness Celebration, the THOR began to hold services every Saturday at 6:00 p.m. at the home of the Overseeker. However, the group eventually began to grow too large for the Overseeker's house to accommodate, necessitating a change in the THOR's structure. It was decided by the Overseeker that the THOR needed new accommodations, which were eventually to be found by the Overseeker and his wife one day while shopping near their home in Ogburn Station. The large building was eventually leased with option to buy by the church. This building is where the THOR currently resides, meeting every Saturday at 6:00 p.m.

LEADERSHIP STRUCTURE

The AALG is a leadership organization which is organized around a central head figure, known as the Chief Elder. The position requires that the candidate be a presiding elder of one of the seven regional branches of the AALG for seven years. Since the THOR was founded less than seven years ago, no one in the THOR is eligible for the position yet. The THOR and the AALG are currently led by the Overseeker (or the Alpha House King) and his wife, the Omega House Queen. Because the Overseeker is the only presiding house elder, he is the only individual in line for the position of Chief Elder, which is not currently being occupied. The Overseeker's primary duties are to act as the organizational head whose purpose is to create other ministries and houses of Rastafari, in addition to tending to the organizational needs of the THOR and giving sermons at the Sabbath services.

The next individual in the leadership hierarchy is the Pastor of the THOR, who was appointed to his position by the Overseeker soon after the church was formed. The Pastor is the local ceremonial head, usually introducing all of the individuals who are giving sermons and lectures to the THOR during services. Additionally, the Pastor often gives sermons himself and oversees the audio recording of the Sabbath services.

In addition to the Overseeker and the Pastor, the THOR has a number of middle-level authorities known as Deacons, who are male elders of the group responsible for helping the Overseeker and Pastor in their duties, as well as providing guidance to the members who require assistance in their spiritual journey.

A number of other offices are held by less experienced members of the group. Positions such as Minister of Information, Drum Leader and the Overseeker's Armor Bearer. These positions are occupied by members who the Overseeker feels have demonstrated a complete submission to Jah's word and have dedicated themselves to the church.

Although the primary positions in the THOR (i.e., Overseeker, Pastor, Deacons) are held by males, female members also hold official positions in the group as well. Although the Alpha Queen does organize Biblical study sessions and occasionally makes short sermons, the female-held positions are primarily administrative rather than leadership oriented, such as treasurer and secretary of the THOR.

Through this manner of handing out positions to those who are demonstrating promise of future accomplishments, the Overseeker hopes to increase not only the church membership, but the quality of the individual's relationship with Jah as well. This is illustrated in the Overseeker's comment: "That's what I'm looking to, not only just physical growth, as far as numbers, but growth for the individuals who are there as well. Because, from that point, then others will come. I want those that are there to be strong, I want the links to be equal. So we can pull the weight without any of the links breaking."

However, the Overseeker has also initiated programs aimed at increasing the size of the Rastafari population in not only the surrounding area but nationwide as well. One such program has been the development of the prison ministry, which is perceived as a means to rescue those in the "belly of the Babylonian beast" from following the corrupt ways of the larger society.

SYMBOLS OF "JAH POWER" AND INDIVIDUAL SELF-IMAGE

During the course of my preliminary ethnographic fieldwork with a group of Rastafari in the North Carolina Triad area, the Triad House of Rastafari (THOR), I began to notice a number of symbols that were used quite frequently by the members to present their identity as believers in Haile Selassie. These symbols, which were displayed by members in their presentation of self, were misunderstood by outsiders, who, members said, often confuse them with the black power movement rather than with "Jah power."

Therefore, the purpose of this project was to understand the manner in which Rastafarian symbolism is both interpreted and incorporated into the self-image of the individual Rastafari adherent. Additionally, this project was aimed at understanding how the Rastafari perceive those who display Rastafari symbolws but are not followers of Selassie, and how this use of Rastafari symbolism by non-Rastafari contributes to their perception of self.

It was expected that the distinction between the actor's personal interpretation and the group's shared meaning would be observed in the responses of individual members to questions regarding their interpretation of cultural symbols particular to the religion of Rastafari. During the analysis of interview transcripts, particular themes in symbolic interpretation which were group-mediated were expected to have arisen. It was also expected that personal responses would appear as well, although they should have been less similar to each other than were the group-mediated responses.

Based on the current model and the proposed hypotheses, it was expected that responses would reflect particular aspects of the individual's life, such as their personal status, position in the church, age, ethnic background, manner of entrance, and the like. Particular attention was paid to the issue of power as it related to the members' use of symbolism to present their identity as Rastafari.

Members' responses appeared to conform to the project's original hypotheses, which held that although variance would exist, a general level of uniformity would still be observed. Specific themes were observed in informant's symbolic interpretations that, although the syntax and terminology may have varied, were fairly consistent with one another in content. I was able to discover a number of themes in the responses of the informants which can be summed up as:

1. Belief in a return to a more natural state of being;
2. The desire to return everything to Jah;
3. The concept of "vibrations" and
4. Interaction of power and symbolism.

I will discuss each of these themes in turn, beginning with belief in a more natural state of being. Throughout my interviews with the members of the THOR, I was consistently faced with the idea of Rastafari as a more natural alternative to the modern society. This was demonstrated in the Rastafari's responses regarding their choice of diet, hairstyles, use of the herb, and the colors of the Ethiopian flag. This desire to return to what is perceived of as a more natural existence is consistent with the rural origins of the Rastafari movement in Jamaica as well as its contemporary position in a modern industrial world. As the aim of the Rastafari is to separate from what is perceived as a corrupt, depersonalized, and money-driven "world," the natural tendencies of the movement have been to head in the opposite direction, which is toward a simplification of reality through a return to a natural way of life.

Symbolic aspects of the Rastafari's life are altered to adapt to this naturalist perspective, such as the elimination of unnatural toiletries (although they can be corporately manufactured natural goods, such as herbal or organic toiletries) and a change in personal grooming habits (such as combing and cutting of the head hair, shaving facial hair for men and body hair for women, and a cessation of wearing makeup by females).

The growing of dreadlocks is of major significance, as they are the epitome of naturalism to the Rastafari because they need no grooming. Rastafari grow locks by just washing their hair and refusing to comb or brush afterward. The resulting locks are endowed with spiritual power which emanates from within the pure soul of the Rastafari who has given his life to Jah. This power is often called upon in the Rastafari's daily interactions with what is perceived of as the "Babylonian establishment," which attempts to drain the power of the individual through subversive means.

Regarding the second theme in their responses to my interview questions as well in daily interactions with the Rastafari, constant reference to Jah or Haile Selassie were made. Over the course of a conversation, an individual would often chant out "Jah!" to which all those in the immediate vicinity would respond by finishing, "Rastafari, Haile Selassie I." This perpetual focus on "the Most High" is what Rastafari feel separates them from society rather than the overt symbols which they display to outsiders to present their external image as Rastafari. The true Rastafari can be anyone who carries himself in an "upful way," as one member told me: "A lot of times a person is Rasta and they don't know they are a Rasta or they don't acknowledge him. Those type vibes. You have some real crucial vibrations about you, you know. You conglomerate, you put them all together, you know? Give thanks Rastafari."

Thus, a Rastafari is not only someone who displays the external symbols associated with Rastafari, but anyone who possesses the mentality of a "Rastaman" (though not necessarily displaying the outward manifestations of Rastafari identity). The Rastafari way of life is one which involves a constant awareness of the individual's interconnectedness with all other facets of reality. The true Rastafari is perceived as the individual who is a part of Jah through both physical deeds and mental attitude.

The Rastafari perception of the individual is one which holds a dualistic orientation to human existence. According to the Rastafari belief system, the physical and the spiritual aspects of the individual's life must be united in order for the person to become one in the eyes of god. This personal relationship with Jah is one that is manifested in many symbolic ways by the Rastafari. However, the primary means by which the Rastafari include Jah into their lives is through constant prayer and the "chanting up of his hola (holy) name." This was deduced through reflecting on the manner in which the Rastafari responded to my questions, not necessarily the content of their answers. However, the Rastafari did speak of Jah in almost all of the questions that I asked, thus demonstrating the importance of including the name of Jah in their day-to-day interactions.

The concept of vibrations, the third theme, was one that appeared to take on a large amount of significance in the manner in which the Rastafari perceived reality. The dualistic notion of good and bad vibrations is one which surfaces in every aspect of the Rastafari's existence, from the clothes that they wear and the words that they say to the food that they eat and the emotions that they sense from other people during their day-to-day interactions. These vibrations can affect anything in the individual's life, which is perceived as having three distinct parts – mind, body, and spirit.

Thus, a person must take care to avoid negative vibrations, which can approach an individual from any of the three parts of the human experience:

mind, body, or spirit. However, individuals can help to defend against the negative vibes that they may encounter by emanating nothing but positive vibes. Positive vibes act as a sort of "forcefield" which shield the Rastafari from the negative vibes they encounter in their forays into the "Babylonian World." One member even referred to his dreadlocks as antennae that could pick up vibes.

These vibes can be perceived by the Rastafari in a number of ways, although they are usually interpreted as being positive if they are of Jah and negative if they are of the "world" (which stands in bi-polar opposition to the "earth,"which is the physical entity of the planet earth).

This fundamental aspect of the Rastafari belief system is one that appeared to dominate all of the interactions that the Rastafari engaged themselves in, even to the point of structuring the members' conversational topics based on their perception of the impact that their word-sound may result in. This can be clearly illustrated in my interactions with a member who had caught himself talking about the weather conditions, which he claimed were similar to those that cause tornadoes. Upon realizing that he was talking about tornadoes, he stopped himself and said to the other I-dren (brethren) that he had to watch out for what he was saying. The member explained that by focusing on such a topic, he was empowered to call down the vibrations on the earth accidently, just by thinking about vibrations such as tornadoes and the like. This clearly demonstrated the extent to which the Rastafari incorporate the concept of vibrations into their everyday actions and perceptions of reality, which is ordered along these bipolar avenues of orientation that ultimately concern themselves with the balance of symbolic power.

Throughout my fieldwork with the THOR, I noticed, in relation to my fourth theme, that one core feature of the Rastafari use of symbolism was its ability to enhance the "power" (economic/political prestige) of the members in their interactions with those of the Rastafari community (as well as a perceived enhancement of power over the larger society in which they dwell).

Since the Rastafari maintain themselves as a distinct group outside of the perceived state of "Babylon," an interaction between the them and the larger society (both of which possess varying degrees of power over the other in their day-to-day interactions) is implied. The forces of "Babylon" exert their power in such forms as police harassment, persecution of the Rastafari, and the oppression of others through economic or physical force. This type of power is one that can affect the physical body of the human being, which may ultimately lessen the control individuals have over their life, thus depriving them of vital power in their daily interactions.

Based on my observations with the THOR, it appeared that the Rastafari ideology focuses on the notion of power in many forms. Selassie is viewed as the incarnation of the Biblical God, who after returning in his savior character as Jesus Christ, has now returned in his "kingly character" to judge those who will enter into the kingdom of Heaven. This image of an all-powerful God who has returned to the earth in the clothing and position of a dominant figure in history is an indication of the enhancement of status that the members of the THOR assign to both Selassie and the religion of Rastafari. Thus, their affiliation with the Rastafari way of life enhances their own power which they can then use in their interactions with those of "the world."

The issue of power can be illustrated in a number of examples which demonstrate the symbolic ways in which power relations are recognized and maintained by members. As was mentioned earlier, the locks of the Rastafari are perceived as centers of personal power by some members, such as the member who spoke of his locks resembling antennae which could sense the "vibes" of his contextual surroundings. By way of contrast, the covering up of the female's locks in a sense inhibits or mutes their displays of power, while the uncovered state of the male Rastafari enables them to actively make use of the power of their locks in whatever situation they encounter. Additionally, the length of the locks also functioned as a barometer of the amount of power the individual had in commanding respect from other "dreads" as well. Although locks were not the only factor considered when assessing an individual's level of involvement in Rastafari, the locks did, nonetheless, function as an easily seen and recognized facet of Rastafari adherence that provided varying degrees of respect and power in interactions with other members according to the length of the individual's locks.

Throughout their interactions, therefore, the Rastafari are constantly involved in the presentation and maintenance of their identity through the use of symbolism. This presentation of Rastafari symbolism can be viewed on one level of abstraction as an attempt to access the power that is perceived by members to reside in the Rastafari way of life. This can be done by simply wearing their locks uncovered or by speaking in the I-ric form of language, which is an alteration of the English language. The I-ric language often involves the placing of an *I* or some other word that is perceived to have positive connotations in the front of a word to change its character. This is often used when a word happens to rhyme with something that could be interpreted as negative or related to sickness or death. *Dedication,* for example, is transformed through the I-ric to *livication.* The term *Unity* is changed in order to symbolize the oneness inherent in the word, to *I-nity.* This is opposed to its original form which emphasized the U in unity, which is in direct opposition to the I, or self. The I-ric is used to sanctify a particular word or phrase, as one elder in the church told me:

In Rastafari, you will hear them say I-tinually, meaning continually, I-rit meaning spirit. The reason why they put I in the front like that is because of InI (individual and Jah). See, I stands for Rasta. Its just to put the spirit on it, put the vibes on it. You know, to make it a more powerful I-bration. That I, just stand on the I vibration. It doesn't make you go from hell to heaven, but it just survives. Forming our own language and tongue and putting the spirit in front, which is the I. Always put God in front of everything, 'cause that is where the I vibrations comes from, putting God in front.

This focus on linguistic symbolism is another important aspect of the Rastafari identity, as has been observed by other researchers such as Velma Pollard (1990) in her work with the emergence of the Jamaican Rastafari language structure (I-ric) in the eastern Caribbean (St. Lucia in particular). In my observations, the THOR impresses upon its members the necessity of being able to speak to anyone on the street about Rastafari. As was mentioned by the members frequently, "Word sound is power," and if the Rastafari does not have the correct word sound, they have no power that they can call on in times of crisis, such as when dealing with those of the world who are trying to chant down Rastafari." Handouts are often distributed by the elders at meetings which have been written in the I-ric, thus allowing new members to become familiar with the new vocabulary. This is very important since "word sound is power" and through the correct "word sound" the member can acquire the full power of the religion of Rastafari. This is recognized by the members, who actively try to increase their understanding of the I-ric terminology and their use of Rastafari symbolism to distinguish themselves from the people of Babylon.

WORLDVIEW

At the basis of all Rastafari interactions is their concern as to whether these interactions will add positive or negative energy to their lives. As Rastafari interact with others, they are viewed as being an entity which accumulates the vibes (or types of energy) that they encounter. These vibes, if negative, must then be either cleansed from the individual through prayer, or even such measures as anointing the person's forehead with oil that has been blessed. Over the course of my fieldwork, I observed the elders of the house anoint the Overseeker's forehead with oil to help him in ridding his body of a sickness that had been caused by the negative vibes he had accumulated over the course of his daily interactions. Additionally, I observed several purification rituals which all had as their ultimate goal the replacement of negative vibes with those of a more positive nature.

An example of one such ritual was the process the Rastafari used to cleanse the negative vibes from marijuana that they had obtained from non-Rastafari. As this marijuana, or "herb" as they preferred to call it, was usually purchased from someone who had not grown it themselves, the herb had picked up all of the "vibrations" it had encountered along the way. These vibrations may have included harm or injury to one of the people in the distribution chain due to money, which is perceived to be a construct of the evil Babylonian system. Therefore, there are ritualistic measures used by the Rastafari to purify the herb before the member accidentally ingests these negative vibrations which have become part of the herb's aura. Members would hold the herb up in the air and chant for Jah (God) to cleanse the herb from all of the negative vibrations that it had acquired. All of those who were in attendance would exhort such phrases as "Fire" (perceived as the cleansing and purifying agent of Jah), or "Yes I, Rastafari" (meaning that they are in agreement with the member offering the prayer). The herb was then perceived as purified and safe to be used, whereupon it would be distributed to those who were in attendance. The herb would then be rolled up into marijuana cigarettes, or "spliffs" as the Rastafari called them. Depending on the amount of herb available, members would either share a few spliffs among them or, if the amount of herb available was prodigious, each individual would roll and smoke his own spliff. Use of the herb as a sacrament was viewed by many of the members as a means of increasing the "positivity" of their "I-brations" and allowing a closer channel of communication between them and Jah (thus gaining greater symbolic access to the ultimate positive vibration).

Therefore, as the Rastafari interact with others in their environment, they must be constantly aware of the type of vibes they are encountering and emanating. This in turn helps to shape their behavior, such as their choice of vocabulary, diet, clothing, mannerisms, and sexual behavior (the Rastafari perceive promiscuity and adultery as behavior that is sure to bring on negative vibes). This worldview influences every aspect of the individual's life.

INDIVIDUAL VARIATIONS

Individual variations appeared to be related to a number of context-specific variables, such as social standing in the church, as well as particular interpretations based on historical connections that the individual has with the particular symbol or topic.

Social standing in the church appeared to have a significant influence on the member's interpretations and presentation of specific symbols. For example, those members with the highest status in the church made the least use of the herb among those I encountered. What is more, even when these individuals consumed the herb, it was in a different manner (usually only eaten or made into a tea) than that of the average member (who usually smoked it in the form of large spliffs or in a "bowl" or pipe). This difference in symbolic use of the herb enabled those with higher status in the group to legitimate their elevated positions (and thus greater personal power) as well as provide for easily identifiable means of differentiating themselves from the general masses of the group. (Other means of displaying differences in status did, however, exist, such as more elaborate style of dress and spatial locationing in the room during ceremonies.) Whereas those with the highest status in the group did not consume the herb during their "reasoning," those less involved in the upper leadership tended to smoke more herb during their "reasoning sessions" (which consisted of periods of heavy conversation usually revolving around biblically-related topics). Additionally, it appeared that those who had a history of excessive drug or herb use prior to the acceptance of Rastafari did not consume a large amount of the herb due to their conscious rejection of their previous lifestyle.

Social status in the church also appeared to influence the types of responses I obtained to my interview questions. Those in the leadership hierarchy (as well as those actively seeking those leadership positions) were more likely to cite biblical scriptures in their answers to particular questions. This is more than likely a result of the elders' greater familiarity with the Bible due to their extended involvement with Rastafari as well as their use of biblical scripture to bring on the "word sound" of "Jah power." As the Bible (generally the King James Version) is the final word for all the members of the THOR and it is defended vehemently by the elders of the church, the knowledge and use of Biblical scripture implies a greater familiarity with the general precepts of the religion of Rastafari. This enhanced focus on, and knowledge of the Biblical scripture thus demonstrates the significant accumulation of power that the elders possess over those who do not attempt to familiarize themselves with the root of the Rastafari way of life, the Holy Bible. Members are encouraged by the elders to attend Bible lessons which are held to enhance the member's knowledge of the Bible (Revelations in particular, although the entire Bible is read and quoted from), thus adding power to their lives through the incorporation of biblical elements into the members' cultural repertoire.

Members who played a significant role in the everyday functioning of the THOR appeared to have their responses colored by their own churchly responsibilities. These individuals would offer more thorough explanations of the symbolism included in the THOR's banner, and they had more knowledge about the relation of the use of these particular symbols in the presentation of the group's identity. However, this is to be expected as they played a significant role in determining what symbols would be displayed by the group in such formal ways as the actual decoration of the banners.

However, social standing in the church was not the only variable that affected an individual's interpretation of particular symbols associated with the Rastafari way of life. A person's level of involvement in the reggae music scene also influenced his/her perception of the importance of reggae in the spiritual quest.

Those members who were personally involved in the reggae music scene (i.e., disc jockeying or performing in a reggae band) appeared to place a higher emphasis on the importance of reggae music in the religion of Rastafari than did those who were not personally involved in such activities. However, although those who played in musical groups or DJed for radio stations appeared to have the greatest relationship with the musical aspect of Rastafari, all members that I spoke to mentioned the importance of reggae in their conversion to Rastafari.

Many members stated that their introduction to Rastafari came through listening to reggae music, which initially appealed to them because of the soothing and "natural" beats of the music itself. However, as the individuals listened to reggae for an extended period of time, they began to discern particular passages in the music that appeared to have biblical or spiritual roots. This then prompted these members to seek out information about Rastafari, either through written sources or personal acquaintances they had with actual Rastafari. After learning more about Rastafari, all of the members stated that they began to incorporate aspects of Rastafari into their lives.

However, it appeared that often an individual had begun to display the symbolic characteristics of Rastafari prior to accepting Selassie, resulting in a rather fluid transition into the group. This can be illustrated in one member's statement when I asked him, "How did you become introduced to Rastafari?" "A friend gave me a book; he said , 'You know, you might like this.' It was *The Rastafarians* by Leonard Barrett [1988]. Read that, and I was already into reggae music scene and I had started growing locks, so it just automatically fit into that cycle. That somebody had handed me that book with my lifestyle being like that at that point in time. It fit along with my lifestyle so I just got right into it."

Thus, as the individuals had already incorporated many of the physical elements of Rastafari into their perception of self, the resulting association with the THOR eventually led to an increased focus on the spiritual aspect of the Rastafari way of life. One attribute of the religion that appeared to be important in the member's entrance and acceptance of Rastafari was the similarity of Rastafari to Christianity. All of the members I spoke with were originally from Christian-oriented families, although a number of members mentioned that they had some relatives who were Islamic (both Nation of Islam and Orthodox Islam) as well. This familiarity with the Bible and its teachings allowed the members to syncretize the teachings of Haile Selassie with the biblical scripture, resulting in a creation of the Rastafari way of life. As the religion of Rastafari is actually the embodiment of the ideals set forth by the Christian Bible, the actual belief system of the religion is very similar to that of many Christian churches. However, one major difference that the Rastafari stress is that many Christian churches do not focus on the Revelations of St. John, which are of critical importance to the religion of Rastafari. The Rastafari emphasis on the

Revelations gives a sense of urgency in changing the current racist and oppressive societal conditions, as the end is near and the time to correct these circumstances is now.

MEMBERS' PERCEPTIONS OF SYMBOLISM

The members of the THOR are acutely aware of the importance that symbolism has in the Rastafari identity. This is illustrated in one member's comments on the symbolism he identified with when he first joined: "Everything, man, the herb, the hair, the peace, love, one aim, one destiny, one God, just love. The atmosphere that Rasta stood for."

However, as this member progressed in his learning about the religion of Rastafari, he began to place greater significance on other aspects of Rastafari, namely the behavioral patterns recognized by other Rastafari brethren as those of a Rastafari. This change was reflected in the member's display of a number of symbolic gestures, which he performed: "Through the music, through my percussion playing and how I separate myself from society. The way of my style of eating, eating vegetarian food, possibly wearing a red, gold and green toboggan to cover my locks in the winter or whenever I feel like wearing my locks up. Wearing something with colors that represent Rastafari. The way I carry myself mostly."

Although the Rastafari realize that they are actively displaying this symbolism, they are very conscious as to its misuse for reasons other than "chanting up His Majesty's name." As one of the elders said to me when I asked him how he felt about these symbols being used to portray Rastafari: "Oh it don't portray Rastafari, those are just things that are there, red, gold and green too. You have to have something to express yourself, know where you are coming from. So they are just things that are there to express the movement. They are just things that are there, ain't got nothing to do with being or being not, they are just things that are there."

RASTAFAKE-I

Rastafari-associated symbolism, when used by those who are not Rastafari, can actually have the effect of identifying the person as not a Rastafari, but a Rastafake I. One member described a Rastafake-I to me as: "Somebody that would say Rastafari, claim to be a follower of Rastafari but actually commit themselves in acts that are not of Rastafari. Such as sexual indulgence, being drunk and lustful, just to name a few. Those type of things if a person calls themselves a Rasta, but yet does all of these things."

Thus, although the Rastafari realize the importance symbolism holds in the presentation of their identity as followers of Selassie, they eschew the use of this symbolism by those who are not practitioners of the faith. Harsh criticism is directed toward those who are Rastafake-I, a term denoting an individual who displays some of the symbols of Rastafari adherence but does not follow the strict behavioral code of the biblical Nazirite vow nor act in a manner that the members feel, "is of Rastafari."

However, many of the Rastafari I spoke with admitted to being similar to a Rastafake-I at one point in their life, especially when telling me about their introduction to Rastafari. This concept is clearly illustrated in one member's perception of his use of the term "Rastafari" before he "came to know Selassie": "I didn't even know Rasta and I would have told you that then, but I was of the vibration of saying the name itself, you know what I am saying? Rastafari, Jah Rastafari! [yells loudly in a drunken sort of manner as if impersonating himself while he was a Rastafake-I]. Even then, Jah would not be with it, just Rastafari. It just had the ring."

Therefore, it appears that although it is an abomination to be a Rastafake-I, it is one phase in the continuum of the acceptance of Selassie as the Supreme Deity, which may represent a liminal stage in the conversion to the Rastafari way of life for a number of individuals. What's more, this awkward phase of entry into Rastafari is often later mentioned in humorous stories among members during reasoning sessions or even formal sermons. On many occasions, I have observed members relating their initial attempts at associating with Rastafari to others in a way which demonstrated the process of growth in their knowledge of Selassie.

CONCLUSION

The research on which this chapter is based was an attempt to understand the importance of Rastafari symbolism to the individual member. This was done, first, by determining the awareness of each individual's personal interpretation of these symbols and the relevance it had to their perception of self, and second, by assessing the group's ascribed meaning. Group meaning was determined by comparing all of the individual responses and then determining the common themes in interpretation of particular symbols. Through this focus on the dualistic nature of symbolic interpretation, it was hoped that a more holistic understanding of the nature of Rastafari symbolism could be discerned.

BIBLIOGRAPHY

Andrews, Amy. "One Aim." *Winston-Salem Journal.* Nov. 6: A1- A5, 1995.

Barrett, Leonard E. *The Rastafarians: Sounds of Cultural Dissonance.* Boston: Beacon Press, 1988.

Barth, Fredrik. *Ethnic Groups and Boundaries: The Social Organization of Culture Difference.* Boston: Little, Brown and Co., 1969.

Barton, Richard W. "Signs, Contexts, and the Narrative Structure of Practices." *Studies in Symbolic Interaction* 6 (1985): 113-147.

Burns, Thomas A., and J. Stephen Smith. "The Symbolism of Becoming in the Sunday Service of an Urban Black Holiness Church." *Anthropological Quarterly,* 51(3): 185-204, 1978.

Campbell, Horace. "Rastafari: Culture of Resistance." *Race & Class,* 22(1): 1-22, 1980.

Campbell, Horace. *Rasta and Resistance: From Marcus Garvey to Walter Rodney.* Trenton N.J.: African World Press, 1992.

Chevannes, Barry. *Rastafari: Roots and Ideology.* New York: Syracuse University Press. 1994.

Cohen, A. P. *The Symbolic Construction of Community.* New York: Tavistock Publications, 1985.

Cohen, Abner. *Two-Dimensional Man: An Essay on the Anthropology of Power and Symbolism in Complex Society.* Berkeley: University of California Press, 1974.

Faith, Karlene. "One Love–One Heart–One Destiny: A Report on the Rastafarian Movement in Jamaica." In *Cargo Cults and Millenarian Movements.* G. W. Trompf, ed. New York: Mouton De Gruyter, 1990, pp 295-341.

Firth, Raymond. *Symbols: Public and Private.* Ithaca: Cornell University Press, 1973.

Furst, Peter T. *Flesh of the Gods: The Ritual Use of Hallucinogens.* Prospect Heights: Waveland Press, 1990.

Geertz, Clifford. *The Interpretation of Cultures.* New York: Basic Books, 1973.

Gerlach, Luther P., and Virginia H. Hine. *People, Power, Change: Movements of Social Transformation.* New York: Bobbs-Merrill, 1970.

Kearney, Michael. *World View.* Novato: Chandler & Sharp, 1984.

Kertzer, David L. "Flaming Crosses and Body Snatchers." In *Applying Cultural Anthropology.* Aaron Podolefsky and Peter S. Brown, eds. Mountain View: Mayfield, pp. 1994, 217-225.

Lewis, William F. *Soul Rebels: The Rastafari.* Edited by Young Gregg, Joan. Prospect Heights: Waveland Press, 1993.

Lyman, Stanford M., and William A. Douglas. "Ethnicity: Strategies of Collective and Individual Impression Management." *Social Research,* 40(2): 344-365, 1973.

McCann, Ian. *Bob Marley: In His Own Words.* London: Omnibus Press, 1993.

McCracken, Grant. *The Long Interview.* Newbury Park, Calif.: Sage, 1988.

Miller, Marian A. L. "The Rastafarian in Jamaican Political Culture: The Marginalization of a Change Agent." *The Western Journal of Black Studies,* 17(2): 112-117, 1993.

Morrison, Silburn "Mosiah." *Rastafari: The Conscious Embrace.* Brooklyn: Itality Publishing House, 1992.

Nettleford, Rex M. *Mirror, Mirror: Identity, Race and Protest in Jamaica.* Kingston: William, Collins, & Sangster, 1970.

Pollard, Velma. "The Speech of the Rastafarians of Jamaica, in the Eastern Caribbean: The Case of St. Lucia." *International Journal of Social Language,* 85: 81-90, 1990.

Rubin, Vera, and Lambros Comitas. *Ganja in Jamaica.* Paris: Mouton & Co., 1975.

Sahlins, Marshall. "Colors and Cultures." *Semiotica,* 16: 1-22, 1976.

Schouten, John W. "Selves in Transition: Symbolic Consumption in Personal Rites of Passage and Identity Construction." *Journal of Consumer Research,*17: 412-425, 1991.

Shibutani, Tamotsu. "Reference Groups as Perspectives." *American Journal of Sociology,* 60: 562-69, 1955.

Simpson, George Eaton. *Religion and Justice: Some Reflections on the Rastafari Movement,* 286-291, 156 (4),1985.

Smith, Michael Garfield, Roy Augier, and Rex Nettleford. *The Rastafari Movement in Kingston, Jamaica.* Kingston: Institute of Social and Economic Research, 1960.

Stokes, Martin. *Ethnicity, Identity and Music: The Musical Construction of Place.* Providence: Berg Publishers, 1994.

Stromberg, Peter G. "Ideological Language in the Transformation of Identity." *American Anthropologist,* 92(1): 42-56, 1990.

Turner, Victor. *The Forest of Symbols: Aspects of Ndembu Ritual.* Ithaca: Cornell University Press, 1967.

Turner, Victor. *On the Edge of the Bush.* Tucson: University of Arizona Press, 1985.

United States Census Bureau. *1990 Census of Population and Housing.* City of Winston-Salem, North Carolina, Washington D.C.: Government Printing Office, 1991.

Waterman, C. A. *Juju: A Social History and Ethnography of an African Popular Music.* Chicago: University of Chicago Press, 1990.

12

The Nation of Islam

Mike Taylor

The transatlantic slave trade was made illegal in 1808, abolished in the British Empire in 1833, and, in 1865, a constitutional amendment in the USA prohibited slavery forever.

In spite of all this, the psychological consequences of slavery continue. Slavery itself exercised a degrading effect both on the minds of slavetraders and on their victims. Many members of the dominant culture continue to think of themselves as inherently superior to the descendants of the slaves, who are having to fight a hard strnggle to achieve the full respect due to them.

At present, in both the US and Great Britain, there is a tendency to affirm the dominant culture, yet to downplay the contribution of those who are regarded as alien and not really "part of the family." A number of responses by "minority" groups is possible, for instance: avoidance of people perceived as representatives of the dominant culture, acceptance of dominant cultural values, or aggression. One increasingly popular option is that known as "Black Nationalism," with its implication of ethnic separatism.

"BLACK NATIONALISM"

In the USA, the term "black" is used of any person considered to have African ancestry. The term "white" is, therefore, used of those considered to have no African ancestry of any kind. Black Nationalism reacts to this by inverting the status quo. Black Nationalism, therefore, advocates the unity of all blacks, emphasizing their distinctiveness from whites. However, it goes further than this in viewing all blacks as superior to whites, the blacker the better, emphasizing their past glorious heritage and a glorious future for them, aiming to put whites at a psychological disadvantage. Accordingly, cultural symbols which tend to make whites feel alienated are particularly emphasized.

Some Black Nationalists espouse separation. Separatists believe that people of African descent cannot hope to attain freedom and equality in the US, and they advocate either a return to Africa or territorial separation within the US.[1] The Nation of Islam under Elijah Muhammad taught that blacks should not mix socially with whites, and should develop their own businesses and have their own separate government.

The Nation of Islam espouses an extreme variety of Black Nationalism, and for this reason it is vital that it be understood.

MARCUS GARVEY AND THE UNIA

The first significant Black Nationalist movement was that of Marcus Garvey.[2] Born in Jamaica, Garvey (1887-1940) founded in 1914 a movement called the Universal Negro Improvement Association (UNIA), the aims of which included the promotion of unity among the African diaspora, as well as the strengthening of independent African states. Perhaps inspired by Zionism, Garvey wanted to build a state on the African continent based on a high level of technical and professional excellence to which black people from all over the world would be attracted.

A man of vision, Garvey soon established headquarters in New York which became the center for his organization, which certainly by 1920 had attained world significance. A number of organizations were established snd staffed, including the UNIA's Black Star Steamship Line that would link the black peoples of the world in commerce and trade and transport African Americans back to their African home. Although Garvey's movement was essentially political and social, he also attacked the presentation of God and Jesus as Caucasians.

Garvey's activities eventually drew opposition, but it was his lack of business acumen that was the downfall of this bold and highly imaginative enterprise.

NOBLE DREW ALI AND THE MOORISH SCIENCE TEMPLE

While the political dimension was dominant in Garvey's movement, the religious element was clearly dominant in the Moorish Science Temple of Noble Drew Ali (1866-1929).[3] Whereas all previous black revolutionary movements in the US had been built on neo-Christian foundations, Drew's organization was the first to be based on explicitly Islamic symbolism. Born in

North Carolina, Timothy Drew felt that if some identity between African-Americans and Oriental people could be established, African-American ethnic pride would be enhanced. Probably because identification with sub-Saharan Africa would not have been prestigious in those colonial days, he chose instead to identify with North Africans, whom he called "Asiatics." Accordingly, Drew ultimately decreed that African Americans were really "Asiatics," believing that they would be liberated by a discovery of these alleged ethnic roots.

In 1913, Drew established a "Moorish Science Temple" in Newark, New Jersey, issuing "Nationality and Identification Cards" to his followers. In 1927, after moving to Chicago, he produced a book which he called *The Holy Koran of the Moorish Temple of Science*, very different from the Islamic *Qur'an*. Drew's Koran was actually a booklet of 64 pages, divided into 47 chapters and an epilogue. Overall it can be viewed as comprising three parts, the first being allegedly historical and dedicated to John the Baptist and Jesus. It is said, for example, that Jesus went to India "with Prince Ravanno," studied "the man's Law," preached in Benares, went to Egypt, was crucified by the Jews, appearing later to Apollo and to the priests in Heliopolis, and so forth. In fact, this section follows almost word-for-word *The Aquarian Gospel*, Levi Dowling's 'psychic' production, first published in 1911. Minor alterations were made, such as changing "God" to "Allah" and removing blatantly pantheistic expressions. Its second part (chapters 20-44) is concerned chiefly with ethics, and the last part explains the historical and 'racial' basis of the new religion. Among other things, it teaches that the "Moorish Americans" must be united under Noble Drew Ali, who was heralded by Marcus Garvey, just as Jesus had been heralded by John the Baptist.

Drew's movement took root in many major U.S. cities, some members coming from Garvey's movement. Drew was seen as a prophet and "the Reincarnation of Mohammed." Belief in "Asiatic" identity and perceived citizenship of Morocco, as seat of the Nation, in addition to North American citizenship, freed members to dispense with the labels imposed on them, such as "Negro," "black," "colored,"or "Ethiopian" and instead to regard themselves as "Moors," "Moorish Americans" or "Asiatics." The terms "el" or "bey" were attached to members' names to demonstrate their "Asiatic status." Although ostensibly Muslim, the cult's transitional nature is evident from its retention of many features commonly associated with Christianity, particularly the prominence given to Jesus and love. Drew was very familiar with Freemasonry and hence esotericism is evident, with belief in a higher and lower self, and the honouring of all "prophets," including Buddha and Confucius. Despite their hostility to whites, the Moors saw themselves as the nucleus around which a world of truth, peace, freedom and justice must be built.

Sincere, aware of his own limitations, and desiring to extend the movement, Drew encouraged other, better educated people into positions of leadership.

However, the growing movement was increasingly seen by such people as an opportunity for private gain, and less discriminating members were duped into buying spurious literature and artifacts allegedly connected to the their "Asiatic" heritage. Naturally, these leaders grew rich and, seeing Drew as the main obstacle to fuller exploitation, marginalized him. During a power struggle within the leadership, and while Drew was away, one of Drew's rivals was killed. When Drew returned to Chicago, he was arrested and charged with murder. However, he was never brought to trial as he died mysteriously soon after being released on bail. His death was attributed either to police brutality or to murder by a leadership rival.

After Drew's death, various strands of power arose within the Moorish-American community. Today it is estimated that membership is about 10,000 spread over fifteen cities across the US.

WALLACE D. FARD

The ultimate failure of Garvey's and Drew's movements left a powerful residue of feeling among the African-American working class. The deepseated resentment against "racial" indignities remained, but it lacked a vehicle for its expression. All of this was aggravated by the great Depression of late 1929.[4] At that time, a number of groups were competing for the allegiance of the African-American working classes, but none had a leader of sufficient charisma or ability to transform the Garveyite and Moorish passions into a new force in which religious and political energies were fused.[5]

It was just at this time, in July 1930, that a likeable but mysterious peddler, known as Wallace D. Fard (or "Farad") suddenly appeared in the black ghetto of Detroit.[6] He was thought to be an Arab,[7] although his precise ethnic identity is still uncertain.

He was welcomed into the homes of culture-hungry African-Americans who were eager to purchase his silks and artifacts, which he claimed were like those worn by black people in their homeland across the sea. The desire for information about their "homeland" led to Fard's holding meetings from house to house throughout the community.[8] The many ailments, such as rheumatism, aches and pains, experienced by the people in the northern climate[9] also made them eager to heed Fard's instructions concerning diet, which he claimed would cure them. He told them to avoid all meat of "poison animals," such as hogs, ducks, geese, 'possums, and catfish, as well as stimulants, particularly liquor.[10]

He also used the Bible as a textbook to teach them about their supposed true religion,[11] which he maintained was not Christianity, but rather the religion of the black men of Asia and Africa. He told them that the Bible was not the proper book for the Black Nation, but provided it was carefully interpreted, it could be made to serve until they could be introduced to the Qur'an. Influenced strongly by Drew Ali, Fard worked out his agenda by presenting a package of value systems which closely followed the profile of Drew's paradigm.[12]

Fard's later teaching contained increasingly bitter denunciations of the white race, and, as his prestige grew, he began to attack the Bible in such a way as to shock his hearers and bring them to an emotional crisis. People experienced sudden "conversions" and became his followers.

As the house-to-house meetings became inadequate to accommodate the audiences, a hall was hired,[13] named Detroit's Allah Temple of Islam. House meetings were discontinued and informality of contact between Fard and the African-Americans was replaced by a tightly knit organization. Members were examined before acceptance, and a hierarchy was established. At this point, some of Drew's followers began to pledge themselves to Fard.[14]

Each proselyte, in order to be initiated, was required to write a letter asking for his "original"or "Islamic" name. When he received this name, the "slave name" given his ancestors by the whites was discarded.[15]

Fard described himself to his followers as having been sent to awaken his "uncle" (the "Black Nation") to the full range of possibilities in a world temporarily dominated by the "blue-eyed devils." His followers all believed him to be a Prophet sent to bring "freedom, justice, and equality" to the black men "in the wilderness of North America, surrounded and robbed completely by the Cave Man [sic]."[16]

Amazed by his boldness, African-Americans became increasingly alert to the subtle discriminations which they faced daily.[17] The North had been presented to them as a promised land, but the worst features of ethnic prejudice were still there, though thinly camouflaged by "sweet talk about equality."[18]

Fard taught his followers about the deceptive character of whites and helped them relive, at least in fantasy, the glorious history of black Afro-Asia. He utilized literature of various kinds, including Watchtower Bible and Tract material and some of the literature of Freemasonry, to bring the people to "a knowledge of self." Some of the illiterate were taught to read so that they could learn firsthand about the past greatness of their race.[19]

Despite encouraging his followers to read, Fard warned that the words of whites were not to be taken literally, as they were incapable of telling the truth, but that their writings were symbolic and needed interpretation. To supplement the "symbolic" literature of the whites, Fard himself wrote two manuals for the movement. Fard's *The Secret Rituel of the Nation of Islam* was, and still is, transmitted orally; it is memorized verbatim by the students at the movement's parochial schools and has become an oral tradition. *Teaching for the Lost Found Nation of Islam in a Mathematical Way* for registered Nation members resembled a series of riddles. Fard had to struggle to retain control after the movement began to grow, yet, within three years, the organization had become so effective that he was able to withdraw almost entirely from active leadership. He had set up the temple and established its ritual and worship, and had also founded a University of Islam (actually a combined elementary and secondary school) dedicated to "higher mathematics," astronomy, and the "ending of the spook civilization." He created the Muslim Girl Training (MGT) Class and the General Civilization Class (GCC), which taught "Muslim" girls and women the principles of home economics and how to be proper wives and mothers. Finally, "fear of trouble with the unbelievers, especially with the police, led to the founding of the Fruit of Islam (FOI)—a military organization for the men, who were drilled by captains and taught tactics and the use of firearms."[20] A Minister of Islam was appointed to run the entire organization, aided by a staff of assistant ministers. Each of these men was selected and trained personally by Fard, who gradually stopped his public appearances and eventually disappeared from view.

Not much was ever known about Fard. He claimed to have come from Mecca and usually referred to himself as Mr. Farrad Mohammed or Mr. F. Mohammed Ali. He was also known as Professor Ford, Mr. Wali Farrad, and W. D. Fard.[21] One of his earliest converts recalls that, on one occasion, the "prophet" said, "My name is W.D. Fard and I came from the Holy City of Mecca. More about myself I will not tell you yet, for the time has not yet come. I am your brother. You have not yet seen me in my royal robes."[22] He was, of course, also known as "The Prophet."

Inevitably, many legends clustered around this mysterious figure. One view was that Fard was a black Jamaican whose father was a Syrian Muslim, another that he was a Palestinian Arab. Some of his followers believed him to have come from the tribe of Koreish, the tribe of the founder of classical Islam. Fard announced himself to Detroit police as "the Supreme Ruler of the Universe," and at least some of his follwers seem to have considered him divine.[23]

ELIJAH MOHAMMAD

One of the earliest officers in the movement under Fard was Elijah Mohammad, born Elijah Poole in Sandersville, Georgia, on October 7, 1897.[24] He was one of thirteen children born to Wali and Marie Poole. His father was a Baptist preacher,[25] and his grandparents had been slaves owned by a white family named Poole.

Elijah completed the fourth grade at school and when he was sixteen he left home. In 1923, with his wife Clare (née Evans) and two children, he moved to Detroit, Michigan. Poole worked in factories, holding several different jobs, including one as a supervisor, until the Depression of late 1929.[26] About a year later, he came under the influence of Wallace Fard, with whom he speedily developed a close relationship. At Poole's initiation, Fard gave him the "original" surname "Karriem."[27] In 1932, Poole established, what two years later became the Southside Mosque (later Temple No.2) in Chicago and apparently ran it for some time.[28]

That year Fard went to prison because a Detroit Nation member was convicted in 1932 of a sacrificial killing of one of his "brothers."[29] Fard was ordered out of Detroit on May 26, 1933. The same year he went to Chicago, where he was arrested almost immediately and imprisoned. Each time he was arrested, he sent for Elijah Karriem; it was claimed, that Karriem might "see and learn the price of truth for us (the so-called Negroes)."[30]

When Fard was trying to evade the police in 1933, he sought refuge with Poole in Chicago. Poole's dedication to Fard doubtless cemented their bond, for Poole soon became Fard's chief minister and gradually assumed leadership of the Detroit temple. Fard soon conferred full administrative responsibility for the movement on him, giving him this time the surname "Muhammad," and began grooming him as a successor.[31] Although opposed by moderates in the hierarchy, Poole became Fard's most trusted lieutenant and was eventually chosen as chief Minister of Islam. A number of Detroit members objected to Elijah Mohammed's position of favor with Fard, some of his antagonists rejecting his second renaming and nomination as chief Minister of Islam. When Fard mysteriously disappeared in June 1934, only four years after his arrival, leaving Muhammad as his obvious successor, it became rumored that Muhammad had induced Fard to offer himself as a human sacrifice. This was in line with the common belief amongst Fard's followers that any Nation member who sacrificed himself could become "Savior of the world." The rumours were never substantiated; nevertheless, Fard is now honored by Nation members everywhere as the "Savior."[32] Fard's nomination of Elijah Mohammed as his successor ensured the continuity of the Nation and that same year the paper *Muhammad Speaks* was started.

After Fard's disappearance, members soon lost their aggressiveness and the movement, to which Fard had drawn between 5000 and 8000 adherents,[33] began to decline in size and power. Quarrels came to the surface, and the moderates drove Elijah Mohammed, with his wife and family of six sons and a daughter, from Detroit to Temple No. 2 in Chicago.[34]

Muhammad designated Temple No. 2 as the new headquarters of the movement and began to reshape the movement under his own highly militant leadership. Fard became deified and called "Allah." Elijah Muhammad, who had served "Allah," naturally assumed the mantle of "Prophet" that "Allah in person" had worn during his Detroit mission and presented himself as the sole "Messenger of Allah." Human sacrifice was never again mentioned as a "Muslim" doctrine. The most important change, however, was Elijah Muhammad's determination to bring every African-American into the "light" as he saw it. His faction became known as the "Temple People" and their meeting places as "Muhammad's Temples of Islam."[35]

In 1934, having refused to transfer his child from a University of Islam to a state school, Elijah Muhammad was found guilty of "contributing to the delinquency of a minor,"[36] and placed on six months' probation. This experience gave him firsthand acquaintance with the process of the law. As his chief minister, Muhammad appointed a Haitian, Theodore Rozier, who had never known Fard. Other factions objected as Rozier "never saw the Savior" and that this "second-hand revelation" did not qualify him adequately for the role. Underlying this may have been an objection to Muhammad's audacity in identifying himself as the only channel for Fard's message. At this time, the movement made only small inroads into the African-American community. Elijah Mohammed preached that he and his followers should not serve in the U.S. Army, and in 1942 he was arrested by the federal authorities in Chicago, serving time in prison,[37] and thus enabled to identify with young men who were in prison and so to communicate with them on their own terms. Recruitment of convicts became a specialty of the Nation and it was in prison, in 1947, that Malcolm Little, later to become Malcolm X, was recruited into the movement by relatives and entered into correspondence with Muhammad.[38]

Muhammad's association with Fard," the Supreme Being among all Black Men," gave him a status and power that were never successfully challenged. He proclaimed: "I am with Allah [God] and He [Allah] is with me."[39] He was known not only as "Messenger" and "Prophet," but also as "Spiritual Head of the Muslims in the West," "Divine Leader," and "The Reformer." His ministers referred to him most often as "The Honorable Elijah Muhammad" or "The Messenger of Allah to the Lost-Found Nation of Islam in the Wilderness of North America." Wherever Muhammad spoke, growth in temple membership immediately followed, and while the movement was growing, he traveled widely. But, later, advancing age and the administrative burden kept him close to Chicago. He operated from his Chicago headquarters, Muhammad's Temple of Islam No. 2. Administrative policy was set mainly through written directives and conferences in Chicago, and enforced through a few lieutenants of demonstrated loyalty. Malcolm X was appointed his personal assistant.[40]

MALCOLM X

Malcolm X was born Malcolm Little in Omaha, Nebraska, about 1925. He was one of eleven children and, like Elijah Muhammad, the son of a Baptist minister. Early on his family moved to Lansing, Michigan, where the outspokenness of his father, a Garveyite, was resented by local whites. When Malcolm was only six, the family home was burned down by the Ku Klux

Klan. Subsequently his father tried to become more economically independent by building his own shop in a predominantly white area, but he was soon found with "his head bashed" and his body mangled under a train.[41] The poverty-stricken family was eventually broken up and Malcolm sent to an institution for boys, where the white housemother was kind to him.[42] Soon Malcolm was attending school, but being the only African-American and a brilliant student, he incurred the resentment of both teachers and pupils. He was ideally gifted for the legal profession, but prejudice was such that he was advised to think instead of a trade such as carpentry.[43] He left school, moved east and took up a delinquent life. By his late teens, he was involved in the fringes of the Harlem underworld, becoming known as "Detroit Red"[44] and earning big money.[45] In 1947, while in the maximum-security prison in Concord, Massachusetts, Malcolm was drawn to the Nation of Islam through the visits of one of his brothers and letters from other relatives who had joined the Detroit Temple. His conversion was clinched through correspondence with Elijah Muhammad.[46] Malcolm was a person essentially loyal to those he trusted and, accordingly, for seventeen years, he demonstrated unshakable loyalty to Muhammed.[47] His "X" signified the rejection of his "slave-name" and the substitution of a mathematical unknown to represent his now-unknown original African name.[48]

Elijah Muhammad relied heavily on the close-knit coterie of Nation leaders, particularly his chief aide, Minister Malcolm X Shabazz, once minister of the powerful Temple No. 7 in Harlem and one of the few ministers granted an "original" (or Arabic) surname. [49]

Malcolm X was an energetic organizer and speaker. Whereas Elijah Muhammad spoke almost exclusively to African-Americans, Malcolm X frequently appeared at colleges and universities and was a popular radio and television guest. He toured the US regularly, visiting temples, organizing new ones, motivating missions and newly-founded cell groups, conducting rallies and fundraising campaigns, and generally serving as Muhammad's troubleshooter and spokesman.[50] Malcolm X expanded the agenda of the Nation into a full blown Black Nationalism,[51] but his desire to make contact with black people worldwide was restrained by the will of Elijah Muhammad. Malcolm became increasingly troubled by certain features of the Nation, and only his personal loyalty to Elijah Muhammad caused him to suppress these doubts.[52]

Shortly after Malcolm was appointed National Minister, President John F. Kennedy was assassinated on November 22, 1963. In a press interview following this event, Malcolm indicted white America for creating the climate of hatred and violence in which such an outrage could occur. In a meeting in New York, Malcolm expressed the view that Kennedy's murder was a case of "chickens coming home to roost." He added, "Being an old farm body myself, chickens coming home to roost never did make me sad; they've always made me glad.[53]

The next day, Muhammad announced Malcolm's suspension for 90 days, prohibiting him from exercising any ministerial function and from making any public statement.[54] Malcolm accepted this judgment, but when he was not reinstated and became aware that his life was under threat, other doubts which he had been suppressing started to burst forth and disillusionment set in.[55]

Early in March 1964, Malcolm withdrew from the Nation of Islam and formed his own organization, The Muslim Mosque, Inc., followed by its secular counterpart, the Organization of Afro-American Unity, which he felt reflected the ideals of Black Nationalism more faithfully than did the Nation.[56] During 1964, he traveled extensively in Africa and the Near East, including making the pilgrimage to Mecca. He claimed that it was the sight of so many people of different tone and ethnicity mixing together freely that made him realize that white people were not *intrinsically* racist.[57]

Shortly after his return to the US, he was assassinated on February 21, 1965. One of the three assassins was caught, together with two suspects. Although an ex-member of the Nation, he denied being part of a Muslim conspiracy.[58] After the death of Malcolm X, Minister Louis Farrakhan became Muhammad's national representative in spiritual matters, while Muhammad's son-in-law and supreme captain of the FOI, Raymond Sharrieff, travelled the length and breadth of the US keeping the Nation in order.[59] Elijah Muhammad, having suffered most of his life from severe bronchial problems,[60] died of congestive heart failure on the morning of February 25th, 1975. On Savior's Day February 26th, the designation of his son, Wallace Deen Muhammad, as successor was made public.[61]

THE REFORMS OF W. D. MUHAMMAD

Immediate power struggles were resolved by the overwhelming affirmation of Wallace as the Chief Minister of the Nation by ministers from across the country on Savior's Day, 1975. By March 1975, the title of "Chief Minister" had given way to "The Honorable Wallace D. Muhammad, Supreme Minister of the Nation of Islam." [62]

Wallace, a close friend of Malcolm X, always inclined toward classical Islam rather than Nation mythology, and was disciplined by dismissal or excommunication at least three times.[63] Finally, however, Elijah Muhammad himself seemed to have accepted that the Nation would have to move in Wallace's direction.[64] Long before he assumed leadership in the Nation, Wallace had determined that the true uplift of his people lay in the security of the international Muslim confraternity rather than in an isolated Black Nationalism. Once confirmed as leader of the Nation, Wallace, or Warith, as he became, lost no time in reforming it and initiating a process of movement into the larger world of Islam.[65]

Fard was declared mortal and demoted to teacher/prophet, and the memory of Elijah Muhammad, though still accorded honor, was reconsidered in the perspective of his times and limitations. Whites were to be recognized on their merits as individuals rather than as intrinsically evil sons and daughters of Yakub.[66]

By late 1975, many Universities of Islam had been closed, and in 1976, Warith replaced them with the Clara Muhammad Elementary and Secondary Schools, in memory of his mother, Sister Clara Mohammad.[67]

Authority was decentralized and businesses were turned over to private ownership when it was discovered that the Community was actually debt-ridden. The FOI and MGT were disbanded, all members were "advised" to exchange their military style garments for modest simple dress, and "X" surnames were replaced by Arabic and African names.[68]

By 1976, the transition from the Nation of Islam to a more mainstream Islamic community open to all peoples was nearly complete. In 1977 the name "Nation of Islam" was changed to "the World Community of al-Islam in the West," *Muhammad Speaks* became *Bilalian News* and "Ministers" were called "imams" ("models"). Minister Wallace became Imam Warith Deen Muhammad and initiated classical Islamic guidelines and standards for Imams.[69]

However, in 1977, Imam Silis Muhammad openly condemned all Wallace's changes and left the movement, taking a small number of members with him to establish a new Nation of Islam along the old lines. Even though this community formed alliances in several cities[70] with other groups of varying ethnicity, it maintained its Black Nationalist thrust. Based in Atlanta, it has a substantial following with an estimated eighteen to twenty congregations scattered across the US.[71]

Imam Louis Farrakhan also left the Community in 1977, some two and a half years after Warith's reforms began. He took a larger share of Community members with him to re-form the Nation of Islam along the old lines. In this way, the Community once known as the Nation of Islam had by 1978 divided into three factions—two groups identifying themselves as "the Nation of Islam," and one identifying itself as "the World Community of al-Islam in the West" (WCIW). Each of these communities offered variations of the themes introduced by the original Nation of Islam under Elijah Muhammad.[72]

Inevitably other factions also developed. Apart from Silis Muhammad's and Louis Farrakhan's "Nations," two other groups have subsequently made their own claims either to be the legitimate continuation of the "Nation of Islam," or to be its only authentic resurrection. One of these is headed by John Muhammad of Detroit, blood brother of Elijah Muhammad.[73] Another movement claiming to be "the Nation" was established in Baltimore, Maryland, by Emmanuel Abdullah Muhammad, of whom it is said that he will reign as

"The Caliph" until the return of Allah, conceived as Wallace Fard. At least eight other movements claim the "Nation of Islam" as their heritage, yet have developed independent doctrines and have adopted alternative names. One such is the "Five Percenters."[74]

During the 1980s, both Louis Farrakhan's and Warith Muhammad's communities continued to grow. The WCIW worldview underwent further expansion and it was renamed The American Muslim Mission to reflect this. The *Bilalian News* was renamed the *World Muslim News*, then the *AM Journal,* and finally the *Muslim Journal.* Community members ceased to be "Bilalians" and were renamed "Muslim Americans." Louis Farrakhan pursued coalitions with Native and Latin Americans on social issues. Silis Muhammad's somewhat slower expansion aimed at publicizing the plight of African-Americans on the world stage.[75]

Each community is working to expand its base further and simultaneously support an American Islam, whilst retaining links with the Muslim world as a whole. Elijah Muhammad's legacy is still evident as each community attempts to apply the practical self-awareness and knowledge that he provided.

LOUIS FARRAKHAN

The man who has done most to bring about a restoration of Elijah Muhammad's original teaching is Louis Farrakhan.

Louis Haleem Abdul Farrakhan was born Louis Eugene Walcott on May 11, 1933, in the Bronx, New York.[76] His father was from Jamaica and his mother was from St. Kitts. At the age of three, his mother moved to Boston, where he and his older brother were brought up. He grew up a devout Episcopalian and, like Malcolm X, was a highly able school student, but with particular musical gifts. In September 1953, he married his childhood sweetheart, Betsy, who had been brought up a Roman Catholic, and he left college after his junior year to engage in show business and provide for his new family. He became popular in the Boston area as a calypso singer and dancer, as well as a generally accomplished vocalist and musician. In February 1955, while headlining a show on Chicago's Rush Street called Calypson Follies, he attended the Nation of Islam National Savior's Day Convention, He was recruited into the Nation by Malcolm X and accepted the teachings of Elijah Muhammad.[77]

After living in New York and training under Malcolm X, Louis was recommended by Malcolm X to head the Boston Temple of Islam where he served as minister for nine years (1956-1965)[78] under the name Louis X, Although Louis had been Malcolm X's protégé, he unhesitatingly denounced Malcolm's 1964 defection from Elijah Muhammad in the strongest terms.[79]

In May 1965, just three months after the death of Malcolm X, Elijah

Muhammad appointed Louis to succeed Malcolm as Minister of Temple No. 7 in New York City, building it up to become the strongest in the Nation of Islam. Seventeen businesses, three schools, five major Temples, and a host of satellite Temples scattered throughout the New York area were opened.[80] He also used his musical gifts in promoting the Nation. His unusual ability to speak and expound Elijah Muhammad's message attracted thousands of people in the New York area to the Nation. The largest gathering of African-Americans in the history of Harlem turned out on Randall's Island on May 31, 1974, to hear Louis deliver the Black Family Day Speech, About one year later, in June 1975, after the death of Elijah Muhammad, before a vast crowd in Madison Square Garden, Louis was removed from his position as the Minister of New York City.[81] Then, the following month, the leadership moved him to the West Side of Chicago. No official explanation has been published, but it may be that Imam Warith had some presentiment of Louis's possible future influence. After a few months, Louis himself "decided he would no longer use his voice as a minister."[82]

At first, Farrakhan accepted his new invisibility, but gradually he came to believe that Imam Warith's reformation was aimed at cloaking the entire vision of Elijah Muhammad and dismantling its infrastructure. To be so near to the scene of this destruction and yet so far from having the power required to stop it eventually drove Farrakhan to a decision. In 1977, as a result of visiting the Near East, Africa, South and Central America, and Europe, Farrakhan decided, after seeing a worsening in the condition of black people, that he should use his ability to help black people in the only way he could see that would be of benefit to them, namely: through the teachings of Elijah Muhammad. Accordingly, Farrakhan left Warith's World Community of Islam in the West to reform Elijah Muhammad's Lost-Found Nation of Islam in the Wilderness of North America. The parting was peaceful, and relationships among all the various factions have remained good. One possible factor of significance could be that some of Farrakhan's eleven children had intermarried with some of Elijah Muhammad's grandchildren. This fusion seems to have set the tone in establishing a climate of coexistence for a whole spectrum of variously focused Muslim groups.[83]

Since 1977, Louis Farrakhan has traveled throughout America, as well as visiting the West Indies and Africa on lecture tours, bringing "the message of The Honorable Elijah Muhammad for the unity of Black people."[84] During the years 1977-1990, Farrakhan made considerable strides in rebuilding the Nation of Islam. He began by reassembling the infrastructure of his "new" Nation solidly and unequivocally on the foundations laid by the original builders. The teachings about the nature of Allah, Yakub, the white man, Armageddon, and the like, were reinstated. The original declaration of "What the Muslims Believe" and "What the Muslims Want" remain intact. The paper *Muhammad*

Speaks was resurrected as *The Final Call*. Muslim entrepreneurship was once again made an important aspect of the faith. In the face of escalating unemployment, the Nation sought to take care of its own as Elijah Muhammad had taught it.[85] Once the reconstructed Nation began to reproduce the organizational style so familiar to the era of Elijah Muhammad, hundreds of members who had simply fallen away rather than accept Imam Warith's changes hurried back. Some brought in new recruits. Farrakhan[86] and, in November of that year, Farrakhan asserted: "the Honorable Elijah Muhammad is not physically dead."[87]

Farrakhan's anti-Jewish reputation has generated a reluctance among US colleges to allow him on their campuses, yet he remains popular among African-American students.[88] In 1986, he was barred from entry to the UK, a ban that still applies. For the last few years, Farrakhan has made a strong impact on African-American communities by going into churches and preaching the unity of all black people and maintaining that Muslims, Christians, and people of other persuasions have the capability to join hands as brothers and sisters and work together.[89] Thus, although Farrakhan opposes the cardinal tenets of Christianity, he is not antagonistic to Black Christians as individuals. In 1990 Farrakhan was permitted to address the Continental Muslim Council, a body representing mainstream Islam in the US. In the course of his address he affirmed his commitment to the Shahadan (the basic confession of Islamic belief), and on the strength of overt support from Imam Warith Muhammad among others, Farrakhan was accepted for membership on "profession of faith."[90]

THE BASIC TENETS OF THE NATION OF ISLAM

The Nation of Islam, under Elijah Muhammad, taught a range of key concepts, which are today endorsed by Louis Farrakhan, ranging from notions about the first God to the first religion of black people.

According to the Nation, there were several gods from the beginning of time, such that one God lives and dies and passes his knowledge and godship from one to another.[91] This occurs in cycles of 25,000 years, and therefore each god is not eternal.[92] The first God is said to have created himself from triple darkness.[93] He was a man and not a spirit, or "spook."[94] All these gods are actually "Blackmen,"[95] although the 'god' of the present cycle is said to be half black and half white, and to have come to earth as Master W. D. Fard.[96]

It is also taught that there is a committee of 24 gods, one of whom acts as Judge or "God" for the others, becoming "God of gods," while the other 23 do the work of getting up the future of the Nation.[97] Different gods have different functions, so that one god created the sun, another created the moon, and another created the stars and earth.[98] This committee makes history once every 25,000 years.[99]

These gods are really human beings; they make mistakes, marry, eat food, have sex and produce babies, so that one of the gods, named Alfonso, visited Europe, married a white woman, and produced a daughter. This was a mistake, and the lesson concerning this actually portrays Alfonso ("God") as saying, "Oops, we missed that time."[100]

Human beings are viewed by the Nation as consisting of two distinct races, one black and the other white. The "Black man" is self-created[101] and, therefore, the "Original Man,"[102] as well as the "maker and owner of the universe," including planet earth.[103] The black race consists of the only true human beings, who were here in the beginning.[104]

The original religion of the "Blackman" is said to have been Islam and their God, Allah.[105] All "Black men" are god,[106] but Allah is the supreme "Blackman" and, therefore, "God of gods."[107] Allah is thought to be present within all black people.[108] Clearly this bears little resemblance to the Islam which was taught by Muhammad (A.D. 570-632) in Saudi Arabia. Whereas Muslims believe that the Arabic Qur'an is the final book from God, the Nation teaches that both Bible and Qur'an were written by the scientist-gods appointed to arrange history.[109] The present books are only intended for this particular cycle of 25,000 years and will both be superseded by the "Last Book" which will take the Nation into the Hereafter.[110]

Black people are said to be "descendants of the Asian black nation and of the tribe of Shabazz.[111] Sixty trillion (60,000,000,000,000) years ago, a great explosion is said to have divided the planet into two parts; one part is called "earth" and the other "moon."[112] At that time, the Tribe of Shabazz came with this part, the "earth."[113]

The descendants of the Tribe of Shabazz, the black people, are said to be good and highly religious by very nature.[114] Islam is said to be their natural religion.[115] They have the nature of God and so can evolve to such a high mental level that they can themselves become gods.[116]

"Brown," "Yellow" and "Red" people are thought to be the "brothers" of black people,[117] whereas the origin of the white race is explained by the activities of another dissatisfied scientist-god, Dr Yakub. In 4000 BC, Dr Yakub wanted to cause trouble on the earth so he decided to breed a race of people[118] who were evil by nature,[119] a "grafted race,"[120] which was "white"[121] or "Caucasian."[122] This took place in "Pelan" (Patmos) in the Aegean Sea.[123]

This "white race is said to be "a race of devils"[124] and "the man of sin."[125] The "white man" is presented as "a great deceiver, liar and a murderer by nature."[126] Whites are regarded as "a people who by nature are evil, wicked, and have no good in them."[127] In fact responsibility for this state of affairs is actually passed back to the original righteous blacks since Dr Yakub was black. It was he who devised the "white race," who taught them wickedness and how to rule the "Blackman."[128]

This race was "made to rule the nations of earth for 6000 years."[129] Accordingly, the religion which the white man taught was actually obedience to himself.[130] Elijah Muhammad wrote that "this present world was sentenced to death when the Man of Sin was made and all who follow him."[131] It was at this time, according to Elijah Muhammad that "Islam first temporarily ceased to dominate mankind."[132]

Interracial hatred is explained in the following way. Because the white man has a different god or father from the black people, it is inevitable that he should hate black people.[133]

Since its beginning 6000 years ago, the "white race" brought trouble upon the original people of the earth, especially the black people. Therefore "the righteous black nation" will labor "under the wicked rule of the devil for 6,000 years."[134] During this period Allah sends prophet after prophet to predict "the coming of God" who would appear at "the end of the world"[135] to deliver the "Blackman" from white rule. The white race is said to have invented Christianity as a supreme device for keeping black people in ignorance of their true identity and nature.[136] Elijah Muhammad wrote that from A.D. 570 (the birth of Muhammad in Arabia) until 1555 (the beginning of the transatlantic slave-trade), Islam kept the "devils" and Christianity bottled up in Europe.[137] This period culminated in a period of unprecedented tribulation for black people in the shape of the transatlantic slave trade when, it is said, the black people are said to have been "deceived and brought into America by a slave trader whose name was John Hawkins in the year 1555."[138]

The period of slavery persisted for 400 years (A.D. 1555 to 1955), during which time the "devils" were "loose" or free to travel over the earth and deceive the people.[139] This period of 400 years was prophesied (Genesis 15:13) as a time when the "so-called Negroes would have to serve (the white people)"[140] and is believed to have ended in 1955,[141] in fulfillment of the prophecy.

The slavemaster taught the slaves to eat the wrong food, especially "hog," in order to make them sick and shorten their lifespan,[142] and also stole their identity by taking away their names.[143]

Christianity is viewed as a system of psychological control to dominate the minds of black people;[144] for example: worshipping a "blond blue-eyed God,"[145] being content with their lot,[146] motivating them to be passive and not to defend themselves,[147] and to pray for their oppressors.[148] Jesus is said to be nothing more than a prophet of Islam[149] and, therefore, unable to hear prayer: only Allah can do that.[150]

As a result of having his identity, his name, his diet and his religion stolen, the black man has become "mentally dead," [151] made "blind, deaf and dumb by this white race of people"[152] and still "kept in slavery by the slave-master's children."[153] Consequently, they are "without the knowledge of self or anyone else."[154] They "remain asleep to the knowledge of self."[155] Therefore, the white man's religion (Christianity), church and his names are the three chains of slavery that hold black people in bondage to them. black people are free only when they reject them.[156]

Throughout the ages, prophets have been sent by Allah to predict "the coming of God," who would appear at "the end of the world." The "end of the world" here is taken to signify "the end of the white race."[157] This "true God was not to be made manifest to the people until the God of evil (devil) had finished or lived out his time which was allowed him to deceive the nations."[158] Then the end of the white race as a dominant power would end and their punishment would be administered.[159] Allah is said to have come to the "Blackman" from Mecca on July 4, 1930 in the person of W. D. Fard,[160] the second son of Alfonso and his European wife.[161] In this way, Fard took the place of "Allah" and Elijah Muhammad becomes his prophet, in place of the Muhammad of classical Islam.[162] Fard announced that the whites were soon to be judged. But although the time was said by him to be imminent, he also stated that it was conditional upon the "Blackman" waking up to his true nature and right to the whole earth.[163] The strongest judgments were due to come upon the US, but that it would be delayed until all black people had heard the call.[164]

The primary object of Elijah Muhammad's teaching was to bring "the so-called Negroes" to "the Knowledge of Self."[165] They had to become aware of their real identity (members of the Nation of Islam), their true place of origin (Asia = Africa), their real names, their real language (Arabic), their true God (Allah), their original religion (Islam, as interpreted by Elijah Muhammad), their glorious past and superior nature. This self-knowledge would lead to their "redemption."[166] Wishing to concentrate the emphasis of his people upon their struggle in the present, Elijah Muhammad regarded belief in an afterlife as a distraction.[167] Therefore, in Nation teaching, all references to an afterlife, whether in the Bible or in the Qur'an, are dismissed as "spook religion" and accordingly applied instead to conditions on the earth.

Heaven and hell are not places or states to which people are consigned after a judgment of all people by God. Rather they refer to conditions in this life, which must be brought about by the efforts of the "Blackman." So, according to the Nation," Islam . . . makes hell and heaven not two places but *two conditions of life*" neither being possible," unless it is brought about by our own efforts or making."[168]

Elijah Muhammad taught that every "Blackman" who "accepts the religion of Islam and follows what Allah has revealed" to him will begin enjoying "the above life" or the "Hereafter" right now.[169] He wrote: "It is true that God has come to sit us in heaven, but not a heaven wherein we won't have to work." [170]

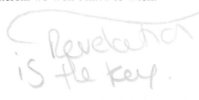
Revelation
is the key.

He wrote that "Allah" had made clear what constitutes heaven on earth, namely: "Freedom, Justice, Equality; money, good homes and friendship in all walks of life."[171] He taught that "Allah" offers "the righteous Heaven (riches) while they are alive."[172] He wrote of an "eternal heaven," by which he meant a good life on earth after the judgment of the whites. He stated that "hell . . . is not eternal," but by "hell" he meant the bad conditions suffered by the black people in this life.[173] Resurrection is reinterpreted as referring to a "mental resurrection" which results from the preaching of "truth" to those who have become "mentally dead" under the influence of "the devil's falsehood." Elijah Muhammad argued that there is nothing left to rise from the dead of a body which has decayed or been burnt, and so on, and actually maintained that the Old Testament does not teach physical resurrection at all.[174]

For Elijah Muhammad, the very purpose of Islam was to raise "the so-called Negroes" from "their mentally-dead condition."[175]

The hereafter is used as a term to designate the condition on earth after the hated whites, and their black lackeys, have been destroyed.[176] Elijah Muhammad resented any presentation of Christianity that gave the impression that the oppressed would have a good afterlife and so would be induced to bear passively the oppression in this life.[177] He believed that good things were available for the "Blackman" even in this life, just as much as for the white.[178]

The time of judgment, instead of following a physical resurrection, was believed to be a historical event that would take place in this life.[179] The Islam of the Nation was simply an instrument in the hands of "Allah" to "separate the righteous from the evil-doers" even now.[180] In effect, this meant a separation between "black and white" people."Allah" was said to be even "now pointing out to the nations of the earth their rightful places" and the judgment will bring an end to wars over the occupation of land.[181] The first target for judgment will be the US, but not until "the so-called Negroes" have heard the truth.[182]

The "awakening" of the 'black man' is said to be "the last step in the Resurrection and judgment of the world."[183] Therefore, the greatest desire of the white man is that the black people should remain asleep.[184]

It might be thought that the Nation's future would be good for all black people. On the contrary, it is prophesied that only 144,000 will be saved. The 16,856,000 black people who will not accept the Nation's teaching will suffer judgment along with whites, although Muhammad hoped that the prophet could be proved wrong and that more could be saved![185]

The "white race," or "world," is to be destroyed by Allah at the end of the age, although by natural calamities rather than by a directly supernatural work.[186] One instrument of judgment was said to be a special man-made planet, called "the Mother Plane," which looks like a UFO.[187] While the earth is being bombed, African-Americans will be taken up into this plane and out of the earth's atmosphere for a thousand years.[188] According to Mustafa El-Amin, a former Nation member, Minister Farrakhan has often said that he had a vision that he was on the Mother Plane with Elijah Muhammad and that he was warned that the US would bomb Libya.[189] The Nation could look forward to a "Hereafter," that is "seeing and living under a ruler and a government of righteousness, after the destruction of the unrighteous."[190] But there will be no place for whites in this "Hereafter," which is a continuation of the present bodily existence in which the Nation can make "unlimited progress."[191] "What is meant by the Hereafter? It means, 'After the destruction of the present world, its power and authority to rule,' More specifically, it means, 'After the present rule of the Man of Sin.' "[192]

It goes without saying that the message of the Nation of Islam is only for the "Blackman." whites are deemed incorrigibly evil[193] and, now that their 6000 years are completed, they are worthy only of destruction.[194] For black people, however, there is still hope. They can be forgiven by Allah for their waywardness if they repent.[195] But those who do not join up quickly will be judged.[196]

All of this deviates from orthodox Islam, which teaches that God is the supreme and invisible Being, Creator of all things, and that his only prophet is Muhammad of the Qureish tribe (570-632). It also teaches the existence of a world of spirits and that people will be judged by God after a physical resurrection. Islam also maintains that people should be obedient to the teachings of the *Qur'an* and certain *Hadith* (or "traditions").[197] The non-Islamic nature of the Nation is evident also in its approach to Islamic practices, such as the dress code, fasting, prayer, observance days, and Temple conduct. The Nation is stricter in its dress code for men, but less strict in its code for women. Nation men usually wear a suit, white shirt, and bow tie. They have close-cut hair and shave off all facial hair. When required, they wear the red and blue FOI uniform. Women cover their hair, wear long dresses and never expose their body in public.[198]

Fasting occurs in December, as opposed to Ramadhan, although the Ramadhan fast is optional,[199] as are certain other practices which would be considered obligatory in mainstream Islam.[200] Formerly, the major holiday for the Nation was February 26, a celebration of the birthday of W. D. Fard, believed to have been February 26, 1877, but more recently Minister Farrakhan instituted October 7 also as "Savior's Day," in celebration of Elijah Muhammad. Some of his followers observe both occasions as "Savior's Day."[201]

NATION RULES OF CONDUCT

In their day-to-day living, ordinary *Nation* members are governed by a strict code of private and social morality considered appropriate to divine black men and women in their capacity as true rulers of the planet.[202]

Certain foods, such as pork and corn bread, are forbidden on the grounds that "they are a slow death" to those who eat them. Many other foods common to the diet of African Americans, especially in the southern states, are forbidden on the grounds that they constitute a "slave diet" and "there are not slaves in Islam." Lamb, chicken, fish, and beef are approved, but all foods must be strictly fresh. The hog is considered filthy—"a poison food, hated of Allah"— and was never intended to be eaten, except by the "white race."[203]

Nation members are warned against overeating. In general, one meal a day is considered sufficient. Tobacco is forbidden. Certain temple activities are considered morally binding, and lapses can be swiftly punished. For example, Nation members are required to attend two (and occasionally more) Temple meetings a week. In unusual circumstances, they may be excused if permission is secured in advance, but those who fail to attend without such permission are suspended. Male members are also expected to "fish for the dead," or go into the streets in search of potential members, and unsuccessful "fishermen" are penalized. A strict sexual morality is also said to be vehemently enforced, any philanderer being answerable to the FOI, a quasi-judicial militia. Courtship or marriage outside the Nation is discouraged, and constant pressure to join is put on spouses who are nonmembers. Divorce is frowned on, but permitted. No female member may be alone in a room with any man other than her husband. [204]

Officially, Nation members are exhorted never to initiate violence, but only to retaliate against those who are violent toward them. However, remarks by Malcolm X would suggest that this policy has also been used to justify attacks upon those who are felt to threaten the movement as a whole.[205]

There was at one time a strong emphasis on the equality of the ministers and the "brothers," all tending to live similarly in terms of housing and visible goods," but there is some recent evidence that this ideal of brotherly equality is being modified in its application to the life-styles of some of those closest to the center of the power." [206]

Although the Nation went heavily into debt during the time of Elijah Muhammad,[207] being in debt is discouraged, as far as individuals are concerned, and thrift is encouraged. Money must not be wasted, and no members are expected to live beyond their means. Eventually the hope is that no Nation member will have to work for a white.[208]

These standards are generally so high that many people find the pressures too great and leave the movement. People leaving the movement for these reasons, however, still feel that the Nation is basically right, the problem being a failure in themselves as individuals. Thus, although they "give up trying" to live up to the standards, they retain the Nation mindset. This phenomenon facilitates the dissemination of this mindset throughout a catchment much wider than the confines of Nation membership. Thus its ideals and mythology have become widely influential amongst African-Americans in general.

NATION GOALS

The goals of the Nation of Islam are never fully spelled out, not because such goals do not exist, but probably in the interests of diplomacy.[209]

Basic goals are the unity of all African-Americans in a country of their own.[210] It is believed that the white nations will destroy each other and that the Black Nation will inherit the spoils.[211] A basic belief of the Nation is "racial separation," and personal relationships with whites should, therefore, be severed immediately. Economic severance is said to be under way, but political severance is a future goal. Only with complete racial separation will the perfect harmony of the universe be restored.[212]

The Nation is against intermarriage between races. Nation members are convinced of their superior racial heritage, therefore, there should be no more mixture.[213] The white race will soon perish, and when that happens, the merest trace of white blood will consign its possessor to an inferior status.[214]

Elijah Muhammad saw his mission as including the repurification of all, biologically. Not until this has been accomplished can African-Americans assume their rightful place of dignity and leadership among the triumphant Black nations of the world.[215]

There is ambiguity in statements concerning the requirement of land. Although the Nation has often mentioned the alternative of leaving the US, this possibility is never emphasized.[216] More often it is stated that land in the US is required,[217] perhaps "four or five states"[218] or "nine or ten states would be enough,"[219] and the Southwest has featured prominently in speculation.[220]

There are indications, however, that Elijah Muhammad did not really consider the physical separation of races in the US a viable prospect and that he considered that white Americans should return to Europe: "The wicked must be punished for their wickedness poured out upon us. . . . This country is large enough to separate the two (black and white), and they both [could] live here, but that will not be successful. The best solution is for everyone to go to his own country. . . . The native home of the white race is Europe.[221]

SOCIAL DIMENSIONS

The Nation of Islam of today is constantly seeking to extend its influence beyond its membership. Louis Farrakhan has succeeded in arresting the attention of the entire African-American and Caribbean community by his determination to unite all blacks regardless of religious persuasion. Consequently, his audiences are made up of large numbers of professing Christians and Rastafarians. Conversely, he has been invited by a number of Christian ministers to speak in their meeting places. He has commended himself to outsiders by championing a number of issues that are a great cause of social concern. The escalating breakdown of marriages in the US and Western' society as a whole is seen as a threat to the foundations of society. By contrast, the proclamation of the family as the key element in a stable society is a feature of the Nation.

Rehabilitation of convicts has been on the Nation's agenda from the outset. This is done by convincing the ex-convict that he fell into crime because he was ashamed of being black and had been conditioned not to respect himself. Then he is convinced that being black is a blessing and accordingly he must clean himself up and live a life of decency and respect.[222]

A similar approach is used in combating the drugs problem.[223] In the words of Farrakhan, "There is a reason why a man seeks drugs and that reason is that the man does not have a healthy love and a healthy respect of self. But when a man knows himself, and loves himself, he will not poison himself or destroy himself.[224] His antidrug stance is also clear in a number of speeches,[225] Farrakhan claimed that Elijah Muhammad had, by this means," combatted drugs more effectively than any drug program ever put forth by the government."[226]

Since 1984, through the efforts of Dr. Abdul Alim Muhammad and Dr. Barbara Justice, the Nation has undertaken work with AIDS patients and the licensing of new therapy. Although opposed by the general medical community, the Nation medical team continues its work, retaining significant support from the African-American community.[227]

Cleaning up crime is also on the Nation's program. Private security firms, such as "New Life Self Development" and "X-Men," are on the increase. Together with N.O. I. Security Agency, Inc. [NOISA], based in Washington, DC, and frequently advertised in *The Final Call* newspaper, these are said to hold about $10,000,000 in contracts at nine public housing developments in Baltimore, Maryland, Washington, DC, Chicago, IL, Buffalo, NY, and Dayton, OH. These firms claim to have reduced crime levels and to have reduced vacancy rates where they operate,[228] and the success of the NOISA operation has made US national news.[229] On the face of it, this sounds very good. But to whom is the Nation accountable when it undertakes these operations? Is there any court of appeal if a person is wrongly taken to be a drug-dealer?

Again, it cannot be overlooked that the Nation has throughout its lifetime entertained links with white supremacist groups, such as the Ku Klux Klan and the American Nazi Party, under the leadership of George Lincoln Rockwell, who attended *Nation* rallies on June 25, 1961, and February, 25, 1962, where he spoke briefly.[230] This continues even today. In the *National Front News*, issued in mid-1988, a photograph appeared of a National Front leader observing a Nation antidrug operation in Washington DC, evidently part of the very operations reported so favourably in *The Final Call*.[231] In 1992, attention was drawn to these disturbing features in a front-page article in *The Weekly Journal*, a publication that claims to present news from a black perspective.[232] It is significant that the Nation of today and white supremacist groups have three particular emphases in common: the belief that the human race can be subdivided into distinct races, the political goal of ultimate racial separation, and a tendency to use the Jews as a scapegoat for the problems in the world of today, Particularly they share a belief in a conspiracy in which the Jews are alleged to be the key players.

RAP AND CONVERSION

One of the attractions of the Nation for young men is its link with the entertainment world and particularly the hip-hop culture. The conversion of Cassius Clay to Muhammad Ali is well known. But other celebrities have had contacts with the Nation, such as Michae Benett, Shaquille O'Neal, Spike Lee, Leo X Chester, Andre Harrell, Tupac Shakur, and Ice Cube. Indeed according to *Voice* reporter Dionne St Hill, "Rap, more than any other music genre, has proved a fertile ground for young converts." West Coast rapper Kam became a Nation member while in hospital recovering from a near-fatal shooting, and Eclipse mouthpiece, MCD, was converted through Leo X Chester and attends the West London Study Center.[233]

A number of others have accepted aspects of the Nation's message, although they are not members. These use rap to attack the system, as they see it, and to present an alternative value-system based on those aspects of Nation thinking that they accept. Examples of this are Chuck D of Public Enemy and Ice Cube, whose record *Lethal Injection* [234] included a speech by Dr. Khallid Muhammad, former National Spokesperson for the Nation, but now somewhat distanced by Farrakhan because of the anti-Jewish vitriol in his notorious Kean College speech.[235]

In general, the Nation appeals more to the younger age range (15-30) and particularly to males. A major factor in its appeal is the perceived irrelevance for today's youth of the "Black Pentecostal" churches, which are perceived as female-dominated and are, therefore, failing to generate appropriate role models for young men.

In Great Britain, family events, referred to generically as "edutainment," are currently held under the auspices of P.O.W.E.R. (People Organized and Working for Economic Rebirth) on bank holidays at Hammersmith Town Hall, London, with professional comedian Leo X Chester ("Mr Edutainment himself") usually headlining.

Professor Eric Lincoln estimated US membership at between 70,000 and 100,000 in 1994.[236] However, a more recent estimate, made by a student of

Islamics, is that formal membership in the US is no more than 20,000, many attenders at public meetings being professing Christians. He has contrasted this with Warith Muhammad's membership estimated at 400,000.

CONCLUSIONS

On the one hand, the Nation of Islam can be seen as a cult that plays upon the aspirations of the African-American and Caribbean communities, providing for them a powerful, but fanciful mythology, thus countering disinformation in one direction with confusion in another.

On the other hand, the Nation can be seen as a pacesetting movement with a leader whose finger is on the pulse of Black issues, and with whom considerable numbers of black people are proud to identify. In a sense, both perspectives are equally true. One thing is clear: the influence of the Nation is far greater than would be expected from its small membership. If the Nation did not exist, the inevitable vacuum would have to be filled. Anyone who desires to supplant the Nation's influence will have to surpass the level of esteem in which Farrakhan is held and develop an even more compelling framework in which members of the African diaspora become aware of their true stature.

NOTES

1. Clifton E. Marsh, *From Black Muslims to Muslims: The Transition from Separatism to Islam, 1930-1980* (Metuchen, NJ: Scarecrow Press, 1984), p. 18.

2. The information on Marcus Garvey and the UNIA is derived from the following: Peter B. Clarke, *Black Paradise: The Rastafarian Movement* (Wellingborough: Aquarian Press, 1986), pp. 27, 36-44; Edmund Cronon, *Black Moses*. Madison: University of Wisconsin Press, 1948, pp. 16-17, 41-47, 65-70, 107-132, 176-187; E. U. Essien-Udom, *Black Nationalism: A Search for an Identity in America;* (Chicago: University of Chicago Press, 1962), pp. 36-43, 46, 48-49, 55-56, 59-63, 95, 98, 130, 132, 333, 347; C. Eric Lincoln, *The Black Muslims in America.* 3rd ed. (Trenton, NJ: Africa World Press, 1994), pp. 47, 52-61. Adib Rashad, *Elijah Muhammad and the Ideological Foundation of the Nation of Islam* (Hampton, VA: U.B. & U.S. Communications Systems, 6/1994), pp. 36-52, 121.

3. The information on Noble Drew Ali and the Moorish Science Temple is derived from the following: Anon. "A New Islam in America," in "Current Topics," in: *Moslem World*, 25 New York, NY: 5. Zwemer, January 1935), pp. 78-79; G. H. Bousquet, "Moslem Religious Influences in the United States," in *Moslem World*, 25 (New York, NY: S. Zwemer, January 1935), pp. 40-44; Essien-Udom, *Black Nationalism*, pp. 18, 33-36, 43, 45-46, 48, 60-61, 63, 66, 167, 346-347; Arthur H. Fauset, "Moorish Science Temple of America," in J. Milton Yinger, (ed.). *Religion, Society and the Individual*

(New York: Macmillan, 1957), pp. 458-507; C. Eric Lincoln, *The Black Muslims in America.* 3rd (Trenton, NJ: Africa World Press, 1994), pp. 47-52, 257; Aminah Beverly McCloud, *African-American Islam* (New York: Routledge, 1995), pp. 10-18, 54-56; Gordon Melton, J., "Black Muslims," in "The Eastern Family (Jews and Muslims)," in Gordon Melton, J., *The Encyclopedia of American Religions* (Wilmington, NC: McGrath Publishing, 1978), pp. 339-340; Rashad, Adib. *Elijah Muhammad and the Ideological Foundation of the Nation of Islam.* Hampton, VA: U.B, & US Communications Systems, 6/1994, pp. 53-91.

4. Marsh, *From Black Muslims to Muslims*, pp. 25-38.

5. Lincoln, *The Black Muslims in America*, p. 62.

6. Beynon, Erdmann Doane. "The Voodoo Cult among Negro Migrants in Detroit," in *The American Journal of Sociology,* 43(6), July 1937-May 1938, p. 895. According to Beynon, "The cult received the name 'Voodoo' solely because of cases of human sacrifice" (p. 894). Fard is said to have lived in Detroit from July 4, 1930, to June 30, 1934.

7. Ibid., p. 896.

8. Ibid., p. 895.

9. Ibid., p. 899.

10. Ibid., p. 901.

11. Beynon, "The Voodoo Cult among Negro Migrants in Detroit," pp, 895-896.

12. Marsh, *From Black Muslims to Muslims* p.44; Muhammad, Wallace D., July 25, 1979, quoted in Ibid, pp. 41, 107.

13. Beynon, "The Voodoo Cult among Negro Migrants in Detroit," p. 896.

14. Ibid., p. 900.

15. Ibid., p. 901.

16. Prophet W. D. Fard, *Teaching for the Lost Found of Islam in a Mathematical Way,* Problem No.30, quoted in "The Voodoo Cult among Negro Migrants in Detroit," p. 897.

17. Ibid., p. 898.

18. Ibid., p. 899.

19. Ibid., p. 900.

20. Ibid., p. 902.

21. Ibid., pp. 896-897.

22. Sister Carrie Mohammed (Mrs Carrie People), quoted in ibid., p. 896.

23. Ibid., p. 897.

24. Lincoln, *The Black Muslims in America,* pp. 15, 179-180, 257.

25. Lincoln, *The Black Muslims in America,* pp.257; Essien-Udom, *Black Nationalism,* p. 74.

26. Lincoln, *The Black Muslims in America,* p. 180; Essien-Udom, *Black Nationalism,* pp. 74-75.

27. Beynon, "The Voodoo Cult among Negro Migrants in Detroit," p. 901.

28. Essien-Udom, *Black Nationalism,* pp. 68-69; Lincoln, *The Black Muslims in America,* p. 180.

29. Beynon, "The Voodoo Cult among Negro Migrants in Detroit," p. 903; Essien-

Udom, *Black Nationalism,* pp. 226-227.

30. Elijah Muhammad, *The Supreme Wisdom: Solution to the so-called Negroes' Problem.* 2nd ed. (Chicago, IL: University of Islam, 1957), p.15.

31. Lincoln, *The Black Muslims in America,* pp. 180.

32 Ibid., pp. 180-181.

33. Beynon, "The Voodoo Cult among Negro Migrants in Detroit," p. 897.

34. Lincoln, *The Black Muslims in America,* p. 16.

35. Ibid., p. 181.

36. Ibid., p. 186.

37. Ibid., p. 181; Essien-Udom, *Black Nationalism,* pp. 4, 67-69.

38. Malcolm X, *The Autobiography of Malcolm X,* with the assistance of Alex Haley (London: Penguin, 1968), pp. 248-288.

39. Muhammad, *The Supreme Wisdom,* p. 43.

40. Lincoln, *The Black Muslims in America,* p.182.

41. Malcolm X, *The Autobiography,* pp. 79-90; Lincoln, *The Black Muslims in America,* pp. 189-90.

42. Malcolm X, *The Autobiography,* pp. 93-112.

43. Ibid., pp.117-8; Lincoln, *The Black Muslims in America,* p.189.

44. Malcolm X, *The Autobiography,* pp. 121-243; Lincoln, *The Black Muslims in America,* p.189.

45. Lincoln, *The Black Muslims in America,* pp. 190.

46. Malcolm X, *The Autobiography,* pp. 244-287.

47. Lincoln, *The Black Muslims in America,* pp. 190.

48. Marsh, *From Black Muslims to Muslims,* p. 55.

49. Lincoln, *The Black Muslims in America,* p. 188.

50. Malcolm X, *The Autobiography,* p. 398; Lincoln, *The Black Muslims in America,* p. 188.

51. Sande Smith, *The Life and Philosophy of Malcolm X* (London: Bison Books, 1993), p. 6.

52. Malcolm X, *The Autobiography,* pp. 396-429; Smith, *The Life and Philosophy of Malcolm X,* pp. 49, 53-54.

53. *New York Times* (February 12, 1963), quoted in Lincoln, *The Black Muslims in America,* p. 191.

54. Malcolm X, *The Autobiography,* pp. 410-411; Lincoln, *The Black Muslims in America,* p. 191.

55. Malcolm X, *The Autobiography,* pp. 404-413, 416; Smith, *The Life and Philosophy of Malcolm X,* p. 53.

56. Smith, *The Life and Philosophy of Malcolm X,* pp. 54-55; Lincoln, *The Black Muslims in America,* p. 191

57. Malcolm X, *The Autobiography,* pp. 38-39, 447-456.

58. Marsh, *From Black Muslims to Muslims,* pp. 83-86; Malcolm X, *The Autobiography,* pp. 58-66; Smith, *The Life and Philosophy of Malcolm X,* pp. 68-73; Lincoln, *The Black Muslims in America,* p. 191.

59. Lincoln, *The Black Muslims in America*, p. 182.

60. Malcolm X, *The Autobiography*, p. 396.

61. Lincoln, *The Black Muslims in America*, p. 263.

62. Aminah Beverly McCloud, "Epilogue," in Lincoln, *The Black Muslims in America*, p. 273.

63. Wallace D. Muhammad, (July 25, 1979), quoted in Marsh, *From Black Muslims to Muslims*, pp, 90, 112-113.

64. Marsh, *From Black Muslims to Muslims*, pp. 91, 114.

65. Aminah Beverly McCloud, "Epilogue," in Lincoln, *The Black Muslims in America*, p. 274; Aminah Beverly McCloud, *African-American Islam* (New York: Routledge, 1995), pp. 72-76.

66. Lincoln, *The Black Muslims in America*, p. 265; McCloud, "Epilogue," p. 274.

67. Lincoln, *The Black Muslims in America*, p. 265; McCloud "Epilogue," p.274; McCloud *African-American Islam*, p. 77.

68. McCloud, "Epilogue," p. 274; McCloud, *African-American Islam*. p. 78.

69. McCloud, "Epilogue," p. 274; McCloud *African-American Islam*, pp. 75-76.

70. For example, Atlanta, Georgia, and Los Angeles.

71. Lincoln, *The Black Muslims in America*, p. 267; McCloud, "Epilogue," p. 274.

72. Lincoln, *The Black Muslims in America*, p, 267; McCloud, "Epilogue," pp. 274-275.

73. McCloud, *African-American Islam*, pp. 83-84.

74. Lincoln, *The Black Muslims in America*, p. 267.

75. McCloud, "Epilogue" p. 275.

76. Lincoln, *The Black Muslims in America*, p. 268.

77. Abdul Akbra Muhammad, "Biography," in *Who is Louis Farrakhan? And What is the Nation of Islam?* (London: The Nation of Islam Headquarters, 1995).

78. Ibid.

79. Lincoln, *The Black Muslims in America*, p. 268.

80. Abdul Akbra Muhammad, "Biography" p. 2.

81. Ibid., pp. 2-3; Lincoln, *The Black Muslims in America*, p. 268,

82. Abdul Akbra Muhammad, "Biography" p. 3; Lincoln, *The Black Muslims in America*, p. 268.

83. Lincoln, *The Black Muslims in America*, p. 268.

84. Abdul Akbra Muhammad, "Biography" p. 3.

85. Lincoln, *The Black Muslims in America*, p. 269.

86. McCloud, *African-American Islam*, p. 82.

87. Louis Farrakhan, in *The Final Call* (November 1984), quoted in McCloud, *African-American Islam*, p. 78.

88. Lincoln, *The Black Muslims in America*, p. 269.

89. Abdul Akbra Muhammad, "Biography," p. 3.

90. Lincoln, *The Black Muslims in America*, pp. 268-9.

91. Mustafa. El-Amin, *The Religion of Islam and the Nation of Islam: What is the Difference?* (Newark, NJ: El-Amin productions, 1991), p. 4.

92. Ibid., p. 5.

93. Elijah Muhammad, *Our Saviour Has Arrived* (Newport News, VA: United Brothers Communications Systems, [1974]), pp. 41, 43, 46; El-Amin, *The Religion of Islam and the Nation of Islam*, p. 4.

94. Elijah Muhammad, *Message to the Blackman in America.* 3rd ed. (Newport News, VA: United Brothers Communications Systems, 1965), pp. 1-7, 9-10, 14-15, 18-19, 54.

95. Ibid., pp. 108-9.

96. El-Amin, *The Religion of Islam and the Nation of Islam*, p. 5.

97. Elijah Muhammad, *Message to the Blackman in America,* p. 108.

98. El-Amin, *The Religion of Islam and the Nation of Islam*, p. 4.

99. Elijah Muhammad, *Message to the Blackman in America,* pp. 108-9.

100. El-Amin, *The Religion of Islam and the Nation of Islam*, p. 5.

101. Elijah Muhammad, *Message to the Blackman in America,* p. 42.

102. Elijah Muhammad, *The Supreme Wisdom*, pp. 38-39; Elijah Muhammad, *Message to the Blackman in America*, pp. 42-43, 53-54, 118, 183, 186-187, 215-216, 229, 244, 266, 281, 289, 290, 294, 297, 317-318.

103. Elijah Muhammad, *The Supreme Wisdom*, p. 38; Elijah Muhammad, *Message to the Blackman in America*, pp. 53, 109.

104. Elijah Muhammad, *The Supreme Wisdom*, pp. 19, 38-39; Elijah Muhammad, *Message to the Blackman in America*, pp. 53, 88.

105. Elijah Muhammad, *The Supreme Wisdom*, pp. 36, 50; Elijah Muhammad, *Message to the Blackman in America*, pp. 70, 80.

106. Elijah Muhammad, *The Supreme Wisdom*, p. 23.

107. Elijah Muhammad, *Message to the Blackman in America*, pp. 246, 108.

108. Malcolm X, in "The Hate that Hate Produced" (television documentary), *Newsbeat,* presented by Mike Wallace and Louis Lomax on WNTA-TV, New York (July 10, 1959), quoted in Lincoln, *The Black Muslims in America*, p. 71; Elijah Muhammad, in "The Hate that Hate Produced" quoted in Ibid., p. 69; McCloud, *African-American Islam,* p. 29.

109. Elijah Muhammad, *Message to the Blackman in America*, p. l08.

110. Ibid., p. 97, 108.

111. Elijah Muhammad, *The Supreme Wisdom*, p. 33; Elijah Muhammad, *Message to the Blackman in America,* pp. 3, 14, 20, 31, 51, 64, 92, 131, 137-138, 243, 266, 299.

112. Elijah Muhammad, *Message to the Blackman in America*, pp. 31, 110.

113. Elijah Muhammad, *The Supreme Wisdom*, p. 33; Elijah Muhammad, *Message to the Blackman in America*, p. 31.

114. Elijah Muhammad, *The Supreme Wisdom*, p. 36; Elijah Muhammad, *Message to the Blackman in America*, pp. 108-122.

115. Elijah Muhammad, *The Supreme Wisdom*, p. 31; Elijah Muhammad, *Message to the Blackman in America*, p. 80.

116. El-Amin, *The Religion of Islam and the Nation of Islam*, pp. 13-14. Elijah Muhammad, *The Supreme Wisdom*, pp. 26, 25, 24; Elijah Muhammad, *Message to the Blackman in America*, pp. 6-7, 303.

117. Elijah Muhammad, *The Supreme Wisdom*, p. 38-39; Elijah Muhammad, *Message to the Blackman in America*, pp. 121, 222, 228, 267.

118. Elijah Muhammad, *The Supreme Wisdom*, p. 38.

119. Elijah Muhammad, *Message to the Blackman in America*, p. 23.

120. Elijah Muhammad, *The Supreme Wisdom*, p. 21; Elijah Muhammad, *Message to the Blackman in America*, pp. 28, 53, 228, 244, 266-267.

121. Elijah Muhammad, *The Supreme Wisdom*, p. 24, 38; Elijah Muhammad, *Message to the Blackman in America*, pp. 228, 244, 266-7

122. Elijah Muhammad, *The Supreme Wisdom*, p. 27; Elijah Muhammad, *Message to the Blackman in America*, pp. 28, 36.

123. Elijah Muhammad, *Message to the Blackman in America*, pp. 114, 116, 125-6; El-Amin, *The Religion of Islam and the Nation of Islam,* p. 28.

124. Elijah Muhammad, *The Supreme Wisdom*, p. 23, 25, 27; Elijah Muhammad, *Message to the Blackman in America*, pp. 2-6, 8-9, 11, 21, 23, 51, 60-61, 90, 98-106, 108-109,116-123, 127, 135-136, 185, 215, 218, 228, 230-231, 236, 262, 270, 282, 294, 296, 313-314, 328; Malcolm X, *The Autobiography*, pp. 105, 286, 312, 354.

125. Elijah Muhammad, *The Supreme Wisdom*, pp. 17-18, 24, 25.

126. Ibid., p.18.

127. Ibid., p.15.

128. Elijah Muhammad, *Message to the Blackman in America,* pp. 103-122;. El-Amin, *The Religion of Islam and the Nation of Islam*, pp. 36-37.

129. Elijah Muhammad, *The Supreme Wisdom*, p.42, see also p. 29; Elijah Muhammad, *Message to the Blackman in America*, pp. 2-4, 6, 9, 28, 32, 42, 53, 70, 74, 83, 88, 94, 100-2, 107, 111, 125, 128, 133, 142, 241, 243, 266, 270, 293, 300, 303.

130. Elijah Muhammad, *The Supreme Wisdom*, p.42; Elijah Muhammad, *Message to the Blackman in America*, p. 2, 6.

131. Elijah Muhammad, *The Supreme Wisdom*, p. 25.

132. Ibid., p. 29.

133. Elijah Muhammad, *The Supreme Wisdom*, p. 27; Elijah Muhammad, *Message to the Blackman in America*, pp. 24, 32, 94, 102.

134. Elijah Muhammad, *The Supreme Wisdom*, p.24; Elijah Muhammad, *Message to the Blackman in America*, pp. 83, 100; Elijah Muhammad, *Our Saviour Has Arrived,* p. 42.

135. Elijah Muhammad, *The Supreme Wisdom*, p.43; Elijah Muhammad, *Message to the Blackman in America*, pp. 3, 13.

136. Elijah Muhammad, *The Supreme Wisdom*, pp. 13-14; Elijah Muhammad, *Message to the Blackman in America*, pp. 18, 47, 60, 70, 83-84, 97, 99, 101, 221.

137. Elijah Muhammad, *The Supreme Wisdom*, pp. 42-43; Elijah Muhammad, *Message to the Blackman in America*, p.3.

138. Elijah Muhammad, *The Supreme Wisdom*, p. 15; Elijah Muhammad, *Message to the Blackman in America*, p.230; Elijah Muhammad, *Our Saviour Has Arrived,* p. 190.

139. Elijah Muhammad, *The Supreme Wisdom*, pp. 43; Elijah Muhammad, *Message to the Blackman in America*, p.3.

140. Elijah Muhammad, *The Supreme Wisdom*, p. 16; Elijah Muhammad, *Message to the Blackman in America*, pp. 5, 6, 20, 29, 36, 38, 44, 54, 63, 96, 102-104, 177, 179,182, 194-195, 209, 211, 216, 223-224, 237, 243-244, 271, 282, 295, 298-299, 308, 312, 314, 317.

141. Elijah Muhammad, *The Supreme Wisdom*, p. 16; Elijah Muhammad, *Message to the Blackman in America*, p. 38.

142. Elijah Muhammad, *The Supreme Wisdom*, p. 11; Elijah Muhammad, *Message to the Blackman in America*, pp. 17, 247.

143. Elijah Muhammad, *Message to the Blackman in America*, pp. 54-55, 43, 45, 47, 63.

144. Elijah Muhammad, *The Supreme Wisdom*, p. 13, 14; Elijah Muhammad, *Message to the Blackman in America*, pp. 18, 47, 60, 70, 83-84, 97, 99, 101, 221

145. Malcolm X, *The Autobiography*, pp. 319-320, 257, 354.

146. Ibid., pp. 257, 298, 424.

147. Elijah Muhammad, *The Supreme Wisdom*, p. 13; Malcolm X, *The Autobiography*, pp. 257, 313.

148. Elijah Muhammad, *The Supreme Wisdom*, p. 13.

149. Ibid., p. 16.

150. Elijah Muhammad, *The Supreme Wisdom*, p. 34; Elijah Muhammad, *Message to the Blackman in America*, pp. 3, 26, 32,

151. Elijah Muhammad, *The Supreme Wisdom*, p. 34, 36; Elijah Muhammad, *Message to the Blackman in America*, pp. 19, 50, 66, 97, 131, 249, 264,

152. Elijah Muhammad, *The Supreme Wisdom*, p. 11; Elijah Muhammad, *Message to the Blackman in America*, pp. 51, 65-66, 249, 267.

153. Elijah Muhammad, *The Supreme Wisdom*, p. 11; Elijah Muhammad, *Message to the Blackman in America*, p.47.

154. Elijah Muhammad, *The Supreme Wisdom*, p. 11.

155. Elijah Muhammad, *The Supreme Wisdom*, p. 34; Elijah Muhammad, *Message to the Blackman in America*, pp. 20, 31, 34, 36-37, 44-45, 51, 108, 220, 242, 244-245, 301, 306.

156. Elijah Muhammad, *The Supreme Wisdom*, p. 14; Elijah Muhammad, *Message to the Blackman in America*, p. 26.

157. Elijah Muhammad, *The Supreme Wisdom*, p. 43; Elijah Muhammad, *Message to the Blackman in America*, pp. 3, 13.

158. Elijah Muhammad, *The Supreme Wisdom*, p.42.

159. Ibid., pp. 33, 29, 18.

160. Elijah Muhammad, *The Supreme Wisdom*, p. 11, 13, 15, 17, 24; Elijah Muhammad, *Message to the Blackman in America*, pp,13, 16, 17, 19-20, 24-25, 27, 33, 42, 46, 49, 51, 53, 106, 141-142, 145, 155-6, 172, 179, 187, 233, 237, 242, 246, 259, 267, 269, 281, 325.

161. El-Amin, *The Religion of Islam and the Nation of Islam*, p. 5.

162. Elijah Muhammad, *Message to the Blackman in America*, pp. 231, 233; M. Amir Ali, *Islam or Farrakhanism.* (Chicago, IL: The Insitute of Islamic Information & Education, [c. 1991]), p.l.

163. Elijah Muhammad, *The Supreme Wisdom*, p. 34, 41; Elijah Muhammad, *Message to the Blackman in America*, p. 32.

164. Elijah Muhammad, *The Supreme Wisdom*, p. 11; Elijah Muhammad, *Message to the*

Blackman in America, pp. 13, 18.

165. Elijah Muhammad, *The Supreme Wisdom*, p. 11; Elijah Muhammad, *Message to the Blackman in America*, pp. 39-43.

166. Elijah Muhammad, *The Supreme Wisdom*, p. 11, 24, 41; Elijah Muhammad, *Message to the Blackman in America*, pp. 32, 39, 42.

167. Elijah Muhammad, *The Supreme Wisdom*, p. 30; Elijah, Muhammad, *Message to the Blackman in America*, p. 32.

168. Elijah Muhammad, *The Supreme Wisdom*, p. 35; Elijah Muhammad, *Message to the Blackman in America*, pp. 76-77, 97.

169. Elijah Muhammad, *The Supreme Wisdom*, p. 26.

170. Ibid., p. 19.

171. Ibid., p. 15.

172. Ibid., p. 33; see also: Elijah Muhammad, *Message to the Blackman in America*, pp. 22, 304.

173. Elijah Muhammad, *The Supreme Wisdom*, p. 44; Elijah Muhammad, *Message to the Blackman in America*, p. 76, see also pp. 97, 168, 188-190, 200, 237.

174. Elijah Muhammad, *The Supreme Wisdom*, p. 36.

175. Elijah Muhammad, *The Supreme Wisdom*, p. 34; Elijah Muhammad, *Message to the Blackman in America*, p. 168.

176. Elijah Muhammad, *The Supreme Wisdom*, p. 25-26; Elijah Muhammad, *Message to the Blackman in America*, pp. 83, 107, 247, 303; see also p.288.

177. Elijah Muhammad, *Message to the Blackman in America*, pp. 168, 304.

178. Elijah Muhammad, *The Supreme Wisdom*, p:.33, 28.

179. Elijah Muhammad, *The Supreme Wisdom*, pp. 41, 38; Elijah Muhammad, *Message to the Blackman in America*, pp. 53, 100, 254.

180. Elijah Muhammad, *The Supreme Wisdom*, p. 16; Elijah Muhammad, *Message to the Blackman in America*, pp. 38, 46, 63, 98, 208, 254.

181. Elijah Muhammad, *The Supreme Wisdom*, p.38; Elijah Muhammad, *Message to the Blackman in America*, p. 53

182. Elijah Muhammad, *The Supreme Wisdom*, p. 11; Elijah Muhammad, *Message to the Blackman in America*, pp. 5, 17, 46-48, 51-52, 88, 129, 172, 249, 268-281, 288, 298,

183. Elijah Muhammad, *The Supreme Wisdom*, p. 17; Elijah Muhammad, *Message to the Blackman in America*, pp. 13, 18.

184. Elijah Muhammad, *The Supreme Wisdom, (op. cit.)*, p. 17; Elijah Muhammad, *Message to the Blackman in America*, pp. 5, 11, 25.

185. Elijah Muhammad, *The Supreme Wisdom*, p. 41; Elijah Muhammad, *Message to the Blackman in America*, p. 46.

186. Elijah Muhammad, *The Supreme Wisdom*, p. 14; Elijah Muhammad, *Message to the Blackman in America*, pp. 17, 290-1.

187. Elijah Muhammad, *The Supreme Wisdom*, p. 14; Elijah Muhammad, *Message to the Blackman in America*, pp. 17-18, 290-91, 293.

188. El-Amin, *The Religion of Islam and the Nation of Islam*, p. 25.

189. Ibid., p. 26.

190. Elijah Muhammad, *The Supreme Wisdom,* pp, 24, 25, 39; Elijah Muhammad, *Message to the Blackman in America*, pp. 17, 51, 265.

191. Elijah Muhammad, *The Supreme Wisdom,* pp. 24, 25, 26; Elijah Muhammad, *Message to the Blackman in America,* p. 303.

192. Elijah Muhammad, *The Supreme Wisdom,* p. 25.

193. Ibid., p. 39.

194. Ibid., pp. 35, 24; Elijah Muhammad, *Message to the Blackman in America. (op.cit.,),* pp. 17, 36, 46, 49, 90, 280.

195. Elijah Muhammad, *The Supreme Wisdom,* p. 11.

196. Ibid., pp. 35, 36, 41.

197. Ali, *Islam or Farrakhanism,* p. 6.

198. El-Amin, *The Religion of Islam and the Nation of Islam,* p. 29.

199. Ibid., pp. 30-31.

200. Ibid., pp. 32-34.

201. Ibid., pp. 34-35.

202. Lincoln, *The Black Muslims in America,* p. 76.

203. Elijah Muhammad, *The Supreme Wisdom,* pp. 21-22, 42; Lincoln, *The Black Muslims in America,* p. 76.

204. Lincoln, *The Black Muslims in America,* p. 77.

205. "The Black Muslim movement: An assessment." Malcolm X in "Contact" panel discussion program, WINS Radio, New York (February 18, 1965), hosted by Stan Bernard, in Malcolm X, February 1965: *The Final Speeches.* Ed. Steve Clarke (New York: Pathfinder, 1992), pp. 184-211. Appearing with Malcolm X was former Nation member Aubrey Barnette, who had been assaulted under instructions from Malcolm when Malcolm was in the movement. Aubrey had written an article in the *Saturday Evening Post* (February 27, 1965) entitled "An Ex-Official Tells Why the Black Muslims Are a Fraud."

206. Lincoln, *The Black Muslims in America,* p. 86.

207. McCloud, "Epilogue," p. 202. See also: Malcolm X, "The Black Muslim Movement." p. 202.

208. Lincoln, *The Black Muslims in America*, pp. 85-90.

209. Ibid., p. 79.

210. Elijah Muhammad, *Message to the Blackman in America*, pp. 223-224

211. Lincoln, *The Black Muslims in America,* p. 82.

212. Ibid., p. 83; Elijah Muhammad, *Message to the Blackman in America,* pp. 216, 258-259, 272, 301, 314.

213. Elijah Muhammad, *Message to the Blackman in America. (op. cit.),* pp. 33, 107, 115.

214. Lincoln, *The Black Muslims in America,* pp. 84-85.

215. Lincoln, *The Black Muslims in America,* p. 85.

216. "Mr. Muhammad Speaks," Pittsburgh Courier (July 16, 1960), quoted in ibid., p. 91.

217. Elijah Muhammad speech in Washington, DC, quoted in *The Islamic News* (July

6, 1959), quoted in: Lincoln, *The Black Muslims in America*, p. 91; Malcolm X at the Boston University Human Relations Center, February 15, 1960, ibid., p. 92.

218. *Chicago Daily Defender* (March 5, 1960), in Lincoln, *The Black Muslims in America*, p. 91; see also: Essien-Udom, *Black Nationalism*, pp. 260-261.

219. Malcolm X, in a radio interview aired on Boston, MA (April 2, 1960), in Lincoln, *The Black Muslims in America*, p. 91.

220. Lincoln, *The Black Muslims in America*, p. 218.

221. "Mr. Muhammad Speaks," p. 93.

222. See: William J. Peterson, *Those Curious New Cults.* 2nd ed. (New Canaan, CT: Keats Publishing, 1975), p. 125.

223. Malcolm X, *The Autobiography* , pp. 363-367.

224. Louis Farrakhan interviewed on television in Bermuda, in Louis Farrakhan *Seven Speeches* (Western Kentucky University and The Final Call, 1992), p. 145. Original edition published 1974.

225. *How to Give Birth to a God*, speech (Chicago, Illinois, July 26, 1987), in Louis. Farrakhan, *Back Where We Belong: Selected speeches.* Ed. Joseph D. Eure and Richard M. Jerome (Philadelphia, PA: PC International Press, 1989), pp. 94, 108; and *Minister Farrakhan speaks at Morgan State University,* speech (Murphy Auditorium, Morgan State University, Baltimore, MD, October 30, 1983), in ibid., p. 129.

226. Louis Farrakhan interviewed on television in Bermuda, in *Seven Speeches* p. 145.

227. McCloud, *African-American Islam,* p. 83.

228. Tyrone 2XA McKeiver, "A Model for Community Policing," in *The Final Call* 14(11), March 29, 1995, p. 3.

229. McCloud, *African-American Islam,* p. 83.

230. Malcolm X, February 1965: *The Final Speeches,* p. 279.

231. "Multi-Racists on the Run," in *National Front News* NFN 109 (London: National Front [mid-1988], p. 1.

232. Heenan Bhatti, "Farrakhan and Far Right Join Hands," in *The Weekly Journal: News from a Black Perspective,* Issue 14 (London: The Voice, July 30, 1992), p. 1. See also Andrew Bell, "Unholy Alliance. Leaders of the National Front have been holding secret meetings with members of the black community in a bizarre attempt to set up joint campaigns promoting racial separatism," in *Time Out* Issue 932, (London: Time Out, June 29-July 6, 1988), p. 11.

233. Dionne St. Hill, "One Nation under a Groove," in: *The Voice* Issue 645 (London: The Voice, April 4, 1995), p. 22.

234. *Lethal Injection* was released in 1993 by Priority in the US and by Island Records of London, on December 6, 1993.

235. Dr Khallid Muhammad, *The Secret Relationship Between Blacks and Jews.* (November 29, 1993). In response to this speech, the AntiDefamation League took out a full-page advertisement in the *New York Times* incorporating extracts from the speech. It stated, "Minister Louis Farrakhan and the Nation of Islam claim they are moving toward moderation and increased tolerance. You decide." Excerpts out of sequence, from a transcript of remarks by Khalid Abdul Muhammad, Nation of Islam national spokesman,

at Kean College, NJ, November 29, 1993, in the *New York Times* (January 16, 1994), p. 11.
   236. Lincoln, *The Black Muslims in America*, p. 269.

13

Santería and *Curanderismo* in Los Angeles

Brian McGuire and Duncan Scrymgeour

Los Angeles is infamous as a city of religious heterogeneity. Due to a complex series of social and economic factors, the City of Our Lady, Queen of the Angels has historically supported manifold variations of traditional religion in addition to hosting a remarkable amount of spiritual innovation. Although volumes of work have attempted to answer the theoretical challenges these phenomena raise, missing from much of the literature is analysis of the religious variation found in the differing Latino communities that comprise the largest ethnic group in America's most demographically diverse city. Through immigration and the resulting importation of indigenous religious traditions as well as considerable religious creativity employed upon arrival, the Latino communities have enriched the Angeleno religious continuum while expanding their own religious identity.

Our interest is situated in what have often been called "folk" religions, that is, those traditions that have responded to the immediate spiritual, social, and physical needs of their adherents while historically operating outside the authority of institutionalized religion. We are concerned with the manner by which these traditions are maintained in Los Angeles, how they serve both to strengthen Latino identity and to act as a buffer against acculturation, and the way the peculiar characteristics of Los Angeles and its place-specific Latino experiences transform these traditions as they inform one another. In particular, we have focused on the juxtaposition of a fundamentally African religion, *Santería* and how it is received by practitioners of traditions native to Mexico subsumed under the umbrella term *Curanderismo*. Certain questions confronted us. Although large numbers of Cubans have immigrated to the U.S., they reside most visibly in the urban centers surrounding New York and Miami. The number of Cubans living in Los Angeles, though increasing, has never been substantial. Although 59 percent of the population of Los Angeles County is Latino, only one percent of the Latino population is Cuban, while a full 89 percent are Mexican or Central American (1990 U.S. Census). How then does *Santería* , a principally Cuban expression of Yoruba religion, continue to thrive in a city whose Latino community is dominated by natives of Mexico and Central America? In what way does *Curanderismo* lend itself to the propagation of *Santería* , and what socio-political realities facilitate this cooperation?

We discovered that the structural similarities of both religions render *Santería* assimilable by many Mexicans raised in *Curanderismo* traditions. Since both are Latin religions, a natural linguistic connection exists. The visual symbol systems historically imposed on both traditions by Roman Catholicism act as a coding system, and differences amount to variation in visual dialect rather than language. *Santería* and *Curanderismo* provide similar functional challenges as systems of physical, psychological, and social healing, yet only *Santería* offers the security of a larger religious community. This sense of community is essential as nativist feelings among Anglos in Los Angeles and subsequent changes in the political and social tenor of the city have made life for Latinos increasingly difficult. Thus, very real fears about continued residence, employment, and social organization have favored *Santería* as a system that provides a sense of community, within a religious setting that is familiar. In the botanicas—functioning as apothecaries, libraries, religious supply shops and spiritual centers to both traditions—we observed a distinctly African religion quietly evangelizing Mexicans and Central Americans, expanding definitions of identity and providing fundamental human services in the face of an increasingly hostile social context.

In the course of our examination, we use terms that although standard for Los Angeles require some explanation. The term Latino reflects a system of classification that is principally linguistic in nature. Latino then refers to those people who have immigrated from the Spanish-speaking countries in North, Central, and South America and those citizens of the United States who claim descent from those countries. By contrast, the term Anglo is used to designate English-speaking citizens of European descent. We realize that these terms have only relative meaning and are clumsy at best, but we have used them in place of alternate terms like *white* and *Hispanic* because they are used by the individuals who are the subject of our study. Likewise, the term *Curanderismo* poses some problems. It is a collective term for a series of different material and spiritual healing strategies. Within its indigenous context, sectarian divisions have been observed between its practitioners based on the nature of their approach (Finkler, 1985: 43). Other researchers feel that the *Curanderismo* practiced by Latinos in the United States constitutes a more structured whole, its practitioners competent at some level within a variety of methods (Trotter & Chavira, 1981: 61). Our study confirms the latter observations, at least in Los Angeles, and so we use the term in its broadest possible application. By contrast, our use of the term *Santería* is more specific and reflects Yoruba religion as it is practiced in its distinctly Cuban flavor. Although other forms of Afro-Caribbean religion are represented in Los Angeles, Cuban *Santería* facilitates the most contact with Mexicans living in the greater metropolitan area, and we have chosen therefore to make it the focus of our study.

METHODOLOGY

Casual observations concerning the growing number of *Santería*-oriented botanicas in areas with sizable non-Cuban Latino populations was our first indication that *Santería was* making inroads into the general Latino populace. A comparison of the sites of these botanicas to census blocks composed of non-Cuban Latinos confirmed our observations, and we set about attempting to explain it. We utilized a number of approaches in our attempt to understand the appeal of *Santería* to Latinos raised in the traditions of *Curanderismo.* There is a fair amount of literature available on *Curanderismo,* much of it concerning *Curanderismo's* existence in the United States, but relatively little concerns its practice in the peculiar environment of Los Angeles, and that which does predates what we believe to be fairly substantial political and social changes in the character of the city having far-reaching consequences for Latinos and Anglos alike. Likewise, most of the information on *Santería* in the U.S. concerns the Cuban communities of Miami and New York. The information available on *Santería* as it is practiced by Cubans living in Los Angeles is limited, due undoubtably to the relatively small size of the community. Whenever possible we have reviewed existing literature in an attempt to understand the progress that had been made previously. Most of our information concerning the relationship between Cuban *Santeros* and their Mexican clientele was obtained through interviews conducted with representatives from the communities in question. They provided an emic interpretation of their respective traditions and their functions which proved invaluable to our attempt to understand the manner by which *Curanderismo* acts as a point of departure and *Santería* as a destination. We have, therefore, attempted to let the adherents of both traditions speak for themselves, while respecting their desire for anonymity. All had perspectives on their religious devotion that extended outside their immediate concerns, and we have attempted to consider these interpretation as much as we have our own.

SIGNS OF CURANDERISMO

The members of La Raza [Mexicans and Mexican-Americans] do not divide the natural and the supernatural into separate compartments as Anglos do. A harmonious relationship between the natural and the supernatural is considered essential to human health and welfare, while disharmony precipitates illness and misfortune. (Madsen, 1964: 68)

Visitors to Los Angeles who drive along the city's main avenues and through its large Latino neighborhoods may spot curious metal signs placed above simple storefronts or notice flyers randomly pasted on telephone poles. These advertisements are normally in Spanish, sometimes in English, and they solicit the services of "Curanderas" or "Espiritistas." Some are professionally rendered, most less so, and often include small graphic silhouettes of gypsies hunched over crystal balls, astrological symbols, or the image of a Catholic saint, the words "health, money, and love" inscribed next to phone numbers and imaginative names like "La Senora Amelia" or "Hermana Marta." Although these notices may seem whimsical to the uninitiated, they are indications of the presence of a broad assortment of professional curanderos, practitioners of a variety of Mexican and Central American healing and spiritual traditions known collectively as *Curanderismo.*

Curanderismo, which comes from the Spanish verb *curar,* to heal, manifests itself in many different forms. Some of these methods are physical while others are spiritual or psychic. There are curanderos who utilize chiropractic methods of healing and manipulate bones and muscles in order to reflexively alter points of distress throughout the body. Others seek to heal the body though the imposition of herbal poultices or potions; still others cleanse the body by ritually sweeping it clean of pollution or by anointing it with specially prepared oils. The curanderos who market their services are often spiritual healers who rely on the manipulation of electric currents or spiritual entities to cure their patients. Whatever the method, the role of the curandero is central to the indigenous contexts of many Latino immigrants to Los Angeles and plays a large part in alleviating fears of physical hardship upon arrival.

Although *Curanderismo* has been in the Southwest portion of the United States for centuries, the rise in Latino immigration during the second half of this century makes its presence more visible. *Curanderismo* is fundamentally a survival of indigenous pre-Columbian religions, encrusted with colonial religious ideologies and symbol systems that acts as a form of folk medicine in many parts of Latin America (Aguirre Beltran: 1963, 73-81; Marzal, 1985: 39-74). Its many disciplines reflect the historical periods that contributed to its development. Therapeutic massage and the lengthy taxonomies of medicinal flora are the inheritance of its Mayan and Aztec origins. The missionary Catholicism of Spain and its attending hagiolatry are evident in the devotion to saints mediated through the use of statuettes, candles, holy cards, and chromo lithographs. The reliance on energies and currents, often conducted through trance mediation, are the legacy of the scientific spiritualism of Allan Kardec and Amelia Solar which spread through Mexico and Latin America during the nineteenth century.

Etiologically, *Curanderismo* orients physical and social ailments within a complex network of physical and spiritual causes. Physical well-being and social security are understood to reside in a state of equilibrium that can be disrupted by material, mental, or spiritual forces. *Curanderismo* catalogs a number of physical ailments that can be caused by inappropriate amounts of otherwise normal emotional states. Some of the better known include *Mal de Ojo*, or the evil eye, a condition that generally affects infants or young children whose spiritual immaturity leaves them victim to the unintentional psychic influence of others, normally expressed through an overabundance of affection. *Susto,* or fright, is the result of a shock great enough to force the soul temporarily from the body. *Mal Puesto* occurs when the subject has fallen prey to witchcraft and *Aire* is the result of bad or cold air that enters the body in varied fashion. These conditions along with intense emotional states like anger *(coraje)* and envy *(envidia)* have somatic consequences and often result in fevers or intestinal discomfort, back pains, and headaches. Likewise, unfulfilled social expectations such as the lack of romance, financial success, or pregnancy may be the manifestations of negative energy summoned from simple jealousy or the manipulation of witchcraft in addition to other less sinister causes that lie outside standard social relationship dynamics.

Once the balance that governs physical and social well being has been disrupted, the problem my prove difficult to correct. Often, preventative measures can be taken by an individual to avoid common ailments and mishaps. Herbal formulation taken internally can prove effective, as can petitions to particular saints or other holy persons identified with health and good fortune. For Mexicans and Central Americans, these devotions are often directed toward saints that have national relevance. For Mexicans, both the virgins of Guadalupe and San Juan are candidates for direct petition and ritual devotions and certain historical figures known for their ability to heal are also called on to intercede, though these popular healing "saints" are unrecognized by the institutional church. As in biomedical systems of healing, when individual attempts at prevention and cure have failed, the services of a professional are normally sought.

Curanderos are those who have been initiated in any number of proven therapeutic disciplines and shown through their effectiveness that they possess a specific gift for diagnosis and healing. Methods for both vary according to discipline. Trotter and Chavira have recorded a number of methods in their survey of curanderos operating in South Texas. "Diagnosis can be accomplished in may ways: . . . reading cards for the patient, or sweeping the patient with eggs, candles, lemons, or other objects and then burning these objects. . . . The curandero can make a diagnosis by observing the color, size, and shape of a patient's aura, or through mental readings or mental telepathy" (Trotter & Chavira, 1981: 154). In Los Angeles, aura reading and telepathy are prevalent, as are spiritual readings conducted through trance mediation. The curandero prepares him or herself for the trance, utilizing the body as a conduit for a beneficial spirit to present itself and diagnose the particular ailment. Spiritual readings can also be conducted through object mediation, as the spirit directs the movement of cards or other objects of divination, after which the curandero supplies the appropriate interpretation. Treatment naturally depends on the results of the diagnosis. It can take the form of herbal formulations or it may require a cleansing that is performed with an egg, sage, or a collection of special branches. Often the cleansing requires the imposition of higher powers, a saint traditionally associated with healing, for example, or the spirit of a famous human healer whose power to effect a cure has been retained after death. In this manner the patient and the curandero are linked through the spirit or saint to God, who is regarded as the ultimate source of healing.

It must be noted that generally *Curanderismo* is a complimentary system of affecting physical, mental and social well being. It is not strictly substitutionary. Many of our informants utilize both standard bio-medical systems of healing and methods found in *Curanderismo* in varying degrees. In the same way, *Curanderismo* operates within the enormous structure of practiced Catholicism. It does not strictly repudiate it. Most of our informants participate to some degree in the sacramental life of the Roman Catholic Church while benefiting from *Curanderismo* without contradiction. *Curanderismo* enhances medical treatment and spiritual counseling in that it recognizes and treats physical ailments and their causes outside the understanding of the bio-medical approach while countering social crises for which the church has made no sacramental provisions.

SANTERÍA IN LOS ANGELES

Santería is the worship of the orisha, anthropomorphic deities who act as intermediaries between the material world and *Olodumare,* its Creator. It shares the main corpus of its spiritual beliefs and liturgical practices with the religion of the Yoruba of West Africa known as If· and is the Cuban manifestation of the Yoruba religious diaspora. The orisha characterize various human emotional states and social institutions, that is, love, war, marriage, and commerce, in addition to atmospheric elements like thunder, fire, and the sea. They have an essential gender identification and are fraternally related, children of *Olodumare.* The origin myths of the *orisha* reveal that they marry, experience jealousy and fear, and argue among themselves (Efundé, 1978).

The term *Santería* roughly translated means "saint worship" and refers to the association of Yoruba deities with various saints and Marian manifestations of Roman Catholicism. This association developed as a means of cultural survival for the Yoruba who were brought to various Caribbean countries as a human resource during the slave trade. Although forbidden to practice their native religion, Africans made use of Catholic hagiolatries by associating aspects of Catholic narratives to those of the *orisha*. Associations developed so that *Shango,* the *orisha* of thunder and lightning, became identified with St. Barbara, Yemaya, the *orisha* of the sea with the Virgin of Regla, Ogun the *orisha* of iron with St. Peter, and so forth. These associations did more than merely disguise the *orisha,* they provided new and more culturally relevant objects of worship.

This dual perspective is easily recognized in many of the material productions used in *Santería* devotions whether they be candles, badges, or chromolithographs. Graphic representations of the saint or Marian apparition rendered in romantic styles are subtitled with the name of their *orisha* complement. Frequently these images are assembled around a central Christian image like the crucifixion.

The familial context of the *orisha's* relationships are enforced by their association with members of the family of saints and is extended to their followers. Each worshiper is ritually chosen by two *orisha* for whom the worshiper will serve as an asiento or seat. These two *orisha* become the subject of special individual devotion and will reward proper obeisance with divine protection. In this respect, *Santería* empowers an individual and allows the participant to develop a unique and personal bond with the divine. Possession of the devotee by the *orisha* is considered a desirable sign of this bond and occurs most frequently during communal invocations known as *bembe.* Devotees are known as children of their *orisha,* fictive family relationships that also provide the context for congregational devotion in the *casa templos.*

The *casa templos* or temple houses are spiritual homes where the religious family will gather for all religious and social activity. The head of the casa templo is the *Santero/a,* or *babalawo,* the priest whose "children" gather at for all corporate devotion and to seek the pastoral guidance from the *Santero.* The casa templo is the foundation of the religious community. It is also the home of the spirits of the ancestors and the *orisha.* Here, altars to the *orisha* are erected and their sacred objects are maintained. During gatherings, levels of sacred initiation and physical limitation are the only means of differentiation, hierarchies of class and gender, are ignored and even the most simple of tasks are shared equally among the children. The involvement of the entire religious family is necessary. Everyone is involved in the exaltation of the *orishas,* and in so doing develops a closer personal relationship with them. The ultimate spiritual goal of the believer is to develop the qualities within himself that are an inherent part of the character of each individual *orisha.*

Like *Curanderismo, Santería* maintains a belief in balance and which is held in a reciprocal tension between spiritual and material planes of existence. A central tenet of *Santería* is the belief in *aché*, the essential energy that pervades all of creation. *Aché* is the power to make things happen, an active force that emanates from *Olodumare* and maintains a complex system of balance based on a multitude of exchanges. All devotional offerings, from simple petition to blood sacrifice, are preformed to replenish *aché* and the *orisha* are the major channels in this cycle of restoration.

In Los Angeles, The casa templos are nestled in both urban and suburban areas open only to the initiated. The public face of *Santería* is found in the botanicas, shops that provide goods and services to practitioners of both *Curanderismo* and *Santería* though they are operated primarily by Santeros. Here statuettes are available along with devotional items and extensive herb and plant stores. Botanicas provide non-Cuban Latinos with direct access to the *Santería* religion and Mexicans and Central Americans who seek the services of curanderos are introduced to *Santería* through them.

THE CONNECTION

Although *Santería's* origins are African and *Curanderismo* is the legacy of the indigenous peoples of the Continental Americas, the influence of Spanish Catholicism and the imposition of the Saints have created symbolic bridges for both systems. Most of our informants who had contact with *Santería* initially through the botanica had originally gone to purchase items necessary for rituals common in Curanderismo. Familiar efforts at healing that are unsuccessful require new methods often available without the direction of a curandero. The Santeros who run most of the botanicas are themselves healers and logically direct their clientele in a manner consistent with *Santería.*

The systems of *Curanderismo* are often as enigmatic from the standpoint of the afflicted as is the science of biomedicine. Loyalty to both methods require faith in the culturally established value of the practice in addition to the effectiveness of the treatment. The Latino cultural framework of *Santería* and its *Santeros,* its recognition of spiritual and physical equilibrium, and the familiar Catholic symbols involved in its devotionals are all accommodating to those familiar with *Curanderismo.* Indeed, many of our *Santero* informants stress this accommodation and take pains to provide systems of healing with the specific cultural references of their Mexican and Central American clientele in mind.

Yet a question remains. Even though structural similarities between the two traditions are clearly present, why would *Santería* appeal as a religious system to people raised with a similar yet culturally distinct system? Why not remain within the religious system that is most familiar? It's likely that the proximity of both traditions to one another would account for a certain amount of crossover, but cultural conditions specific to Los Angeles have encouraged Latinos who previously resolved social and physical affliction with *Curanderismo* to turn increasingly to *Santería* as a complete form of religious devotion. Recent events have emphasized the need for new forms of community, and *Santería* has responded at least partially to that need.

LOS ANGELES

The last five years have not been kind to Los Angeles. A series of natural disasters, floods, fires, and the 1993 earthquake have compounded to help emphasize a financial crisis that has beset the city since a recessionary period began in 1990. The current situation stands in sharp contrast to the economic success of the 1980s, a period notable for the number of undocumented workers who left the depressed economic conditions and civil war in their native countries and crossed California's southern border to participate in the what they hoped would be a continuous economic boom. Nativist reaction to the rapid increase in the Latino population accelerated the creation of gated communities and enclaves populated by middle and upper class Anglos (Flusty, 1994). After four officers of the Los Angeles Police Department were acquitted in the videotaped beating of Rodney King, an African-American motorist stopped initially for speeding, Los Angeles erupted in four days of arson and rioting that left 51 people dead and caused more than $1 billion worth of property damage. Latino participation in the riots was emphasized by the local media, confirming nativist fears that the immigrant Latino population posed a threat to the stability of the city. The previous mayor of Los Angeles, an African-American Democrat, was replaced with an Anglo Republican and in the next statewide election voters overwhelmingly approved Proposition 187, which barred all undocumented aliens from the most basic of human services in an attempt to stem the continuing tide of immigration and persuade those undocumented Latinos already residing in the city to return to their countries of origin. Although Proposition 187 has yet to be implemented due to organized protest of its constitutionality, many services slated to be denied have been the subject of increased restriction. Education and health, two areas earmarked by Proposition 187, have been constrained by the projected closing of USC-County Medical Center, a chief provider of health care to working class Latinos, exacerbated by the pending termination of affirmative action programs in the University of California, which provides race-based admission assistance to Latinos and African-Americans from disadvantaged backgrounds. All of these social conditions have had obvious consequences for Latinos, both undocumented and resident aliens.

IDENTITY

When immigrants leave the familiar surroundings of their homelands and move to Los Angeles, the result is always disorienting. This confusion is exacerbated when moving from a rural to an urban environment and when the political climate is antithetical to the very notion of continued immigration. Normally, immigrants rely on the fraternal and charitable organizations of preestablished communities of their countrymen in addition to a variety of state and federal agencies to provide the support they require to begin functioning as individuals and integrating themselves into the larger economic and cultural life of the city. In Los Angeles, however, the vast majority of immigrants from Mexico and Central American have immigrated illegally, and fear of discovery inhibits many of them from utilizing the few services that exist to assist them. For those who do utilize the health, education, and other human services, as we demonstrated earlier, continued access is far from certain.

In addition, Latino immigrant communities in Los Angeles were historically composed of Mexican nationals. Currently, a broad spectrum of Latino nationalities are represented in growing numbers, and the economic niches that were once occupied predominantly by Mexican immigrants are the subject of increased competition by different Latino peoples. What was once a Chicano minority—specifically Mexican immigrants and Mexican-American—within the larger population of Los Angeles has become a Latino majority. As this has occurred, individual national groups have begun to think of themselves not only as Salvadoreos, Guatemaltecos, or Mexicanos, but also collectively as Latinos, a class that is dominant demographically though oppressed politically and economically. The formation of a broader Latino identity is therefore favored in place of separate national identities because of the increased diffusion of separate nationalities in Los Angeles as well as the strategic possibilities in overcoming marginalization by a broad Anglo identity that continues to reassert itself.

In this way, Mexicans and Central Americans who are raised with *Curanderismo,* can make the transition to *Santería* while remaining distinctly Latino. This is a relationship that is peculiar to Latinos. African-Americans who become involved in Yoruba religion generally do so in a form that is more purely African. Centers of Yoruba religion like Oyotunji Village in South Carolina and Imole Olumo Akinwale Yoruba Temple in Los Angeles seek a return to original African forms of worship, devoid of Catholic imagery and the influence of colonial religion. As such, they more clearly represent opportunities for American Blacks concerned with recovering "authentic" cultural experiences stolen from them during the course of slavery (Youngstedt, 1989; Brandon, 1993: 114-120).

Anglo participation in *Santería* is minimal, though it may be growing. However, although most Anglo practitioners of *Santería* are undoubtably sincere in their devotion, there can be little question that their initial encounter with *Santería* was novel. It is an "exotic" religion for Anglos, and their interest must be one of discovery.

COMMUNITY

New forms of Latino community are necessary to properly confront the increasingly challenging conditions of Los Angeles. Strictly secular forms of community are apparent in the formation of everything from street gangs to Latino-dominated trade unions, and new religious communities have been formed under the auspices of a variety of pentecostal organizations. The Venezuelan theologian Otto Maduro has observed that this spread of pentecostalism is largely a rediscovery of collective identity, and he credits the success of pentecostalism to its ability to create "a sense of community, of being personally recognized and welcomed, of connecting in a more permanent and warmer way with other human beings, of being treated as an equal, of not being despised and marginalized" (Torrens 1993). The intimate organizations that surround the small pentecostal churches that exist in Los Angeles have analogues in the casa templos of *Santería*.

Although the curandero and his patients operate within a communal structure in their original context, these interpersonal relationships do not survive immigration and are difficult to establish upon relocation. The organizational framework of the Casa Templo in *Santería* provides a setting that is familiar and supportive while remaining small and intimate enough to respond adequately to the individual needs of its members. Because of the specific notions of kinship that *Santería* engenders through the Casa Templo, emotion, spiritual and often financial support is available in a family-oriented setting.

CONCLUSION

Curanderismo is a method of maintaining physical and social equilibrium within specific social contexts. Its specialists provide services to communities throughout Mexico and Central America where, by performing rituals of diagnosis and treatment, they alleviate anxiety and perform important functions of healing. In Los Angeles, the systematic and institutionalized marginalization of Latinos creates the need for new and pervasive forms of communal identity. *Santería,* an African religion practiced by Cuban and other Spanish-speaking Caribbeans, provides a sense of community better able to withstand the social and economic exclusion peculiar to Los Angeles. Through shared cultural and religious structures, Latinos raised in the traditions collectively known as

Curanderismo are introduced to *Santería* in the neighborhood botanicas common to both traditions and discover a belief system that responds to their physical, social, and spiritual needs.

BIBLIOGRAPHY

Aguirre Beltran, G. *Medicina y magia: el proceso deaculturación en la estructura colonial.* Mexico City: Instituto Nacional Indigenista, 1963.

Brandon, G. *Santería from Africa to the New World: The Dead Sell Memories.* Bloomington and Indianapolis: Indiana University Press, 1993.

Finkler, K. *Spiritualist Healers in Mexico.* New York: Bergin & Garvey, 1985.

Flusty, S. *Building Paranoia: The Proliferation of Interdictory Space and the Erosion of Spatial Justice.* Los Angeles: Los Angeles Forum for Architecture and Urban Design, 1994.

George, V. *Santería Cult and Its Healers: Beliefs and Traditions Preserved in Los Angeles.* UCLA Master's Thesis, Los Angeles, 1980.

Karade, B. *The Handbook of Yoruba Religious Concepts.* York Beach, Maine: Samuel Weiser, 1994.

Kiev, A. *Curanderismo: Mexican American Folk Psychiatry.* New York: Free Press, 1968.

Madsen, W. "Value, Conflicts and Folk Psychotherapy in South Texas." In *Magic, Faith and Healing: Studies in Primitive Psychiatry Today*, ed. Ari Keiv, London: Free Press of Glencoe, 1964.

Malinowski, B. *Coral Gardens and Their Magic.* 2 vols. London: George Allen and Unwin, 1935.

Marton, Y. *The Dancing of the Orishas in Los Angeles and the Pan-Yoruba Spiritual Tradition.* UCLA Master's Thesis, Los Angeles, 1986.

Marzal, M. *El Sincretismo Iberoamericano.* Lima: Fondo Editorial de la Pontificia Universidad, 1985.

Murphy, J. *Santería: An African Religion in America.* Boston: Beacon Press, 1988.

Roeder, B. *Chicano Folk Medicine from Los Angeles, California.* Los Angeles: University of California Press, 1988.

Torrens, J. "U.S. Latinos and Religion: An Interview with Otto Maduro." In *America.* August 14, 1993.

Torrey, E. *The Mind Game: Witchdoctors and Psychiatrists.* New York: Bantam Books, 1972.

Trotter, R. & Chavira, J. *Curanderismo: Mexican American Folk Healing.* Athens: University of Georgia Press, 1981.

Youngstedt, S. "Resisting Racism and Constructing Cultural Identity: African Americans and the Imole Olumo Akinwale Yoruba Temple in Los Angeles." UCLA Doctoral Dissertation, Los Angeles, 1989.

14

Some Thoughts on Syncretism in Suriname Creole Migrant Culture, as Reproduced by Migrant Women in the Netherlands

Ineke van Wetering

The subject matter discussed here, the religious beliefs and ritual practices of migrant Creole women in the Netherlands, undeniably belongs under the heading of what used to be loosely called "syncretism." Creole "folk" religion as practiced by a rural and nowadays mostly urban population in Suriname has been welded together out of African elements, Christian and non-Christian. The cultural complex is an outcome of a long historical process of interpenetrating cultures, in rapidly changing contexts. The adherents, Creoles, are a group of mixed descent; the element they share is some African strain. In contradistinction to most Maroon groups in Suriname, they insist on being called Christians, and there is no reason to deny this claim. At the same time, they see themselves as the guardians of a cultural heritage that owes much to a by-now-almost-mythical "Africa." There also is no basis to doubt that the aggregate is, in fact, a system and deserves to be called a "culture." The issue adressed here is the use of the term "syncretism" to denote and account for both the character and the resilience of the cultural complex usually referred to as *Winti*.[1]

Nowadays it is felt that notions like syncretism are ideologically charged (Droogers 1989; Stewart and Shaw 1994:5; Van der Veer 1994:196), and, in order to be useful, should be reclaimed from such meanings. All authors stress that associations of impurity or a lack of authenticity, attributions made in religious studies, are to be be discarded. The positive connotations it received in anthropology, in the older "acculturation" studies for instance, are found equally wanting. Whether the newly-evolving "creolization" approach, which these writers (1994:2) briefly mention, has more to offer, remains to be seen. As an outline for a new program, Stewart and Shaw (1994:2,7) propose to focus on processes of religious synthesis and upon discourses of syncretism, which involves attending to the workings of power and agency. In short, they recast the study of syncretism as the politics of religious synthesis. This field has been inadequately explored in Suriname.

The relevance of power and agency for the study of culture, rightly underlined, leads to other questions. As Comaroff and Comaroff have stressed, power and culture are closely intertwined. The idea of culture embraces both systemic features, an orderly worldview with related practices, and fields of inchoate, emergent and contested meanings. Following Bourdieu, they argue that part of culture is taken for granted, internalized or naturalized; representing power in its nonagentive mode. In the agentive mode, people actively shape their own and others' lives. For the first aspect, they use the term "hegemony;" the latter is referred to as ideology. As they summarize the distinction: "Hegemony, at its most effective, is mute; ideology invites argument" (1992:28-29).

Stewart and Shaw (1994:18) have noted an objection to the potential bias in their conception of syncretism as agency. Whereas they acknowledge the fact that cultural syntheses may become uncontested, reproduced without discursively available intentionality, they raise the question whether syncretic practices that no longer are consciously syncretic should still be described as such. Often, in the latter case, we simply speak of culture, or of a new culture born. Here, we will look into the case of *Winti* to see which notions have heuristic value. If the concept of syncretism is to be restricted to conscious attempts to harmonize worldviews regarded as separate, and to contested meanings, would it then apply to *Winti*? Do terms like hegemony and ideology, as defined by the Comaroffs, contribute to a clarification of the issues at hand? There will be occasion to return to these questions below.

SURINAME AS A SHOWPIECE OF "AFRICA IN THE NEW WORLD"

At the time when the study of African-American religions was in its infancy, the term "syncretism" was new and exciting. It opened up a field of studies that seemed to do justice to the experiences of a population sector in the complex modern world that was mostly thought of as deprived of a culture of its own, that would be worthy of anthropological interest. When, in the 1920s, Melville and Frances Herskovits turned to the worldview of the descendants of the one-time slaves, and in that pursuit went at great lengths to explore the lifestyles of urban women in Paramaribo, they did break new ground and were far ahead of their times. The mixing of cultures was at the heart of their interests. Also, they had a keen eye for women's forms of agency. If, at present, the concepts they used—syncretism, revitalization, and acculturation—are contested, regarded as inadequate, or discarded as of little analytic value, this is not because the approach of former generations was different from present concerns.

We do well to remember that many of our present criticisms have been voiced earlier. Academic ancestors like Herskovits (1958: XXII-XXIII) who used these concepts as tools, simultaneously expressed a wariness toward a conception of culture as a homogeneous entity or a "mosaic," and stressed processes of merging. As the danger of representing our predecessors as espousing cultural holism and statics is not always successfully evaded, Stewart and Shaw (1994:5-6) did well to remind us of continuities in anthropological thinking.

In retrospect, a concept like syncretism seems unwieldy rather than irrelevant, and the way the notion was applied in the past strikes posterity as haphazard. We should realize, perhaps, that the fields of research staked out were wide. Anthropologists seem to have run in like a pack of eager young dogs. In a study of Creole beliefs in Suriname—counting more than 600 pages—Herskovits and Herskovits ([1936] 1969) do not make use of the concept of syncretism at all. Although they had noted its significance in other, mostly Latin American or Roman Catholic contexts, they seem to have dropped the concept in their Suriname studies. There, they were after "Africa in the New World." This, however, does not imply that a concept like syncretism is automatically to be regarded as irrelevant or useless.

The form of syncretism observed, by Melville Herskovits (1937) and others, in black Roman Catholicism—a worship of African gods behind a mask of Christian saints—is not conspicuous in Suriname. Although many Creoles are Roman Catholics now, the Protestant churches, notably the Congregation of Evangelical Brethren, Herrnhutters, or Moravians had made a first and lasting impact on the worldview of the lower classes, among whom the guardians of the African heritage are to be found. As Bastide (1971:162-163) has stressed, syncretism has taken different forms in Protestant America, and Surinamese Christianity could certainly be interpreted along lines set out by this author and his followers (see, for instance, Simpson 1978).[2]

As if to lay the specter of "wild thinking" in his predecessor Herskovits, Bastide (1978) underlines that it makes no sense to study "Africanisms" as loose aggregations of cultural elements, or to approach a religion as a mere mixture of folkloric traits. In a firmly sociological, Weberian style, Bastide analyzed cultural complexes and the interpenetration of civilizations against the backdrop of the articulating institutional forms. Also, he takes the fact into account that the civilizations involved are part of a world system, and that its contradictions affect the worldview of those experiencing its effects.

This line has been pursued by Mintz and Price (1976, 1992), who dispense with the term syncretism. Cultural materials, they stress, are best seen as an aspect of the growth of institutions or the relations between the persons involved. Like Bastide, they stress the role of contradictions in the social system. Apart from the rapid development of local cultures, they note an enhanced appreciation of individualism and an expectation of continued change and dynamism. In their view, institutions were forged to further the interests of groups or categories, for the creation of social codes on the one hand, and for innovation and individual bricolage on the other. This program, well suited to a study of religious aspects of Creole culture, has only partly been carried out so far.

POLITICAL ECONOMY AND CREOLIZATION

In Caribbean studies no less than in other fields, regional ethnographic traditions intersect with disciplinary histories and discourses (cf. Stewart and Shaw 1994:13). In the post-World War II period, political economy has been high on the Caribbeanist agenda, to the detriment of ethnography (cf. Carnegie 1992). There were good reasons to opt for this research strategy. From a very early date capitalism has been the dominant mode of production in the area, and the plantation system, very modern for its time, provided the model for the organization of society (Mintz 1971:27, 36). The in many ways laudable preoccupation with political and economic issues, with domination and resistance themes, has apparently deterred students from moving ahead in the direction of culture studies. Up until now, the attempts to contextualize the world views of those dominated and exploited are few and far between. Anthropology seemed to be on its way out.

Recently, though, the Caribbean has been rediscovered as an area that might bring its students into the anthropological vanguard. The Caribbean was presented as a model of modern, post-modern, and even post-cultural society; "Caribbean" was presented as synonymous with "syncretic" (Clifford 1988:95), with the mixing and merging of traditions. The fact that the indigenous Amerindian population had ceased to be a political factor, that the area could not boast an "authentic" cultural tradition of its own but had been host to various import groups, supports the argument. In the Caribbean, the notion of culture as a homogeneous or coherent whole, and the study of a confrontation or dialogue between cultures and traditions-as-wholes never has been viable. Rather, the area is taken as a product of western expansion. A familiarity with mass migration, and incorporation into various forms of capitalism, would mark the region as an ideal site to explore processes of cultural amalgamation in a modernist setting. As Marcus (1986:165-166) has observed: "ethnographers interested in problems of cultural meanings have not generally represented the ways in which closely observed cultural worlds are embedded in larger, more impersonal systems."

To obviate some of the connotations involved in notions like syncretism, the concept of creolization was introduced. Drawing upon fieldwork experiences in Guyana, Drummond (1980) has suggested a change in focus for students of culture. Taking a clue from linguistic studies, he suggests that we speak of a cultural "intersystem" or "continuum." As in language use, people understand different ways of speaking, but are fluent only in some. In Creole languages, people will follow different rules simultaneously, which often results in inconsistencies and contradictions. In cultural matters the same is to be expected; cultures he regards as overlapping sets of transformations or continua. Our program should be to look closely at cultural exchanges in various contexts.

Drummond's ideas have been taken up in a stream of globalization studies. Hannerz (1987), for instance, thinks highly of this project and winds up by proclaiming this approach the future direction of all culture studies.

Processes of bricolage, or creole processes, that used to be thought of as characteristic of small, post-colonial or ethnically fragmented societies are, in fact, going on everywhere in the world now. Thus, the culture concept we knew is a thing of the past: "We are all creolized." In a sense, there is common ground in creolization and syncretism studies: all cultures are either syncretic or creolized.

A difference, however, would lie in the mechanisms singled out as moving forces. Whereas most syncretism studies would not be explicit on this issue—it is not a determinate term with a fixed meaning (Shaw and Stewart 1994:6), which is probably one of the main reasons why the concept has been dismissed—the creolization model would allow for cultural dynamics free from material conditions, an option that remains largely unexplored by political economists. Most students, from Bastide to Mintz and Price to Hannerz, would opt for a semi-autonomy, and not make much of the linguistics part. There is a gap between materialist and interpretive approaches that, as yet, seems hard to bridge. Reconciling the best of political-economy research and the best of cultural analysis in anthropology is a difficult task, Marcus & Fisher (1986: 85-86) state. They, however, proceed to define this as primarily a problem of representation or textual construction.

Hannerz keeps a firm footing in the materialist tradition. Enthusiasm for the new trend does not keep him from a careful stipulation of conditions, which introduce some restrictions on general applicability. Hannerz (1987:552) will speak of creolization only if culture contact involves people who draw upon two different cultural sources or traditions. Further, there should be a time span that allows for development and integration, and for socialization into the new complex for new generations. Another assumption is, that culture has a built-in political economy.

Recently, Mintz (1996) has expressed doubts whether the introduction of the terms "globalization" and 'creolization" brings the promised advance. It has struck him that so many of the new terms have been derived from Caribbean studies: "The term 'Caribbean' is enjoying great metaphorical popularity." The area is thought of as emblematic of modern conditions of migration and adaptation. This, in Mintz's view, obscures the uniqueness of both the

Caribbean and other areas. He reminds his readers that cultural creolization, as understood by Caribbeanists, is more specific than the oft-cited "mixing and merging of cultures" that looks so much like syncretism. Indigenization involves "the refashioning of cultural materials from more than one source, materials being transmuted into a remarkable *tertium quid*, neither African nor Eurasian but American. Creolization did not average out, or marry neatly together, the parental cultures" (p. 302).

Mintz prefers to narrow down his conception, whereas many scholars regard syncretism or globalization as processes that may encompass indigenization or "localization" but have a wider range. Stewart and Shaw (1994:7) observe that all cultures have composite origins and are continually reconstructed through ongoing processes of synthesis and erasure, and will focus on such processes and discourses of syncretism. Droogers (1989: 13-15) similarly defines syncretism as an open-ended process that may or may not result in a new synthesis.

Mintz also rejects the idea that the linguistic analogy is fruitful for cultural analysis: "language is not culture, only a part of culture; it is not organized 'just like culture,' but differently" (p. 301). The main drift of his argument is that all processes of cultural exchange have to be historicized. In the same vein, Peel (1989:199 ff.) cautioned against a too-ready adoption of constructivist notions in cultural studies, and advocated to making genuine contact with people's actual experience, with "a history that happened."

Other constraints neglected in the creolization model are those imposed by ethnicity. The change in outlook is based on the observation that students, in modern contexts, are confronted only rarely with social divisions and boundaries that are clearcut, or with people that follow one cultural model only. Yet, this does not imply that the ethnic approach is wholly superseded. As Norton (1983) observed, there are limitations to the creolization model. It hardly makes sense to deny the reality of group boundaries or ethnic tensions. There is more to culture-building than negotiations of meaning between unattached parties. Whereas it should be granted, that the workings of modern societies will produce an increasing number of persons who are inadequately integrated in any social system, the role of institutions and interests, and the attractions of belonging, may outweigh other considerations. In fact, part of the cultural work performed in creolization processes is aimed at the maintenance of solidarities within the bosom of in-groups or in rebuilding threatened identities. The complexity of social life can neither be subsumed under the term of ethnicity, nor can it be explained by creolization only.

Such reservations are worthy of note, as ethnicity has been a dominant factor in Suriname, for instance in national politics (Dew 1978; Kruyer 1973). Internal differentiation and the high rates of migration have made the mobilization of the Creole group a pressing but arduous task. Among Surinamese immigrants in the

Netherlands, an impressive endeavor is made to maintain relations and supportive networks across the Atlantic. Religion is one of the channels for recruitment. In the specific syncretic form to be discussed here, religion is very much part of this process. This is one of the few uncontested insights about *Winti* (Wooding 1981). As ties of kinship are under constant stress, a great amount of social entrepreneurship is needed to achieve anything like the desired objectives (Van Wetering 1987). This involves a constant effort to maintain a common code and shared views, and makes for improvisation and bricolage at the same time.

NATIONALISM AND MULTICULTURALISM: ANTI-SYNCRETISM?

While academic debate took its own course, the syncretism issue was taken up in Suriname's political arena. This was part of the emancipatory strivings of a Creole intelligentsia which, since the fifties, had aimed at a re-evaluation of an Africa-derived cultural heritage, and resistance against postcolonial imperialism (Voorhoeve & Lichtveld 1975). Until 1971, the practice of Winti was prohibited by law, and generally looked down upon as "idolatrous" and backward in circles of the respectable and the established in society. Young Creoles who had been abroad hoped to change this. They searched for authenticity, and looked for a proper identity for a new nation in "our own thing" or Wi Egi Sani, as the cultural movement was named. To this effect, the authenticity and self-sufficiency of the African-American religion was stressed.

Wooding (1981: 1, 271ff., 290) has been one of the main champions of this view. In his major work, devoted to the worldview and religious practices of rural Creole communities, he depicts *Winti* traditions as carrying on in almost "unadulterated" form, and he explicitly denies the relevance of the syncretism concept. *Winti* is boldly represented as African, and untouched by the Christian creed of a dominant class. Although Wooding (1981: 275, 290) allows for a limited degree of syncretism with Amerindian cosmology—the Amerindians are taken as allies in a common struggle against cultural imperialism—he regards the respective traditions as separate, not fused.

This construction betrays an uneasy compromise between ethnicity and nationalism. These principles are often at loggerheads (Eriksen 1993), and this is also true of Suriname Creole cultural politics. In fact, the effects of ethnicity and nationalism on *Winti* are contradictory. Whereas ethnicity calls for an authentic, undiluted Creole identity, nationalism should stress elements in worldview that are shared with other ethnic groups. Christianity, the religion of the one-time oppressor, is thought unfit as a support for either ethnicity or nationalism. Amerindians, as a numerically and politically insignificant grouping, are unthreatening to the larger Creole group, and thus welcome to be taken up into the system. Wooding's ideas have been well received among a young Creole elite, who regard them as a fountainhead of true knowledge of their tradition and a basis for group identity.

The fact that religious culture was systematized and laid down in written form was new for *Winti.* What used to be an ill-defined, informal, mainly private realm of belief and practice was carried into the open, public field, to be scrutinized and potentially appropriated by all and sundry. This was looked at askance by the many traditionalists among the lower classes, who were barely literate and used to think of *Winti* as a cultural resource firmly under their control. As both ethnicity and nationalism were accepted as ideologies among the rank and file of the Creole group, their criticism was not voiced openly.

In the mid-1970s when Suriname achieved political independence, many of its citizens fled the country to settle in the Netherlands. The ethnic traditions and strategies practiced in the home country were well adapted to the new situation, where ethnic groups could claim rights to their own culture, and subsidies for its promotion. So, it was not too long before actions were taken to "lift the taboo on *Winti.*" Initiatives were mostly taken by social workers, active in youth clubs or health agencies. They advocated the view that the life of migrants from Suriname had been beset with a great number of difficulties aggravated by psychosomatic problems. Youth workers hoped to keep the kids off the streets and out of mischief by assembling them in centers where they could play traditional musical instruments, to bolster up their self-respect and identities. These activities fitted well into the existing patterns in the wider society, which were extended with some clubs catering to specific ethnic categories.

Other spokesmen hoped to gain National Health Service acceptance for *Winti* ritual treatment. To this end, and to enhance an appreciation of tradition both within and beyond the ranks of the Creole group, books were published, often in a popularizing style. Lectures on *Winti* were taken up in programs catering to a public interested in alternative worldviews and health care systems. In these publications, *Winti* is represented as a cultural system, valid in itself, and to some extent reified. On the other hand, syncretism is not denied in these accounts. On the contrary: a Christian identity is stressed as essential for all Creoles, as is the compatibility of both traditions (H. Stephen 1983, 1986; Banna and Moy 1991). Like Wooding's book, these publications contribute towards a codification of tradition. *Winti* is presented here as the combined result of ethnicity, of nationalism and of incorporation in a multicultural society.

Like ethnicity and nationalism, multiculturalism has contradictory effects. On the one hand, it prompts objectivation, and a corresponding tendency to erase all traces of cultural mixing. On the other, the striving toward acceptance in wider circles makes for a stress on shared elements with other religious systems, Christianity included. An added advantage of the acceptance of such influence is that it will lend credibility to *Winti,* which is too often lacking in the eyes of the respectable. But again, all propaganda-making runs counter to a tradition of secrecy and is frowned upon by many traditionalists: *Winti* used to be part and parcel of "covert culture" and should remain so, as far as they are concerned.

Multicultural society thus provides stimuli for change. Strategies may may take the form of a strengthening of non-syncretism claims, as Stewart and Shaw (1994:8-9) have noted, although they equally found cases where syncretism was stressed and reinforced. A forecast about what direction will be taken seems difficult to make. Also, both processes can occur simultaneously; paradoxical effects are within the range of expectations. In modern contexts, it seems to make little sense to classify religions, or characterize developments within religions, as either uniquely syncretic or anti-syncretic. The distinctive forms of syncretism and anti-syncretism that arise are dependent on historical circumstance, manners of incorporation in a wider society, and concomitant differential developments within religious communities.

At present, internal struggles on these issues take place among Suriname Creoles in the Netherlands. Here, we will see in what other ways multicultural society has affected Creole religious culture.[3] As we will note, all authors discussed so far have made relevant points about syncretism or anti-syncretism; no particular view is either right or wrong.

SYNCRETISM IN CONTEMPORARY WINTI PRACTICE

To properly assess these effects we should, first, be careful to make a distinction beween what happens in the private and in the public realm. *Winti's* history as a religion of a subject group has marked it as a discourse to be hidden from outsiders and has promoted a double outlook or double consciousness (cf. Scott 1990:43). This is characteristic of both religious and non religious manifestations of Creole culture (cf. Budike & Mungra 1986:135 ff.). *Winti* adherents entertain significant relations with others occupying a lower-class position, but they are also taken up in patronage relations with persons who are better off. Since Melville and Frances Herskovits did their fieldwork, the proverbial guardians of culture are elderly women ([1936] 1969:9). This is still true in the Netherlands now: the hard core of participants in *Winti* is female. To a great extent, women are able to define what *Winti* is and should be. As heads of households, they make significant investments in social networks comprising other women and kinsfolk of various stations in life. As active agents, representatives of their families, and intermediaries with the outside and middle-class world, these women stress forms of syncretism. Withdrawal into the private realm is a form of appropriation; the carrying over of Christian worship into the home on special occasions, such as birthdays and wakes, guarantees a measure of control. Thus, agency and the politics of religious synthesis, the elements stressed by Stewart and Shaw, are quite marked. Yet, conscious striving is only part of the process of cultural reproduction.

The conscious and explicit aim of *Winti* adepts is to preserve "their culture." So a first question is what they understand by "their culture" and in what way they present it to the world beyond. When discussing this with outsiders—which, as indicated above, they are reluctant to do—the women will stress the domestic part. Participation in *Winti* rituals as such smack of "social problems" and "sliding down the social ladder," when one's steps are dogged by *winti,* suspicion immediately arises that low-ranking, magic-working spirits are involved. So this is disclaimed, but home rituals (*oso sani*), which show an obvious amalgamation of Christian and non-Christian worship dedicated to the human soul, is thought of as quite respectable and a marker of identity. As these rituals have been described elsewhere (Schoonheym 1980; Van Wetering 1995b), the details will be skipped here. The soul or self, to be harmonized with a Supreme Being, is held to be a container of various *winti.* In fact, each person's self is regarded as host to representatives of three classes of *winti;* a male power, either African or Amerindian, a female power, and an inner demon. The former, spiritual parent-figures or *dyodyo*, are compared to Christian guardian angels.

The classification into three powers indicates that a wide-ranging pantheon of powers has been compressed into a manageable form. In fact, the cult of the deities lying dormant in the self amounts to a packaged form of religion, suited to the needs of individual, city-dwelling immigrants. Likewise, the center of worship is domestic—a shrine, in a corner of the living room or in a bedroom where the paraphernalia of each spirit are kept.

When women describe what the forces in the self are like, and when they impersonate these in trance, they present images of the deities. This image-making activity draws heavily upon material from dreams, that is, unconscious material. Dreams are accepted as messages from the spirit world, and so have an impact upon the reproduction of culture. All sorts of so-called day-residues surface, derived from commonplace, day-to-day experiences, and this contributes to the fusing of cultures.

The representation of one of the main *winti* in the cosmology, Aisa or Mother Earth, bears this out. This female sacred figure, worshiped as the main *winti* in the pantheon by men and women (Sedoc 1979; H. Stephen 1983, 1986), is pictured as definitely Creole and thus, to some extent, derived from African models. Her attributes, clothes and ornaments, and many of the sacred songs dedicated to her, point to her plantation origin and her role in the city. This implies that she is represented as looking with favor upon Christian hymns (cf. H. Stephen 1986:46). And, in fact, such hymns are sung in her honor on ritual occasions.

The images, or collective representations, are products of subjective experience. Figures appearing in dreams are interpreted as belonging to a certain class of supernatural beings. They are recognized by personal appearance and behavior, and all sorts of concrete details. Women report they dream about "an old woman from Africa," wearing cloth of a certain fiber and color, who advised the dreamer to do something or refrain from a certain course of action. That specific type of cloth had been seen in a shop the day before, and this was taken as a sign that the dreamer, who had hesitated to buy such an expensive piece, should do so and add it to her shrine's devotionalia. The "African" female figure was classified as an *Aisa*. The dream images are made to fit in a familiar scheme; they are canonized in this way and add to the cultural repertoire.

Small wonder, then, that the supernaturals, though classified as African or Amerindian, mostly resemble familiar, contemporary, and real-life personages. Mother Earth mostly appears as a typical mother or grandmother figure, dressed in traditional *koto misi* costume. Amerindian spirits wear uniform caps, emblems of the authority of state administration. A typically African *Kromanti* spirit will be seen in an impeccably white suit, and so is cast in the model of a dignified Creole church elder. The inner demon is represented as a doll, a little boy in navy suit with a matching cap. Devotees keep these dream-inspired paraphernalia in store, to wear when the spirit takes possession of them. This situation invites and induces syncretism, which is, however, hardly acknowledged as such.

This implies that it would not do, as Werbner (1994:215) suggests, to make a distinction between religious and cultural merging. In *Winti,* there is a long tradition of sacralization of the secular. That western valuables, status symbols, trade goods—varying from alcoholic beverages to pieces of cloth and furniture—would be appropriated and given new meanings was within the range of expectations. That they were taken up as pleasing to the spiritual powers is another step, though perhaps less surprising than would seem from a modernist viewpoint. Through the workings of the imagination, by dreams and visions, associations were and are made between such goods and the wishes of the unseen powers. Many of the spirits' paraphernalia betray their origin in early globalizing processes. Screened off from the questions of prying outsiders, *Winti* or "the culture," is naturalized in this form, and should be regarded as authentic. Thus, part of the process of cultural reproduction is unconscious.

Though fostered in private life, the representations are carried over into the public domain. Most rituals are small-scale affairs, to which personal relations, mostly kin, are invited. There are gradations of privacy, though. On feast days, Creole women strive to turn their homes into public spaces. Anniversary festivities are, for instance, singled out for such purposes. Introduced as part of European culture, and blended with West African, notably Ghanian, notions about a sacred identity connected with one's day of birth, these parties are among the main props of group mobilization. Processes of sacralization and elaboration are notable. The feast usually starts the night before, on one's personal "New Year's Eve." This part is dedicated to the cult of the personal soul. For these preliminaries, only one's intimates are invited. The birthday proper is an event that draws ever-widening circles of friends and relations; a large number of guests is much-desired and gives prestige to the organizer. Festivities often open with an improvised Christian service in the home. Later in the day, and pre-eminently at night, a climax is reached in the dancing party. Typical Creole dishes are served for meals; and live music, equally ethnic, is regarded as an almost indispensable part. Extremely "creolized" as the party is, often a move towards deeper levels of "authenticity" can be observed. In many parties, there is a clear break between the general and the *Winti* part. All day and night a lot of cultural mixing may go on, but suddenly, around midnight, both Christian and secular music will stop and the drums will be carried in. From then on, preferably till daybreak, *Winti* music will be played. A desired high point is the moment the celebrant will reach the trance state to honour his or her special *winti*. The impersonation of the spirit, for which the medium relies on inner motivation, conscious and unconscious, reinforces collective representations.

The disjunction between the two ritual phases can be brought in to underpin the views of the Herskovitses and Woodings, that there is a tendency to keep the two religions from fusing. Christian overtures can be looked upon as an outer shell or cloak shielding off the inner sacred part of the *winti*. Such protection is characteristic of the private world of *Winti* adepts, in the semiprivate context of ethnic celebrations. Thus, this is not only to be observed in syncretism of an indigenous system with a Roman Catholic cult, but also in an amalgamation with Protestantism.

There seems to be more to this than a mere separation, though. Believers harp upon the necessity of starting a ritual with Christian prayer and hymn-singing. This is regarded as a means of building up spiritual power and tension. Expressions of the "other" forms of worship have been taken up into an encompassing system, a new cultural complex. That this is probably not fortuitous is corroborated by the work of Pitts (1989). In a fascinating study of an Afro-Baptist congregation in Austin, Texas, he observed a binary structure in ritual: a sequence of two enacted frames. There is a long, stultifying, unexciting beginning that seems to imitate archaic European custom, followed by a trance phase. In his view, there is a relation between these sequences; the first serves as a necessary preparation, a warm-up, for the trance experience. Pitts has noted a similar structure in other African-American ritual traditions, and *Winti* could be added as an example.

This would be inconsistent with Bastide's (1971:153 ff.) view that "true syncretism" with Protestantism is impossible. He foretold that missionary work, carried out in depth, would lead to an eradication of Africanisms. His—and Herskovits'—corresponding insight, that the most common process in this case would be a "reinterpretation"—of biblical figures and practices, such as angels, baptism, and exorcism—is not necessarily the whole story or the most significant feature. *Winti* believers, unaware of the African precedents and American counterparts mentioned by Pitts, or of a transfer of old symbols into a new, disguised, context, insist on the wholeness and authenticity of their practices.

Whether the term "reinterpretation" is well suited to account for these structures and processes is another matter. Obviously, more is involved than a new interpretation; another system of knowledge about the workings of the human psyche seems to be involved. Conceivably, this type of knowledge or experience has been conserved and is put to use. Whether this knowledge is applied consciously or not is hard to say: participants are not given to theorizing on this matter. The system is presented as "tradition," which is based on and transmitted as experience.

The idea that Protestantism, relying on abstraction," The Word," and averse to imagery, would be less suitable for syncretism than its Roman Catholic counterpart does not stand up to scrutiny, either. *Winti* adherents take up Protestant religious ideas with ease, and deal with abstractions as they find these embedded in imagery. They will "translate" ideas into images and material objects, in a style inspired by primary process thinking going on in dreams. Thus, they go about this in an "African" manner, creating visual supports for ideas and associations. When assembling items for a shrine in the home, for instance, a believer reared in both worlds, *Winti* and Moravian, may think it necessary to rest his or her *kondi,* the central pole known as a fetish from West Africa (MacGaffey 1975), on a bible. To this end, he or she buys a secondhand copy and puts it at the base of the construction. This is a concrete, literal expression of a personal conviction, truly Christian, that life should be based on holy scriptures. Janzen (1977:70) has noted the significance of dreams for the fabrication of such objects, and compared them to Greek icons, symbolizing a religious experience. For *Winti* practitioners, the production of such fetishes is an equally symbolic activity.[4] To an observer it may smack of "magic," and thus be set apart from mainstream Christian practice. Indeed, the meaning of the object is practical, and thus akin to "magic," intended to further an aim. In this case this would mean: to be a help in keeping the Christian convictions alive by evoking all sorts of associations. But such objects may serve other purposes as well.[5]

Doubts about the merits of a distinction between magic and religion have been voiced frequently (Lowie 1948:147; Van Baal 1985:55). The magical practicality of actions such as these does not set them apart as a lapse into paganism, as has been inferred,[6] but rather suggests a connection with spiritualism or mysticism. The religious mixture would fall under the heading of "philosophical syncretism" (Peel 1968:136) or "natural religion" (Van der Veer 1994:197-198). At an abstract level, the fusion of African and European thought is real. It would be wrong, however, to infer, as Van der Veer seems to do, that this type of spirituality is relegated to the private sphere of life only, and has no political consequences. As among some Christian groups, it counts among Creoles as the sole basis of spiritual authority, in public and in private.

To sum up: ritual and imagery rest on both a transmission of deeply-ingrained, semiconscious elements that have been proven to be valid by experience, and on conscious appropriation of power symbols derived from different traditions.

WINTI IN PUBLIC

Arguments derived from "natural religion" or philosophical syncretism are called upon to support Winti's claims upon recognition and equivalence, whereas many aspects that look like magic are hidden from public scrutiny. The former are acceptable to middle-class believers (cf. Peel, 1968), whereas the latter only partly so, or not at all. Many of the covert but lingering beliefs— unacceptable to Christian orthodoxy—are nevertheless cherished by lower-class adepts as "authentic" and markers of identity. These make sense when regarded as products of social forces. It has been argued (Van Wetering 1995b) that body symbolism, notably beliefs expressing fears of a loss of vital power and the dangers of pollution, stems from ambivalences about social relations. The cultural complex centering around the soul or self can be regarded as a transformation of slave experience, which has been reproduced by an economically marginal population sector among the Creoles.[7] There is a sedimentation of historical experience here, worked out into a cultural code, that is not shared to the same extent by middle-class Creoles, and not made public, or only reluctantly so.

When "the culture" is brought into the open and publicized, in the form of multicultural shows, radio broadcasts, lectures, or theater plays, a different attitude prevails. Then, the organizers are representatives of the ethnic group who are in closer contact with the outside world than the common *Winti* adept. They will belong to a new middle class, rather than the rank and file, and are often placed in positions to get access to subsidies. In order to bring "the culture" into the limelight, however, they need performers who are willing and able to show to a public what *Winti* is like. The performers, who often live off welfare allowances, are keen to earn some extra money and will oblige. They know how to drum and to sing the songs associated with the diverse spirits. Also, they can be trusted to make such a spectacle convincing to an audience, which members of the middle class would not do well. The public is expected to be interested in exotic features such as possession and trance. Thus, the performers who, from an early age, are familiar with these phenomena and the cultural ways to express such contacts with the deities, go through the movements. They take great care, though, to avoid getting personally involved and letting their tutelary spirits really take over: "I will not hazard my own deity in this affair," it is said. Thus, such shows lack authenticity for the believers. On the other hand, they will make an effort to create a proper impression.

The staging is the outcome of negotiations between organizers and performers. The organizers have their own ideas of what is acceptable to the outside world. In order to avoid all connotations of paganism, they introduce changes. Unwilling to submit to the dominant culture by calling upon the Christian God, as will happen in private rituals, but striving to present their own religion as equally worthy, they introduce a Supreme Being who is truly Creole and African: *Anana.* This name of the creator-god is invoked to open a performance. This would not happen in the inner circle. Neither in West Africa nor in Suriname is the Supreme Being an object of public worship (cf. Peel 1968:125; Schoonheym 1980:51; Venema 1992:140). The novelty is an instance of "invented tradition," on the spur of multiculturalism. In a sense, the innovation makes for continuity by reinforcing a "double outlook," what is said and done in public is different from what is considered "real" in private.

The relevance of class is clear. Those who, through social background, education or profession have entered a wider world and subscribe to middle-class norms, have different views of what is essential in culture. They will legitimate *Winti* in abstract, almost psychologized, terms (Van Wetering 1995a). Also, they are more willing to negiotiate than the common believers, who are taken up in dense networks and accept the culture as a social code.

Conflict surfaces in public discussions. The costs of *Winti* rituals, for instance, are a bone of contention. For those who entertain aspirations toward middle-class status, rituals can be modest: small things may bring great pleasure to the soul or self. They will refer to traditional norms: in a legendary past the huge fees ritual specialists demand for their services today were unheard-of; they would be content with 32 copper cents.[8] Lower-class adepts take an entirely different position. In their eyes, *Winti* is not a religion to be professed in private only. Although they never explain or discuss their attitude—this is regarded as a middle-class practice that is shunned—this is borne out in ritual practice. *Winti* is not an individual pursuit, but is part of the life of a collectivity. Money invested in rituals is not regarded as wasted. Adherents identify with the folks back home and insist on the obligation to return to the home country for the performance of rituals. Notions about illness and affliction are attuned to this requirement (Van Wetering 1997). A net effect is a transfer of money, often considerable sums, which help the economically hard-pressed to survive. There is an obvious link here between religion and supportive networks.

A similar difference of opinion between the members of different classes crops up when issues of bricolage are at stake. Although innovation is legitimate when inspired by a *winti*—an attitude that makes for a certain amount of individualism—this freedom is kept within bounds. Traditional authority, exerted by the elderly and public opinion, sets definite limits to improvisation. Belief in herbal remedies is a case in point. In the inner circle of *Winti* adepts, only herbs freshly brought from Suriname are regarded as effective in ritual treatment. It is conceded that one can get some temporary relief by using substitutes, but one should not postpone laying hands on the right herbs for too long. Such herbs are for sale on ethnic markets and in the numerous ethnic shops in the Netherlands' big cities now. As a rule, they are expensive, but magical effects are attributed to them. Some middle-class believers hold that it is feasible to apply herbs that have been grown in Europe, arguing that God has given his natural remedies for all ills in all places. Also, some adherents accept that it is possible, in a state of emergency, to "re-baptize" certain herbs in order for them to take effect. One adresses the plant, saying: "We need herb X, properly speaking, but it is not at hand. Now I ask you, plant Y, to replace X, and so I re-baptize you, I call upon you and your forces to do what we need now." Such solutions are not regarded as final, though.

These alternatives were discussed in public lectures. As mentioned above, nowadays lectures are given by cultural brokers to gain acceptance for *Winti*. As a rule, the speakers are male. Although many female healers are practicing, they, like their male counterparts within their circle, fear a loss of reputation as experts if they should squander their shared cultural resource in open debate. So the speakers are, as a rule, persons who straddle the class-line. The audience mostly consists of persons who have not been raised in *Winti*-practicing families but look expectantly to their own culture. Lacking a proper traditional background for access to knowledge, they have recourse to modern, western-style means of communication: books and lectures. In these contexts, a heated controversy about the potential of endive flared up. One cultural innovator confessed having applied endive in an herbal ablution. Some conservatives were horror-stricken and reacted vehemently from the back benches, others laughed profusely. The speaker was put into a difficult position: to legitimize such options would undermine his reputation, to outlaw them would alienate part of the public.

CULTURE, RELIGION AND IDEOLOGY

Several issues have been adressed here: first, the relevance of the term syncretism. It was assumed that the concept would primarily have a denotative value: to draw attention to a field of interest that has been inadequately explored. From the start it was clear that there would be little use in assigning the term to some congregations and denying it to others. In the case of *Winti,* the merging of world-views and practices is obvious. Much depends on definitions. If we follow Peel (1968:129) and Stewart and Shaw (1994:17-18) in applying the concept only to conscious attempts at harmonizing religious systems, Winti would be ruled out.

If, as suggested by Droogers (1989:20), contestation is taken as essential in syncretism, the term would apply. Cultural struggles are manifest, but are not always carried into the open. The *Winti* faithful choose the weapons that suit them best—secrecy about cultural resources and withdrawal from public scuffles being a main strategy. It is fully realized that elite groups need backing to legitimate their ethnic or hegemonic pursuits, and refusal to cooperate presents a formidable nuisance value. The best expression would perhaps be negative contestation.

When we look at the attempts made by an emergent elite in a multicultural context to politicize *Winti* as an ethnic group's culture, these seem to meet the stipulated conditions for speaking of syncretism. Yet, as we have seen, the results are paradoxical. There is both a merging of traditions and an enhanced stress on *Winti's* self-sufficiency. Moreover, in *Winti* this is, as yet, a marginal phenomenon.

If we rephrase the question in Droogers's (1989:13) terms: "What exactly is mixed: religion, culture, ideology?," we come closer to a key issue. *Winti* has been defined as a "culture," and religion—notions and practices regarding the sacred—is part of a way of life. This way of life has been characteristic of a sector of society, a peripheral sector rather than a class, which expressed its preoccupations in a religious idiom and appropriated a dominant sector's religion, regarded as a source of power. This is true in a philosophical sense: *Winti* adepts try to ferret out the secrets of effective spiritual power, and add what looks promising in endless processes of bricolage. The resultant cultural complex is accepted as a code that marks a class boundary within the bosom of the ethnic group.

Within the circle of adherents, *Winti* is "naturalized," informal, non-verbal, internalized and experiential. To state that "naturalized" implies "axiomatic," even "unconscious," and for that reason, hegemonic and "non-agentive," as Comaroff and Comaroff (1992:28-9) seem to suggest, would be to go too far in this case. A binary opposition between hegemony and ideology—one mute, the other open to debate—and the two to be bracketed by the "culture" concept, is not to be found here. *Winti* believers are fully aware that their belief system is under attack, and they argue back in their own way. The hegemony concept, with its Foucaultian connotations, seems of little use in elucidating policies of cultural contestation of those who are neither mute nor given to debate.

The term "ideology" is relevant when referring to the emancipatory strivings of the new elite. A middle class orientation directs their policies toward consciously formulated aims, and they welcome opportunities for contestation. A striving for hegemony within the ranks of the ethnic group is also manifest, a necessary condition to meet the challenge of the outside world. If the ideal is to make *Winti* a real part of a multicultural society, this approach is the only viable one. Their problem however, as indicated above, is a lack of support from the rank and file. Moreover, the term "hegemony" is used in a conventional but slightly different sense from what the Comaroffs had in mind.

There is another argument that detracts from the relevance of the "hegemony" concept: the "double consciousness" referred to above. *Winti* believers realize that they live in two worlds, one sanctioned by an inner circle, one controlled by outsiders. None of the two is completely "hegemonic," as individuals, people know how and when to switch codes, to cross boundaries between these worlds. In order to be able to negotiate this, they have to be constantly aware of difference. Some cultural values are internalized, or ingrained at a deeper level, than others. But one is conscious that the latter should be kept secret, and, as a consequence, one behaves "situationally." The tradition of managing these differences is a long one, and has become second nature, and is not, I therefore assume, synonymous with hegemonic.

NOTES

1. This term literally means "winds," and it refers to the invading spirits that are assumed to take possession of human beings. Another term to denote the cultural complex is *afkodrey* (literally, superstition), which carries no negative associations for the adherents— or, for the younger generation mostly, *kulturu* (culture).

2. This would imply looking at African elements in Protestant churches, whereas the topic of this chapter is: Christian elements in *Winti*.

3. The data that form the basis of this chapter have been gathered mostly in Bijlmermeer, an Amsterdam suburb where many Creoles settled in the 1970s. Zuiver Wetenschappelijk Onderzoek, or Foundation for Scientific Research, sponsored the research project in the period 1984-1987. The main research method applied was that of anthropological fieldwork: participant observation.

4. It is not far-fetched to assume that Herrnhut pietism has reinforced this, resting as it does on inner experience. On this issue, more research is needed.

5. This is not meant to do away with the reservations voiced by missionaries about some other consequences of syncretism. An argument as presented by Peel (1968) and Kiernan (1994) about Zionist churches could easily be duplicated by one on *Winti*, although I will not attempt this here. These authors' acceptance of believers' claims— that they are Christians, not syncretists—is sympathetic, but it raises questions. Although Peel denies that academians should have a say in the matter, he winds up by attaching a label to religious organizations, to decide which is or is not syncretist. Kiernan (1994) argues in the same vein (cf. Stewart and Shaw 1994:15).

6. See, for instance, the reference to Sundkler in Stewart and Shaw (1994:14).

7. This is in line with the arguments of Bastide (1978:XVII), Scott (1990) and

Comaroff and Comaroff (1992), who look upon religion as a response to contradictions in a mode of production, and expect magic in its various forms to spring from the ensuing predicaments. These are felt more acutely by the poor and dependent than in circles of the better-off. This would go far to explain that Winti mainly is a lower-class affair.

In studies of popular belief, in Europe and beyond, related arguments have been presented which would hold for *Winti*. Taussig (1977), Thoden van Velzen and Van Wetering (1988), Jane Schneider (1990) and Pina Cabral (1992) advocate the view that popular religion, or "animism" as we know it, should be regarded as reactions—defensive and ambivalent—to encroachment by political and economic forces impinging upon marginal sectors. The problem of "magic" thus is the product of a power struggle.

8. This is what is mentioned frequently, but is presumably part of a myth. There was an ideal of disinterest; it was left to the discretion and gratitude of the client to pay what was regarded as fair. Recompense was given not only in money but also in kind.

BIBLIOGRAPHY

Banna, Yuri, and Yok Moy. *De Voorouders en Haar Winti.* Amsterdam, 1991.

Bastide, R. *African Civilizations in the New World.* New York: Harper Torchbooks, 1971.

Bastide, R. *The African Religions of Brazil.* Baltimore/London: Johns Hopkins University Press, [1960] 1978.

Budike, Fred, and Bim Mungra. *Creolen en Hindostanen.* Houten: Unieboek, 1986.

Carnegie, Charles V. "The Fate of Ethnography: Native Social Science in the English-Speaking Caribbean." *New West Indian Guide* 66 (1&2): 5-25, 1992.

Clifford, James. *The Predicament of Culture.* Cambridge, Mass.: Harvard University Press, 1988.

Comaroff, John, and Jean Comaroff. *Ethnography and the Historical Imagination.* Boulder Colo.:Westview Press, 1992.

Dew, Edward M. *The Difficult Flowering of Suriname: Ethnicity and Politics in a Plural Society.* The Hague: Nijhoff, 1978.

Droogers, André. "Syncretism: The Problem of Definition, The Definition of the Problem" (7-25) in: Jerald D. Gort et al. (eds.), *Dialogue and Syncretism: an Interdisciplinary Approach.* Grand Rapids, Mich./Amsterdam: Eerdmans and Rodopi, 1989.

Drummond, Lee. "The Cultural Continuum: a Theory of Intersystems." *Man* (N.S.) 15 (2): 352-374, 1980.

Eriksen, Thomas Hylland. *Ethnicity and Nationalism: Anthropological Perspectives.* London/Boulder, Colo.: Pluto Press, 1993.

Hannerz, Ulf. "The World in Creolization." *Africa* 57 (4): 546-559, 1987.

Herskovits, Melville."African Gods and Catholic Saints in New World Negro Belief." *American Anthropologist* 39: 635-43, 1937.

Herskovits, Melville J. *The Myth of the Negro Past.* Boston: Beacon Press (1941) 1958.

Herskovits, M. J., & F. S. Herskovits. *Suriname Folk-Lore.* New York: AMS Press (1936) 1969.

Janzen, John M. "The Tradition of Renewal in Kongo Religion" (69-115) in: N. S. Booth, Jr. (ed.), *African Religions.* New York: NOK Publications, 1977.

Kiernan, J. "Variations on a Christian Theme; the Healing Synthesis of Zulu Zionism" (69-84) in: Charles Stewart and Rosalind Shaw (eds.) *Syncretism and Anti-Syncretism.* London: Routledge, 1994.

Kruyer, G.J. *Suriname, Neo-Kolonie in Rijksverband.* Meppel: Boom, 1973.

Lowie, Robert H. *Primitive Religion.* New York: Liveright, [1924] 1948.

MacGaffey, Wyatt. "Fetishism revisited: Kongo Nkisi in Sociological Perspective." *Africa* 47 (2): 172-184, 1975.

Marcus, George E. "Contemporary Problems of Ethnography in the Modern World System" (165-93) in: James Clifford & George E. Marcus (eds.), *Writing culture.* Berkeley: University of California Press, 1986.

Marcus, George E. & Michael M. J. Fisher. *Anthropology as Cultural Critique.* Chicago/London: University of Chicago Press, 1986.

Mintz, Sidney W. "Enduring Substances, Trying Theories: the Caribbean Region as Oikoumene" *The Journal of the Royal Anthropological Institute* 2 (2): 289-311, 1966.

Mintz, Sidney W. "The Caribbean as a Socio-Cultural Area" (17-46) in: Michael M. Horowitz (ed.) *Peoples and Cultures of the Caribbean.* Garden City, N.Y.: Natural History Press, 1971.

Mintz, Sidney W., & Richard Price. *The Birth of African-American Culture: An Anthropological Perspective.* Boston: Beacon Press, (1976) 1992.

Norton, R. "Ethnicity, 'Ethnicity' and Culture Theory." *Man* 18 (1): 190-191, 1983.

Peel, J. Y. "Syncretism and Religious Change." *Comparative Studies in Society and History.* 10:121-141.1968.

Peel, J. Y. "The Cultural Work of Yoruba Ethnogenesis." (198-215) in: Elizabeth Tonkin e.a. (eds.), *History and Ethnicity.* ASA Monographs 27. London: Routledge, 1989.

Pina Cabral, J. de. "The Gods of the Gentiles are Demons" (45-61) in: Karen Hastrup (ed.), *Other Histories.* London: Routledge, 1992.

Pitts, Walter. " 'If you caint get the boat, take a log': Cultural Reinterpretation in the Afro-Baptist ritual." *American Ethnologist* 16 (2): 279-293, 1989.

Schneider, Jane. "Spirits and the Spirit of Capitalism" (24-53) in: Ellen Badone (ed.), *Religious Orthodoxy and Popular Faith in European Society.* Princeton, N.J.: Princeton University Press, 1990.

Schoonheym, Peter. *Je Geld of . . . je leven.* (transl. *Your Money or . . . Your Life*) Utrecht: Institute of Cultural Anthropology Utrecht. Mededelingen 14, 1980.

Scott, James. *Domination and the Arts of Resistance: Hidden Transcripts.* New Haven/London: Yale University Press, 1990.

Sedoc, N. O. *Aisa Winti.* Paramaribo, 1979.

Simpson, George E. *Black Religions in the New World.* New York: Columbia University Press, 1978.

Stephen, Henri J. M. *Winti: Afro-Surinaamse Religie en Magische Rituelen in Suriname en Nederland.* Amsterdam: Karnak, 1983.

Stephen, Henri J. M. *De Macht van de Fodoe Winti. Fodoe Rituelen in de Winti-Kultus in Suriname en in Nederland.* Amsterdam: Karnak, 1986.

Stephen, Michele. "Dreaming and the Hidden Self: Mekeo Definitions of Consciousness" (160-186) in: Gilbert Herdt and Michele Stephen (eds.), *The Religious Imagination in New Guinea.* New Brunswick/London: Rutgers University Press, 1989.

Stewart, Charles, and Rosalind Shaw. *Syncretism/Anti-Syncretism: the Politics of Religious Synthesis.* London/New York: Routledge, 1994.

Taussig, Michael. "The Genesis of Capitalism Amongst a South American Peasantry: Devil's Labor and the Baptism of Money." *Comparative Studies in Society and History* 19: 130-155, 1977.

Thoden van Velzen, H. E., and W. van Wetering. *The Great Father and the Danger: Religious Cults, Material Forces and Collective Fantasies in the World of the Surinamese Maroons.* Leiden: Koninklijk Instituut voor Taal-, Land- en Volkenkunde, 1988.

Van Baal, J. *Symbols for Communication.* Assen: Van Gorcum (1971), 1985

Van der Veer, Peter. "Syncretism, Multiculturalism and the Discourse of Tolerance" (196-211) in: Charles Stewart and Rosalind Shaw (eds.) *Syncretism / Anti-syncretism.* London: Routledge, 1994.

Van Wetering, W. "Informal Supportive Networks: Quasi-Kin Groups, Religion and Social Order among Suriname Creoles in the Netherlands." *The Netherlands Journal of Sociology* 23 (2): 92-101, 1987.

Van Wetering, W. "Demons in a garbage chute." (211-232) in: Barry Chevannes (ed.), *Rastafari and Other African-Caribbean Worldviews.* London: Macmillan, 1995a.

Van Wetering, W. "Transformations of Slave Experience" (271-304) in: Stephan Palmié, (ed.): *Slave Cultures and Cultures of Slavery.* Knoxville: Tennessee University Press, 1995b.

Van Wetering, W. "Women as *Winti* Healers: Rationality and Contradiction in the Preservation of a Suriname Healing Tradition" (243-261) in: Hilary Marland et al. (eds.), *Illness and Healing Alternatives in Western Europe.* London: Routledge.

Venema, Tijno. *Famiri nanga Kulturu: Creoolse Sociale Verhoudingen en Winti in Amsterdam.* Amsterdam: Het Spinhuis, 1992.

Voorhoeve, Jan, & Ursy M. Lichtveld. *Creole Drum.* New Haven/London: Yale University Press, 1975.

Werbner, Richard. "Afterword" (212-5) in: Charles Stewart and Rosalind Shaw (eds.), *Syncretism / Anti-syncretism.* London: Routledge. 1994.

Wooding, Charles J. *Evolving Culture: A Cross-Cultural Study of Suriname, West Africa and the Caribbean.* Washington D. C.: University Press of America, 1981.

15

The African Diaspora in the Netherlands

Gerrie ter Haar

INTRODUCTION

According to Dutch government statistics, in 1993 almost 91,000 Africans were living in the Netherlands (Centraal Bureau voor de Statistiek, 1994). This figure represents only those who have been able to legalize their presence and does not include the large number of illegal Africans who are in the country but whose presence remains officially unknown. Many of the most recent African migrants are Christians from West Africa. They are mostly Ghanaians, but there are also significant numbers from Nigeria, Sierra Leone and Liberia. Recent research has estimated the total number of Ghanaians in the Netherlands, that is, including non registered ones, at 15,000, 10,000 of whom were believed to live in Amsterdam (Van 't Hoff 1992). In 1994, the total number of officially registered people from Ghana was over 7,000 (CBS 1994). This shows a decrease compared to previous years and, again, does not include any illegal immigrants. Due to their numbers, the Ghanaians can be said to constitute real communities, particularly in the form of Christian congregations (ter Haar 1994 and 1995).

Ghanaians, like other labor migrants, live mostly in the big cities in the Netherlands where their chances of employment are highest. The majority live in Amsterdam, the capital city, and particularly in the southeast district, commonly known as the "Bijlmer," which houses a great variety of migrant communities, including many Africans. With almost 100,000 officially registered inhabitants, the southeast district is the largest district of Amsterdam, containing some minority groups large enough to deserve explicit mention in government statistics. About half of the Bijlmer population is of non-Dutch origin, the largest minority group being constituted by Surinamese. Other groups explicitly mentioned in the statistics are Antillians, Turks, Moroccans (including other North Africans), and "South Europeans," including Spanish, Portuguese, Italians, Greeks, and (former) Yugoslavs. The many West Africans living in the Bijlmer and largely of Ghanaian origin fall within the category of "other foreigners" which in 1992 comprised slightly less than 10,000 people (*Zuidoost in Cijfers* 1992). In 1994 the number of different nationalities living together in this particular district of Amsterdam was recorded at sixty-five (Southeast 1994). Depending on their size and substance these different groups have established their own networks which help them to survive in their new environment, that is full of difficulties. They are faced with unemployment, housing problems, and criminality at a time that the general atmosphere in the Netherlands is becoming increasingly hostile toward foreigners from the poorer parts of the world.

One particular social network for many migrant communities in the Bijlmer is formed by the religious organizations, of which there are at present some forty different ones,with the number continually increasing. Muslims and Christians of various sorts, Hindu groups, and Winti[1] adherents, can all be found in this particular district of Amsterdam (De Jonge 1994, Oomen and Palm 1994). The African communities represent only one aspect of that kaleidoscope of religions, albeit an important one. To a large extent they are responsible for the growth and flourishing of the Christian churches in the Amsterdam Bijlmer. By 1995, there were some twenty different churches or church groups under African leadership in the Bijlmer, varying in size, and mostly founded by Ghanaians (ter Haar 1995b). Apart from these African-led churches, there are substantial numbers of Africans who belong to one of the Catholic churches or to other denominations such as the Seventh Day Adventists. The rapid growth of African-led churches is a relatively new phenomenon that reflects the influx of Ghanaians into Dutch society since the early 1980s. This latest migration trend is connected to the political and economic changes in Ghana during that time (Nimako 1993). On arrival in the Netherlands, many Ghanaians found shelter in the Bijlmer, where soon they also started to worship together. In practice this often meant a small number of people congregating in an apartment and sitting around the kitchen table to pray together and read the Bible. The increasing numbers of participants forced most groups to look for more suitable accommodation.The emergence of full churches is a very recent development, in fact one of the last few years.

One of the major problems of all religious groups in the Bijlmer is the lack of space to worship (De Jonge 1992). At the time that the Bijlmer district was built, in the 1960s, provision was made for only one church building to accommodate some of the traditional Dutch churches. Almost thirty years later a completely new picture has emerged as a result of the influx of non-Dutch people. Some groups have come to share buildings on a temporary or permanent basis, others have been able to obtain their own space, usually at great financial cost, entirely paid by membership donations, while others are still coping with the present inadequate situation. The majority of groups are Christian, many of which have found shelter in one of the empty spaces under the multistory car parks, or in places such as an old shop or supermarket, or they may congregate on Sundays in one of the community houses in the Bijlmer. What they have in common is, literally, their invisibility.

This chapter attempts to analyze the situation of African Christians in the Bijlmer, with a view to understanding better the situation of their communities. I will make particular use of the classic theory of Arnold van Gennep concerning rites of passage (Van Gennep 1975) and its further development by Victor Turner (Turner 1969). Rites of passage are rites that can be found in all cultures and are connected to important phases of life. They mark the transition from one phase to the other and thus help in the resolution of a life crisis. Or, as Van Gennep defines it, these are "rites which accompany every change of place, state, social position and age" (quoted in Turner 1969: 80). This describes well the African communities under discussion. Their rituals have been designed to cope with a life crisis resulting from the transition from one part of the world to another and the change of status involved.

By borrowing Van Gennep's concept of "rites of passage" to explain the situation of African religious communities in present-day Western Europe, I apply a theory originally designed to explain rituals occurring in small-scale societies rather than those occurring in modern, secular mass societies.

I will further base myself on Victor Turner's analysis of ritual as a process (Turner 1969). His concepts of communitas and liminality, which he developed on the basis of Van Gennep's work on rites of passage and which he applied to both religious and secular situations, sheds a particular light on the meaning of ritual behavior as presently practiced among African Christian communities in the Bijlmer. The social context in which the ritual process takes place has changed, and so has the naure of the life crises which many Africans face today. They have become of a sort that does not simply affect small-scale communities, but global ones created by migration between continents. This is certainly so with the large-scale migration processes of today. At the same time, much of the social setting has been influenced by a process of secularization that has reduced the meaning of rites in modern times, particularly in the Western world. But, as has been stated by others, there is no evidence that a secularized urban world has lessened the need for ritualized expression of an individual's transition from one status to the other (Kimball 1975), and the same, I believe, can be said of specific communities.

THE AFRICAN-LED CHURCHES IN THE BIJLMER

In discussing the religious life of African-led churches in the context of Western European society, I will particularly base myself on my experiences in one of them, the True Teachings of Christ's Temple, the largest of the churches under African leadership and the longest in existence. Over the years the True Teachings of Christ's Temple has grown from a small house congregation into a fully-fledged church which is housed under one of the car-parks in the Bijlmer. Although there are some differences between this church and the other African-led churches in the Bijlmer, the general pattern is rather similar. The True Teachings of Christ's Temple, therefore, can be considered to function as a model for African Christianity in the Netherlands. Some outstanding features of this from a Western perspective are the importance of prayer and fasting, the intensive use of the Bible and praise-giving during worship, public testimonies, and general pastoral care. An additional element which is of importance in the European context is that all churches see themselves as charged with the task of evangelization. They call themselves international churches in that they declare themselves explicitly open to non-African believers, irrespective of their race or color. In practice, however, these churches attract black people almost exclusively, from Surinam and the Antilles and from various African countries, mostly from Ghana and Nigeria. There are also similarities in their structural organization. One normally finds the congregation under the leadership of a male pastor assisted by a number of church officials with varying responsibilities. A board of elders, a pastoral board and a welfare committee, as well as a financial board are among the most common structures, consisting of both men and women. They are known for their choirs and accompanying bands, and for their youth activities. They run their own creches and organize Sunday schools and other activities, depending on their accommodation. Finally, and most significantly in the context of Dutch society, each and every one of their churches is always full on Sundays.

The True Teachings of Christ's Temple officially became a church in 1988 when it was registered by the Dutch Chamber of Commerce. That year, after some wanderings similar to most religious communities in the Bijlmer, the congregation bought the former accommodation of the Jehovah's Witnesses, which could hold some 350 people. Five years later the hall had already proved far too small. In 1994 an extension project was completed that allows room for some 600 people. The leader and founder of the church is Rev. Daniel Himmans-Arday, commonly known as "Brother Daniel," who comes from Accra, the capital of Ghana. In spite of his involvement with the Ghanaian migrant community in the Bijlmer his own presence in the Netherlands is not related to this latest migration trend. It is the result of a religious experience as a young man in Ghana, when, during a serious illness, he was promised recovery in a vision and received a divine call to preach the gospel overseas."You will be well, you will travel into the other continents and bring back lost souls (who will be made equally well on the account of your testmony) into My Vineyard" (Himmans 1986). In the late 1970s he arrived in the Netherlands, where during the years to follow he became involved in the lives of his fellow Ghanaians as they started to come and live in the Bijlmer. In the meantime he undertook theology studies in Europe preparing himself for his future task. His success as a pastor owes much to his charismatic personality.[2]

Church doctrine and practice in the True Teachings of Christ's Temple are derived from what is believed to be prescribed by the Bible and therefore seen, as the name indicates, as the "true teachings" on which Christianity is based. The sermons, presented in the form of "lessons" focusing on a particular theme, are a central element in the Sunday services. As in all other churches in the Bijlmer, a connection is always made between the lessons to be taken from the Bible and the present-day situation, and a line is drawn from the universal meaning it entails to its individual application. In the True Teachings of Christ's Temple two sermons are normally given, the first one in Twi, the principal language of Ghanaians in the Netherlands and one of the main languages of Ghana, and the second one in English. The sermon in Twi is by the second pastor with the rank of "Apostle" and is simultaneously summarised in English. It is followed by a full sermon in English by the reverend pastor, who elaborates further on some of the issues under discussion. The atmosphere is generally relaxed, joyful, and attentive. People may come and go as they like although many will sit through the hours-long sessions of preaching, praying, reading, singing, dancing, and music with apparent pleasure. Much time and attention are devoted to individuals.

Sunday worship will normally start with attention to personal matters during the so-called "morning devotion," when some of the junior pastors, known as the *Holy Children*, lead the congregation in songs and prayer, encouraging people to put their requests before God. They wear white robes with a colored trim, like the Pastor and the Apostle. Often, the Pastor himself will conduct special healing prayers and, if necessary, pray over individual people. He is known for his spiritual gifts. As in other African-led churches, the awareness of the presence of evil as a potential threat to humankind is prevalent and is openly addressed. Preventive action may be taken, for example, by the use of incense in the building, as well as the use of the rosary during prayers. These are practices that are unique to the True Teachings of Christ's Temple and are not always approved of by other congregations. The True Teachings of Christ's Temple also lights candles during services, another individual characteristic that is disapproved of by some other churches.

Bible reading and Bible lessons are important aspects of the Sunday services. The leaders of the church are supposed to set an example for others by their life style. To further spiritual growth the pastors and "evangelists," a group of men and women who want to live up to the principles of the church and carry these further, engage in regular prayer and fasting. The male evangelists are called *Faith Brothers* while the women are known as *Divine Sisters*. Like the pastors, they can be recognized by their special dress. They have their seats at the back of the church, with the church elders. They are responsible for maintaining discipline during services, for answering any queries or providing translation if needed, and they take care of the children. The evangelists and elders both participate in carrying out the rituals of the church, such as the naming and dedication of a child.

Ritual practice is more developed in the True Teachings of Christ's Temple than in any of the other churches. It appears well-adapted to the needs of the congregation; it is related to their life conditions in the Netherlands and, more particularly, in the Bijlmer district of Amsterdam. These are often conditions of uncertainty, and extreme worry. The majority of Africans in the Netherlands have come to find a job that will enable them to secure a future for themselves and their families. The church provides a place where they receive encouragement in their endeavors through the spiritual underpinning of their lives (cf. E. Turner 1992). At the same time it constitutes a community of equals where people in similar circumstances can share their experiences. That way the church provides a social network for basically marginalised people who depend on each other's support. Love and unity, mutual concern and understanding, solidarity, and practical support are constantly stressed, and are expressed through word and action.

In the following I will give some examples of ritual behaviour in the True Teachings of Christ's Temple which, in a different way, demonstrate the same need. The ritual acts involve the whole congregation and require the active participation of all ritual functionaries in the church.

RITUAL ACTS OF PURIFICATION

Purification rituals or, more simply, ritual acts, may be performed in a number of ways. They are a symbolic expression of the awareness of the existence of evil that requires effective action to counter it. Evil forces can be warded off by calling upon the power of the good forces people believe in, that is, the power of Christ or the power of the Holy Spirit. People may also seek protection by burning incense which spreads a pleasing fragrance and is therefore known in various religions as a cultic means to ward off evil forces or spirits and attract good ones. The True Teachings of Christ's Temple bases the use of incense on various Biblical references, such as Exodus 30, which give prescriptions for the building of an altar for burning incense. The burning of incense is also seen as representing the prayer of good Christian people, as expounded in the Book of Revelations (Ch. 8: 3-5).

The most common and obvious symbol for purification in the True Teachings of Christ's Temple, as in many religions, is the use of water. The sprinkling of holy water, that is, water that has been blessed by an ordained minister, takes place on various occasions, such as   at the end of the dedication ceremony, which will be described later in more detail. In this ceremony, during which a newborn child is "committed into the capable hands of the Lord," the sprinkling of holy water onto the congregation refers to the power of God as it is expressed through water and which is believed to work miracles. Evidence for such miracles is found in passages from the Bible, for example, in 2 Kings 5: 13-16, which tells of the miraculous healing of Naaman, the army commander of the Syrian king. Purification and healing, the example shows, go hand in hand. The same is true for the use of water in the dedication ceremony. It is a symbolic act expressing the belief that God can heal people from whatever troubles they may have. In the context of a dedication ceremony it expresses the belief that he can also heal barrenness and use his miraculous powers to provide children even to those who may—humanly speaking—have no hope of conceiving. At the same time the sprinkling and washing with water as practiced in the True Teachings of Christ's Temple are meant as a symbol of love and equality in the sight of God. We find the clearest expression of that on New Year's Eve, when, during a night-long service, every individual's feet are washed with water by the Apostle and subsequently blessed with oil by the Pastor. Purification and restoration are merging here into one act that is to symbolize the love of God for all humankind, irrespective of time and place.

The most common symbolic use of water, however, is through sprinkling as a simple act of purification. There is no particular time or moment during services set aside for this purpose, nor does it take place as a regular part of the weekly service. Rather different from traditional Dutch churches, much is said to depend on divine inspiration (which by definition cannot be channeled in the conventional way), while at the same time much room is left for improvisation within the broader framework of the service. The sprinkling with water may take place at the beginning of the service, before the so-called morning devotion. One of the Holy Children goes around the church hall sprinkling water from a white plastic jar. Once the hall has been purified the necessary conditions have been created for the power of God to manifest itself during and through the prayers that will follow, conducted by the pastor. There is no set pattern, and the following description is just one example of a purification rite carried out in this church.

The pastor enters the hall joined by the junior pastors. They kneel down in front of the hall, facing the congregation, whose members follow their example. In the meantime the sprinkling of holy water continues. The pastor starts praying to purify the hearts and minds of everyone and to remove all evil. He calls upon the Lord to remove the evil forces that are believed to be acting against the well-being of individual people as well as of mankind as a whole. In his prayers he will refer to Satan as the ultimate source of evil or otherwise express the belief in satanic powers that work against God's essentially good creation. In his prayers the pastor shows an acute awareness of the fact that many people in his congregation are troubled physically or spiritually or otherwise under the pressure of forces they feel unable to control. He will therefore call upon the power of Christ and ask for "spiritual blessings" for all in order to drive Satan away. He may address Satan directly by pointing out that this is a holy place, sanctified and dedicated to the Lord, and that therefore Satan is not wanted in this area. It is a powerful prayer which is said in the knowledge that as an ordained minister the pastor is not acting in his own right but on the authority of "our Lord Jesus Christ." This challenging of Satan may have a visible effect on those who indeed feel oppressed by evil in some way. Some of the members of the congregation may fall into a state of trance and start shaking, thus showing the tumultuous effect of the prayers for healing and purification.

When the prayers are concluded, that is, when Satan is believed to have been effectively removed from this area, the pastor addresses himself to the congregation. He will assure the members that the Lord has purified them and warns them against going into any "dark places," where Satan is believed to be active and where they can easily come under the influence of Satanic powers. He emphasises the power of prayer and how the Lord is changing man's heart that way. He will call on the believers to open their hearts and to receive the Lord. All will then say the Lord's prayer together. This may be followed by a special prayer which is first said by the pastor and repeated by the congregation which is standing up with their hands raised. It may go as follows: "Unto you I commit my whole body; the forces from inside and outside have no control over me; let me walk free; because of your blood I am redeemed." Once again, the congregation may call upon the Lord to cast out evil forces, with the words "cast them out, cast them all out, I will be free." Subsequently the congregation will submit itself to God by stating that "I belong to you," and ask for his protection. "Let me proclaim your glory, I need you always; protect me and protect my family; protect my feet, my eyes, my mouth, so that everything will be in glory to your name. Help me, touch me and set me free." Often the session is ended with the Lord's prayer and with reciting the "song of togetherness," Psalm 133, which is in praise of brotherly love.

THE DEDICATION CEREMONY

As in all African-led churches, the True Teachings of Christ's Temple pays special attention to children. Parents take their children to church from a very young age. Babies usually stay with their mothers for whom special seats are reserved in such a way that they can easily walk in and out to look after them during the service. The older children follow Sunday school classes in a separate room but participate during part of the service. Everything is aimed at preparing the children for a Christian way of life and instilling Christian values and principles. In that context the first time a child enters the church after birth is seen as a very special and joyful occasion which is accompanied by a special ritual, the so-called dedication ceremony.

The dedication of a new-born child normally takes place after three months, when the mother has recovered from giving birth and will resume church attendance. Both parents will proudly present the child to the church community to which the new-born baby will also belong from now on. This takes place in the presence of a host of relatives and friends, who are not necessarily members of the church but may just accompany the parents for this special occasion. Parents and other participants dress in their best clothes, the parents often in white as a symbol of purity. During the service they will be seated in the front rows of the church, with the child that is to be dedicated to God. After the service has ended but before the closing prayer, parents and child with all who have accompanied them leave the church hall to re-enter it in procession. In the meantime the Church Mother announces the ceremony by reciting the relevant passage from the Bible which explains the need for dedication. This is taken from the gospel of Luke, Ch. 2: 23, which speaks of the need to dedicate every first-born to the Lord. After that the Church Mother also leaves the hall while the choristers rise from their seats and sing, joined by the congregation.

Then, the Holy Children, preceded by the Apostle, enter the hall solemnly in their white robes and without their shoes. They kneel down at the front of the church before the altar, facing the congregation. Once they have knelt down in this sanctified space the full parade enters with the parents in front, the mother carrying the baby. They are preceded by the Faith Brothers and Divine Sisters and followed by other church functionaries such as elders and members of the welfare committee. They enter through the center aisle while the choir is singing, and they walk in procession around the church hall. When they are back in front the Faith Brothers turn left while the Divine Sisters turn right, after which they kneel down joining the Holy Children. The parents remain standing in the middle, in front of the center aisle with their backs to the congregation, facing the altar. The Church Mother positions herself behind them and takes the baby from the mother. The pastor opens proceedings with a short speech, followed by prayer. The Apostle reads from the Bible the story of Hannah (I

Samuel 1: 26-28) who has been longing for a child and finally had her prayers answered. Then the pastor leaves the altar and, while the choir starts singing again, he goes around blessing all those who have knelt in front and those sitting in the front rows, who are mostly family or friends. When he is finished the choir falls silent so that the actual dedication can take place.

The Apostle takes the child from the Church Mother while the pastor stands in front of the parental couple, who have also taken off their shoes and knelt down. The Apostle, who is standing behind the parents, hands the child to the pastor, who hangs his rosary around its neck. He lifts the child up in the air for everybody in the church to see, walking from one side to the other, presenting the child to the congregation. He introduces the child as a gift from God to the community. "Children of Israel," he proclaims, "here is the gift which the Lord has given us." He then sprinkles the child three times—in the name of the Father, the Son, and the Holy Spirit—with blessed water from a jar held by the Holy Head, the senior of the Holy Children. In the same way he blesses the child three times with blessed oil, applying the sign of the cross on the forehead. Finally he kneels down with the child to make it touch the floor with its feet, again three times in the name of the Father, the Son, and the Holy Spirit. He directly addresses the child which for the first time in its life has literally set foot in the house of God. Although the actual wording may differ, the meaning of this act is clear: the church is introduced as the ultimate place of security. It is presented as a place of asylum and a safe haven where she or he can always go and which will always be open to him or her even though the whole world may have abandoned them. This is the house of God, where the power of God is believed to be present and all evil will be warded off, a place where Satan cannot enter. It is a moving and meaningful sign in an environment full of uncertainties.

At the end the pastor returns the child to the parents, pointing out once more that the newborn child is a gift from God and that they are its stewards. He impresses on them that the child has been entrusted to them by the Lord. They should take good care of it so that it will grow up in good health and prosperity. He then blesses both child and parents. Finally, he pronounces a blessing for the whole community, expressing the hope that the blessing of children may also be bestowed upon others. In doing so he may sprinkle the community with water as a symbolic act of purification and a sign of God's miraculous power and fatherly love.

All those who have been kneeling will then get up for the thanksgiving part of the ceremony to start. The mother, or both parents, express thanks to the Lord, usually beginning with a hymn. Surrounded by relatives and friends, the mother may inform the congregation about problems during pregnancy or at childbirth that were successfully overcome. She may tell about her longing for a child or her long waiting, or any other circumstance related to the new-born child. After this testimony there is singing and dancing animated by the choir and the band. Finally the procession leaves the hall while parents and family then return to their seats at the front. The whole ceremony lasts for about half an hour and will be concluded by the pastor with a prayer. Soft drinks and cakes will be distributed among the congregation to conclude the celebration.

THE FOOT-WASHING RITUAL

Once a year, on the eve of the New Year, a special ritual is performed in the True Teachings of Christ's Temple to mark the transition from the old to the new year. Following the example of Jesus as described in the New Testament the feet of every member of the church are washed and blessed with oil while prayers are said over them.

The service starts in the evening and lasts into the early morning, as a few hundred people need to be served this way. In order of arrival the individual names are written down on a list that will be worked through during the night-long service. The night is spent in singing, praying, Bible reading and preaching by the various evangelists. Tea and sandwiches are served through the night. From time to time a number of individuals' names are called out, some ten at a time, for the foot-washing ceremony.They queue up at the pastor's consultation room which they enter barefoot. When it is their turn the faithful enter the front room one by one for one of the junior pastors to wash their feet with water from a plastic tub. This water is regularly changed by some helpers. The person then enters the senior pastor's room, stepping into another little tub for the pastor to bless their feet with oil, making the sign of the cross. He does the same on the forehead while saying a short prayer for the person and blessing him or her. In cases where a person does not speak English, the language of communication used by the pastor, somebody will translate what is said. Only when every individual has been served this way will the service be concluded. At the end of the service all the pastors and evangelists queue up in front of the church hall to shake hands with every individual member to wish them happy New Year.

In practice this means that the service goes on for some twelve hours, during which most people remain in the church. In the prayers during the service regular references are made to the need to be washed anew by Jesus, and God's protection is sought against attacks from the "Evil One." The washing of the feet and the blessing with oil have symbolically prepared the congregation for the year to come. The washing has purified them from whatever evil may have affected them, while the blessing with oil is meant to provide protection against any Satanic attacks. The end of the year is seen as a particularly vulnerable period, during which Satan will try and strike a final blow and when spiritual protection is needed more than ever.

RITUAL IN TIMES OF CRISIS

The emphasis on purification, the need to ward off evil, the sharing in the power of Christ, and the offering of a secure place in the church are all ritual underpinnings of the teachings of the church. Church teachings and doctrines are all related, in one way or another, to the day-to-day situation in which people live. There is a constant awareness that the marginalization of most Africans living in the Bijlmer, in itself already the most marginalized district of Amsterdam, can easily lead them into difficulties. Drugs, prostitution and the danger of contracting AIDS, drunkenness, and theft, all social evils to be found in the conditions of a marginalized society, can easily turn from potential into real dangers for migrant communities. One of the most noticeable things in the True Teachings of Christ's Temple, therefore, is the creation of a safe place, not just physically in the form of a church hall but, more importantly, in a ritual sense. The church constitutes a sanctified space which has been set apart as the place of the Lord and can neither be entered nor touched by Satan. Incense and holy water are means to secure the place's purity and sanctity, safe from evil. Whoever enters the place under the spell of Satan will be able to rid themselves of evil by calling upon the powers of Christ through the Holy Spirit. The ritual is controlled by an ordained minister who is considered spiritually too strong to be affected by Satan. Rituals are performed in an orderly manner. Physical signs of spiritual presence, whether it is believed to be of a good or an evil spirit, signs of the presence of God or of Satan, are accepted as a normal effect of the ritual act that is performed and dealt with without disturbing the proceedings.

The environment is particularly full of risks and dangers for young people, who form the majority of the church members. Hence the dedication ritual is particularly meaningful, as it most explicitly symbolizes the idea of the church as a safe haven from the moment of birth. Love and unity, brotherhood and solidarity, sharing and communication are constantly promoted in word and action, including in ritual action. For example, a "chain of the Spirit" may be formed during or after healing prayers, healing referring not simply to physical problems but particularly addressing the social problems that have a disturbing effect on people: joblessness, homelessness, and lack of formal identity documents. Ritual action is aimed at linking people together, as they are all victims of the prevailing political climate in Western Europe and the Netherlands.

These ritual responses to life crises may be usefully analyzed with the help of Van Gennep's "rites of passage" model. In this particular case, the life crisis has been set in motion by some form of upheaval in the home countries in Africa: war, poverty, unemployment, lack of education, food shortages, and so on. It is this type of life crisis which oblige people to leave their home countries for unknown and insecure places. Here, they tend to live a marginal life while they try to merge with their new environment. In other words, these migrant communities are going through an important transitional phase of life which, like other "life crises" such as birth, puberty, marriage and death, requires ritual or ceremonial validation. The rituals in the Bijlmer church communities accompany this new type of life crisis and help in making the transition.

Van Gennep identified a regular pattern in the rites of passage which allowed him to develop a classification by distinguishing three major phases: separation, transition and incorporation, in English translation also referred to as stages of separation, marginal or liminal, and aggregation. I am particularly concerned with the second phase, the phase of transition, or liminality which is vital to all rites of passage and marks the most sensitive phase in the ritual process. The African communities in the Bijlmer have gone through the phase of separation and are now in the most delicate phase of their life crisis, the transitional or marginal phase, which is marked by liminality. It is this phase—elaborated upon by Turner—which is vital to their eventual successful incorporation into Dutch society. Hence, we may argue, all ritual behavior in these communities is aimed at achieving internal strength and stability in order to overcome their liminality and prepare for moving to the third and last phase of incorporation, namely as an accepted part of the new society, or Dutch society in this case. The crisis arising from the transition from Africa to Europe has a disturbing effect on the community concerned as well as on most of the individual members. Ritual behaviour is aimed at restoring the balance through spiritual empowerment coupled with practical action to solve individual problems. Jobs, housing, documentation problems, and so on, are all recurrent themes of prayer and preaching in church services.

I will move to Victor Turner to explore in more detail the characteristics and consequences of the second phase of the transitional cycle, the liminal phase (Turner 1969: 81 ff.). Characteristic of the liminal phase is the ambiguity that goes with it. Liminal persons belong neither to the community from which they have come nor yet to a new community. Such is the case in the Bijlmer district of Amsterdam. Africans living in the Bijlmer have left their original communities in their home countries and are not part of these any more; nor do they yet form part of the Western community where they have come to live. They are indeed, as Turner puts it," betwixt and between the positions assigned and arrayed by law, custom, convention, and ceremonial" (ibid.: 81). Liminality, as he says, goes with marginalization and structural inferiority, with low status and structural exclusion. The issue of demarcation lines being drawn by the European community is constantly and openly addressed in these churches.

The characteristics of liminality can all be found among the African communities in Amsterdam which, in spite of their size and numbers, are marginalized in Dutch society. There are, of course, individual exceptions, but as a group the statement holds true. This can be demonstrated from their social as well as their geographical position. They are concentrated in the least popular district of town where they live in the huge tower-blocks which in the 1970s-1980s were vacated by many Dutch citizens who had come to find the living conditions of the Bijlmer intolerable. Socially, the majority of Africans are equally marginalized, in the sense that most of them have unskilled jobs and relatively low wages while at the same time many are forced to live in hiding as they lack the official papers which allow them a legitimate place in Dutch society. In other words, many of them have no recognized status in the wider society of the Netherlands, which is characteristic of their liminal situation: "the passage from lower to higher status is through a limbo of statuslessness" (Turner 1969: 83). The people concerned are aware of this and determined to turn things to their advantage during the liminal phase by moving away from their lower status and achieving a higher status in the Netherlands. The church communities in the Bijlmer play an important role in helping them to achieve that. They provide the institutional context for a form of ritual behavior that is geared to help individuals make the transition from one stage to the other, from separation from an old community to incorporation into a new one.

Liminality, in given circumstances, as Turner has shown, is represented in various ways, such as by lack of possessions, passiveness, or humility. Most significant, however, are the comradeship and egalitarianism that are promoted in this phase and that lead to a form of homogeneity which has been labeled by Turner "communitas." It stands for a model of society or a modality of social relationship which, according to Turner, emerges recognizably in the liminal period, representing a rather unstructured and undifferentiated community, or even communion, of equal individuals who submit together to the general authority of the ritual elders (ibid.: 82 ff.). This is relevant to the case of the Bijlmer, where we can discern a similar pattern, with details varying according to the specific situation. The teachings in the various churches are clearly designed to emphasize this communitas aspect. Love, equality, sharing, firmness, and discipline are among the qualities which recur in the "lessons," as the sermons are often called, and other admonitions during church services. The emphasis on communitas is also important as the members of the church, although mostly coming from one specific region in Ghana, all bring their different personal backgrounds and different individual experiences, as well as their own hopes and expectations. They gather in these churches as individual beings in-between two communities: the one of the past and the one of the future.

The authority of the church leadership is (as is normally the case in churches) generally accepted and followed, even if it is only because one cannot easily evade it. The leadership is clearly aware of the importance of promoting and cultivating communitas in these marginal communities as a prerequisite for successful integration in Dutch society. In order to integrate, they need to find and develop a new identity. In the given circumstances this new identity does not lie, as is often suggested by outsiders, in their "Africanness," which sets them apart as a different and separate community in Dutch society, but in their Christianity, which allows them to become part of the world community or, indeed, the Western community. The majority of the African migrant communities in Holland are Christian and as such they identify themselves with the Netherlands as a basically Christian country. In such a context, they feel little need to emphasize their own identity as Africans, or specifically *African* Christians. They have understood that this would contribute to their isolation in society rather than bringing them into the mainstream of Western Christianity. Therefore, Africans in the Bijlmer tend to stress their identity as *Christians* and not as Africans, while their churches do not call themselves (as others often do) "African churches" but international churches.

Communitas, as Turner sees it, is essentially a relationship between concrete, historical, idiosyncratic individuals who are not segmentalized into roles and statuses but confront one another in the manner of Martin Buber's "I" and "Thou," that is in a mutual relationship between total and concrete persons (ibid.: 119, 124). That is precisely what one finds in these Bijlmer communities that in doctrine and practice favor an egalitarian model that, ideally, should lead to a form of solidarity that is not based on the contrast with others. The notion of demarcation is virtually absent, as their solidarity is with the marginalised which also comprises members of other faith groups. Christianity is preached not as a dogma but as a way of life which contains a solution to all human problems. Demarcation, by emphasizing the differences among believers, offers no solution to the problems of these communities. On the other hand, stressing shared human values does help in the solution of their problems in life.

Communitas, it should be added, is the predominant element of one particular phase in the life process, the transitional or liminal phase, and as such is not a permanent condition. The communitas that emerges during that phase is born out of a condition of crisis and may well be called a "communitas of crisis" (cf. Turner 1969: 143). Turner makes a distinction between three different types of communitas, which represent three different phases in the transitional process: an existential, a normative, and an ideological communitas as it develops over time from a rather unstructured and spontaneous into a more structured model (ibid.: 120). The Bijlmer communities can best be compared to the normative communitas model, as they find themselves in a period where they need to mobilize and organize resources and require a degree of social control among members of the congregation in pursuit of these goals. Thus, from an existential communitas, often in the form of small house congregations, they have organized themselves into a more enduring social system, more structured and with an adapted institutional context. The step to an "ideological communitas" has not yet been made but seems inevitable in the course of time.

CONCLUSION

We have seen how in the Bijlmer district of Amsterdam the content of people's beliefs and the way they give expression to them are formed by the specific conditions of their life. These are not the circumstances of "traditional" Africa, nor of modern Africa, but first and foremost of modern Europe. I have described these circumstances for Africans in the diaspora in Europe as conditions of great difficulty, resulting from the transition from Africa to Europe and leading to marginalization and structural exclusion in their new environment. I have shown how the African-led churches are of vital importance in accompanying the life crisis that goes with the transition, and I have tried to explain ritual behavior in these churches along the same lines. In order to try and understand ritual behavior among African Christian communities in the Netherlands one should not base the argument on the African situation, but rather seek one's points of reference in the context of present-day Europe. This is not to diminish the meaning and influence of traditional African cosmology in the European situation, but to bring out the dynamic interaction of tradition and modernity of African religion in new circumstances. In this case, that is, in the case presented here, the emphasis of many Africans on their Christian identity is striking.

Marginalization and the resulting struggle for survival are the main factors that define ritual behavior in the most recent migrant communities in the Bijlmer, notably the African ones. While the inner frontiers in the European Union are gradually being removed to further integration among various peoples, new demarcation lines are being drawn in order to be able to exclude certain other categories. The content and tone of the recent political debate in Europe on migrants and illegal workers is a logical consequence of this policy of demarcation. Significantly, the demarcation lines are largely racially determined, so that in practice a predominantly white community is consciously separating itself from a largely black community. This situation also applies to the Netherlands and includes the sphere of religion.

The need for demarcation also manifests itself on the side of the white Christian communities, which seek to separate themselves from black Christian communities in their midst. This may not be immediately apparent due to the intellectually liberal discourse often to be found in Western Christianity which stresses the right of Africans to maintain their own identity. This need is also expressed in the conventional view of many scholars of religion, or theologians for that matter, who use the same argument to describe and analyze the position of African Christians. For African Christian communities in the West, however, in present conditions, it runs against their interests to emphasise their African-ness as it helps to put up barriers rather than remove them, especially as they are blacks living among whites. Instead, in their own discourse, they set great store by the concepts of mutual love and unity, first among Christians of all denominations and irrespective of race and color, but also among all human beings, irrespective of their creed. Belief in Christ, rather than functioning as a strict line of demarcation, is stretched to encompass others who want to be part of the group, even if on an occasional or temporary basis. As such, African Christians in the Netherlands continue a religious practice characterized by openness and flexibility which can be considered a hallmark of African religiosity in general.

NOTES

This article is an updated and adapted version of Ter Haar 1995b.

1. Winti is the indigenous religion of the Surinam people; it was carried there from West Africa at the time of the slave trade.

2. I am using the term "charismatic" here in its everyday sense as well as in the sense of somebody with a special attraction based on perceived special powers, in this case healing.

BIBLIOGRAPHY

Centraal Bureau voor de Statistiek (CBS). *Niet-Nederlanders in Nederland,* Januari 1994.

De Jonge, J. *Soms was er Geen Plaats in de Herberg: Een Religieuze Kaart van de Bijlmermeer.* A report commissioned by the Stuurgroep Vernieuwing Bijlmermeer Amsterdam, 1992.

De Jonge, J. *"Halverwege de Hemel": Religieuze Kaart van Amsterdam-Zuidoost.* Amsterdam: Mozeshuis, 1994.

Himmans, D. *Light on the Scriptures.* London: Oval Press, 1986.

Kimball, S. T. "Introduction," in A. Van Gennep, *The Rites of Passage.* Chicago: University of Chicago Press, 1975, p. xvii.

Nimako, K. *Nieuwkomers in een "Gevestigde" Samenleving: Een Analyse van de Ghanese Gemeenschap in Zuidoost.* (A research report commissioned by the Stadsdeel Zuidoost.) Amsterdam: Stadsdeel Zuidoost 1993.

Oomen, M., and J. Palm. *Geloven in de Bijlmer: Over de Rol van Religieuze Groeperingen .* Amsterdam: Het Spinhuis, 1994.

Southeast: Quite a City District. Amsterdam: Stadsdeel Zuidoost, 1994.

ter Haar, G. "Afrikaanse Kerken in Nederland," *Religieuze Bewegingen in Nederland* 28: 1-35, 1994.

ter Haar, G. "Ritual as Communication: A Study of African Christian Communities in the Bijlmer District of Amsterdam," in J. G. Platvoet and K. van der Toorn (eds.). *Pluralism and Identity: Studies in Ritual Behaviour.* Leiden: Brill, 1995a.

ter Haar, G. "Strangers in the Promised Land: African Christians in Europe," *Exchange* 24 (1): 1-33, 1995b.

Turner, E. *Experiencing Ritual: A New Interpretation of African Healing*. Philadelphia: University of Pennsylvania Press, 1992.

Turner, V. W. *The Ritual Process: Structure and Anti-Structure*. Harmondsworth: Penguin Books, 1969.

Van Gennep, A. *The Rites of Passage*. Chicago: University of Chicago Press, 1975.

Van 't Hoff, G. *Leeronderzoek: "Migratie van Ghanezen."* M.A. thesis, University of Amsterdam, 1992.

Zuidoost in Cijfers. Amsterdam: Stadsdeel Zuidoost, 1992.

16

From Africa into Italy: The Exorcistic-Therapeutic Cult of Emmanuel Milingo

Vittorio Lanternari

For more than twenty years, and in some cases from the end of the Second World War, Europe has seen the arrival and the spread of a variety of new religions and sects, received with renewed and always more widespread eagerness by an expanding range of social classses. From the US came the Pentecostals, the Mormons, and Jehovah's Witnesses. From Asia, Buddhist sects and a sect of Korean origin (Unification Church). More recently Japan has launched, besides its electronic and car industries, religious sects that are no less influential than these powerful organizations (for example, Soka Gakkai and Rissho Kosei-Kai). The multiplication and expansion of new religions is having an impact on various interests and, depending on the case, causing serious concern at an institutional level and in the wider society as a whole. The Catholic Church has been forced by these developments to reflect on its own situation.[1] Social groups, family or˙anizations and courts have been mobilised to respond. Large numbers of young people hasten to new prophets. Women and men "vibrate" to the calls that alternative preachers make to rescue "spirituality." If we consider the mixing of new religions and of syncretism at an intercontinental level, between America, Asia, Europe, and Africa, it was possible until recently to distinguish two predominant areas of origin and two prevalent directions of diffusion. India, Korea, Japan, and America (particularly California) were the areas of origin, except that the US is a secondary area of origin for oriental religions since many oriental gurus have transferred to the US.

The principal directions of diffusion are, respectively, from Asia to the US, Europe, Africa, and Australia, and from the US to Europe, Africa, and South and Central America. Once the West was virtually the sole provider of religion to the Third World, which was the receiver pure and simple. However, a situation has now developed in which the relationships, once clearly identifiable, between the cultures that gave and those that received, between areas of origin and areas of diffusion, are becoming destructuralized and more complex, to the point where the Third World of Africa and Central and South America, is also increasingly confirming itself as an area of origin along with Asia, particularly the Indian subcontinent and East Asia, in respect to the West (Europe, North America) which is increasingly a receiver. We are witnessing a process that is overturning the missionary itineraries constructed by the Christian Church throughout the centuries. In some ways, Christianity is also returning toward the West, remolded and elaborated by the Third World and the great cultures of Asia.

In this way, religious movements of African origin as well as the syncretism of traditional religions with Christianity, are found today in London and throughout Great Britain in the form, for example, of the "Church of the Cherubims and Seraphim" strongly represented among Nigerian immigrants. But the socio-religious Rasta movement, that originates from Jamaica, has attracted not only West Indian immigrants but also large numbers of English youth and has also spread widely in Europe. If Africa is the "land of the missionary" for sects such as the Jehovah's Witnesses, Hare Krishna, The Family of God, Mahikari, and also the Bahai, the Moonies, and Japanese Buddhist movements including Soka Gakkai, by the same token African spiritual guides now constitute an integral part of the religious landscape in Paris, being consulted and followed not only by African immigrants but also by the French in search of new sources of psychological assurance on the symbolic and religious level. [2]

In Italy, the "Case of Emmanuel Milingo" has been part of Roman religious life since 1983. It is the case of a Catholic African priest (a bishop, in fact) who carries and spreads a cult of healing, that is capable of mobilizing an impressive number of followers from all social classes, by revitalizing with a language and a tangibly African style archaic and subjective uses of magic and witchcraft. We can consider a case in point:

A woman affected by physical illness and mental disturbances (who could not eat, was hearing voices, was afraid of her own son), presented herself one day," Malingo recalls. He continues. "She told me she had tried to recover in a psychiatric hospital but without success. I tried the treatment typical of traditional Catholicism: I prayed with her in the conventional way, I gave her confession, I said mass. No good came of it. Then I tried hypnosis. While the woman was in a state of unconsciousness, I prayed with particular intensity. The prayer touched me in soul and body, all of me. I felt absolutely at peace. My body was cold. It was impossible to do anything. The woman had undoubtedly completely recovered.[3]

For Emmanuel Milingo, Bishop of Lusaka (Zambia) since 1969, before being suspended from duties in 1982, and now (since 1983) a priest, healer, and exorcist in Rome, this case "revealed" to him that he had been granted by God the gift to heal the sick and to defeat Satan and all other evil spirits.

The reported episode, and the therapeutic procedure activated in him, offer a paradigm of the successive activities practiced by Milingo as a healer. It is these therapeutic procedures themselves, which from 1973 (the year of "revelation") he had applied in Africa, that brought him into conflict with the local and European clergy, with the African bishops and Rome. In fact, Milingo was not accepted in Lusaka, where the clergy was largely European and was not prepared to recognize in him the role of spiritual healer and guide, or to accept aspects of his culture of origin. It is true that Milingo showed a rigid intolerance of the rational, scientific mentality and of its supporters. He attacked experimental psychology, and also theologians who, he said, rendered themselves easy prey for the Devil because of their neglect of man as a living entity. Without being given the means to defend himself and without the usual process of investigation being carried out, he was recalled to Rome and was barred from practicing as a priest and bishop in Zambia.

Milingo represents a novel case of an African who has founded a Christian faith-healing cult interwoven with ritual forms and ideologies from the African tradition, but who nevertheless forcibly proclaims total adhesion to the Catholic Church. In this he distances himself from the rich stream of charismatic African personalities who, in accepting Christianity and spreading their new churches, syncretised to varying degrees, stress their own individual autonomy in respect to the historical missionary church; not to mention those churches that controversially assumed (in the colonial era) the label "separatist." Nevertheless, Milingo shares with a series of prophets and charismatics, the tendency to reinterpret Christianity in "African" terms, not only in liturgy and ritual, but also in doctrine.

Since his forced migration to Rome, Milingo has set himself up as the protagonist of a socio-cultural and religious process without precedent in European history. With the sweeping call to action that in the whole of Italy is associated with his name and that of his cult to which flow hoards of pilgrims time and again, Milingo is turning into the promoter of a Catholicism in which archaisms that in popular Christianity ordinarily remain untouched are being reborn and revived. This has come about by virtue of the evident similarities in ideology and structure between popular Catholicism and traditional African religions: the belief in sorcery, witchcraft, the ideology of the Devil, possession, and the rituals of exorcism. Thus, with Milingo, sub-Saharan African religion makes its appearance in Europe, mixing itself with popular Catholicism. From another perspective, it finds an echo in the ideology of Satanism, officially and independently relaunched with insistence and vigorous calls to action by recent popes. Certain fundamental elements of African religion, through Milingo, come to resemble closely and fuse with tenets of Christian origin, and the novelty of such a syncretic mix that results from this gives rise to an extraordinary proselytistic effectiveness. A population is desperately searching, in the present condition of collective psychic unease and of crisis where matters of faith and morality are concerned, for new and original ways of salvation, respond eagerly to Milingo's call.

In Italy, Milingo has intensified and extended contacts, already started while in Africa, having participated in a conference at Ann Arbor, Michigan, in 1976 with the charismatic movement, that offers him support and appreciation. Ordinary priests actively participate in his meetings in official dress, collaborate in his cult, accompany him in prayer, descend among the crowd to administer the eucharist and to bless and anoint the postulants.[4] Certain appointed lay people collect donations.

The most salient and characteristic feature of the cult initiated by Milingo is seen in the ritual of faith healing that he practiced in public among the throng of the gathered faithful in the vast expanse of the church (until January 1987) and later in a hall adapted for monthly meetings. In this ritual the observer recognises the unmistakable charismatic authority that emanates from him and is the primary nucleus of his power to attract. The inspired preaching, the recitation of sweeping invectives against all the forces of evil, the quotation of dramatically effective biblical passages, create a climate of fervent participatory tension and encourage choral responses to his precise and provocative questions. The symbolic-religious system generates an unusual degree of vitality that impacts upon the collective psyche which as a result is subdued. Milingo becomes the paternal mitigator of every suffering, the conqueror of evil.

As a charismatic leader, he exudes a "sense of a mission, of authority, of communion with God."[5] He claims to have received from God the "gift" to perform miracles of faith healing. When Milingo denies that it is a question of his "charisma" and affirms that it is a question of "power", he evidently intends to rule out any question of "human talent" (charisma) so as to underline that it is a question of divine "power": in this way his activity becomes opportune and all accusations that official Catholicism might make about prevarication are forestalled. Milingo insists that it is from experiences of inspiration that he receives when enraptured in the course of prayer, or in dreams and visions, that he obtains the certainty that he has been endowed with a gift. Such experiences are renewed, he says, with every new patient, at least on those occasions when he practices individual faith healing. It is not by accident that he evokes the experience of Paul the Apostle, elevated to the Third Sky and who plausibly during prayer saw Our Lord as the model for his experiences.[6] His inexpressible spiritual experiences, which cannot be shared by others, represent the primary argument adduced as proof of an unquestionable authenticity of his divine inspiration. From a socio-psychological and socio-anthropological point of view, the problem of the reciprocal understanding between the leader and the assembly of the faithful—the latter expecting, and inwardly rejoicing at, this authentication, the former presenting it with the certainty of satisfying collective expectation—imposes itself as one of primary importance.

Faith in him persists, confirmed by him each time, in his ability to communicate with the world of spirits, or the World in Between, as he calls it: that is, a world that is the intermediary between man and God, betweeen himself and the divine. The protective and benvolent spirits are identified sometimes, in accordance with the African tradition, as the spirits of dead ancestors, sometimes—following the Christian model—as the angels of the Bible, or the saints of Catholicism.[7] But the world of the spirits is ambivalent: and the evil spirits coincide, according to Milingo, with malignant powers, already the object of belief among the Ngunis and the Shonas from which our charismatic himself originates—and on the other hand correspond to, and blend with, the unitary figure of the Devil in the biblical representation. The Devil himself, however, in Milingo's speeches, decomposes into a multiplicity of beings. He distinctly mentions demoniacal entities such as Satan, Beelzebub, Astaroth, Lucifer and so forth. He also evokes other beings, clearly from the African tradition. These are the evil spirits and the spirits of the dead, the latter traditionally presented as ambivalent, acting at times as guardian spirits, and at other times as punishing and destructive entities.[8] The African inheritance of this sector of Milingo's mental world is very much alive and determines an arduous and discordant mixture or alternation of ideas. Milingo himself concedes that he has to be cautious when talking of his experiences with the world of spirits, mainly in consideration of the reservations felt by the official clergy with regard to his way of reliving Christianity. "Years ago"—he says on this subject—"I told a group of priests that I was able to speak to the dead and the evil spirits. But they muttered the formula anathema *sit*, that is, 'be cursed.'"[9] So Milingo can—as he himself declares—converse with witches, with the Devil, and more generally with the devils from whom he can get information on the nature and the cure of individual ailments. In that respect, the episode he recounts of an encounter with a postulant, whose true nature he ascertained through communication directly received from the devils, seems significant to me. Fully sharing in the archaic witch ideology inherited from his original Zambian culture, Milingo—referring to the woman who approached him—says, "The demons confessed to me that she had been handed over to them by a Mrs X. who was one of their agents in a quarter of Lusaka."[10] There he pointed at her as a witch. On close analysis, this is typical, traditional behavior of the "witch-hunters" who rage among Shonas and Ngunis, as well as in other societies of sub-Saharan Africa. These "witch-hunters" are generally pointed at by Milingo as "the worst witches," because they are inspired by spirits he considers evil. Nevertheless he shares some of their ideological presuppositions, despite operating—for his part—on God's inpsiration. Besides, a reading of texts written by Milingo since his Zambian days shows that he acknowledges the active presence of witches, and of a surprising variety of spirits, inherited from the local original tradition. Some are connected, for their intervention, with individual days of the week, others with distinct types of illness. Then one can count spirits or groups of spirits called Ngozi, who act malevolently as authentic witches, and come from people who lived operating witchcraft. Others, the Midzimu, are the spirits of the dead who are gone to heaven. Finally Milingo, in his first writings, composed in Africa or shortly thereafter, insists on the Shave, or Mashave, spirits. These bring psychological illness. In fact they cause uncontrollable possessions:[11] a kind of psychological disorder whose therapy, according to the Shona-Nguni cultural tradition (and that of many other African societies), is entrusted to a traditional priest, called nganga in the case of the Shona-Nguni. In Lusaka, the nganga is traditionally the one who, endowed with mystical powers and inspired by spirits, can diagnose, cure and prevent diseases. His powers derive from spirits who visit him in dreams or during a trance and guide him with various signals. During the ritual conducted by nganga, a dance with choral singing takes place, and the nganga himself, wearing his ceremonial dress, enters a state of trance-possession. At this point the spirit speaks with the nganga's voice, and an assistant listening, interprets and reports to the postulant the spoken oracle.[12] The ritual, as far as the patient is concerned, involves the latter's inclusion within the cultural group. In this way his person, and with it his illness, become socialized. The patient is set on a process of more or less durable cultural initiation, until he can control his spells of possession within predetermined ways and times, that is, in direct correlation with his participation in the rite: a participation whose continuity will easily induce the once "persecutory" and harmful spirits to perform their action in a beneficial and therapeutic way. These are the ways of traditional exorcism as practiced in African culture.[13] If one looks at the cult practiced by Milingo in Rome (and occasionally in other Italian cities) from the viewpoint of its African connections, it is impossible to miss the fact that it has in common with the beliefs and the practices of traditional religion widespread in African societies a fundamental layer of ideas concerning witches and spirits, deemed to be responsible for all sorts of evils, the ideology of possession by spirits (now by the Devil), and the procedures originally intended for healing practices in respect to patients afflicted by psychological disorders (now exorcism of diabolical possession). As indicated above, spirits and witches continue to be present in Milingo's speeches and public exorcisms; but now they are accompanied by the Devil, in whose image they occasionally tend to be cast. The critical moment in the cult's sessions comes at the point of the sermon in which the leader of the cult pronounces out loud and in order the list of ills: a list drawn up following criteria of an empirical order (for example "eye and throat complaints, chest problems" but also "cancer, diabetes, etc."). The recitation of this list is always followed by the exorcistic formula: "Away evil spirits! Away with witchcraft! Away Satan!" Also by the recital of the biblical Psalm 59 ("free me, O my God, from my enemies, from my assailants give me refuge . . . Raise yourself to my aid and intention. You, God of the people, God of Israel, have no mercy on the wicked. They return at night, they snarl like dogs and roam the city . . . "). This frequently gives occasion for crises of desperation and cries torn with terror. The public is clearly induced, by suppositions supplied by the preacher, to feel in these words the "living" presence of Satan, far from recognizing that which the text of David really contains, that is, the prayer of the warriors against the enemies that threaten to subdue the nation of Israel. In such a way, the God of the armies is reinterpreted; better still, he is awakened as a God that fights a Satan who threatens the subject who listens and prays. The figure of Satan, in effect, pervades with his harrassing presence the entire course of the ritual.

There are good grounds for thinking that there could be a relation—not coincidental but predetermined—between the outbreak of individual crises, at least in the majority of cases, and the behavior of the preacher in his choice of themes, tone of voice— in short, his method of communication.

The procedures following the exorcism consist of two consecutive but distinguishable stage and involve the use of techniques (verbal, gesticular, placement of the hands, shouting, threatening . . .) suited to stirring up the crisis of "possession" in the patient; and then there is the insistence in ordinary prayer and the use of techniques to engage good spirits in order to overcome the crises. The religious service practiced today by Milingo in Italy is characterized by so called "possession" among the faithful: in reality these are psychic crises, for the most part violent, and taking a variety of forms; such as shouting, cursing, shivering, weeping, disordered motor agitation, convulsions. This was also a striking feature that was already present in the cult that Milingo practiced in Lusaka. In Rome those seized by the most acute forms of crises are assistants predisposed to possession and others predisposed to being carried away.

It needs to be borne in mind that Milingo's first existential and cultural experiences were shaped by a traditional rural culture. He was born in 1930 and lived until he was 12 years old in a village (Mnukwa) in eastern Zambia. He spent his childhood helping his parents with livestock and in agricultural labor, before embarking on seminary studies that led to his ordination as a priest in 1958.[14] In the city of Lusaka, where the population is typically multiethnic, and where Milingo carried out his ministry as priest and later as archbishop, the dominant religious culture is influenced by elements of various components from different ethnic traditions.[15] Thus, Milingo, born in the Nguni culture, was as a matter of course influenced by the Shona culture of Zimbabwian origins. Therefore, it is not surprising that various categories of spirits remembered by him come from a source, from Shona culture, as a recent study has shown.[16]

If we then look at the form of exorcism practiced by Milingo we find a precise parallel with that of the Zambian prophet Peter Mulenga, founder of a Christian syncretist church called Mutumwa Church.[17] Adrian Hastings raises the point: "To fully understand Milingo's ministry of faith healing, it should be placed in the context of African as well as Christian traditions, in as much as both already interact between themselves throughout the whole of modern African society."[18]

At this point it seems useful to document what we know about certain important characteristics of the religious cult that Milingo practiced at the beginning of his episcopal ministry in Africa, when he began to develop his innovative and personal interpretations of the Catholic cult, which very soon was to provoke, among the other local bishops, and therefore among the representatives of the Vatican, concern and alarm which in the end resulted in his removal from office. In private correspondence written in 1977, an Italian missionary, Father Kikito Sesana, then present in Lusaka and personally interested in extending his knowledge of the new religious forms produced in Africa by Christianity, at the level of practical religion, informed the present writer of certain peculiarities that he had had occasion to observe directly in Milingo's religious services, and of the particular reactions of the followers during healing sessions. Milingo conducted in that period four faith healing sessions a week, two on Tuesdays, two on Fridays. Sesana reports, "After a preparation that for Catholics is confession and for the others a spiritual— Sesana did not consider all of Milingo's followers to be Catholic—Monsignor Milingo calls a group of around ninety people into a room." He continues "often many of the Africans came from far away (Kenya, Malawi, Rhodesia, etc.). After a brief reading from the Gospel starts the prayer, and immediately 15-20 of those present react with manifestations of possession. There are those who weep hysterically, those who bark like dogs, those who roll around the floor, etc. This lasts for an hour, with the Bishop the only one to pray, he does so out loud, moving among those present, placing his hands on them and calming the possessed, sprinkling holy water, etc."

Fr. Sesana further noted: "The Bishop is absolutely convinced of having carried out faith healing—from cancer to sterility to name but two." Now for those with direct experience of Milingo's cult in Italy, it is inevitable that they will make make comparisons of various structural analogies with what happened in Africa. The calender of healing sessions has changed; in Rome it is only the first Monday of every month. As for the location of the cult, from the "room" in Lusaka it has moved to a church (until 1986), and then to a grandiose conference room in one of Rome's big hotels (Ergife). The number of followers, from the 1,300 in Lusaka, has risen to several thousand, with monthly pilgrims coming from all parts of Italy. G. ter Haar[19] informs us that the faith healing sessions, until then conducted by Milingo in his house twice a week, were suspended by order of the conference of the local bishops in 1977. With serious effort, Milingo, nevertheless, succeeded in obtaining authorization to restart his faith healing, on the condition that there be only one session a month in the Cathedral of Lusaka; that is, by agreeing to follow the same calendar that is now prudently observed in Italy. Haar also tells us that the 90 faithful seen by Father Sesana at every session was soon to become 500 and later around 1300. The rapid and sweeping success in Lusaka prompted the church hierarchy to take measures to limit Milingo's influence. Likewise in Italy today the widespread appearances of the Bishop on TV and the expansion of his cult to numerous centers on the outskirts of Rome, have brought about Papal intervention to stop him.

In Italy also, Milingo plays the role of the charismatic leader, especially at the most solemn part of the service when the exorcism of the spirits and demons takes place. It is at this time that the congregation responds and the atmosphere is charged with an excitement and enthusiasm that are highly contagious. A violent and emotional climate fills the air; anxiety, fear and near panic reign as the members of the assembly reach a climactic emotional peak, entering into psychically altered states of consciousness and, as interviews suggest, behave as if demoniacally possessed. Such manifestations of crisis and so-called "possession" in Rome replicate the behavioral model of Milingo's faithful in Lusaka. In reality the analogy of the behavior of the two congregations from such different environments and culture can only be explained by the fact that it is evidently the same charismatic leader, Milingo, who employs the same techniques to untrap and "release" the crises that afflict the possessed. In this way he comes to have control over them and to provide the faithful with a real chance to escape from these crises and embark on the path to salvation, protected from evil. Milingo's approach is traditional and involves the blessing water, salt, oil, clothing, and various objects brought along by the faithful— conducive to elevating the mood of his followers until the end of the service, which is remarkable for its dramatic moments.

Father Sesana in 1977, before the first and then still informal liturgical and therapeutic assemblies of Reverend Milingo, took the trouble to note that "The principal happenings during the course of his *healing sessions* were part of the traditional culture of the people of Zambia, and in intention the explanations given by the Bishop"—the missionary noted—"were based 90% upon typically African reasons. Only in the smallest degree did he follow modern *healing* movements of the US."

The observations of the Catholic missionary seem, for the most part, to be valid for the Milingo cult in Rome, except for the fact that his relations with the charismatic movements of the United States and Europe have had an immediate and direct impact and today he finds in them important and legitimating parallels.

It is important to insist here on the peremptory and threatening tones that

Milingo adopts when hurling attacks against witchcraft, evil spirits, black and white magic, curses, in summary, Satan—all of which are indications of physical ailments, psychic disturbances, anxiety, and so on. Milingo spells out a long list of misfortunes of the body and soul: organic illnesses, mental illnesses, moral vices, wicked deeds, perverse feelings. In short, illnesses suffered are mixed together with "wrong" deeds consciously performed, suffering and guilt are promiscuously joined together as the single product of the occult forces of evil. In the climate of emotion and terror thus generated, reactions are spontaneous and a contagious fear spreads through the people and contrition, remorse, and even panic ensue. In such an exceptional climate as this, there is an irresistible need, felt throughout the whole assembly of the faithful, for miraculous help, for salvation from the menaces and attacks of the Demon. The eruption itself of cases of so-called "possession" among those present, creates an acute fear of the living presence of Satan, whose threats are now actual and are believed to be immediate. As a result the exorcistic intervention of the leader assumes vital importance. He becomes, for the mass of the faithful, the bountiful and indispensable savior and as a result all come to depend on him. While he insists he is only an instrument in the hands of God, he becomes an object of personal veneration.

This operation is repeated in Rome by every charismatic African prophet before a crowd disconcerted by the move from village to city, by the disintegration of inherited socio-cultural structures, and by the emptiness, both psychological and cultural, created by modernization, the sense of insignificance caused by the conflict with the new, limited, but indigestible models of life and culture. Many of the new charismatic African prophets come to help with the spiritual welfare of the people and then intervene to help with every moral and physical ill of the African masses who are to a greater or lesser degree conscious of the crisis situation that they are in. Milingo finds in Rome a similar enthusiastic reception from people of all social classes who find themselves searching for meanings and values that will refill the emptiness left by the uneven and disconcerting change in the old way of life, and by the depressing and degenerate aspects of present day social organization: they are searching for a source of power to overcome the sense of bewilderment and impotence felt due to the lack of community.

The range of ills that Milingo claims to be able to tackle with adequate therapies is vast. There is practically no affliction, be it physical or moral or spiritual, that he cannot attempt to cure. Nor do any of his followers have any doubts concerning his extraordinairy ability as a faith healer.

An article written in Lusaka in 1981, *The Demarcations*, is an eloquent testimony to faith in his healing powers. It is recounted by the patient herself, Karen Swanson, an American psychiatric worker. In 1980 she turned to Milingo as she was suffering from a state of serious astenia, high blood pressure, dysfuntion of a kidney, enlargement of the heart, discopatia with acute pains—enough for doctors to view surgery as inevitable. She does not write of the nature of the treatment applied by Milingo and does not say that she was diagnosed as suffering from diabolic posession. She says simply that the treatment immediately stopped the pain and restored her blood pressure to normal.[20] Adrian Hastings has a point when he observes that Milingo followed two different models of practicing therapy, depending on the case. Basing myself on direct observations made in Rome, not always including an investigation of the patients, Milingo sems to combine, in a manner difficult to appreciate from the standpoint of our rational methodical assumptions, the exorcistic model which assumes that the illness is the result of diabolical possession, and the medico-charismatic model, according to which the cure is effected by the "power" conceded to Milingo by way of divine gift. It would be extremely difficult for an external observer to distinguish the possessed from those with illnesses of other kinds. What is more, the criteria for differentiation does not seem to distinguish between what are known as psychic and what are known as organic illnesses. Certain clear psychic disturbances are treated as common complaints, while sterility can be ascribed by the healer, to the intervention of a demon, which requires cure by exorcism.

The effectiveness of Milingo's therapy also obviously depends on the degree of unconditional abandon by the patient ending in hypnosis that ensues while the charismatic leader prays for the patient, placing his hands on the head or suffering parts of the body. The report of the patient Mother Gacambi of her own clinical relationship, a relationship transcribed by Milingo in his *The Demarcations*, illustrates the particular nature of the therapeutic techniques, both charismatic and ritual. It shows that the objective was the elimination of suffering by means of hypnosis and also provides information on what actually took place in the healing session. Standing beside the sister seated on the couch, Milingo induces her to sleep. Closing her eyes, the sister "feels" Milingo "enter into communion with one familiar to him," and she hears him talking to various parts of her body. He cries, "O heart, in the name of Jesus, pump blood to all parts of the body." When MIlingo calls by name the pelvic bones to return to their place, she perceives inside her something that moves in a confused way. Then she hears Milingo invoke Jesus and Mary the Virgin. Next she senses being called and awaken from sleep, helped by Milingo taking her hand.[21] Clearly the climate that is created in the meeting with the charismatic leader based as it is on foundations of faith easily produces a condition in which the patient is inclined to abandon the state of ordinary consciousness and of controlled criticism; it can therefore facilitate an inclination to undergo hypnosis. It is in these conditions that the symbolic language, behavioral and verbal, of the healer can have an effect on the patient. The face, the hands, the mannerisms, the style of speaking of the one presiding all assume for the patient considerable symbolic value and powerful significance.[22]

Already the invocation of the demon, out loud and at high pitch, predisposes and stimulates those in the audience who are more psychically predisposed to respond in such a way to abandon the state of ordinary consciousness and ultimately enter into "possession." In the highest state of this experience the subject adopts stereotypical behavior that he/she knows to be characteristic of those "possessed" and knows is expected by the general audience. The "possessed," to some extent perform what is expected of them. However, the spectacle has a disturbing effect on the audience, who become frightened and interpret what is happening as demonic possession.

The charismatic individual in our case generates a particularly high level of collective emotional response with his threats and tirades against evil spirits. It is worth pausing briefly on the psycho-cultural dimensions of these reactions. The mental climate that results at a collective level due to the influence of a leader identified as one with occult powers who receives visions and is capable of dealing with demons and spirits causes all, but most notably the psychically or mentally ill and the weaker subjects, to react according to a precise behavioural pattern, both mental and physical. This is the stereotypical and preconstituted scheme that fits with the collective symbolic imagery of the "Devil" and "demonic possession." It is this imagery, already a long established as a cultural tradition, that re-emerges, at least for the average person, in the Gospels, where the "possessed" is a salient figure. For the subject who is now exposed to the influence of ritual-therapy, this image will be greatly reinforced and evoke the models of the dominant culture and those transmitted through the family.

Milingo's ritual call that re-evokes the living presence of demons and spirits has the effect of bringing to life in those present both the Gospel imagery and the Gospel model of possession. Those present who believe themselves to be possessed act according to the imagery and the model. This is also a possible means of escaping from suffering, especially where other attempts at a cure have failed. A close look suggests a "theatrical" element in the "possession"; that has a pre-exorcistic phase when the spirits and demons are evoked—and an exorcistic phase, when they are scattered. The rite itself can also be interpreted as giving rise to a crisis in a psychologically predisposed form that is designed to relieve another crisis previously induced. In other cultural contexts, M. Leiris and I. Lewis, have witnessed similar theatrical aspects in "possessions" by the spirits.

We find, in the context of Milingo's therapy, a ritual process that reveals aspects similar to the process that, on a corresponding psycho-socio-cultural level, induced witches to confess during the time of the Inquisition. The witch was a product of coercion and psycho-culturally determined by the "collective imagination": socially shared and personally stored, so as to lead the subject into recognizing it as typical and to "confess." Likewise the "possessed" is a psycho-cultural creation ritually determined by a similar collective "image." "The taranta of tarantismo" studied by Ernesto de Martino in his *La terra del rimorso* (1962), and the argia studied by Clara Gallini in *La ballerina variopinta* (1988) are also the creations of a collective imagination. While it is through the ritual itself that the original illness can be overcome it is equally important to have the participation of a community that shares the experience and perception of the sufferer for "possession" to occur.

All that has been said so far invites reflection on the power generally ancipite del rito which acts as the initiating factor in the crisis produced. Those suffering from illnesses that are more difficult to treat are those who receive through the ritual the strongest stimulus to enter into a critical state of possession or trance. The proof can be seen in certain cases of so-called therapy, practiced in Taranto, by a faith healer and an exorcisitc priest, both followers of Milingo. The cases are from the research of Anna Maria Albano's fieldwork undertaken for her thesis.

The first case concerns T, 24 years old and employed as a secretary in a private office. This woman was afflicted by various disturbances—anorexia, migraine, fits of dizziness—that forced her to leave her job and persuaded her to consult a local faith healer, a practicing exorcist passionately devoted to Milingo (the "new messiah" in his words) and then the local priest, who was also a charismatic exorcist and follower of Milingo.

The diagnosis was of witchcraft and the witchcraft in question was treated as diabolic. In this specific case, the "spell" had been cast by an acquaintance of T, who had already attempted, by another "spell," to kill her own fiancé "accidentally." During a spiritual session this same woman had evoked an evil spirit against T that produced the actual afflictions. It was the local priest, a follower of Milingo, who carried out the exorcism, with the faith healer and the researcher Albano also present. To us, the behavior adopted by T following the priest who performed the exorcistic ritual seems particularly significant. Suffering from common psychosomatic illnesses the woman "realizes" in the presence of the priest and the ritual exorcist an immediate change in the nature of her her illness and its symptoms, following the scheme of diabolic possession. In fact she shouts, spits, and lurches around until she is approached with a cross and sprinkled with holy water. It is clear that the patient takes on the role of the "possessed," adapting herself to the scheme implicit in her and already noted in her upbringing and actually suggested to her from without by the actions and formulae of the priest exorcist. It is the ritual, thus, that produces such behavior—or rather, the "crisis"—following precise traditional stereotypes.

A second case considers R, mother of a young man whose wife she is so averse to that she procured from a witch recipes and instruments to bewitch her. But it was the mother herself who fell ill with unusual complaints: anxiety, insomnia, anorexia, hearing things (suspicious noises at night). She turned to the same healer and priest mentioned in the preceding case, who collaborated in curing psychic illnesses and underwent exorcism. Her condition was diagnosed as being due to submission to Satan. The submission, significantly, induces the context of "doing evil" and of "undergoing suffering." (It is seen that Milingo unifies ills passively suffered with errors, faults, "sins" committed as belonging to a single "satanic" category.)

Exactly at the moment when the priest places his hands on the woman's head to exorcise the demon, she enters into a critical state of violent agitation. She paws the ground, shouts, pushes the priest away, and gets angry with "the old man" (a figure straightaway interpreted by the healer as "the Lord.") Only later on does she calm down, stop, and agree to recite the rosary. As in the preceding case, this also demonstrates the rapid change of the original signs of psychic illness, diagnosed from vague and nonviolent symptoms, into the precise form of "possession" typified by an aggressive manner toward the priest, who is seen as the "enemy of Satan."

We have just seen, in brief digression, some behavioral similarities between the patients treated by Milingo—with his call to a precise symbolic imagery—and the two cases treated by other healers, also using the methods and symbolic imagery of Milingo himself. Other parallels can be made with Pugliese tarantism and Sardinian *argism*. All this offers useful elements for decoding the broad comparative range of the world of ideas and the related therapeutic system that our charismatic African—and, in his own way—Catholic, operates through the direct evocation of demons and spirits.

There is yet another instance of how the logic of symbolic effectiveness functions in the course of the ritual performed by our charismatic. As just mentioned, ingredients and various objects—water containers, oil jars, bags of salt, family clothes and photos, rosaries, crosses, sacred images, and so on, are brought each time by the participant to the meeting. In the concluding part of the cermony the celebrant invites the audience to take out and hold up in the air the bottles and other objects, and upon them, in succession, he pronounces the formula of blessing-exorcism. The entire operation, in the mind of the assembly, now predisposed to respond positively, is charged with powerful symbolic effect. The tension is demonstrated on every face, and immediately afterward, there is the visible relaxation of the tension that signals the perception that supernatural protection has been obtained. Water, oil, blessed salt, become "medicines" and substances to protect from all adversities. Milingo has written : "Whatever I want to use as a medicine to heal, becomes effectively a medicine" and to integrate the religious sense into this claim he adds: "He who leads is precisely Jesus."[23] In effect, the crowd leaves the meeting feeling and looking uplifted. There is a widely felt sense of liberation, of renewed faith in the victory over the forces of evil, a sense of reassuring protection. The system of symbols, in the intense climate of participation that marks the whole celebrative ritual, is undeniably working on the psychological plane. Against this background Milingo appears in an edifying and psychologically positive light. It is also the case that his activities are unedifying and psychologically unhelpful.

In the presence of subjects who show signs of hate towards him, cursing him, Milingo suggests that they are clearly possessed by demons. Cursing and hate toward sacred objects is the most common sign in the ancient Christian tradition of a diabolical presence. But Milingo condemns, as people under Satan's control, whoever shows incredulity at, or suspicion of his therapeutic and exorcistic practices. It is, therefore, possible that one of his assiduous and faithful followers in hearing another express suspicion, incredulity, and criticism of the Monsignior, will see in that person the Devil personified. At least one case of the kind has been verified by a psychiatrist, whose help was sought by a woman, a victim of persecution by an ex-friend. The last mentioned, after hearing from the first woman a critical account of Milingo and his therapies, was denounced publically as one possessed by the Evil One. From that moment this person, a tradeswoman by profession, hit upon extremely difficult times due to the loss of clients, and what is more she felt that she was being shunned by the public. The psychological consequences were such that she had to turn to a psychiatrist.[24] The result of the story we were able to ascertain personally, in the course of a public meeting. The patient labeled by Milingo as "possessed" was handed over by him to the assembled crowd to be mocked as if she were less than human, a beast. In a meeting (healing session), while the assistants carried a number of possessed women out of the room shouting and overcome by psychomotor agitations, we heard Milingo declare harshly, "These are not human beings." Later he would certainly have been able to practice on these patients "suitable exorcistic techniques" in the confines of a closed room. But the effect upon the faithful, those who believe in Milingo and the Devil without reserve, is undoubtedly to avoid from fear and contempt the so called "possessed." At this point the question poses itself: how is this behavior to be reconciled with that demanded, by professional ethics, of a psychiatrist in treating psychic patients, or simply with the behavior required of anyone in the presence of the psychiatrically ill? The influence that Milingo is capable of having on people is certainly ambivalent: positive and beneficent, but capable of producing negative and malicious effects.

We can now look at the developing relations between the Monsignor and official Catholicism, having already pointed to his forced transfer from Africa to Rome. After being dismissed from the position of Archbishop of Lusaka but still maintaining the tile of Bishop, and after a two-year enforced wait in Rome, Milingo was authorized by the Pope to practice his ministry as a healer outside of his African homeland.

In Rome also interference from the traditional clergy resurfaced. Milingo was obliged after January 1987 to leave the Church of the Argentines of Rome (Argentini di Roma), where he had been practicing his cult. He had no other church to go to and so was forced to locate in a secular location, l'Hotel Ergife. The macroscopic dimensions assumed by the "Milingo phenomenon" in Italy and the not-easily-controlled mass demonstrations inevitably had the effect of creating a reaction of reserve and fear in the Catholic Church.

Toward the beginning of 1988 news leaked out of racketeering by dishonest followers who had organized a system of profiteering from Milingo's activities, unknown to him. Without scruple they arbitrarily requested the payment of sizeable amounts, which they appropriated, as payment for admission from those who crowded the doorway of the charismatic, desperately seeking entrance. Milingo clearly had to intervene and end the abuse. The episode shows, however, that in the expectant climate in which ordinary people look for miracles, corrupt business speculation can surface and feed off what is strictly a spiritual cult, inspired by a leader who is perceived to be a wonder worker. A religion that seeks to provide spritual therapy leaves tiself open to such corruption in an unscrupuluous and cynical society where people easily yield to the allurement of the miraculous.

The fears and reservations that had been mounting at an increasingly rapid pace within the Catholic Church in Rome came to a noisy and decisive head in the first days of January 1989. Without warning the cult's first meeting of the month was refused permission to proceed. The crowd of pilgrims and the faithful, bitterly disappointed and dismayed, waited in confusion and agitation. Milingo did not appear in public, and from then up to the time of writing he has not held another service. This seems an opportune point to review—leaving to one side Milingo's amazing success in Africa and Italy—why he was removed from Zambia and why the Vatican intervened and forced him into silence. We begin with the forced extradition from Africa before considering what happened and is happening in Rome, which we discuss in our conclusions.

Having alluded to the implicit syncretism created by Milingo between the complex of African witchcraft and the Judeo-Christian tradition regarding the doctrine and figure of Satan, it is worth pausing briefly to reflect on the relationships between this syncretism and popular Italian culture. If the revitalization of witchcraft is a conspicuous part of our theologian-healer's doctrine and reveals a continuity with African traditions, it also has much in common with the popular beliefs of our homeland in Italy. In Italian civilization, both lay and secular, the complex of beliefs involving witchcraft, sorcery, and evil occult powers—a complex already dominant at the level of official doctrine in the culture until the sixteenth and seventeenth centuries—has neither been obliterated nor extinguished by industrialization or the dominance of scientific thought. It has survived in the most hidden recesses of popular religion in spite of the processes of rationalization and the demystification of ancestral prejudices: processes that predominate in most advanced circles with the most advanced outlook. The advent of Milingo in the midst of Italian culture, far from constituting a radical innovation, points up and revitalizes an archaic mentality already officially removed, but only partly hidden and one that has recently been resurrected even in official circles by the last two popes with their proclamations that re-evaluate the role of Satan in human society. All Milingo's faithful in fact relive—and this is evidenced by statements from followers—the atmosphere of former centuries, of medieval and Renaissance times, that links our culture with that of traditional African society. In this respect it seems appropriate to talk of the relationship Milingo has with popular Italian culture, of a "short circuit" between two energy poles in contact, from which flames that are capable of starting a fire burst forth. The climate of Milingo's meetings is effervescent and often touches the ignition point. Bypassing the mathematical logic of the electronic and space revolutions, and alongside the new science-fiction mythology, the renewed mythology of the Devil, of witches and spirits, takes up space and encamps itself. As a defense against these fantastic beings, the miracle of salvation is earnestly begged for.

But the Milingo phenomenon. if its true nature is not to be misunderstood, cannot be reduced to its anti-modern component. Nor can it be reduced to its Manichaean fundamentalist component, whose totalizing vision of the world depicts a perennial struggle against the impenetrable forces of evil that lie in ambush, ready to divert man from God. Away from the ideology of witchcraft and spirits, Milingo's religion opens itself to the powerful Christian mystical theology of the redemption. It offers the faithful the reassurance of protection that comes from the realization that the metahistoric plane acts on the individual psychic plane. The search for health becomes the search and promise for total salvation. It is not by chance that exorcism is sustained by collective prayer, its essential nucleus. The appeal to religious values—whether in Africa or in Rome—offers a society that is lacerated by tormenting imbalances and crises, compensation brought about by a convulsive and disorganized process of transformation.

It should not be forgotten that Milingo's religion was born in the *urban* culture of Africa (Lusaka): a culture characterized by the break-up of territorial ties at the level of the village, of social bonds, of clans, of lineages and of large extended families, that are the typical heritage of rural African society and that confer on it a fundamental unity. Today in these rural cultures illness is often interpreted or explained as a sign or effect of a breakdown, due to man's errors, of the ethical-social ties that were the basis of community life: and in many cases the spirits carrying the illnesses punish the transgressors, in defence of these ethical-social values or rituals. But in the environment of the city, where these ties and values are obscured or lost, the illness remains—for a pre-scientific culture—the province of supernatural forces of evil that obscurely originate in transgressions and human responsibility. Only when it is a question of witchcraft and sorcery are human actions seen to be at the roots of illness: for the rest the evil spirits and Satan are responsible.[25] In such conditions Milingo and other modern African healers like him influenced by Christianity—the prophet Albert Atcho from the Ivory Coast is a good example[26]—rediscover in the biblical representation of Satan a figure that, fits in with the need to adapt in the sense of "modernize" the old system of beliefs about Evil and its origins which can no longer be traced to a "social network" which by now is extinct or has badly broken down. The figure of Satan also fits in an equally appropriate way, the need to attribute illness to a supernatural entity, an exponent of evil— beyond human action and in itself a negation of values. However, if in Africa the success of Milingo and of others like him can be explained in terms of socio-cultural motivation, by reference to the two factors mentioned above that concern a society by now unhinged—more in the cities than in the villages— from its social structures and its traditional cultural models, the great success that he has had in Italy must be accounted for differently. The reasons why Milingo re-emerged with vigor and a sort of new official position—that of a priest, or better still, of an African Bishop—in an old belief system and in a situation of compelling need for help and protection of an alternative nature, was due to the almost moribund nature of official religion, administered in orthodox, bureaucratic, and conformist ways. Given the nonexistence in Italy of the cognitive substratum in force in Africa that transfers illness to the ethical-social or ritual world, given the conditions of crisis or inadequate medicine or psychiatry compared to the levels of illness of this kind, and given the increasing imbalance between the potential creativity of individuals and the limitations or the boomerang effect of their efforts, Italy provides a favorable terrain for the revival of the explanation of evil in the world, by recourse to demonic ideology. The Devil, in conditions where the rational and critical mentality is abandoned, can well satisfy the need to explain evil: that for which a person's actions are responsible, and also that which is passively borne, pertaining as it does to intrinsic human limitations.

At this point, after having underlined the peculiar and the most interesting factors that Milingo's cult, in our opinion, has raised in the Italian socio-cultural situation, it is now time to summarize what were from the beginning in Africa, and what are now in Italy, the factors causing most concern in the Catholic Church with a view to explaining the Vatican's restrictions on Milingo's activities.

Regarding the relationship between Milingo and the Church while he was in Zambia, I have referred to the enquiries on this matter made by Gerrie ter Haar.[27] For Haar the practical and doctrinal factors that determined the removal of Milingo from the archdiocese of Lusaka are essentially the following: (1) The exceptional charisma earned by the healer-exorcist among the indigenous peoples, making him dangerous, in a period of serious socioeconomic crisis, for the country because of the criticism he mounted methodically against all iniquity and oppression. Moreover, he created serious embarassment for the local bishops, placed in the impossible position of adopting pastoral practices analogous to those, totally arbitary in their view, initiated by Milingo and which people had come to expect of them. (2) His decisive defense of "African identity" in a reinterpretation of Christianity contrasted African Christianity to White Christianity, for him too "theologized," that was seen to incur the risk of provoking a slide toward "paganism and superstition." (3) The doctrine of the *World in Between* that postulates the existence of a united world of spirits, good and bad together, with which Milingo himself can directly communicate in his therapeutic and exorcistic activities. (4) An unacceptable confusion between this "world of spirits" and the Christian conception of the Holy Spirit. (5) A series of doctrinal opinions and practices alien to canonical Catholicism: apparent identification made between "evil spirits" and the Devil; the notion of illness as a possible effect of witchcraft or a consequence of sins; the close identification of religion with faith healing. While this may be the case in African tradition, it is unacceptable as the pivot of spirituality in the Roman Catholic Church.

The contrasts between the official church and the position of Milingo in Zambia, lead ter Haar to conclude that the Church pursues in Africa a decidedly "western" pastoral approach and therefore, we would say, an ethnocentric one. While it is firmly convinced that the African tradition closely links religion and faith healing, it does not examine the problem of possession, which in African culture also occupies a position of enormous importance.

If we now turn to the situation in the last few years in Italy, it can be seen that many of the doctrinal and liturgical elements adopted by Milingo in Zambia are still to be found in vigorous use in the cult he practices in Rome and in the pastoral visits he makes to various Italian cities. In spite of the following that Milingo has drawn from among numerous priests who accompany him in his religious services, the aforementioned elements cannot but reopen the old conflict with the official church. Let us add that there is active opposition to the African Bishop in Italy. The media have highlighted other new factors linked to his presence in the developed world, in the midst of a society in a serious crisis of values and ethico-religious principles. Milingo has been champion of his own cause, and his irrepressible religious spiritual advocay of his cause has certainly played a critical role in the whole affair. He has appeared many times on national television, and has established branches of his exorcistic and therapeutic cult supported by lay and ecclesiastical personnel in dozens of Italian cities. Ultimately the charismatic appeal and a message inspired by principles of sanctity have made Milingo, to his faithful followers, a true "living saint" and object of veneration. If, as ter Haar writes, "Milingo in Zambia smashed the mechanisms in force and the ancestral traditions of the official church, upsetting the entire system," it is possible that in Italy he has, for the second time, produced an upset in the traditions of the church, providing a mouthpiece and resonance box for the implicit and urgent spiritual pulse of the masses in crisis, in search for new, alternative sources of security.

ACKNOWLEDGMENTS

Thanks are due to Dr. G. Stapardi, Oxford University and Mr. A Clarke, Manchester University for helping with the translation of this chapter from the original Italian.

NOTES

1. The "provisional report" of the episcopal cconferences titled *The Phenomenon of Sects and New Religious Movements*, Ed. Dehoniane (Bologna, 1986).

2. Th. Perret, "Les Sectes en Afrique, Id, Les Marabouts des Blancs," *Africa International*, September 1987, pp. 41-45; L. Kuczynski, "Everyday Life and African Divination in Paris," *Anthropology Today* 4 (3), 1988 pp. 6-9.

3. E. Milingo, *The World in Between* (Hurst, London, 1984), pp. 14-15; Healing, Mimeo E Malingo, (Pamphlet, Lusaka, 1977), p.1.

4. The following observations come directly from the team research. Participating were the author, Professor Luigi Frighi, Dr. Margherita Mancini, and Sandra Fersurella, psychiatrist.

5. Adrian Hastings, "Emmanuel Milingo as Christian Healer," in U. Mclean and Ch. Fyfe (eds), *African Medicine in the Modern World*, University of Edinburgh Seminar December 10-11, Dec. 1986 (Edinburgh, 1987), pp 147-171, esp. p. 150

6. Milingo, *The World in Between*, p. 124

7. Ibid. p. 28

8. Ibid. pp. 38-40

9. Ibid. p. 118

10. Ibid. p. 36

11. E. Milingo, *Plunging into Darkness*, mimeo, p. 7; *The Church of the Spirits*, mimeo, p. 4; *The World in Between*, op cit pp. 88,91; *Healing*, mimeo, E. Milingo, Lusaka, 1977 p. 2.

12. R. Frankenberg and J. Leeson, "Disease, Illness, Sickness: Social Aspects of the Choice of Healer in Lusaka Suburb," in J.B. Loudon (ed), *Social Anthropology and Medicine*, (London: Academic Press, 1976), pp. 240-243.

13. V. Lanternari, "Characteristics of Primitive Medicine; Medicine Religion, Values in Tribal Society," in *Medicine, Magic, Religion* (Rome: Libreria Internazionale. Esedra, 1987), pp. 77-84, 100-101; 114-115.

14. E. Milingo, *Liberation Through Christ: African Point of View*. Conference held by

the Archbishop of Lusaka E.M at the Divine World Centre in London, Ontario (Canada) 1977, p. 1.

15. Frankenberg and Leeson, "Disease, Illness, Sickness," pp. 223-258.

16. For example, the Mashave spirits that Milingo talks about are superimposed on other spirits of Nguni origin, cibanda, or Ngulu. Confirmed. C Dillon-Malone, "The Mutumwa Church of Peter Mulenga," *Journal of Religion in Africa* XV (2) 1985, p. 122-141; XVII (1) 1987.

17. Ibid.

18. Hastings, "Emmanuel Milingo as Christian Healer," p. 164.

19. G. ter Haar, "Religion and Healing: the Case of Milingo," *Social Compass* XXXIV (4), 1987, pp. 475-493, esp. p. 481.

20. E. Milingo, *The Demarcations*, p. 57; cited in Hastings, Emmanuel Milingo," pp 153-154. For the case of sterility cured by excorcism, see. *Healing* E. Milingo, Lusaka, 1977, p. 5.

21. Milingo, *The Demarcations*, p. 57, pp. 71-72: cited in Hastings, "Emmanuel Milingo," pp. 155-156. The episodes of faith healing reported by Milingo in *The Demarcations* go back to a period between 1973 and 1980 in Africa. Otherwise he talks about material gathered in the other pamphlet, *Healing*, part of which is incorporated in the volume *The World in Between*. As for the pamphlets partially reproduced in the cited volume, here we have referred (including *The Demarcations*) to original texts.

22. For a problematic, corresponding and parallel view of shamanic therapy, confirm with classic authority of C. Lévi-Strauss, "L'efficacité symbolique," *Revue de l'Histoire des Religions* 135, 1949, pp. 5-27. As well as the work cited there is a new edition by E. De Martino, *La Terra del Rimorso*, (Torino: Boringhieri, 1976); C. Gallini, *La Ballerina variopinta*, (Napoli: Liguori, 1988), p.32-33. For the reports of T and R confirm A. M. Albano, *Magia e Religione in Alcuni Guaritori e Operatori Dell'Occulto a Taranto*, Graduation thesis, (Facoltà di Magistero, Roma, 1988), p.p. 288-291, 294-298. For the theatrical aspects of spirit possession, confirm M. Leiris, *La Possession et ses Aspects Théatraux Chez les Ethiopiens de Gondar*, (Paris: Plon, 1958), I. Lewis, *Le Religioni Estatiche*, (Roma: Ubaldini, 1972), pp. 61-66.

23. Milingo, *Healing,* p. 14.

24. Confirmation. The contribution of Sandra Ferusella included in the contribution of équipe (L. Frighi, V. Lanternari, M. Mancini) presented at the conference in Torino, "Demonologia, Psicopatologia, Transculturalismo," October 1988.

25. Hastings, "Emmanuel Milingo," p. 166.

26. M. Augé, R. Bureau, C. Piault, J. Rouch, L.Saghy, A. Zempléni, *Prophétisme et Thérapeutique. Albert Aicho et la Communauté de Bregbo*, (Paris: C. Piault, Herman, 1975).

27. G. ter Haar, "Religions and Healing: the Case of Milingo," *Social Compass* XXXIV (4), 1987, pp. 475-493.

17

Pseudo-Conversion and African Independent Churches

Victor Wan-Tatah

The expansion of African independent churches in Africa has brought the question of conversion to the fore for a deeper examination. Why have people who once leaped for joy and claimed to have been converted by the preaching of missionaries turned their backs on missions? They no longer abide by the precepts and teachings of their former preceptors, the missionaries and their local agents, the local clergy. In Southern and East Africa, the separation has resulted in the formation of Zionist or Ethiopian-type churches, both of which stress autonomy and independence. The phenomenon of schism among Christian religious bodies and the formation of new religious groups is so conspicuous and frequent in southern Africa that the process of conversion is no longer adequate to explain why people revolt against the established churches to form their own religious groups.

My aim in this chapter is to examine this feature in religion within the broad context of southern African society, with a special eye on the Nazarene Church. We will first look at religious experience as the sum total of what is contained and/or promised in a supposed conversion. We will then examine the facts and make appropriate observations. The second half is devoted to an appraisal of conversion and reconversion and the various effects of the independent movements.

MISSIONARY CONVERSION

In religious vocabulary, conversion designates a process of transformation and new spiritual insight. It is a turning about, a definite change of front, a passing from one state of being to an altogether different state as a definite and specific act, involving different types of emotional experiences—some subtle and gradual, and others intense and dramatic. In the former case, conversion starts from childhood to adulthood. The incremental process is often the result of one's formal religious instruction and the emulation of role models in a religious community to which one belongs. The underlying factor in both cases involves change and acceptance of new ideas and norms within a particular world-view. Therefore, instruction in doctrinal tenets and religious education are preludes to any growth in grace. In Christian theology, instruction on the sinfulness of the human and the consequence of individual guilt and damnation generally precede conversion. In a typical radical experience of conversion, the peculiar and painful experience of conviction of sin is present whether the subject is guilty of actual sins or not. People in these circumstances are made to feel guilty not for specific wrong-doings, but for offenses or sins of a general and abstract nature. The saintly John Bunyan is said to have suffered for months the ordeal of being damned, although he mentions only four sins which he was really guilty of: dancing on the green, playing tipcat, reading the history of Southampton, and ringing the church bells or looking on while other lads pulled the ropes. Jonathan Edwards emphasized during the great Northampton Awakening the need for conversion regardless of specific recollections of sinfulness, and he magnified normal adolescent jollity into mortal sins.

In Evangelical Christian circles, religious revivals have become the accepted method of recruiting church membership. Here is where the Church's potential for a converted constituency is greatest. Revival meetings are ideally suited for radical emotional experiences, and, in reality, they actually produce them. In short, the conversion experience is hastened by revivals.

The Nazareth Church of Isaiah Shembe in South Africa is one indigenous African church that is Zionist in character. Zionist churches according to Bengt Sundkler, are independent churches that are evangelistic, charismatic, and that practice healings. Ethiopian-type churches are more or less political, as opposed to Zionist ones that are spiritualistic. The Nazareth Church, which boasted a membership of about 10,000 in 1967, is rich in ritual and celebrates two great annual festivals.[1] Apart from itinerant Zionist movements there are also Messianic groups that overlap into either Ethiopian or Zionist church types.

Whatever the type, the formation of African independent churches in Africa, though a religious phenomenon, has been triggered by certain socio–political forces. In the first place, their existence, according to David Barrett, is a reaction to Christian missions.[2] Christian missions have always been closely identified with Western colonial encroachments in Africa. Secondly, the propaganda content and methods of gaining converts by missionaries was one of the main reasons for this, when viewed against the background of African traditional culture.

In the 19th century, the predominant missionary attitude was similar to the one during the great missionary expansion of the Counter Reformation. The Spaniards in America and the Philippines felt that all the old religions must be destroyed because they were heathen. In 1531, Bishop Zumarraga ordered from Mexico that more than 500 temples and 20,000 idols be destroyed for this reason.[3] When Catholic and Protestant missionaries came to Africa they pursued a modified version of the Spanish missionary method. Missionaries were hostile to African traditional culture and religion. Compounded with this antagonistic approach to the African way of life, which was considered intrinsically evil, was the unholy alliance between missionaries and their colonial compatriots.[4] To the Africans, these two kinds of foreigners shared a lot in common and aimed at complete control over them. Often, unfortunately, missions did not realize that they were being manipulated by the colonial powers. Religion was used as an institutional means of social control, while congregations were used as vehicles for the pacification of the conquered. Few, if any, missions saw anything positive in African tribal society and religion. For an African to be a Christian, she/he had to reject traditional values and to sever his/her relationships and roots in traditional society. This amounted to self–ostracism. As if that were not enough, converts had to imbibe through formal education Western ideas, dress and behave in a "civilized" way, like the white man. There were, of course, instances where missionaries sided with the natives, or collided with the colonial government. Consequently, there is a paradox in the development of missions and the frantic search for converts in African Christianity. The negative and condescending missionary attitude was balanced by the fervent zeal to give Africans the Christian scriptures translated into the vernacular languages. Bible translations eventually became an effective weapon among talented converts, to challenge the missionary churches. Along with other tools and renewed vision, leaders of African independent churches were able to understand and explain various Christian doctrines in their own terms. Often the independent churches were critical of the missionary churches from which they seceded. The impact of this shift has led to a heavy concentration on the Old Testament part of the Bible, which is in sync with the African world view. Zionist churches demonstrate this in their close identification with the Jews, Mosaic laws, and the acceptance of the one God. There is little or no interest in the New Testament. This same phenomenon occurs in distant and disparate places, as among the Maoris in New Zealand, the Aborigines in Polynesia, and the African diaspora. Consequently, Western missionary efforts at translating scriptures into local languages have awakened in Africans an urge to adapt ancient myths and rituals from the Bible into African culture, without having to accept the rigid anti–pagan code of the missionaries.[5] At the same time, the Judaic pattern has aroused the need for self–determination and liberation from the oppressive presence of their foreign masters. The Zionist and Ethiopian-type African churches are expressions of both the spiritual and political aspects of this liberation.

The basic difference between the Zionist and Ethiopian churches lies in the fulfillment of their messianic hopes: the Ethiopians promise a united and free Africa (political) ruled by the Lion of Judah, King of Kings, whereas the Zionists look to the Judeo-Christian land of Palestine to which Moses and John the Baptist will lead them (spiritual). Isaiah Shembe of the Nazarene Church, as an example of the Zionist hope, regarded himself as the servant of the Lord who had come to wipe away the tears of the people. Claiming to be the Moses of his people he also called himself King of the Nazarenes, as Jesus was called King of the Jews. While he emulated that role, rarely did he mention Christ. The closest he came to Christ was when he described Him as "the One who promised to send the Holy Spirit." Gradually his followers began to look on him as the Black Christ. After his death, Shembe was buried in a big mausoleum and worshipped as a saint. The dead body of the prophet, when seen in visions, often signifies the old African culture now destined to die and rise again in a different form. The Nazarene Church thus seems to have rejected total conversion to Western religion. Its own origins and culture cannot be replaced. Thus, standing halfway between the traditional religion and Christianity, the Nazarenes refuse to completely identify with the former one, or to fully embrace the new religion of the white man. The main reason is that Western missions have used religious ideologies for racial and economic domination of Africans.

Isaiah Shembe blamed the apostle Paul for having invented monogamy in the name of divine revelation. He also accused "whites for distorting the scriptures." Racial segregation, as experienced by the blacks of South Africa, with the support of white Christians, therefore precipitated the founding of independent churches. Religious experience in the Nazarene Church has been shaped by non–religious forces within the society. The racist nature of South African society was not only a political and ideological problem with which the independent churches contend. The increase in the number of Bantu independent churches paralleled the tightening squeeze of natives through drastic land legislation. A native agitator once summarized their cry to whites: "At first we had the land and you had the Bible. Now we have the Bible and you have the land."[6] Dr. Sundkler thinks that the separatist church problem is a corollary of the land problem. Back in 1913 the Natives Land Act made it illegal for Africans to acquire or rent land except within certain zones.

The policy of apartheid was legitimated or justified by theological interpretations of the Dutch Reformed Church. Dr. Sundkler relates an incident that illustrates the consequences of such approval by missionaries. A European woman who worked in the mission at Natal went to visit a missionary center in Durban and, upon meeting a Zulu pastor in the street, greeted him cordially and stopped to chat with him in a friendly, normal way. After a few days, she received a letter from the pastor, thanking her lavishly for having the courage to treat him as a human being and for honoring him by talking to him in the street.[7]

It is not therefore unusual that the separatist movements had an impact on the historic churches. The former were the products of a combination of factors, beginning with a recognition of contradictions in missionary attitudes toward the natives and the Christian principles that African converts were taught. The displacement of Africans from their own land and the resulting frustration and joblessness turned off converts from the new religion to nativistic interpretations of Christianity that fulfilled their basic spiritual and social needs.

The Nazarene Church represents a phase in the religious transformation of its society. Its religious experiences are similar to those of early Christianity when the new faith was struggling to survive in a hostile environment. Then, as in South Africa, the people were seeking a way out of their dilemma through religious regeneration. Now as then, a new church carries within itself contradictions and conflicts that surface when the initial prophetic or messianic phase has ended. When the charisma has been routinized, problems of inheritance and continuity emerge. Accordingly, the second phase of the Nazarene Church is just beginning, following the dominance of the founding figure and his son's succession.

The political, social, and economic oppression by white South Africans of Blacks for decades made the region more vulnerable to disaster than normal. The context of the independent churches yields support to this phenomenon. Elements of millenarianism abound in African independent churches. Their discourse is laced with utopian and apocalyptic imagery. By rejecting the present evil world, the Nazarenes believe that when it comes to an end, they will be the ones to rule thereafter, in the new Jerusalem. It is no surprise that the African independent churches proliferate in the Bantu reserves and in most rural areas, where life is difficult and wretched. People are deprived of basic necessities like decent housing, water, and electricity. A similar phenomenon exists in independent churches in areas outside South Africa, especially in West Africa.

Why the affinity between millennial movements and rural areas? Yonina Talmon concludes that millenarian movements occur among groups that lack political experience or access to political influence.[8] When continually depressed conditions combine with a continual influx of new people, millenarian movements find easy access. Shocks and disasters in both the city and country differ, with more potential for disruptive psychological effects in the latter than the same forces would in cities. Life in the city can be hectic and demanding. In the absence of the extended family, people easily become frustrated and alienated in times of unemployment and uncertainty. For one thing, cities contain more heterogeneous populations, and people are less closely identified with their primary place of residence. The disjunction in the primary environment and one's personal identity creates upheavals which result not only in a feeling that life is meaningless, but present events introduced by secular Western influence are objectively perceived as evil, thus disastrous to the sanctity and security of the traditional world. These fluxes and fears in the revolving picture of the world constituting disaster set the stage for any charismatic leader who upon arrival is likely to capitalize on the displaced individuals' fears and uncertainties. Charismatic leadership, for Max Weber, arises during moments of psychic, physical, economic, ethical, religious, or political distress.[9] Isaiah Shembe's biography reveals this.

CONVERSION AND CATASTROPHE

We have just looked at the vulnerable nature of life in urban areas and the exposure to millennial ideas when the primary localism is threatened. The illnesses that men and women of Zululand suffer, and to which the Zionist Nazarene Church attends, are symptoms of the ailments of their society. The flaws of the microcosm are reflected macrocosmically, and vice versa.[10] When society is sick, prophet–healers are invited to restore health and order. Social problems always have some direct or indirect bearing on the physical well–being of individuals.

We deal here with a society that is not static but dynamic, although members still cling to their traditional styles and ideologies. Apart from the relative deprivation or oppressed condition of blacks, Zululand Zionists are victims of change and modernization. Their traditional world is impinged upon by a modern and non-traditional one, of which Western Christian missionaries are the principal agents. It is this delicate position between stability and change that makes some remote country areas vulnerable and volatile sources of group activity. As a result, the duration of conversion is more or less short-lived and determined by shifting social circumstances: first a switch from one's tradition to missionary religion and on to the Independent Church.

Theologically, when we say that someone has undergone a conversion, we mean that he/she has moved from a point of indifference to one of commitment, from a prior religious persuasion to a new form of piety. The movement involved is made in recognition that the convert has progressed from error to truth. In non-theological terms, conversion, whether secular or religious, is characterized by change and a new orientation measured by new forms of identification, new ideas and association with a different group.

As we found at the beginning of this chapter, when the missionaries began their civilizing and Christianizing missions in Africa, they made many converts, some through tribal chiefs, a method that did not seriously challenge previously held beliefs by individual converts. Later on, after the missionaries had established mission stations, they continued to attract more members through primary and secondary means of socialization. For African independents to have broken away from missionary churches to form their own meant resorting to new attempts in the recruitment of members, especially from among the disgruntled and culturally disenchanted lot. Occasionally, they would utilize conversion methods apparently similar to the missions. Members were products of conversion experiences, but the movements were themselves social discontinuities.[11] That is, they were set apart from culturally dominant modes of belief and action. African independent churches in this sense can be considered as subcultures. Their ideologies emphasized changes in existing cultural themes while promising believers hope and the dawn of God's reign or the reinstatement of the lost golden age.

Individuals' susceptibility to conversion differs. Societies in transition and change are places where existing belief systems do shift frequently and where the plausibility structure is under threat. Programs and ideas that once were taken for granted in the background are propelled to the foreground and become objects of suspicion and scrutiny. Traditional and once-resilient institutions lose their grip on devotees. Individuals looking for stability and certainty more than others, they search for alternatives to old institutions, in keeping with their present circumstances.

Conversion is a possibility only where there is an alternative, hence Peter Berger's use of the term alternation to indicate such an adjustment. In Isaiah Shembe's church, conversion to a millenarian-type movement is frequently accompanied by dramatic physical signs of enthusiasm which constitute symptoms of total conviction. After he/she has been won over, the believer must be reminded over and over again that the transformation is genuine and unshakable. The plausibility of the newly acquired belief increases with the number of people who espouse it, especially one's significant others. They play a major role in the recruit's adjustment process. Growth in the number of people in the church therefore serves a critical socializing function too. The first in a series of catastrophes may well leave the basic attitudinal framework of the adult population intact. But with successive disaster–increments, faith is likely to weaken as the individual finds it difficult to rationalize or explain the horrendous. At the beginning of each disaster event, traditional beliefs are a little shakier than they were before. Disasters can be both socializing and "countersocializing." They work to subvert established norms of a society, through the mediation of family, school, and other social institutions. A single disturbing event may be easily neutralized, but repetitive disasters are bound to undermine one's faith, or undo much of the work that socialization had made possible.

SOCIAL AND POLITICAL IMPLICATIONS OF THE RELIGIOUS MOVEMENT

Independent churches have functioned in precolonial and colonial times more as social mobilization forces, rather than the reconciliation systems that religions are generally supposed to be. Movements in this light present a primary resistance to alien rule. They offer alternate socio-cultural structures in which Africans learn new political roles.[12] African religious movements enable people to make the transition from traditionally diffuse and particularistic forms of leadership to both particularistic and universalistic leader-follower relations. Ironically, this is done through a means of escapism and timidity to face the real and immediate challenges of social change through highly charged apocalyptic images and the introduction of a savior–figure. Now that apartheid is over and blacks have replaced their white apartheid oppressors, the African independent churches will have to adapt to new forms of apocalypticism and Ethiopianism.

There are dangers and a few advantages that can be mapped out from the phenomena of the collective imagination in terms of utopianizing and/or millenarianizing. There is the danger of extremism, which through alienation could become "too much," but there is also the minimal impact of an alienation that is "too little" to cause necessary changes. Moderation is necessary, if we take Durkheim's observation that people commit suicide either because of too much or too little individualization or socialization.[13] Societies become suicidal when they show too much or too little imagination. What is offered in the process of alternation is different from the existing order. The turning around progresses from (1) admitting the admissible, for instance, the dreamed society as objectively presented by the messianic figure; (2) the stage where the imagination ceases to be a plan of escape, and becomes a plan of social protest; (3) the alternative for utopia and millenarianism can be simultaneously defined as imaginary plans of an alternative society: the plan of Elsewhere, the Other.

In the concept of the Black Messiah, whites will be excluded from the kingdom. In post-Apartheid South Africa, however, this vision is not tenable because whites are part of the kingdom. At first, the alternative is hesitant, nostalgic and uncertain, but it becomes consistent, persistent, and convinced with time. It is not simply a mental representation, but becomes an idea–force, operationalized in a social dramatization.[14]

Newly formed African church movements, though living under a cloud of messianic dreams, are a major creative and corrective force in respect to modernization. Whether they are capable of readapting to new circumstances waits to be seen. If there is one thing that has laid bare the hypocrisy of Western missions, it is the absence of love. Whites drove blacks from their land and failed to treat them as equals. According to the theology of the Broderbund, they were heathens and unenlightened. Blacks did not merit God's love. But through the independent churches, blacks can hear of God's love anew. The one difficult question in the post-apartheid era is whether the African community of love can include Afrikaans Christians or people who once oppressed Africans.

The Ekuphakameni community which Isaiah Shembe built is still an apocalyptic reality, held together by Christian love. The Ekuphakameni Church village of the Ama Nazaretha, otherwise known as the High Place, on the outskirts of Durban is a model settlement, whose members are reputed to be morally upright by their neighbors. Will this standard be maintained? It is also the center for a great religious festival every July.

The establishment of communities of love by an African independent church shows that Christianity in its imported version cannot flourish in Africa. David Barrett, in his introspective analysis of this phenomenon, admits this fact as the clue to the religious puzzle.[15] Church historian Stephen Neill says that at the heart of the independent church movement the sin of the white man against the black is unmistakable. It is because of the failure of the white man to make the church a home for the black man that the latter has been persuaded to have a church of his own.[16] Through the reading of scripture in their own languages, the Nazarenes have been able to indigenize their concept of Christian love. The concept has been transformed into a beautiful praxis of genuine African spirituality. Africans understood that the central task of Christianity is to proclaim this love of God in real life. Failure to practice this love by the missionaries, plus their bias against African cultures and society, resulted in the resentment of so-called converts. In the new African community, Africans can now experience heaven on earth.

The failure of Western Christianity to Africa can be summarized in three words: ethnocentricism, lovelessness and isolationism. The conversion of the African into Western Christianity was unsuccessful and superficial at best because the missionaries who sought converts never really knew nor truly converted Africans. They lived in their own world, but they expected Africans to abandon theirs for that of the missionary. African independents never did so. If conversion was pseudo because the natives were suspicious of the white man with his dubious standards, we may hope now that reconversion to African Independency is going to stay in a new nonracial South Africa. Since independent churches are located in rural villages and at crossroads of rapid social change, one can expect the present exhuberance and active recruitment of members to continue with new challenges in a society where racism will become the new enemy. Perhaps mainline churches which have been involved in the actual struggle against apartheid can help independent churches to readapt in the changing environment. Bishop Desmond Tutu is already leading the way by continuously challenging the new government to be ethical and held politically accountable.

The test of success of re-conversion of the African independent churches will be based on their continuing ability to identify and champion social causes for the black masses, and also to continue with healing ritual performances that have always been the staple of a spirituality that is enriching and holistic. The other shortcoming of the Ekuphakameni community is that many young people had to earn their living outside the city, returning to the holy hilltop only on weekends.[17] Shembe regretted this because the youth would be corrupted by the world. He lamented that their earnings would not be controlled by him or his elders. Unfortunately, while these communities give evidence of cohesion and of the work ethic by their devotion to industry, agricultural production, and commercialization, they have remained isolated from the rest of society. But if the independent churches are to play a pivotal role in the transformation of the new South Africa, their future leaders will have to get involved with the rest of society and with other churches that include whites. It is now time for the African independent churches to teach white Christians true love and real Christianity. The process may ironically require the sending of missionaries from independent to white and mainline churches. At least in the new South Africa it calls for a new experience in ecumenism and theological dialogue.

NOTES

1. David B. Barrett, *Schism and Renewal in Africa* (Nairobi: Oxford University Press, 1968), 83.

2. O. Chadwick, *The Reformation* (Harmondworth: Penguin, 1964), 336–337.

3. B. M. Sundkler, *Bantu Prophets In South Africa* (London, Butterworth Press, 1948), 33.

4. Ibid., 32, 35.

5. Michael Barkun, *Disaster and the Millennium* (New Haven: Yale University Press, 1974), 66.

6. Max Weber, *Economy and Society* (ed. Guenther Claus Wittich) 3: 1111–1112. New York, Bedminster Press, 1968.

7. James W. Fernandez, "African Religious Movements" *Annual Review of Anthropology* 7 (1978): 211.

8. Ibid., 101.

9. Ibid., 212.

10. Henri Desroche, *The Sociology of Home* (London: Routledge and Kegan Paul, 1979), 166–167.

11. Ibid., 168.

12. Barrett, *Schism and Renewal in Africa*, 155.

13. Ibid.

14. Fernandez, "African Religious Movements," 217.

15. Barrett, *Schism and Renewal in Africa*, 155.

16. Ibid.

17. Fernandez, "African Religious Movements," 217.

BIBLIOGRAPHY

Annual Review of Anthropology Vol. 7. 1978.

Barrett, David B. *Schism and Renewal in Africa.* Nairobi: Oxford University Press, 1968.

Borhek, James T., and Richard C. Curtis. *A Sociology of Belief.* New York: John Wiley, 1975.

Clark, Elmer. *The Psychology of Religious Awakening.* New York: Macmillan, 1929.

Dessroche, Henri. *The Sociology of Hope.* London: Routledge and Kegan Paul, 1979.

Lanternari, Vittorio. *The Religions of the Oppressed: A Study of Modern Messianic Cults.* New York: Knopf, 1963.

MacMurray, John. *The Structure of Religious Experience.* New York: Archon, 1971.

Parrinder, Geoffrey. *Africa's Three Religions.* London: Sheldon, 1969.

Selected Bibliography

Abimbola, W. *Ifa Divination: An Exposition of Ifa Literary Corpus.* Ibadan: Oxford University Press, 1976.

Achebe, C. *Arrow of God.* Garden City, N. Y.: Anchor Books, 1969a.

Achebe, C. *Things Fall Apart.* Garden City, N. Y.: Anchor Books, 1969b.

Amadiume, I. *Male Daughters, Female Husbands.* London: Zed Books, 1987.

Baer, H. A. and M. Singer. *African American Religion in the Twentieth Century: Varieties of Protest and Accommodation.* Nashville: University of Tenessee Press, 1992.

Barnes, S. T. (ed.), *Africa's Ogun: Old World and New.* Bloomington and Indianapolis: Indiana University Press, 1989.

Bascom, W. *Ifa Divination: Communication Between Gods and Men in West Africa.* Bloomington: Indiana University Press, 1969.

Bascom, W. *The Yoruba of Southwestern Nigeria.* New York: Holt, Rhinehart and Winston, 1969.

Bascom, W. *African Folktales in the New World.* Bloomington, Indiana: Indiana University Press, 1992.

Bastide, R. *African Civilizations in the New World.* New York: Harper and Row, 1971.

Bastide, R. *The African Religions of Brazil: Toward a Sociology of the Interpenetration of Cultures.* Baltimore: Johns Hopkins University Press, 1978a.

Bastide, R. *O Candomble da Bahia.* Sao Paulo: Campanhia Editora Nacional, 1978b.

Bastide, R. *Estudos Afro-Brasiliros.* Sao Paulo: Editora Perspectiva, 1983.

Beattie, J., and J. Middleton (eds.). *Spirit Mediumship and Society in Africa.* London: Routledge and Kegan Paul, 1969.

Boddy, J. *Wombs and Alien Spirits: Women, Men and the Zar Cult in Northern Sudan.* Madison: University of Wisconsin Press, 1989.

Bowie, F., et al. (ed.). *Women and Mission: Past and Present.* London: Berg Publishers, 1993.

Brandon, G. *Santeria from Africa to the New World: The Dead Sell Memories.*
    Bloomington: Indiana University Press, 1993.
Brown, K. McCarthy. *Mama Lola: A Voodou Priestess in Brooklyn.* Berkeley: University
    of California Press, 1991.
Brunner, C. H. (ed.). *African Women's Writings.* London: Heinemann, 1993.
Camaroff, J. *Body of Power, Spirit of Resistance.* Chicago: University of Chicago
    Press, 1985.
Carneiro, E. *Candomblés da Bahia.* Rio de Janeiro: Editora Technoprint Ltd, 1961.
Carybe. *Os Deuses Africanos No Candomble Da Bahia.* Salvador (Bahia): Editora
    Bigraf, 1993.
Chidester, D. *Religions of South Africa.* London: Routledge, 1992.
Clarke, P. B. *Black Paradise. The Rastafarian Movement.* Wellingborough, Northants:
    Aquarian Press, 1987.
Clarke, P. B. "The Dilemmas of a Popular Religion: The Case of Candomble." In S.
    Rostas and A. Droogers (eds.). *The Popular Uses of Popular Religion in Latin
    America.* Amsterdam: Center for Latin American Research and Documentation
    (CEDLA), 1993, pp 95-109.
Clarke, P. B. "Why Women are Priests and Teachers in Bahian Candomblé." In E.
    Puttick and P. B. Clarke (eds.), *Women as Teachers and Disciples in Traditional and
    New Religions.* Lewiston/ Queenston/ Lampeter: Edwin Mellen Press, 1993, pp. 97-
    115.
Clarke, P. B. *Mahdism in West Africa: The Case of the Ijebu Prophet.* London: Luzac
    Oriental, 1995.
Clifford, J., and G. E. Marcus. *Writing Culture: The Poetics and Ethnography of
    Culture.* Berkeley and Los Angeles: University of California Press, 1986.
Crowley, D. J. *African Myth and Black Reality in Bahian Carnaval.* Museum of Cultural
    History-UCLA, Monograph Series Number Twenty-Five, 1984.
Drewal, M. T. *Yoruba Ritual. Performers, Play, Agency.* Bloomington and Indianapolis:
    Indiana University Press, 1992
Droogers, A. "Syncretism: The Problem of Definition and the Definition of the
    Problem," in *Dialogue and Syncretism. An Interdisciplinary Approach.* In J. Gort et
    al. (eds.). Grand Rapids, Mich.: William B. Eerdmans, 1989, pp.7-25.
Droogers, A. "Power and Meaning in Three Brazilian Popular Religions." In Rostas and
    Droogers, *The Popular Uses of Popular Religion in Latin America,* pp.1-17.
Essien-Udom, E. U. *Black Nationalism: A Search for Identity in America.* Chicago:
    University of Chicago Press, 1962.
Fandrich, I. J. "The Politics of Myth-Making: Voodoo Queen Marie Laveaux." In *Social
    Compass, L'Emergence d'une sociologie feministe des religions/ The Emergence of a
    Feministe Sociology of Religion,* Vol. 43 no. 4 (December 1996), pp. 613-631.
Fulup, T. E. and A. J. Raboteau. *African-American Religion: Interpretative Essays in
    History and Culture.* New York and London: Routledge, 1997.
Gilkes, C. Townsend " 'Go and Tell Mary and Martha': The African American Religious
    Experience." In *Social Compass, L'Emergence d'une sociologie feministe des*

religions/ The Emergence of a Feministe Sociology of Religion, Vol. 43 no. 4 (December 1996), pp. 563-582.

Glazier, S. *Marchin the Pilgrims Home*. Salem, Wis.: Sheffield, 1991.

Gleason, J. Oya. *In Praise of an African Goddess*. San Francisco: Harper, 1992.

Harris, J. E. (ed). *Global Dimensions of the African Diaspora* (2d ed.).Washington, D.C.: Howard University Press, 1993.

Hess, D. J. *Spirits and Scientists. Ideology, Spiritism and Brazilian Culture*. University Park: Pensylvania State University Press, 1991.

Horton, R. "Social Psychologies: African and Western." In *Oedipus and Job in West African Religion with an Introduction by R. Horton*. Cambridge: Cambridge University Press, 1983, pp. 41-87.

Horton, R. *Patterns of Thought in Africa and the West. Essays on Magic, Religion and Science*. Cambridge: Cambridge University Press, 1993.

Hunwick, J. O. "Islam in Tropical Africa to the Twentieth Century." In Peter Clarke (ed.), *Islam*. London: Routledge, 1990.

Idowu, E. B. *African Traditional Religion: A Definition*. Maryknoll, N.Y.: Orbis Books, 1973.

Inikori, J. E. *Forced Migration*. London: Hutchinson, 1982.

Laguerre, M. S. *Afro-Caribbean Folk Medcine. The Reproduction and Practice of Healing*. South Hadley, Mass.: Bergin and Garvey, 1987.

Landes, R. *The City of Women*. Albuquerque: University of New Mexico Press, 1994.

Lawson, E. Thomas *Religions of Africa: Traditions in Transformation*. New York: Harper and Row, 1986.

Lewis, I. M. *Ecstatic Religion*. Harmondsworth, Middlesex: Penguin Books, 1971.

Lewis, I. M. *Religion in Context*. Cambridge: Cambridge University Press, 1986.

Littlewood, R. *Pathology and Identity: The Work of Mother Earth in Trinidad*. Cambridge: Cambridge University Press, 1993.

Metraux, A. *Voodoo in Haiti*. New York: Schocken Books, 1972.

Miller, M., and K. Taube. *The Gods and Symbols of Ancient Mexico*. London: Thames and Hudson, 1993.

Mudimbe, V. W. *The Invention of Africa: Gnosis, Philosophy and the Order of Knowledge*. Bloomington : Indiana University Press, 1988.

Murphy, J. *Santeria : An African Religion in America*. Boston: Beacon Press, 1988.

Murphy, J. "Santeria: African Spirits in America." Boston: Beacon Press, 1984.

Omari, M. Smith, From *Inside to Outside: The Art Ritual of Candomblé*. Museum of Cultural History Monograph Series-UCLA, Number 24, 1992.

Olupona, J. K. *African Religions in Contemporary Society*. New York: Paragon House, 1991.

Ortiz, R. *A Morte Branca do Feiticeiro Negro. Umbanda e Sociedade Brasileira*. Sao Paulo: Editora Brasiliense, 1988.

Owens, J. *Dread: The Rastafarians of Jamaica*. Jamaica: Montrose Printery, 1976.

Peel, J. D. Y. *The Aladura. A Religious Movement among the Yoruba*. Oxford: Oxford University Press (for the International African Institute), 1968.

Pereira de Queiroz, M. I. "Afro-Brazilian Cults and Change in Brazil." In J. Beckford and T. Luckmann (eds.). *The Changing Face of Religion.* London: Sage, 1989, pp. 88-109.

Puttick, E., and P. B.Clarke. *Women as Teachers and Disciples in Traditional and New Religions.* Lewiston/Queenston/Lampeter: Edwin Mellen Press, 1993, pp. 97-115.

Ranger, T. "African Traditional Religion." In Stewart Sutherland and Peter Clarke (eds.), *The Study of Religion, Traditional and New Religion.* London: Routledge, 1991.

Ranger, T., and I. Kimmambo (eds.). *The Historical Study of African Religions.* Berkeley: University of California Press, 1971.

Ray, B. *African Religions: Symbols, Rituals and Community.* Englewood Cliffs, N.J.: Prentice-Hall, 1976.

Rodrigues, N. *O Animismo Fetichista Dos Negros Bahianos.* Rio de Janeiro: Civilizacao Brazileira, 1935.

Rodrigues, N. *Os Negros No Brasil.* Sao Paulo: Companhia Editora Nacional, 1977.

Rostas, S., and A. Droogers (eds.). *The Popular Uses of Popular Religion in Latin America.* Amsterdam: CEDLA, 1993.

Shambaugh, C., and I. Zaretsky. *Spirit Possession and Spirit Mediumship in Africa and Afro-America.* N.Y.: Garland, 1978.

Shaw, R. "The Invention of African Traditional Religion." *Religion* 20, 1990, pp. 339-353.

Simpson, G. E. *Black Religions in the New World.* New York: Columbia University Press, 1978.

Sodre, M. *O Terreiro e A Cidade.* Petropolis: Voces, 1988.

Soyinka, W. *Myth, Literature and the African World.* Cambridge: Cambridge University Press, 1976.

Thompson, R. F. *Flash of the Spirit.* New York: Vintage Books, 1984.

Turner, H. "Africa's New Religions." In Stewart Sutherland and Peter Clarke (eds.), *The Study of Religion, Traditional and New Religion.* (eds) London: Routledge, 1991, pp.187-194.

Verger, P. *Les Dieux d'Afrique.* Paris: Flammarion, 1955.

Verger, P. "Notes sur le Culte des Orisa et Vodun a Bahia, La Baie de Tous les Saints au Brasil et a L'Ancienne Cote des Esclaves en Afrique," *Memoire D'IFAN*, No. 51, 1957.

Verger, P. *Lendas Africanas dos Orixas.* Sao Paulo: Editora Corrupio, 1985.

Index

About the Contributors

PETER B. CLARKE is Professor of History and Sociology of Religion at King's College, Department of Theology and Religious Studies and Centre for New Religions at the University of London. Previously he lectured on the History of Africa at the University of Ibaden, Nigeria (1974-1978). He has carried out extensive fieldwork in Western Africa and Brazil, particularly in Bahia.

Recently Peter Clarke was a visiting professor at the University of Stellenbosch, South Africa. He is the founding and present editor of the *Journal of Contemporary Religion* and has written and edited several books on African history and religions that include the following: *West Africa and Islam: A Study of Religious Development from the 8th to the 20th Century* (along with with I. Linden); *Islam in Contemporary Nigeria: A Study of A Muslim Community in a Post Independent State; Black Paradise: The Rastafarian Movement; West Africa and Christianity: A Study of Religious Development from the 15th to the 20th Century; Islam* (with P. Byrne); *Religion Defined and Explained; Mahdism in West Africa: The Case of the Ijebu Prophet* and *New Trends and Developments within the World of Islam.* He is also the author of numerous articles on African history and religion.

VALERIE DE MARINIS is Associate Professor at Uppsala University in the Psychology of Religion and Ritual Studies. She is the author of *Critical Caring: A Feminist Model for Pastoral Psychotherapy.* She also co-edited and contributed to the volume *The Function of Religious and Social Ritual* and was the chief editor and contributor to *Clinical Psychology of Religion: European and American Perspectives on Cultural and Cross-Cultural Issues.*

MUNDICARMO FERRETTI is in the Department of Social Sciences at the State University of Maranhão, Brazil, and is an Affiliated Professor of the Department of Psychology at the Federal University of Maranhão, Brazil. She is the author of numerous articles on Afro-Brazilian religion including "Meu sinal está em teu corpo" (My mark is in your body), co-edited with Carlos Eugenio Marcondes de Moura. Since 1992 she has been carrying out research on non-African spiritual entities in the state of Maranhão along with research on caboclo in Casa Fanti-Ashanti which has resulted in the books *Desceu nu Guma* and *Tambor de Mina, Cura e Bainao na Casa Fanti-Ashanti.*

STEPHEN D. GLAZIER studied anthropology at Princeton University and the University of Connecticut, where he earned his Ph.D. He has conducted research on the Caribbean island of Trinidad since 1976. Currently, Glazier serves as Professor of Anthropology at the University of Nebraska, Kearney. His publications include: *Perspectives on Penteconstalism: Case Studies from the Caribbean and Latin America* (1980); *Caribbean Ethnicity Revisited* (1985); and *Marchin' the Pilgrims Home: A Study of the Spiritual Baptists of Trinidad* (1991). He is general editor of *Anthropology of Religion: A Handbook* (1996) and *Essays in the Anthropology of Religion* (1997).

SIDNEY M. GREENFIELD is Professor of Anthropology at the University of Wisconsin-Milwaukee. He has conducted field research in the West Indies, Portugal, the Atlantic Islands, New Bedford, Massachussetts (in the United States), and Brazil on problems ranging from family and kinship, patronage and politics, the history of plantations and plantation slavery, and entrepreneurship to Brazilian Spiritist surgery and healing and Afro-Brazilian and other syncretized religions. He is the author and/or editor of four books and the producer of five video documentaries (which he filmed, wrote, directed, and edited), and he has published more than one hundred articles and reviews in books and professional journals. He has been the recipient of numerous research grants, including four Fulbright awards, the latest of which will take him to Nigeria.

CHARLES GULLICK received his initial social science education at the Department of Ethnology and Prehistory, Oxford University (1965-1966 Diploma in Ethnology; 1966-1969 B.Litt. and 1970-1974 D.Phil.). He has been on the faculty of the Department of Anthropology at Durham since 1976. His ethnohistorical and ethnographic research has centerd around the Caribbean shore of Central America (cf. his book *Exiled from St. Vincent*, 1976), various West Indian islands (cf. his book *Myths of a Minority*, 1985), the US, Malta, Britain, Scandinavia and the EU. His most recent topic of investigation has been British expatriates including missionaries and business personnel. An M.A in Business and Economic Studies (1990) at the University of Leeds was taken in conjunction with this study.

TINA GUDRUN JENSEN, University of Copenhagen, received her M.A in the Sociology of Religion at the Institute for History of Religions, University of Copenhagen, in 1995. In addition she has a B.A equivalent in Portuguese. Her Master's thesis deals with tradition and innovation in Brazilian umbanda and is based on fieldwork in São Paulo in 1992 and 1994. Another field of study is religion and cultural identity among second-generation Turkish Danes. Her main interests are ethnicity, religious and cultural identity, and pluralism.

OBIAGELE LAKE received her anthropology education at Cornell University in Ithaca, New York. She has been on the faculty of the Department of Anthropology at the University of Iowa since 1990. She has conducted extensive research in Jamaica and other areas of the Caribbean, where she has concentrated on issues of African identity and the social and political-economic position of women in these societies. Her primary focus has been the status and beliefs regarding Rastafarian women in Jamaica. She has also conducted research in Ghana, West Africa, where she collected life histories from Diaspora Africans who have settled there. Her publications include: "The Many Voices of Rastafarian Women," *New West Indian Guide* 68(3&4):135-157; "Cultural Beliefs and Breast Feeding Practices among Jamaican Rastafarians," *Cajanus* 25(4):201-214; "Toward the Formulation of a Pan-African Identity: Diaspora African Repatriates in Ghana, West Africa," *Anthropological Quarterly.* (January), 68(1):21-36. She is currently working on a book on Rastafarian women.

VITTORIO LANTERNARI was a Professor of Ethnology at the University of Rome, "La Sapienza," until his retirement in November 1994. His publications include *La Grande Festa: Storia del Capodano nelle Civiltà Primitive* (1959); *The Religion of the Oppressed* (1960); *Occidente e Terzo Mondo: Incontri di Civiltà e Religioni Differenti* (1967); *Antropologia e Imperialismo e Altri Saggi* (1974); *L'Incivilimento dei Barbari* (1983); *Festa, Carisma, Apocalisse* (1983). One of his volumes, *Dèi, Profeti, Contadini: Incontri nel Ghana* (1988) is the result of his fieldwork in Ghana (1971-1978), among the Nzema people and among some personal representatives of the "spiritual churches."

Lanternari was appointed Visiting Professor of Religion for the Autumn semester 1965 in Columbia University, New York.

ROLAND LITTLEWOOD is Professor of Anthropology and Psychiatry at London University and joint director of the University College Medical Anthropology Centre. His most recent book about the Earth people, *Pathology and Identity: The Work of Mother Earth in Trinidad*, was awarded the Wellcome Medal. He is currently President of the Royal Anthropology Institute.

BRIAN MCGUIRE is in the Latin American Studies Department at the University of California at Los Angeles. His fieldwork in Cuba, Mexico, and Los Angeles concerns Afro-Caribbean Ethnography in addition to Afro-Caribbean religious practice among immigrant populations.

ROBERTO MOTTA is in the Department of Anthropology, Federal University of Pernambuco, Brazil. He has been a visiting fellow at many other places including the University of Paris, and a Senior Fellow in the Centre of World Religions at Harvard. He received his doctorate from Columbia University and has written numerous articles on African-Brazilian religion.

DUNCAN SCRYMGEOUR is at the University of California at Los Angeles and studies Afro-Caribbean religion within the interdisciplinary study of religion program. His fieldwork in New York and Los Angeles concerns the various manifestations of Afro-Caribbean and indigenous Latin American religion within the urban centers of the United States. His most recent work, "Matamoros: Sacrifice and Transformation" is published in *Epoche: The Journal of the History of Religion of the University of California*.

MIKE TAYLOR is a postgraduate student in the Department of Education at King's College, University of London and is the author of a book *Do Demons Rule Your Town?* and a number of booklets, including *Martial Arts—Are They Harmless?*, *The Tarot: Your Questions Answered*, *Hypnosis: Are There Side-Effects?*, *Ley Lines and the Christian*, and *A Brief Survey of Travelling People in North Kensington and Hammersmith*. Mike Taylor is the medical librarian and postgraduate manager at St. Charles' Hospital, London.

GERRIE TER HAAR is based at the Catholic University at Utrecht, The Netherlands, where she teaches history of religion, comparative religion, and African religions. She is a member of the Leiden Institute for the Study of Religions (LISOR) and is also affiliated with the Centre for Resource Studies for Human Development (CERES) of Utrecht University. Her publications include the following: *Spirit of Africa: The Healing Ministry of Archbishop Milingo of Zambia*; *Faith of Our Fathers: Studies in Religious Education in Sub-Saharan Africa*; and *African Traditional Religions in Religious Education: A Resource Book With Special Reference to Zimbabwe*, ed. with A. Moyo & S.J. Nondo. She is presently working on the African religious diaspora in Europe, notably in The Netherlands, on which she is now preparing a book.

WILLIAM R. VAN DE BERG obtained his B.A. degree with honors in Psychology at the University of North Carolina at Wilmington (1992) and his M.A. in Anthropology at Wake Forest University (1996) in Winston-Salem, N.C. Van

De Berg has conducted fieldwork with numerous populations in the North Carolina area, including the Lumbee Native American tribe, a group of Rastafari indigenous to the North Carolina Piedmont-Triad area, and local chapters of the Nation of Islam. He has taught cultural anthropology at Randolf Community College in Asheboro, N.C. and is presently teaching cultural anthropology (spring 1997) and Gender, Race and Class (fall 1997) courses at Appalachian State University in Boone, N.C.

INEKE VAN WETERING completed a Ph.D. thesis on witchcraft in Ndyuka Maroon society (Suriname). During the 1970s her field work area was Suriname Maroon society. In 1988 she published *The Great Father and the Danger: Religious Cults, Material Forces and Collective Fantasies in the World of the Surinamese Maroons* (co-author H. E Thoden van Velzen). In the 1980s she conducted field work among Suriname Creole migrants in The Netherlands. Ineke van Wetering is a senior lecturer at the Amsterdam Free University in the Department of Anthropology and was a visiting professor at the Amsterdam School for Social Science Research in 1995.

Her publications also include "Informal supportive networks: Quasi-Kin Groups, Religions and Social Order Among Suriname Creoles in The Netherlands". *The Netherlands Journal of Sociology* 23 (2), 1987, pp. 92-101; "The Ritual Laundering of Black Money among Suriname Creoles in The Netherlands," in *Religion and Development: Towards an Integrated Approach.* eds. Philip Quarles van Ufford and Matthew Schoffeleers; "Popular Culture and Anthropological Debate: A Case Study in Globalization and Ethnicity," in *Transactions: Essays in Honour of Jeremy Boissevain*, ed. Jojada Verrips; "Demons in a Garbage Chute," in *Rastafari and Other African-Caribbean Worldviews*, ed. Barry Chevannes; "Transformations of Slave Experience," in *Slave Cultures and Cultures of Slavery.*

VICTOR WAN-TATAH is Associate Professor of Philosophy and Religious Studies at Youngstown State University in Ohio. He is a member and past president of the Youngstown chapter of Phi Kappa Phi Honor Society, and a recipient of the Mary Bethune Award for Youth Advocacy of the Youngstown Section of the National Council of Negro Women. He is author of *Emancipation in African Theology.*